"Cultural Complexes and the Soul of America takes Jung's concept of personal complexes and applies it to our national life. The result is a volume full of insight and passion. For anyone interested in the deep forces that shape our politics, this book is a "must read." Thomas Singer has spent 15 years developing the idea of cultural complexes, and now he and his collaborators have produced a work that will be read for a very long time."
– **Senator Bill Bradley**

"Nothing could be more timely or more timeless than this stunning collection by renowned international Jungian scholars and psychologists. *Cultural Complexes and the Soul of America* is a necessary book for today in making conscious what is paralyzing America, the cultural complexes that polarize. Yet the book also superbly articulates the deep psyche at work in any history or culture. This book is about discovering who we are collectively—the end of the illusion of individualism. *Cultural Complexes and the Soul of America* is informed and compassionate, inspired and carefully researched. It offers the reader Ariadne's thread from the labyrinth of the United States as superpower to the possible future of planetary reciprocity —a cultural complex worth striving for."
– **Susan Rowland, author of** *Jung: A Feminist Revision* **(2002),**
The Ecocritical Psyche **(2012), and** *Remembering Dionysus* **(2017),**
and professor at Pacifica Graduate Institute

"With deep reflection, in sadness and in passion, here we have a polyvocal and acute political analysis as a range of brilliant writers addresses today's endless American crises. This timely latest element in the canon of "cultural complexes" deserves to be widely read and appreciated outside the Jungian world as much as inside it. Never before have I seen "the spirit of the times" and "the spirit of the depths" woven together so convincingly. The book is a tremendous example of pluralistic writing. I read it as a kind of conversation, yet one that does not have to have a settled endpoint of agreement. Singer's lifework on what he has called an "inner sociology" enables him to perform as a sublime host or chorus master."
– **Andrew Samuels, former Professor of Analytical Psychology,**
University of Essex, and author of *The Political Psyche*

"America's Puritan roots have endowed its political traditions with fiercer ethics than we see in Europe. We have only to consider the excessive projections of "evil" during the blind aggressiveness of McCarthyism and in the cruelty of the current Trumpian era, all of it contributing to what Richard Hofstadter documented in *The Paranoid Style in American Politics.*

The demonization of one's political opponents has certainly occurred in many places, but more often as a result of tyrannies, not in the context of a supposedly mature democratic system. In this century, Thomas Singer has already contributed greatly to the psychological fertilization of politics, but this present book by Singer and his contributors is the most timely of them all."

– **Luigi Zoja, author of** *Paranoia: The Madness that Makes History* **(2011) and** *The Father: Historical, Psychological and Cultural Considerations* **(2001)**

Cultural Complexes and the Soul of America

Cultural Complexes and the Soul of America explores many of the cultural complexes that comprise the collective psychic-filtering system of emotions, ideas, and beliefs that possess the United States today. With chapters by an international selection of leading authors, the book covers ideas both broad and specific, and presents unique insight into the current state of the nation.

The voices included in this volume amplify contemporary concerns, linking them to themes which have existed in the American psyche for decades while also looking to the future. Part One examines meta themes, including history, purity, dominion, and democracy in the age of Trump. Part Two looks at key complexes including race, gender, the environment, immigration, national character, and medicine. The overall message is that it is in wrestling with these complexes that the soul of America is forged or undone.

This highly relevant book will be essential reading for academics and students of Jungian and post-Jungian ideas, politics, sociology, and American studies. It will also be of great interest to Jungian analysts in practice and in training, and anyone interested in the current state of the US.

Thomas Singer, MD, is a psychiatrist and Jungian psychoanalyst, practicing in San Francisco. He is the editor of a series of books exploring cultural complexes in Latin America, Europe, Asia, Australia, and North America. His interests include studying the relationship between myth, politics, and psyche in *The Vision Thing* and the *Ancient Greece, Modern Psyche* series. He is current president of National ARAS, an archive of symbolic imagery.

Cultural Complexes and the Soul of America

Myth, Psyche, and Politics

Edited by Thomas Singer

Routledge
Taylor & Francis Group

LONDON AND NEW YORK

First published 2020
by Routledge
2 Park Square, Milton Park, Abingdon, Oxon OX14 4RN

and by Routledge
52 Vanderbilt Avenue, New York, NY 10017

Routledge is an imprint of the Taylor & Francis Group, an informa business

British Library Cataloguing-in-Publication Data
A catalogue record for this book is available from the British Library

Library of Congress Cataloging-in-Publication Data
Names: Singer, Thomas, 1942- editor.
Title: Cultural complexes and the soul of America : myth, psyche, and politics / edited by Thomas Singer.
Other titles: Myth, psyche, and politics
Description: Milton Park, Abingdon, Oxon ; New York, NY : Routledge, 2020. |
Series: Cultural Complex Series | Includes bibliographical references and index.
Identifiers: LCCN 2020001327 (print) | LCCN 2020001328 (ebook) | ISBN 9780367272340 (hardback) | ISBN 9780367272357 (paperback) | ISBN 9780429295690 (ebook)
Subjects: LCSH: National characteristics, American. | United States–Civilization–1970-
Classification: LCC E169.12 .C7675 2020 (print) | LCC E169.12 (ebook) | DDC 973.933–dc23
LC record available at https://lccn.loc.gov/2020001327
LC ebook record available at https://lccn.loc.gov/2020001328

ISBN: 978-0-367-27234-0 (hbk)
ISBN: 978-0-367-27235-7 (pbk)
ISBN: 978-0-429-29569-0 (ebk)

Typeset in Times
by Integra Software Services Pvt. Ltd.

This book is dedicated to three extraordinary leaders—Joe Henderson, Tom Kirsch, and Bill Bradley. Their experience and wisdom inspired me to explore the interfaces between mythology, politics, and psyche that are at the heart of *Cultural Complexes and the Soul of America*.

Contents

Figures

Synopsis

This collection of chapters is not intended to offer a comprehensive analysis of its many topics. Rather, each chapter seeks to provide an author's unique perspective about an essential aspect of the American psyche as it wrestles with the most conflicted and emotionally charged issues of our times. I believe that these struggles inform and shape the multifaceted soul of America.

Editor

Thomas Singer, MD, is a psychiatrist and Jungian psychoanalyst who trained at Yale Medical School, Dartmouth Medical School, and the C. G. Jung Institute of San Francisco. He is the author of many books and articles that include a series of books on cultural complexes that have focused on Australia, Latin America, Europe, the United States, and Far East Asian countries, in addition to another series of books featuring Ancient Greece, Modern Psyche. He serves on the board of ARAS (Archive for Research into Archetypal Symbolism) and has edited *ARAS Connections* for many years.

Contributors

John Beebe, a past president of the C. G. Jung Institute of San Francisco, is the author of *Integrity in Depth* and of *Energies and Patterns in Psychological Type: The Reservoir of Consciousness*. He is co-author, with Virginia Apperson, of *The Presence of the Feminine in Film*. John was founding editor of the *San Francisco Jung Institute Library Journal* (now called *Jung Journal: Culture & Psyche*) and was the first American co-editor of *The Journal of Analytical Psychology*.

Jerome Bernstein is a Jungian analyst in private practice in Santa Fe, New Mexico. He is on the teaching faculty of the C. G. Jung Institute of Santa Fe where he served as president from 1993–1998. He was founding president of the C. G. Jung Analysts Association of the Greater Washington, DC Metropolitan Area. He is the author of *Power and Politics: The Psychology of Soviet-American Partnership* and *Living in the Borderland: The Evolution of Consciousness and the Challenge of Healing Trauma*.

Fanny Brewster PhD, MFA, is a Jungian analyst and professor of depth psychology at Pacifica Graduate Institute. She is a multigenre writer who has written about issues at the intersection of Jungian psychology and American culture. *Archetypal Grief: Slavery's Legacy of Intergenerational Child Loss* is her most recent book.

Jules Cashford has a background in philosophy, literature, and psychology. She contributed "Britain: Autonomy and Isolation in an Island Race" to *Europe's Many Souls*, edited by Thomas Singer and Joerg Rasche, and served as co-editor, with Thomas Singer and Craig San Roque, of *When the Soul Remembers Itself: Ancient Greece, Modern Psyche*. Her books include *The Moon: Symbol of Transformation*, *The Mysteries of Osiris*, and a translation of *The Homeric Hymns*. She is co-author of *The Myth of the Goddess: Evolution of an Image*.

Stefano Carta, is professor of clinical and dynamic psychology at the University of Cagliari, Italy, and an honorary professor in the Department of Psychosocial and Psychoanalytic Studies at Essex University, UK.

A Jungian analyst in Rome for over 30 years, he has been president of the Italian Association of Analytical Psychology, and he created the first institutional psychoanalytic group for the study of and intervention within the Italian communities of refugees and migrants. His writing includes more than 100 scientific publications as well as a literary novel. He wrote a short film produced by a psychiatric community, and it has won several national prizes.

Betty Sue Flowers, PhD, is a professor emeritus (UT-Austin) and the former director of the Johnson Presidential Library. She is an international business consultant, with publications ranging from poetry therapy to human rights, including two books of poetry and four PBS tie-in books. Flowers was the series consultant for *Joseph Campbell and the Power of Myth*. Publications include the complete edition of Christina Rossetti's poetry; *Presence: Human Purpose and the Field of the Future* (co-authored); *The American Dream and the Economic Myth*; "The Primacy of People in a World of Nations" in *The Partnership Principle: New Forms of Governance in the 21st Century; Daughters and Fathers* (co-edited); and *Realistic Hope: Facing Global Challenges* (co-edited).

Lynn Alicia Franco is a Jungian analyst and member of the C. G. Jung Institute of San Francisco. She practices Jungian relational psychoanalysis bilingually (in Spanish and English). She focuses on unconscious dynamics of both personal and cultural processes and draws on her multicultural experience as an immigrant to the United States from Colombia SA. She has consulted, organizationally, for UCSF community mental health services and for the Woman's Therapy Center, addressing group dynamics as related to cultural and racial diversity.

Sharon Heath is a Jungian analyst in private practice and a faculty member of the C. G. Jung Institute of Los Angeles. Her three novels comprising *The Fleur Trilogy—The History of My Body, Tizita*, and *Return of the Butterfly*—were published by Thomas-Jacob Publishing. Her chapter "The Church of Her Body" appears in the anthology *Marked by Fire: Stories of the Jungian Way*, and her chapter about tribes formed on Facebook is available in the anthology *Depth Psychology and the Digital Age*. She maintains a blog at www.sharonheath.com.

Steven Herrmann, PhD, MFT, is an analyst member of the C. G. Jung Institute of San Francisco. He has a clinical practice in Oakland, California and is the author of numerous papers, including "Melville's Vision of Evil," several book chapters, and five books: *William Everson: The Shaman's Call; Walt Whitman: Shamanism, Spiritual Democracy, and the World Soul; Spiritual Democracy: The Wisdom of Early American Visionaries for the Journey Forward*, and *Emily Dickinson: A Medicine Woman for Our Times*.

Donald E. Kalsched, PhD, is a Jungian psychoanalyst and clinical psychologist who practices in Santa Fe, New Mexico. He is a senior faculty member and supervisor with the Inter-Regional Society of Jungian Analysts and lectures nationally and internationally on the subject of trauma, its effect on the inner world, and its treatment. His celebrated book *The Inner World of Trauma: Archetypal Defenses of the Personal Spirit* explores the interface between contemporary psychoanalytic theory and Jungian thought as it relates to practical clinical work with the survivors of early-childhood trauma. His recent book *Trauma and the Soul: A Psycho-Spiritual Approach to Human Development and Its Interruption* explores some of the mystical or "spiritual" dimensions of clinical work with trauma survivors. He and his wife, Robin, live in Santa Fe during the winter, and in the summer in Trinity East, Newfoundland, Canada.

Jeffrey T. Kiehl, PhD, is a diplomate Jungian analyst and senior training analyst for the C. G. Jung Institute of Colorado and the Inter-Regional Society of Jungian Analysts. He is also an adjunct professor at the University of California, Santa Cruz, and an adjunct faculty member of Pacifica Graduate Institute, where he teaches a course on ecopsychology. For nearly forty years, he studied climate change at the National Center for Atmospheric Research. He is the author of *Facing Climate Change: An Integrated Path to the Future*, which provides a Jungian perspective on climate change. He lives in Santa Cruz, California.

Joerg Rasche, PhD, DGAP, IAAP, DGST, ISST, is a Jungian analyst in Berlin. He trained in Berlin and Zürich and also trained in sandplay with Dora Kalff. He has published on mythology, music, and cultural issues in relation to analytical psychology. He served as co-editor (with Tom Singer) of *Europe's Many Souls: Exploring Cultural Complexes and Identities.* Former vice president of the International Association of Analytical Psychology (IAAP), he is currently vice president of the German Society of Analytical Psychology (DGAP).

Craig San Roque, PhD, analytical psychologist, has lived in London, Sydney, and Alice Springs, Central Australia, with family links in Europe, San Francisco, and New York. He has had a long association with Thomas Singer and the cultural complex project, contributing to *The Cultural Complex* and co-editing *Placing Psyche: Exploring Cultural Complexes in Australia.* He most recently co-edited and contributed to *When the Soul Remembers Itself: Ancient Greece, Modern Psyche.* His many writings attend to conflicting existential realities and to positive solutions within Australian and indigenous relations.

Ronald Schenk, MSW, PhD, Jungian analyst practicing in Dallas and Houston, is a member of the Inter-Regional Society of Jungian Analysts, having served in many administrative positions including as president. He recently served as president of the Council of North American Societies of Jungian Analysis. He has published essays on language, the city, anger, madness, and the "Trump" phenomenon, as well as four books: *The Soul of Beauty; Dark Night: Imagination in Everyday Life; The Sunken Quest, the Wasted Fisher, the Pregnant Fish: Essays on a Post-Modern Depth Psychology*; and, most recently, *American Soul: A Cultural Narrative.*

Richard M. Timms, MD, received his medical degree from Johns Hopkins School of Medicine in 1967. He is currently a Senior Fellow for the Harvard Initiative on Health, Religion, and Spirituality. A retired professor of medicine at the Scripps Research Institute, he also was division head of Chest Medicine, Scripps Health, and was the former director of Critical Care Medicine, at UCSD. He is chest and internal medicine-board certified. In 1971, he served as director of emergency medicine at Walter Reed Hospital. In 1970, he served as US Army Med Company commander, in the 101st division, in Vietnam.

Alan G. Vaughan, PhD, JD, is an analyst and member of the C. G. Jung Institute of San Francisco. He is a core faculty member in the doctoral psychology programs at Saybrook University and in private practice as a Jungian analyst and a clinical and consulting psychologist. His scholarly interests and publications are at the intersections of analytical and clinical psychology, US constitutional jurisprudence, African historiography and mythology, and African Diaspora studies.

Jacqueline J. West, PhD, is a Jungian analyst practicing in Santa Fe, New Mexico. She is a training analyst in the New Mexico Society of Jungian Analysts as well as in the Inter-Regional Society of Jungian Analysts. She has served as both president and training director of the New Mexico Society and as president of the Council of North American Societies of Jungian Analysts (CNASJA). She is co-author, along with Jungian analyst Nancy Dougherty, of *The Matrix and Meaning of Character: An Archetypal and Developmental Perspective—Searching for the Wellsprings of Spirit.* She contributed the chapter "America in the Grips of Alpha Narcissism" to *A Clear and Present Danger: Narcissism in the Era of President Trump* and also the chapter "Facing the Truth" in *Rocket Man: Nuclear Madness and the Mind of Donald Trump.*

Acknowledgments

Jules Cashford and Craig San Roque have been steadfast members of the "Affinacious Society," which has lent its ongoing support and spirit to this project. LeeAnn Pickrell pulls it all together in her role as copy editor and much, much more. And all of the contributing authors have given generously of their deep reflections on the mysteries of our times.

Introduction

Thomas Singer

The Cultural Complex Series of Books

Cultural Complexes and the Soul of America is the fifth volume in a series of books dedicated to exploring the cultural complex theory. The basic notion of the cultural complex is an extension of Jung's original study of complexes in the individual into the realm of what we have come to term *group* or *cultural complexes*. The goal of the series has been to take this hypothesis into the world to see if it provides a useful lens or framework for understanding some of the dynamics that make societies unique in their identities and conflicts while at the same time having similar underlying structures in the psyches of groups around the world. The essential argument is that cultural complexes are present in every human society but that they vary widely in their content, which can be highly specific to people, place, and time. With both universality and specificity in mind, the series has explored cultural complexes in Australia, Latin America, Europe, Far East Asia, and now the United States.

Over 90 authors have contributed to the cultural complex series, which relies on the observations and sensitivities of those living within specific regions to identify the cultural complexes that are most potent in their societies both in terms of forming identity and causing or expressing political, economic, social, and spiritual disturbance and conflict. Often this puts the authors in the difficult position of having to see "through a glass darkly" (1 Corinthians 13:12)—but the fact is that the living reality of a cultural complex is felt and known most intimately and deeply by those from within a society. Sometimes we can see more clearly when we step outside our culture for a moment to bear witness as participant observers to what we know so personally. To add a non-American perspective to our study of American cultural complexes, however, we have included a group of modern-day de Tocquevilles in the form of Jules Cashford from England, Stefano Carta from Italy, Craig San Roque from Australia, and Joerg Rasche from Germany.

Our authors are what are termed *key informants* in the language of medical anthropology, which offers the following definition of this unique role:

"Key informants must have firsthand knowledge about (their) community, its residents, and issues or problems one is trying to investigate. Key informants can be a wide range of people, including agency representatives, community residents, community leaders, etc."[1] As key informants, our authors use the concept of the cultural complex to observe and reflect on the psychic environment in which they live.

The Psychic Sea

One of the most stunning things that I have had to learn over and over again is that it is not self-evident to many people that there is such a thing as a psyche in which we all swim. It has been my life experience to know that psyche is not only real in individuals, but also exists in groups, often referred to as the *group psyche* or *collective psyche*. Psyche is inside us—forming what I call an *inner sociology*—and all around us, taking many shapes and forms that can shift predictably like the tides or overwhelm unpredictably like a tsunami. Here is how Jung stated it:

> Therefore it seems to me far more reasonable to accord the psyche the same validity as the empirical world, and to admit that the former has just as much "reality" as the latter. As I see it, the psyche is a world in which the ego is contained. Maybe there are fishes who believe that they contain the sea ....[2]

I particularly like the last sentence of Jung's quote because it sardonically makes it clear that the psychic environment in which we swim is much more vast and determinative of how we think, feel, and behave than we might imagine from the perspective of our ego consciousness, which tends to view all things as originating and centering around its own point of view. This kind of ego-consciousness seems to be highly over valued in the intensely individualistic American zeitgeist, as if what we take in from our environment in terms of moods, ideas, and choices is far more in our control than is actually the case. We do not "contain the sea"—*we swim in a psychic sea that surrounds us for better or worse.*

Jung's metaphor of our being like fish who swim in a psychic sea reminds me of one of my favorite books that I read as a medical student when I would retreat to the Yale Medical School Historical Library. There I stumbled on a book by Homer Smith, a physiologist who loved the kidney. He wrote *From Fish to Philosopher* about the kidney's evolutionary development. He celebrates the kidney as being the organ most responsible for amphibians being able to crawl out of the sea some 400 million year ago.[3] The primitive kidney permitted the amphibian to regulate a consistent "internal sea" by filtering and excreting those substances that would be toxic for the organism while retaining those substances necessary to maintain life.

Unlike fish that don't need a kidney as they use the sea as an external filter, we require the maintenance of an essential internal sea. Smith argues that the refinement of the kidney from its amphibian to human form allowed us to evolve from fish to philosopher. For a moment, let us imagine an analogous organ that filters the inner and outer psychic sea in which we live—its emotions, its thoughts, its beliefs, its memories, its images, its behaviors. We like to hope that such a psychic filter might be able to excrete that which is toxic to our survival as individuals and societies while retaining that which is essential for life. Of course what is toxic to one part of our human species may seem essential to the survival of another part. But our individual and collective psychic kidneys (like Facebook and YouTube) are imperfect organs, at best, because their filtering mechanisms are highly influenced by the distillates of previous as well as contemporary generations that determine what is worth retaining and what is worth excreting.

Cultural Complexes

We can think of cultural complexes as being part of the filtering system of the psychic kidney that dwells in each of us and the groups with which we most strongly identify. Distilled over generations, cultural complexes filter and dictate through their own narrative the meaning, emotion, thought, memory, image, and behavior of inner and outer events. Cultural complexes are determinative of what we retain and what we excrete from the psychic sea that surrounds us and exists inside us. In today's hyperconnected world of social media and 24/7 news cycles, we are drowning in a collective psyche that is also filtering, subliminally, what we do and don't take in. If we think of cultural complexes as essential components of the filtering system in our individual and group psyches, they function in the following way:

- *Cultural complexes are autonomous.* They have a life of their own in the psyche that is separate from the everyday ego of an individual or group. Sometimes they are dormant. Sometimes, as when activated by trigger words, they come alive in the psyche and take hold of one's thoughts, feelings, memories, images, and behavior.
- *Cultural complexes are repetitive.* The ongoing life of a cultural complex continues uninterrupted in the psyche of an individual or group, sometimes for generations and even millennia. When they are activated, they are surprisingly unchanged, in the sense that they are recurring, repetitive, and expressive of the same emotional and ideological content over and over again.
- *Cultural complexes collect experiences and memories that validate their own point of view.* Once a cultural complex has established itself, it has a remarkable capacity—like a virus replicating—not only to repeat

itself but also to make sure that whatever happens in the world fits into its preexisting point of view. Cultural complexes are extremely resistant to facts. Everything that happens in the world is understood through their point of view. Cultural complexes collect experiences and self-affirming memories.

- *The thoughts of cultural complexes tend to be simplistic and black and white.* Although they form the core cognitive content of a cultural complex, the thoughts themselves are not complex. They are unchanging and without subtlety. They are rigid and impervious to modification. Indeed, they seem to be impermeable to any outside influence.
- *Cultural complexes have strong affects or emotions by which one can recognize their presence.* Potent knee-jerk affectivity or emotional reactivity is a sure sign that one has stepped on a cultural complex.
- *Not all cultural complexes are destructive; not all cultural complexes are ego-dystonic to the cultural identity of a group or individual.* Indeed, some cultural complexes can form the core of a healthy cultural identity and provide an essential sense of belonging to individual members of the group.

Another parallel set of criteria that I have developed as a way of identifying a cultural complex involves a series of questions about the various types of mental activity that occur when a cultural complex is triggered. A good way to think about a particular cultural complex is to ask the following questions:

- What feelings or affects go along with this complex?
- What images tend to appear with this complex?
- What memories come to mind when this complex is activated?
- What behaviors are triggered by a particular complex?
- What stereotypical thoughts recur with a particular complex?

This book explores many of the American cultural complexes that comprise the collective psychic filtering system of emotions, ideas, and beliefs. At this time in the history of the United States, it is hard for a book like this not to be swallowed by the biggest cultural complex of this era: Trumpism. Nevertheless, I urged all the contributing authors to this volume not to make Trump the center of our inquiry about American cultural complexes. Trump is certainly a potent symbolic carrier and purveyor of some of the United States' most destructive cultural complexes, but his time will come to an end. The national cultural complexes that he embodies, however, will live on well beyond his being president of the United States. Many may argue now and in the future that he is an aberration, but just as many may conclude that he is a well-suited representative of the more virulent American cultural complexes. And there are those who believe that Trump's job has been to dismantle the cultural complex of the elites, progressives, multiculturalists, and other dangerous threats to America.

This book is not about Trump. It is about the collective psyche and cultural complexes that have been part of the national psyche long before Trump came along and will be part of it long after he is gone.

Cultural Complexes and Soul Making

The following comment by Jung leads to the heart of the matter:

> We all have complexes; it is a highly banal and uninteresting fact ... *It is only interesting to know what people do with their complexes; that is the practical question which matters.*[4]

If we extend Jung's insight from personal complexes to cultural complexes, what is most important is not that individuals or societies have complexes. That is just a fact of being human and living in human societies. Of course, when American cultural complexes contribute to the destruction of the country and the rest of the world, it does matter that they exist. But Jung's point is that complexes are naturally occurring "banal" facts of psychological life, whether we are speaking about individuals or groups of people. *And what we do with our complexes matters enormously.* Do our cultural complexes remain unchanged for decades, centuries, even millennia—whether they be about race, ethnicity, gender, religion, or any other primal human concern? Or are cultural complexes transformed over time? The enmity between Christians, Jews, and Muslims seems unchanging and unending for the most part, although scholars can point to notable exceptions such as the *La Convivencia* in Spain, which lasted from the early 8th century to the end of the 15th century and is cited as being a time of tolerance and the creative interplay of ideas between the three religious groups.[5]

Nevertheless, the racism and ethnic scapegoating that infects most societies seems as intractable as it has been for centuries. On the other hand, the homophobia and gender-stereotyping characteristic of cultures around the world seems to be, quite amazingly, in the midst of real and profound change. That cultural complexes tend to be fixed over long periods of time led me to speculate in an article that I wrote for *Spring Journal* in 2007, entitled "A Meditation on Politics and the American Soul," about the relationship between cultural complexes and the soul of nations. I put forth the argument that what we do with our cultural complexes determines not only the fate of our nation but also the nature of our American soul.[6]

About soul, the Nobel Prize winning Greek poet, George Seferis, wrote in *Argonauts:*

And a soul
if it is to know itself
must look
into its own soul:
the stranger and enemy, we've seen him in the mirror.[7]

I believe that each of us as Americans discovers different bits and pieces of "the soul of America" as the personal journeys of our individual lives interface with the unfolding story of our nation's soul journey. When we inquire about the soul of America, I think we need to keep in mind that we are talking about a living interface between the experience of our individual souls and that of the national soul. And if looking into the depths of our personal souls often reveals mysteries, ambiguities, and contradictions, how much more complex is it to reflect on the nature of our American soul? We should begin this inquiry with the recognition that we discover the soul of America only as we discover the story of our own souls. In this volume Lynn Franco and Sharon Heath eloquently demonstrate the unfolding of their personal soul journeys with that of the national soul. If the Hindus speak of Atman (the personal soul) and Brahman (the ultimate reality or soul), perhaps we should think about an intermediary zone and speak of the individual soul and the group soul.

Like any other soul, the American soul seeks incarnation in a specific place, specific time, specific event, and especially in a specific person or groups of people. This specificity of incarnation loves location and the right person(s) at the right moment. Abraham Lincoln, Martin Luther King, and John F. Kennedy come to mind. This very specificity means that many places and times in American history can claim some piece of the American soul as their own. At the same time, the American soul should not be thought of as bound to any particular person or group, any special place on the continent, or any unique time in the nation's history. As a whole, the American soul is much broader than its particularity and specificity, reaching as far back as when the Native Americans first migrated across Beringia at least 15,000 years ago and as far forward as one can imagine hearing Walt Whitman's Barbaric Yawp:

The spotted hawk swoops by and accuses me, he complains of my gab
    and my loitering.
I too am not a bit tamed, I too am untranslatable,
I sound my barbaric yawp over the roofs of the world.[8]

Where do cultural complexes and the soul of America meet? Simply put, I have come to believe that the soul of America is determined by what we do with our cultural complexes. If we do nothing, there is a good chance that the national soul will stiffen and lose its purpose and vitality. It will fall into a kind of mortification or putrefaction. As hard as it is to believe, we could end up, as in the cover image of this book, on our knees in awakening to the burial of the Statue of Liberty, just as actor Charlton Heston does in the 1968 film *Planet of the Apes*. In many ways, the Statue of Liberty stands as the most potent symbol of the soul of America to which Jules Cashford offers an amplification in her brilliant Preface that links the Statue of Liberty, the US Constitution, and the contemporary madness surrounding the cultural complex of the right to own guns in America.

On the other hand, if the people of America, or indeed of any other nation, actively engage with their cultural complexes and wrestle with them, I believe the national soul has a chance for renewal and strengthening. In my mind, active engagement with cultural complexes and the soul making of the US go hand in hand. This is how I said it in 2007:

> My thesis, then, is that the American soul is embedded in our various cultural complexes. Furthermore, our cultural complexes are what give political life its dynamism and its content. Both the energy and the issues of political debate spring from the autonomous, highly charged emotional material of our core cultural complexes. Political life is the natural social arena in which cultural complexes play themselves out. We forge the American soul in our struggle with our cultural complexes. In the political arena, cultural complexes seem mostly to generate heat, division, hatred; they are inflammatory and polarizing; they usually end in a stalemate without any resolution, only to recur in the next election or the next generation; sometimes they are ignored or kept unconscious for decades; occasionally they can be worked out slowly in engagement, compromise, reconciliation, and healing after generations of recurring battle. In short, they behave like complexes. We might now reframe the question about the relationship of politics to the American soul as follows: "What are we doing with our cultural complexes in political life?" Or perhaps the question may be better phrased, "What are our cultural complexes doing with us in our political life?" In order to explore those questions, we need to ask, "What are our primary cultural complexes?"[9]

In the same 2007 article, I created a list of what I considered to be the most urgently pressing cultural complexes of our times. With each of these complexes, the reader might want to refer to the characteristics of complexes I detailed earlier. Each of the characteristics—autonomy, repetition, self-affirming memory, simplistic ideation, potent affect, and identity/belonging—can easily be found in how all of the themes listed here recur throughout history in the American psyche.

Relationship to Money, Commerce, Consumer Goods

One of the highest values in American society has been the accumulation of personal wealth and material goods, often at the expense of or in disregard for the common good. This complex emphasizes individual achievement in the material world. On the positive side of this complex is the promised opportunity for every person to maximize his or her material well-being. The negative side of this cultural complex emphasizes the collective and individual right to eat the world, own the world, amass personal wealth, and continuously increase the "gross national product." In the name of participating in the American Dream, consumerism in the United States has become equated with the highest good.

Relationship to the Natural Environment

Historically, we have been a country of vast and seemingly unlimited natural resources. This has fostered a cultural complex based on the belief that this blessing entitles us to everything we want and that we own everything in the natural world. A growing number of people have come to understand that "stewardship" is the responsibility that goes along with the privilege of vast but dwindling natural resources.

Relationship to the Human Community, Including Family Life, Social Life, and the Lifecycle from Conception to Death

This country was built on a belief in the inalienable rights and freedoms of the individual as much as it was on utopian communalism. A core American cultural complex spins out of the unending dynamic tension between the myth of the self-sufficient individual in opposition to the welfare of the community as a whole and the reality of the community's responsibility to the individual. The good of the whole and all of its members is endlessly challenged by the rights of the individual.

Relationship to the Spiritual Realm

A Puritan heritage launched the country both in dissent and in a tradition of strict belief in moralistic behavior. The belief that the United States has a special relationship to God fuels a sense of national entitlement, which is matched only by a strong tradition of religious dissent, which drives national skepticism about privileged authority, divine or otherwise. Out of these twin foundational attitudes grew the tradition of separation of church and state. Inclusive pluralism and dogmatic fundamentalism are the vying poles of a uniquely American cultural complex that is the psychological inheritance of religious traditions. As in many other countries, the archetypal split between good and evil in the collective psyche projects itself onto many political issues, from the clash over abortion to the debate about the right to bear arms.

Relationship to Race, Ethnicity, Gender—All the "Others"

There have been two distinct poles in the American cultural complex with regard to race, ethnicity, and gender. As much as in any other country in the world, inclusiveness in terms of race, ethnicity, and gender has been part of national character and its proud "melting-pot" history. But ever since the nation's inception, the radioactive background behind the apparent embrace of diversity has been the premise that white, Anglo-Saxon, heterosexual men were destined to dominate the nation.

Relationship to Speed, Height, Youth, Progress, Celebrity

As the "new land," America has always been identified with what is new— a new land with new people and new ideas that every day seems to be faster, higher, younger, ever progressing, and ever renewing itself. The wedding of celebrity, charisma, and ingenuity are forever the hope of the American Dream and American politics. The "new land" gave substance to the belief in the nation's unique "manifest destiny" as God's will.

Relationship to the World Beyond Our Borders

The theme of the freedom of the individual versus the individual's responsibility to the whole is writ large in the cultural complex of the nation's relationship to the broader world beyond American borders. In this case, the nation like its international corporations arrogate to themselves the same rights as the individual whose freedom is viewed as paramount. As an "individual" nation, or an international corporation, for the most part, economic and security interests are placed above responsibility to the global community as a whole. The tension between the freedom of the individual and the individual's responsibility to the whole in this complex joins forces with another cultural complex—a sense of entitlement, which comes from a view of ourselves as Americans as exceptional and therefore as knowing what is best for the world. These two cultural complexes get acted out in peculiar ways—we wage war in other parts of the world in the name of individual freedoms just as easily as we retreat from broader engagement in the world in the name of individualistic isolationism, which renounces responsibility to the broader whole.

More than a decade after first noting these seven areas in which cultural complexes make themselves known, I began to conceive of this volume. Rather than tell the authors what to write about or assign topics, I asked each author to write about what most interested them in terms of the general theme of cultural complexes in the United States. Not surprisingly in terms of the very nature of how a cultural complex functions over time, what emerged is a significant overlap between the themes I focused on over a decade ago and how the group of authors independently ended up circling around the same themes. They did so in uniquely creative and original ways, but cultural complexes are intractable and the more they appear to change, the more they remain unchanged.

Structure of the Book

As the authors began to submit their chapters, I found myself overwhelmed by the task of arranging them into a whole, the structure of which would hopefully reflect the purposes of the book. Initially I had no sense of a coherent narrative or ordering principle. Taken all together, they felt like a *massa confusa*, or chaos that in many ways accurately reflects how it feels to be alive in such confusing times. Is there any real order or sense that can be made out of so many disturbing trends? I shared my *mass confusa* reaction to the book's many chapters with my old friend and colleague, Iden Goodman, before a sense of organic order could emerge between us. Gradually, I began to piece together an arrangement that hopefully honors the *massa confusa* without being swallowed by it.

The first section of the book deals with "meta themes" that are prominent as part of the fabric of many specific cultural complexes. These chapters sketch underlying mythic structures, or what Stefano Carta calls "cultural archetypes," whose presence can be felt in all the apparently disparate conflicts that flood consciousness. Stefano Carta's chapter tracks three dominant themes—infinite space, the Puritan ethos, and the Pioneer spirit—that have run their course in American history and left the country at a dramatic turning point in which traditional values have been turned upside down in what can feel like a medieval carnival with a dangerous fool at the helm. Betty Sue Flowers probes America's purity complex in which the endless pursuit of the triumph of good over evil reflects an almost Manichean split of the world into polar opposites. This split gets played out in divisive projections of one group onto another, not the least of which is how both Republicans and Democrats get caught in the purity complex of projecting good onto themselves and evil onto their opponents. Jerome Bernstein examines the difference between American addiction to what he terms the "Dominion cultural complex" in which Americans seek dominance over everything, including one another, other countries, and nature, and a long-dormant and now reemerging psychological construct of Reciprocity in which we seek a balance with and reverence for all life. Bernstein views Reciprocity as a law of Nature and therein an indispensable compensation in the 21st century for the prevailing Dominion psychology in which a dialogue between the two holds far-reaching implications for how both individuals and groups must go about addressing conflicts in the name of species survival.

Donald Kalsched explores the difference in the American collective psyche between a *dissociative psychology*, in which "the daunting complexities of the real world are simplified and reduced to polarized opposites driven by extreme emotions and primitive defenses" and a *conflict psychology* that cultivates a tolerance in which all the parts of who we are as a people are allowed a voice in the body politic. Joerg Rasche, a German psychoanalyst, takes us on an intimate journey of his American Dream, beginning with his boyhood romance with an imagined America of broad expanses and native vitality. Over time, this gives way to disillusionment as the more shadowy side of America's international bullying proclaims itself to him in the Vietnam era and subsequent military adventurism. He seeks to reclaim his childhood "inner" American freedom, perhaps for Europe if not America. The first section concludes with Craig San Roque's imaginative and visionary parable that offers a chilling glimpse of an America in the midst of devouring itself.

The second section of the book looks at more specific cultural complexes that emerge out of the meta themes. Any one of the specific cultural complexes, or all of them together, can dominate US headlines, blogs, and social media on any given day. The topics covered in the second section are often at the heart of intense political debate from which it would be easy enough to conclude that this is a book about politics. The section's categories of race, gender, immigration, national character, climate change, and medical care are all trigger issues that arouse intense emotion and fiercely divided opinions. But, in fact, the political struggles generated by these issues reflect ongoing deep psychological conflicts in the psyche of the American people.

In the second section, there are three chapters on race. Alan Vaughn examines the psychopathology of racism and white domination that undermine the ideal of a multicultural democracy through the shadowy and tricksterish manipulation of the capitalization of electoral politics, gerrymandering, and voter suppression. Destroying the checks and balances between the judicial, legislative, and executive branches of government further reinforces the cultural complex of libertarianism fused with capitalism to destroy the common good. Fanny Brewster explores how the trauma of entrenched racism infects the American soul of whites and blacks alike by causing a disconnect, even rupture, between ego-consciousness and what Jung termed the Self. And finally in this section, Ronald Schenk takes an unflinching look at how modern mass incarnation of young blacks keeps racism and slavery alive and well. Schenk places this modern phenomenon in the context of the history, mythology, and archetypal underpinnings of crime, punishment, and prisons.

Next we have two very different reflections on gender and cultural complexes. Sharon Heath's chapter makes an essential connection between personal experience/history and cultural complexes. Trump's election and its assault on women as well as ethnic and racial minorities literally hits her in the body as a Jewish woman who knows intimately from childhood the trauma of discrimination on the basis of religious identity compounded by horrific family loss as a result of the Holocaust. Steven Hermann examines the experience of homosexuality and marriage equality through the lens of America's poet of the soul, Walt Whitman. In the poet's challenge to the cultural complex of homophobia, Hermann explores Whitman's uniquely American proclamation of spiritual liberty and democracy.

Lynn Alicia Franco has written a wonderfully personal and, at the same time, widely applicable narrative of the immigrant experience in the subsection on immigration. Conflicts around immigration dominate political and social media, but Lynn takes us deep inside the psyche of the immigrant experience and opens up the personal and cultural dimensions of the immigrant cultural complex.

Another subsection focuses on national character. Jacqueline West develops a narrative of the American character in the 21st century with a horrifyingly accurate portrayal of the kinds of narcissism that have formed a complex of their own in terms of what has come to dominate American values and priorities. John Beebe leads an insightful tour of how the archetype of the child has taken on a new form in its 21st century incarnation as reflected in contemporary film. Current cultural shifts dramatically alter the expectations and aspirations of young people adjusting to a world in which the future is highly uncertain and the present may be all there is.

In the subsection on environment, Jeffrey Kiehl's chapter on climate change explores the profound disconnect between the reality of scientific consensus on climate change and the perception or misperception by the public of this consensus. Dr. Kiehl examines how American cultural complexes contribute to collective denial and inertia to change in the face of overwhelming evidence of impending catastrophic damage to the planet unless we transition away from fossil fuel in the next twenty years.

Finally in the section on healthcare, Richard Timms explores the toll that the practice of modern medicine is taking on medical practitioners, offering a view of one of the many problems challenging the effective delivery of healthcare in the United States. The challenges of balancing efficiency, equity, and quality with regard to everything from drug pricing by pharmaceutical companies to the policies of insurance companies to access to care for all brings to mind Dwight Eisenhower's 1961 warning about the dangers of a "military industrial complex" devoted to the accumulation of power and wealth in the name of protecting the nation. Today we are faced with the rise of a "medical, techno-corporate complex," and, for all its advances, it is becoming its own autonomous, self-affirming cultural complex with many dangerous side effects.

The central focus of this book then is not about politics but about cultural complexes in the group psyche and how they express themselves in society. At the same time the psychology of cultural complexes and the politics of cultural complexes get so interwoven that it can be hard to know which is which. Try to approach these chapters with the notion that you are reading about how cultural complexes get entangled with the American soul as it traverses an imaginary spectrum running from myth to psyche to politics.

Notes

1 "Section 4, Key Informant Interviews," UCLA Center for Health Policy Research, http://healthpolicy.ucla.edu/programs/health-data/trainings/Documents/tw_cha23.pdf.
2 C. G. Jung, "Commentary on 'The Secret of the Golden Flower'" (1929), *The Collected Works of C. G. Jung*, vol. 13, *Alchemical Studies* (Princeton: Princeton University Press, 1968), 75.
3 Homer Smith, *From Fish to Philosopher* (Garden City, NY: Anchor Books, 1953).
4 C. G. Jung, *Analytical Psychology: Its Theory and Practice (The Tavistock Lectures)* (New York: Vintage Books, 1968), Lecture 3, 94. Italics added.
5 Wikipedia, s.v. "La Convivencia," accessed August 28, 2019, https://en.wikipedia.org/wiki/La_Convivencia.
6 Thomas Singer, "A Meditation on Politics and the American Soul" *Spring Journal* (2007): 121–147.
7 Republished with the permission of Princeton University Press, from the *Argonauts* section of "Mythistorema," *Collected Poems*, George Seferis, Revised Edition, 1995; permission conveyed through Copyright Clearance Center, Inc.
8 Walt Whitman, "Song of Myself," in *Leaves of Grass*, Verse 52, lines 1331–1333. From Project Gutenberg, https://www.gutenberg.org/files/1322/1322-h/1322-h.htm#link2H_4_0026.
9 Singer, "A Meditation," 137.

Preface

Jules Cashford

> *America is great because she is good, and if America ever ceases to be good, she will cease to be great.*
>
> Alexis de Tocqueville (1805–1859), *Democracy in America*[1]

The Statue of Liberty, looking out over the sea as a beacon of freedom, has offered the generosity of welcome to the world for over 150 years. It carries perhaps the most inspiring words ever to adorn a statue. They come from a poem by Emma Lazarus, written in 1883, and inscribed on a bronze tablet in 1903 and laid in the pedestal of the statue, seventeen years after the statue had been unveiled:

> Give me your tired, your poor,
> Your huddled masses yearning to breathe free,
> The wretched refuse of your teeming shore.
> Send these, the homeless, tempest-tost to me.
> I lift my lamp beside the golden door![2]

However, the picture on the cover of this book, as many people will know, is taken from the final image of the film *The Planet of the Apes*—directed in 1968 by Franklin James Shaffner, set in the future of 3978, and starring Charlton Heston as the hero George Taylor.

It is the vision of this ruined Statue of Liberty, now half buried in the sand, which allows our hero astronaut to recognize that he is on Earth and has been all the time. He had landed in the distant future, not in an alien world as he supposed. Here in this final scene he realizes that this grotesquely broken and abandoned statue can only have been brought about by humans at war with each other, leaving the planet to be ruled by apes with the "intelligence" of humans. The apes experiment on the humans in the same way that the humans had experimented on the apes.

Kneeling in the long shadow of Liberty's arm reaching upward, the torch long dead—beckoning to no one, pointing to nowhere, the tiny figure bent over in awe and despair—all this tells us that this icon cannot be simply a *sign*, not for him nor for any of us. It is a *symbol*—which means, literally from the Greek, a "throwing together" of two worlds, whose union reminds us of the depths from which it came: those depths that—however we choose to describe them—are in themselves sacred and cannot fail to move us.

The Irish poet W. B. Yeats writes that "an image that has transcended particular time and place becomes a symbol, passes beyond death, as it were, and becomes a living soul."[3] And, further, "Whatever the passions of man have gathered about becomes a symbol in the Great Memory," which is the "Memory of Nature" itself.[4] It follows that such images may have a distinct life of their own, and also, as it were, a mind of their own—even that they make a claim upon us. Why else do these images reappear in new guises throughout generations, over millennia, "dreaming the dream onwards" in "modern dress," as Jung puts it?[5] Is it because they are archetypal images, belonging to all of us, which in some way offer us a mirror to dimensions of our shared humanity, trying to get at the essence, age after age—here, the essence of freedom?

The image itself has, indeed, a long history. *Libertas* was the Roman goddess of freedom, who in Roman times held a torch, and often a *pileus*, a soft cap that symbolized the granting of freedom to former slaves (though sometimes more in principle than in fact); sometimes she also carried a rod required in the ritual that freed the slaves. *Libertas* was figured on the coins of Antoninus Pius in 148 BCE. Liberty and freedom have, though, different origins: *liberty* comes from the Latin, with a Proto Indo-European (PIE) root, and *freedom* comes from Old English and Proto Germanic, both words carrying the undertone of being freed *from* something. In Ancient Greece, the word for *freedom*—*eleutheria*—was embodied in the goddess Artemis: she who was goddess of the wild, animals, childbirth—all that was *not* brought under human rule and constrained (until, perhaps, she appeared on the coins of Alexandria and was called a personification!). Etymologically, in Crete, the name *Eleuthis* relates the Cretan goddess of birth, *Eileithyia*, to the rites of death and rebirth that took place yearly in Greece at Eleusis under the aegis of *Demeter*, goddess of the harvest, and her daughter, *Persephone* or *Kore*, the reborn shoot, beginning as early as 1500 BCE. Vestiges of this may lie in Roman myth in which *Ceres* (the Roman name for Demeter) has a daughter called *Libera*—suggestive of the idea of freedom as a rebirth from enslavement.

The image has other resonances too. The magnificence of the figure herself may have echoes of the Egyptian goddess Isis, given that the designer of the sculpture, Frédéric-Auguste Bartholdi, was fascinated with the art of Egyptian tombs, where Isis was one of the great symbols of rebirth. The placing of Libertas on an island in the sea, as though, when seen from afar, perpetually rising from the waves, recalls Aphrodite, Greek goddess of love and relationship, the first fruit of the separation of Earth and Heaven, and the only one who carries within herself the memory of the whole. Or take the crown of seven spikes, which this copper and steel statue wears. Is it not reminiscent of some portraits of the Virgin Mary, wearing her crown of 12 stars from the Book of Revelation—the numbers 7 and 12 serving in different ways as images of completeness? Just as the inscription itself is evocative of the Sermon on the Mount.

Yet the significance of the statue may also be that it unites archetypal and political realities and is still almost within living memory—we do not have to reach so far back into the past that the country's origins dissolve in a mist of myth. The statue took eight years to construct and was a gift from the people of France in recognition of the friendship created during the American Revolution, and its official title is *Liberty Enlightening the World*. It was shipped across the sea and assembled on the pedestal of what was then called Bedloe's Island, now changed to Liberty Island and dedicated in 1886 by President Grover Cleveland. Whereas it speaks to us now as a universal celebration of freedom from any tyranny, the specific tyrant to be freed from at the time of the American Revolution was the ruthless and repressive British King George III. *Libertas* holds a tablet on which is inscribed the date of the American Declaration of Independence, July 4, 1776, and at her feet lies a broken chain and the cast-off shackles of slavery from Britain. This image was also intended to represent the abolition of all slavery in America and, indeed, for all and any kind of enslavement anywhere.

* * *

Returning to the cover of this book, the blue skies of the film's desolate ending have turned to blood-red, glowering over the horizon, so intense and all-enveloping they feel "doom-laden" or even "doom-eager," as the old Icelandic Sagas have it. This is much more than a sunset: the violence of the encroaching dark reflects and magnifies the devastation of the statue—implicating everything. Only the horse, standing closest to the sea and framed by the white spray of waves upon the shore, casts his own shadow behind him. In a book about the Soul of America, we may wonder whether the "living soul" of the original image has moved on, still with the power to startle us, but in a new way. Is it now pressing us to consider whether cultural complexes are the latest version of a loss of liberty—an enslavement of the mind?

John McCain said: "We are a nation of ideals, not blood and soil." The inalienable right to freedom is one such ideal, given that the country was founded on a magnificent refusal to be a subservient colony, subject to the whims and greed of a tyrannical colonizer, presumably justifying his actions by the pernicious idea of the "Divine Right of Kings." Yet, in any country, Rights of the Individual are inevitably followed with a Duty to the Community, composed of other Individuals with Rights, and also now, we might belatedly add, a Responsibility to the Earth as a whole. Nowhere is this potential conflict more poignantly illustrated than in the people's right to keep and bear arms, stated in the Second Amendment of the US Constitution:

> *A well regulated Militia, being necessary to the security of a free State, the right of the people to keep and bear Arms, shall not be infringed.*

This was written in the 18th century, when the right to bear arms meant the freedom to carry a musket, which took from 15 seconds to a minute to load and reload—time enough for someone to get away. With the absence of prowling Redcoats, eliminating the need for a "well-regulated Militia," the meaning was soon adapted to mean "state militias" made up of part-time soldiers, believed to be a protection against a central government, which was often feared as the latest enemy to freedom. In practice, many people kept their own guns though it was not an absolute right. But whoever stands in for "the other"—state or person, groups of people, or individuals—the gun is never put down. The underlying assumption of the right to carry a gun is that without a gun we would be defenseless, as though still forever fighting a noble cause in an alien land.

Yet, over two centuries later, although the weapons of conflict have altered in ways that could not have been imagined by James Madison and others, the law remains the same. Most of the guns of the 18th century were muzzleloaders with flintlock ignition. These included pistols, muskets, rifles, shotguns (not much different from muskets), grenade launchers, swivel guns, and cannons. Today, to point to the pace of the intervening centuries, a semi-automatic AR-15, invented in the 1960s, can fire over ten rounds per second. In 2017, the Las Vegas shooter modified a dozen rifles to shoot like automatic weapons, using an alteration known as a *bump fire stock*, which makes the firing easier and so quicker. On that night of October 1, 49 people were killed and 53 were wounded: there was nowhere to go. The sheer number of weapons would seem incompatible with a peaceful co-existence; there are proportionately more guns than anywhere else: the United States has 5 percent of the population of the world, and, at the latest figure, 35 percent to 50 percent of guns are in civilian hands.

Even granting the idea its best intention—to give people the freedom to keep themselves and their families and friends safe—it has resulted in a limitation of the freedom of countless others, many of them children, ultimately leaving a whole people on alert—in fear. The horror must be clear to everyone of any political persuasion. But acts of multiple murders in schools, offices, stadiums, and streets bring no concerted response, no resolution of any kind, no presidential leadership. Although barriers to purchasing a gun differ from state to state, it is generally agreed that if you want one badly enough you can get one. Without the "protection" of the

Second Amendment, these atrocities would be called acts of terror and the perpetrator a terrorist.

This suggests that a cultural complex, under the guise of allegiance to the Second Amendment, is undermining a shared structure of value—the sanctity of all human life—without which no culture can flourish.

No rational argument can break through a cultural complex. The arithmetical logic of "more guns equals more deaths" is met with "No bad guns, just bad people." This may be followed by: "All you need is One Good Gun." But then who does *not* think their own gun is good—especially, perhaps, when about to do something they would not want done to them?

From the perspective of the Statue of Liberty, we may ask what has happened to the vision of freedom, once so exhilarating and open-hearted? Is it now conditional on the right to carry a gun? Why else are universal background checks seen as an invasion of privacy, an implicit betrayal of a contract? Even when it comes to the ease of procuring military assault weapons, even after Las Vegas, even after massacres in schools—Sandy Hook (2013), Stoneman Douglas (2018), and all the others—the initial debate founders and then dies out. By contrast in New Zealand, *within a week* of their own massacre on March 15, 2019, all assault rifles were banned: no questions asked; none needed answering.

What seems to underpin the refusal to consider change is the implicit conviction that the original Constitution is a Sacred Text—that what the "Founding Fathers" set down is Sacred Law. Changing it would be sacrilege. When, in the Declaration of Independence, a new sovereignty was born, a new Myth of Origins inevitably came with it, as it does with the birth of all cultures: it was the time of the beginning of things—*in illo tempore*—when order first magically emerged from chaos. Once upon a time is always magical, in myths, fairy tales, and original histories alike; but, subsequently, the magic can go either way: the magic of inspiration, or the magic that becomes a fetish, as with Kurtz in Joseph Conrad's *Heart of Darkness* (and in the film *Apocalypse Now*), in which the originally redemptive idea becomes "something you can set up, and bow down before, and offer a sacrifice to ...."[6]

The great American mythologist Joseph Campbell warned, "Wherever the poetry of myth is interpreted as biography, history, or science, it is killed."[7] Once myth is confused with history, the myth becomes destructive, since what is then called "history" accrues to itself all the poetry of myth, and the result is inflation—endowing oneself with unearned powers. By the same token, the defenders of that "history" become Defenders of the Faith. In this light, the insistence that everyone should have the right to carry a gun may be seen as a *literalization* of the poetic myth of freedom and independence. Could the gun itself have become an unwitting symbol of the lost wilderness of the original freedom? Does it keep alive the re-imagining of origins, once faced with life or death decisions, recalling the idealistic energy of the original enterprise?

If that were so, then surrendering the gun would also be to surrender a dream.

If, as Yeats says, "the first mythology is one that marries us to rock and hill," how are we to imagine the first European settlers arriving in a new land with no mythology except the passionate values of freedom and independence and their own faith?[8] Many, like the Pilgrim Fathers on the Mayflower, were escaping persecution—although the American theologian Thomas Berry, who later preferred to be known as a geologist, used to say incredulously: "We went into this glorious wilderness and all we brought with us was a book!" He continues: *We never thought that this continent, its mountains and rivers and deserts, its forests and wildlife, its birds and butterflies, had anything to teach us concerning the deeper meaning of our existence.*[9]

What they also brought with them, inevitably, was the Western inheritance of a classical and a Judeo-Christian tradition—bringing, in other words, both the virtues and limitations of their earlier thought, but now uncloaked from the civilizations that had once contained them.

In the beginning they would have to be hunter-gatherers, self-reliant, self-sufficient, their lives dependent on their resourcefulness and their guns for food. They wrested a habitation from an unknown wilderness—and sometimes also, it has to be said, from an unknown people who were there before them—inadvertent colonizers in their turn. But for many it was a heroic adventure, embodying the archetypal myth of the hero, venturing into the dark unknown, sustained by ideals, courage, comradeship, and conviction in the rightness of their calling.

The dream of heroism is celebrated and perpetuated in countless American books and films: Herman Melville's *Moby-Dick* (1851), John Stephen Crane's *The Red Badge of Courage* (1895), William Faulkner's *Absalom, Absalom!* (1936), John Steinbeck's *The Grapes of Wrath* (1939), Ernest Hemingway's *The Old Man and the Sea* (1952), and so on. From the sixties onward, the films went all over the world: *Shane, A Fistful of Dollars, Once Upon a Time in the West, Raiders of the Lost Ark, Star Wars, Avatar*—the list goes on and on—all framed by the archetypal fight of good versus evil. Yet the "good gun" always moves on: the young boy, whom Shane saved by killing for his family, is left behind, forever missing him. Strangers who ride in on their horses—suddenly appearing in the bar, the town, the homestead—who sort out the bad guys, they all say they may be back "sometime," but we know they won't, call as we might into the echoing hills. The "good gun" knows better: he does not belong in peacetime.

But 400 or so years later, the mythic challenges of the original hero have now to be found within us, as of course they always were. The essential wilderness is now rarely outside in uncharted territory; rather, it exists within all the individuals who together make up the character of a nation. In that wilderness is both the best and worst of us, reflected most obviously in our allegiances and choices, and at a deeper level in the life we call good. Insofar as the "gun lobby" insists on the constitutional permanence of the Second Amendment, are they not "shackling America to its past," as Jonathan Freedland argues?[10] Once the shackles are back in new form, may we not talk of an enslavement of the mind that undermines the freedom to respond with compassion to the needs of the time?

The interpretation of the poetry of the myth as biography, as well as history, may be even more dangerous, though the one (history) may lead to the other (biography) in ways often too subtle to track. It might be considered that the perpetrators of violence may themselves also be caught in this confusion of myth and personal identity, such that their underlying motives may draw from the same kind of inflation. If the gun is invested with powers beyond itself, then killing with the gun could act as an unconscious *catharsis*—a cleansing of something felt to be evil in others or, more likely, in oneself, which may have been projected outward. If there were such a parallel, it would follow that what is sacred for the gunman in that moment is not the particular human life or lives in front of him in this historical present, with their own right to life. They may have become instead an embodiment of an idea. The act of shooting them, to a mind delusional in that moment, may think itself "exonerated" by the perverted logic of cleansing and purification, even granting a distorted kind of "redemption." This would then be an instance of that same confusion of myth and history that underlies—ultimately—the ease with which the gunman purchased the weapons in the first place.

If there is one consistent opponent to the possibility of rethinking the implications of the Second Amendment, it would be the National Rifle Association (NRA). It is an irony that Charlton Heston, who played the hero in *The Planet of the Apes*, became president and spokesman of the NRA five times, from 1998 to 2003. At the NRA's 129th convention in 2000, just one year after the Columbine High School massacre, he chose to play the actor again. Holding up a replica of a Revolutionary War–era flintlock long rifle, he said:

> *So, as we set out this year to defeat the divisive forces that would take freedom away, I want to say those fighting words for everyone within the sound of my voice to hear and to heed, and especially for you, Mr. Gore: "from my cold, dead hands."*[11]

It was a phrase he repeated at the end of each convention and at the announcement of his retirement, and it has been proudly repeated by many others since—as he must have intended. In fact the NRA, with a membership of about 5 million members, has consistently blocked the possibility of a gun registry and a rule requiring gunowners to hold a license. Indeed Harlon Carter, one-time vice-president of the NRA, implicitly threatened "any politician in America, mindful of his political career" not to challenge their "legitimate" goals.[12] Something, at any rate, seems to have worked.

On the other hand, there are many rural communities all over America— such as, for instance, those in the remote regions of the Appalachians—whose determination to carry on their own way of life, established for generations through customs and music and even their own dialect, has to be honored. Otherwise, as Bill Monroe, bluegrass musician from Kentucky, once put it: "That aint no part of nothin."[13] Any rethinking would not, of course, have to be as absolute as the original—or rather, how the original has been variously interpreted.

Jeffrey Toobin, in his article "Politics Changed the Reading of the Second Amendment—and Can Change It Again," points out that the NRA has "transformed the judiciary and, in the process, rewritten our understanding of the Second Amendment to the Constitution."[14] For the first two hundred years the Supreme Court and academics understood the Second Amendment as conferring the right "to keep and bear arms," *not* on individuals, but only on the state militia, though in practice the two often merged. Toobin refers to David Cole's book *Engines of Liberty*, in which he describes how in the 1970s the NRA set out to change this understanding and eventually convinced individual states to pass gun-rights regulations, and so "fostered a legal culture in which the right to bear arms enjoyed a privileged place"—as well as sponsoring academic research for their cause. In 2008, the Supreme Court rewrote its under-standing of the Second Amendment, concluding that the framers of the Constitution had originally meant to confer this right to individuals.

So here, to turn it around, history is being reinterpreted as myth. That is to say that the sanction of the Founding Fathers is here being co-opted for political ends, which are then—by sleight of hand—justified by the myth! The NRA may find itself "hoist by its own petard"—to use Shakespeare's apposite phrase of 1602,[15] since their actions reveal that, as Toobin says, the Constitution "remains a political document that is subject to the ideo-logical forces of the time," and so can be changed when a new time calls for it.[16] Which leads us back to the Supreme Court, and the original aspir-ation of checks and balances to keep the moral law, followed by a concern that they were put in place by people of good will, long ago, on the assumption that the oath to the Constitution would always take precedence over partisan politics.

Cultural complexes can be seen as those personal complexes that the cul-ture shares and implicitly ratifies—though interpreting them in different ways, when it is sometimes difficult to distinguish some of them from indi-vidual complexes. How crucial is it then that the leader of any culture be beyond all the complexes that have the potential to divide a nation. In ancient cultures the moral character of the leader was believed to have consequences for all the people, and even for the land itself. In Sophocles's *Oedipus Rex*, when Oedipus becomes king in Thebes, not even knowing what he has done, the Earth begins to suffer: the plants shrivel in the fields and the humans and animals do not give birth.[17] We can write this off as a tale of long ago, or we can reflect on the symbolic relationship that Sophocles offers us. The warning is that the leader of any country may not identify himself or herself with the country itself: the role of office and the individual person must be distinct and remain separate. It follows that when someone calls a leader to account for the good of the country—as, say, Tiresias, the blind seer, did to Oedipus—he should not be mocked or banned or accused of "treason."

Yet today there are no Delphic oracles to proclaim "the truth of the gods"—the objective otherness to counter all the warring points of view and decide between them. But there is at least the possibility of trying to bring myth and history into a right relationship to each other, not one confused with, or masquerading as, the other. America was born from a refusal to obey a king who claimed an absolute power, so he could never be wrong whatever he did, whatever he said. Louis XIV of France is often thought to have declared: *"L'État, c'est moi,"* and many others come to mind over the centuries in different countries around the world. One way of understanding how anyone can come to that conclusion about themselves is to wonder whether they believe that the myth of "kingship" belongs to them personally—such that the poetry of myth—its archetypal magic—crowns the *person* who wears the crown, not the crown itself. Then myth and history, as well as myth and biography, in Campbell's phrase, have become dangerously confused. In that case any leader—king, queen, or president—must have constructed a myth of themselves, which to their own mind would put them beyond the personal and cultural complexes to which we are all vulnerable.

So when *Libertas* is sinking into the sand and the torch of Enlightenment is going out, this book asks us to explore the cultural complexes of a nation, in the hope that, if we can become more aware of them they will lose their hold over us, and we may better understand ourselves and each other—and our different points of view—with greater respect.

Notes

1 Alexis De Tocqueville, *Democracy in America*, Project Gutenberg, accessed October 8, 2019, https://www.gutenberg.org/files/815/815-h/815-h.htm.
2 Emma Lazarus, "The New Colossus," originally published 1883. Wikisource, accessed October 8, 2019, https://en.wikisource.org/wiki/The_New_Colossus.
3 W. B. Yeats, *Essays and Introductions* (London: Macmillan, 1968), 80.
4 Ibid., 50.
5 C. G. Jung, "The Psychology of the Child Archetype" (1941), in *The Collected Works of C. G. Jung*, vol 9i, *The Archetypes and the Collective Unconscious* (London: Routledge & Kegan Paul, 1963), ¶271.

6   Joseph Conrad, *Heart of Darkness* (London: J. M. Dent & Sons, 1946), 51. Project Gutenberg, accessed October 8, 2019, https://www.gutenberg.org/ebooks/219.
7   Joseph Campbell, *The Hero with a Thousand Faces*, 2nd ed. (Princeton: Princeton University Press, 1968), 249.
8   W. B. Yeats, *Autobiographies* (London: Macmillan, 1973), 194.
9   Thomas Berry, Introduction to Tom Hayden, *The Lost Gospel of The Earth: A Call for Renewing Nature, Spirit & Politics* (San Francisco, Sierra Club Books, 1976), xiii.
10 Jonathan Freedland, "On Guns and Race, America Is a Nation Shackled to Its Past," *The Guardian*, June 15, 2019, https://www.theguardian.com/commentisfree/2015/jun/19/charleston-shootings-guns-race-america-shackled-to-its-past. See also his "This Sacred Text Explains Why Americans Can't Kick the Gun Habit," *The Guardian*, December 21, 2012, https://www.theguardian.com/commentisfree/2012/dec/21/sacred-text-us-gun-habit; and "Inspired by Trump, the World Could Be Heading Back to the 1930s," *The Guardian*, June 29, 2018, https://www.theguardian.com/commentisfree/2018/jun/22/trump-world-1930s-children-parents-europe-migrants.
11 Charlton Heston, May 20, 2000. Wikipedia, s.v. "From my cold, dead hands," last modified September 7, 2019, https://en.wikipedia.org/wiki/From_my_cold,_dead_hands.
12 Quoted in *The Week*, June 8, 2019.
13 Wikiquotes, s.v. "Bill Monroe," last modified July 7, 2019, https://en.wikiquote.org/wiki/Bill_Monroe.
14 Jeffrey Toobin, "Politics Changed the Reading of the Second Amendment—and Can Change It Again," *The New Yorker*, August 5, 2019. See also David D. Cole, *Engines of Liberty: The Power of Citizen Activists to Make Constitutional Law* (New York: Basic Books, 2016).
15 William Shakespeare, *Hamlet*, Act 3, scene 4, lines 206–207.
16 Toobin, "Politics Changed the Reading of the Second Amendment."
17 Sophocles, "Oedipus Rex," in *Greek Tragedies, Vol. 1*, ed. and trans. David Grene and Richard Lattimore (Chicago & London, University of Chicago Press, 1960), 54.

Meta Themes in American Cultural Complexes

Part I

Meta-Themes in American Cultural Complexes

Chapter 1

Here's Johnny!

American Carnival in Modern Times

Stefano Carta

> *We are, I am afraid, in danger of losing something solid at the core. We are losing that pilgrim and pioneer spirit of initiative and independence—that old-fashioned Spartan devotion to "duty, honor, and country." We don't need that spirit now, we think. Now we have cars to drive and buttons to push and TV to watch—and pre-cooked meals and prefab houses. We stick to the orthodox, to the easy way and the organization man. We take for granted our security, our liberty, and our future—when we cannot take any one of them for granted at all.*
>
> John F. Kennedy, 1960[1]

In the next pages, I will write about cultural, hence psychological, structures that might shed light on the American spirit and its historical crisis. I will call such structures *cultural archetypes*.[2] As a non-American interpreting the American spirit. I am fully aware that what I write will probably describe more about myself and my vantage point than the object of my enquiry. Therefore, I claim no objectivity, even if I refer to historical, sociological, literary, and anthropological sources to make my arguments. My attempt is simply to contribute to an open discussion, a dialectical process between the readers, my object of inquiry, and myself—a process to foster and protect the possibility to think.

My discussion will mostly focus on the "negative" aspects of the American spirit. This does not mean that I "dislike" or demonize the United States while "liking" the Italian or European cultures. I decided to focus more on the critical aspects of the American cultural and psychological world because I think that discussing problematic issues fosters new openings and new possibilities of analysis. At the same time, I am aware that my level of analysis is necessarily a general one, if not a generic one. In fact, how can it be legitimate to write of an "American spirit" as if something could describe in one articulated stroke the immense complexity of a culture? The risk of falling into generalizations and simplifications, which would not reveal but actually conceal, is definitely great. Nevertheless,

I will pursue such a general approach, with the idea that looking for similarities is, after all, the other half of the process by which we look for distinctions and specificity. Like the inductive-deductive circuit, the two always go together. I will begin with an analysis of what might be underlining threads in a fabric that connects American history and the American spirit, from the 17th century to today.

Space, the Final Frontier: A Historical Sketch

Europe is the continent of time, America of space.

Space is the first of three cultural archetypal features that form the deeper fabric of the American spirit. This notion is almost universally accepted by scholars and thinkers from Karl Marx to Frederick Jackson Turner, Perry Miller, or Sacvan Bercovitch, just to name a few.[3] The space these authors refer to is primarily a physical space, or, at least, the immensity of the "empty" physical space that the Puritan pilgrims found when they landed at Provincetown, on November 11, 1620. I will return to this first cultural archetype, but I want to introduce simultaneously the other two: the Puritan spirit of the American pilgrims and the Pioneer mentality. Both are connected to the notion of border (and then frontier), yet in opposite ways. For the European Puritan newly arrived in America, the world was safe only within, whereas the world without was an empty space, where the myth of the errand toward the Promised land acquired a concrete form through a progressive conquest of the immense "empty" American space toward the West. Thanks to the Puritan cultural archetype, the fulfilling of God's grace through predestination acquires a specific cultural form and name—*Manifest Destiny*. This is a destiny, which, with many perilous turns and crises, seems to have held until the first defeat of the United States in Vietnam.

I would like to underline the fundamental religious nature of this foundational cultural archetype, to which the American people and the United States are directly connected mythically, like emissaries, for the will of God and to the accomplishment of His glory through human deeds and workings. For a citizen of the European continent, a continent with no empty physical space to conquer for two millennia, but with a past almost beyond memory (the house where I live was built on 2100-year-old Roman foundations, and Rome itself is the oldest continuously inhabited city on Earth), such a claim sounds close to ridiculous. The point is that such a numinous cultural archetype of "heavenly origin" has been guiding the American spirit since 1620, with an explosive mix of earthly politics and religious faith.[4]

For a European born and living in a crowded (that is, small) place with a huge history, to speak about the "origin" of a country makes no sense. Going back through millennia the European finds so many instances of destructions and re-creations, so many continuities and discontinuities, so much mingling and reshuffling that the idea of an origin of any European country literally dissolves in thin air. It is not the case in the United States, in which one may feel comfortable in imagining an actual real foundational "beginning"—perhaps three of them that are connected in historic and symbolic depth: the arrival of the *Mayflower* in 1620, the arrival of the *Arbella* in 1630, both with their Puritan archetypal shrine, and the Declaration of Independence of July 4, 1776. I approach the foundation of the America spirit starting from these three dates, especially the first two.

The Puritan Ethos and the Pioneer Spirit

For Sacvan Bercovitch, the Puritan character is the essential cultural archetypal force that shapes the whole of American identity.[5] To explain his interpretation, Bercovitch compares the United States with Canada, a country as vast as the US, but with "no mythology." Disconnected from God and from the Puritan myth, Canada's physical space had never been charted as a sacred text like, for instance, Kentucky, nor did its conquest mean the fulfilling of a transcendent destiny toward the triumph of the Good ones against the Bad ones for the fulfillment of God's concealed plan of salvation.

The Puritan cultural archetype brought into the immensity of the American space by the *Mayflower* and the *Arbella* has been continuously active for over 400 years. One of the most numinous images is that of the "City upon the Hill," from the parable of Salt and Light in Jesus's Sermon on the Mount (Matthew 5:14). This image was mentioned by the Puritan John Winthrop in his lecture or treatise "A Model of Christian Charity," which was delivered on March 21, 1630, at Holyrood Church in Southampton before his first group of Massachusetts Bay colonists embarked on the Arbella to settle in Boston.

We must remember this image, as it represents the mythical idea of a fortress of the Good—a space Within, a "city"—that protects and shelters from the symbolic Without. For the Puritan, the "Without" was a physical space, where Evil and Chaos resided. With the official end of the frontier, declared by the American Census in 1890, this "City upon the Hill" eventually coincided with the United States itself:[6] the Country of God, against the meaningless, or mean, "rest." The archetypal force of this image, which stands for the whole Puritan spirit, is evident from its being quoted throughout history.[7]

On January 9, 1961, President-Elect John F. Kennedy used the phrase during a speech to the General Court of Massachusetts:

> I have been guided by the standard John Winthrop set before his ship-mates on the flagship Arabella (sic) three hundred and thirty-one years ago, as they, too, faced the task of building a new government on a perilous frontier. "We must always consider," he said, "that we shall be as a city upon a hill—the eyes of all people are upon us."

Ronald Reagan referred to the same event and image on November 3, 1980, the eve of his election to the presidency:

> I have quoted John Winthrop's words more than once on the campaign trail this year—for I believe that Americans in 1980 are every bit as committed to that vision of a shining "city on a hill," as were those long ago settlers ....

On June 2, 2006, US Senator Barack Obama gave a commencement address at the University of Massachusetts, Boston, in which he also spoke of the "City upon a Hill":

> It was right here, in the waters around us, where the American experiment began. As the earliest settlers arrived on the shores of Boston and Salem and Plymouth, they dreamed of building a City upon a Hill. And the world watched, waiting to see if this improbable idea called America would succeed.
>
> More than half of you represent the very first member of your family to ever attend college. In the most diverse university in all of New England, I look out at a sea of faces that are African-American and Hispanic-American and Asian-American and Arab-American. I see students that have come here from over 100 different countries, believing like those first settlers that they too could find a home in this City on a Hill—that they too could find success in this unlikeliest of places.

We may recognize this archetypal metaphor throughout American literature, art, architecture, and films.[8] From Cotton Mather's (the first Demiurge of the American Imaginary[9]) *Humiliations follow'd with Deliverances*, in which Hannah Swarton is kidnapped (as a punishment) outside by the Indians (the demons) because she had left the "protected city"; to the first American novel, Charles Brockden Brown's *Edgar Huntly or, Memoirs of a Sleep-Walker*, the first real "captivity tale"; all the way to Steven Spielberg's *Saving Private Ryan*, in which an American obsession unknown anywhere else is portrayed once again: to "bring our boys back home" after they have fought for God (for the US) in the wild.[10] Consider also the archetypal wilderness in works such as Herman Melville's archetypal image of the ocean in *Moby-Dick*, the wild of the North in Jack London's novels, to Frances Ford Coppola's jungle in *Apocalypse Now*, or Vietnam in Stanley Kubrick's *Full Metal Jacket*, or the desert in Paul Bowles's *The Sheltering Sky*, just to mention a very few. I anticipate that such archetypal wildernesses all portray the foreseeable outcome of the Puritan schizo-paranoid splitting between Good (Within, "City upon the Hill") and Evil (Without—outside, otherness, wilderness), in which what was repressed and projected comes back to haunt the America spirit.

As Fabio Tarzia and Emiliano Ilardi point out, it is Perry Miller who mediated between the two opposite cultural archetypes of the Puritan spirit and the Pioneer spirit.[11] The Puritan is sheltered in the safety of his predestined goodness. The Pioneer is attracted by the magnet of the wild, empty West. For Miller, the Puritans, who landed on a continent vaster than anything that had ever been imagined in European history since pre-Roman times, were part of a specific religious cult: the doctrine of the Atonement of Grace. In this doctrine, the faithful strike a contract with God, upon which the Pilgrim/Puritan will freely act in order to serve God's grace and hence reveal the life that was predestined. Jesus's death on the cross serves as an opportunity (a holy word, indeed, for the mythology of the "land of opportunity") only to those who are predestined to be saved—that is, for the Good ones. The Bad ones are bad and cannot be redeemed. Therefore, the doctrine of the Atonement acts as a continuous symbolic device to balance the opposite forces of the Puritan and the Pioneer cultural archetypes, producing something like a "Pioneer for God." This balance tipped in the 19th century, when the Pioneer took over and rapidly conquered the seemingly infinite space by projecting the Evil part farther and farther away.

The doctrine of the Atonement has shaped American culture. The United States is the predestined country whose purpose is to realize the Kingdom of God on Earth (unfortunately, since the 19th century this purpose has been transformed into the urge to commodify the Earth, which is rapidly leading to its destruction). Those Others who do not participate in this purpose are purely bad unless they convert. This same Manichean split between Good and Bad has guided the development of the American ethical system, in which those who are Bad are bad, and there is nothing else to be done but punish and ban them. This specific religious credo connects the otherwise oppositional cultural archetypes of the Puritan and the Pioneer. The frontier offers the propulsive challenge toward the exploitation, especially the material exploitation, of space. The Puritan "City upon the Hill" can be expanded beyond the known border through the Pioneer spirit.

In Europe, especially after their oppression by the Bishop of York in 1600, the English Calvinists had literally and symbolically no place to go. There was no space for any errand, as it would easily end up in prison or death. For both—the Puritans and the Pioneers—the immensity of American space, its infinite availability, produced an inflationary increase of their specific mission. For the Puritans it allowed for their conquest of territory for God to expand into the wilderness with a vigor directly proportional to the potential space of the North American continent; for the Pioneers, it allowed them to do the same in the name of human consumption.

Whether space was seen as a negative Evil for the Puritans or as an opportunity for the Pioneers, in both cases it led to the same transformation of space into a commodity, a commodity given by predestination by God's grace. For the Puritan mentality, space was meant for production, whereas for the Pioneer it was meant for consumption. In neither case was space—or, better to say, the wild—approached in a third, very important way, of which Henry David Thoreau in *Walden* is probably the most important prophet: space as a place for contemplation, inspiration, and understanding.

The fabric of what I am calling the "American spirit" has not been created in *vacuo*. In fact, the Puritan ethos was wholly imported from England. The same can be said of the cultural archetype of the Pioneer spirit—which did not originate in the United States, but which was one of the main motivations to emigrate from the old continent in search of a better life. The same would be valid for the radical replacement of the Archetype of the Senex by that of the Puer.[12] The dominance of the Archetype of the Puer did not specifically originate in the United States, although it has been a common feature in the West since the 18th century; and it still seems to be a fundamental, inextricable precondition for capitalism to develop fully as something that, for many (surely for many Americans), is absolutely numinous.

What is important here is the specific character that these features, common to the United States and the whole Western world, acquire when they meet with the archetypal experience of infinite empty space—something that is fundamentally connected with the primal, potential empty container of the Great Mother, a container that may hold the ego but that may also stimulate archaic phallic fantasies of infinite aggressive penetration, movement, activity, creativity, and agency. Such phallic phantasies constitute an important ingredient of the essentially male chauvinist American spirit. The phallic, violent nature of the Puer is always active, always ready to move, to conquer (Pioneer), and to spread democracy among the savages (Puritan). This is why the United States has been in an almost constant state of war since the birth of the American nation.

The spirit of the Pioneer exploded in the 19th century, when it overtook the Puritan archetype, without eradicating it, however, thanks to the structure of the Atonement, which kept intact the relationship of the Pioneer/conqueror to the Puritan God, who reassured the Pioneers that they were entitled to conquer just as the chosen Puritans were entitled to a destiny of salvation. With the "end" of physical space in the 20th century, looking for a more (now symbolic) space to conquer for God's glory (for "democracy"), the United States began to expand all over the world and all the way to the moon with Kennedy's doctrine of the New Frontier and the conquest of outer space.

The end of the frontier at the turn of the 19th century meant a slow and progressive infiltration of the American spirit throughout the Western world, so much so that now some of the American ethos that I am describing actually seems common, at least superficially, in much of the world. Just one example among many: the "pussy-grabber" Donald Trump—whom I describe as a dark, dangerous Trickster—was anticipated more than ten years earlier in Italy by Silvio Berlusconi, another disquieting Trickster himself.

The Italian and the American ethos are quite different in many aspects, but we cannot dismiss the fact that something irrational, unethical, and in many ways "culturally" crazy is trying to enter into our collective consciousness. And if so, there must be not only causes but also reasons and meanings.

Some Psychological Reflections

At this point I would like to reformulate my discussion of these three cultural archetypes in terms of Archetypes and complexes. I do not want to "psychologize"—hence to reduce—the historical and sociological levels of reality. Instead I want to turn the prism and shed some light on another one of its many sides. Therefore, let's start once again from the beginning, which in this case is the Origin of the American Nation. This Origin constitutes a true living myth in the sense of "myth" being a narrative (often implicit) based on numinous unconscious organizers.

The beginning of the beginning was the moment in which the Pilgrims, and especially the Puritans of the *Mayflower* and the *Arbella*, "decided" to leave Europe. I propose, however, that we should not underestimate what these pious men and women were leaving behind. In other words, we should not be polarized just by what they were about to find in front of them. I would like to suggest that this cultural, geographical, and anthropological displacement toward the unknown "New World" must have produced somewhere inside these first immigrants a traumatic sense of loss—a trauma of migration of which we see hardly a trace.[13] I imagine that such a rupture of the cultural shell must have been a loss so deep as to be denied throughout the centuries through a series of manic defenses.

This denial of the enormous loss of an entire "Old World" was made possible not only by the religious Puritan conviction that they were on a mythical errand in search of God and, through good deeds, were aiming to testify to the reality of their predestination. This denial was made possible also by the crossing of the Puritan archetypal structure with that of infinite space. In psychological terms, I might say that the Puritans brought with them a split vision of the world, in which, as often happens, the Good is Within (in the "City upon the Hill") and the Evil is Without (in the wild). Remember, the third archetype, that of the Pioneer, was already lurking in the background, carrying the opposite values of consumption versus production and space as an opportunity versus space as a menace to be morally tamed. The infinity of the physical space that the Pilgrims encountered acted upon them with a numinous force.

If before, in the land of Time (the "Old World," Europe), the historical, cultural, and social past was in front of the Puritans' eyes and the future was behind their backs, now their ontological world rotated 180 degrees. They landed in the universe of possibilities, a universe with no past, in which their errand could actually happen through infinite space and a glorious future. In psychological terms, this represents the denial of the Archetype of the Senex and the advent of the era of the Puer.[14]

Here we see two processes that intersect. The first deals with the relationship between the shadow and the ego. The second involves the Archetypes of the Father, the Puer, and the Senex. And all of these are encompassed by the Great Mother: the infinite available space of the land of opportunities. Within such a space, the Puritan and the Pioneer embody a grandiose child who, in denial of what had been lost and thrust into an immense "Good Breast," is in a constant manic state. This encourages a split between ego and shadow in which all the Bad projected outside into the "objective world," whereas in the world within—the subjective world— only the Good resides.

For the American spirit there cannot be any doubt. When any tragedy strikes the United States from "outside" (for instance, the Great Depression as a shocking break from the archetypal optimism of the Pioneer/Puritan mentality—a break coming from "somewhere else," the launch of Sputnik, the defeat in Vietnam, or the September 11 attacks), Americans always claim these tragedies seem meaningless and inexplicable. "How can anyone hate us?" Americans ask themselves in perfectly good faith. "How can this be if we have done nothing but spread democracy and well-being into the rest of the world where there was only poverty or just plain evil?"

In fact, the archetypal split and projection of the shadow out into the world is a truly foundational characteristic of the American Spirit. Let me provide some clarity by considering two uniquely American celebrations: Thanksgiving and Halloween.

The interesting thing about Thanksgiving (in itself a beautiful celebration I am quite attached to) is that the "thanks" do not really seem to be directed to the Native Americans, who were systematically pushed westward toward the Pacific Ocean and marginalized or exterminated. In a sense, Melville's symbolic ocean was now doubled to include the Atlantic and Pacific as the realm of the White Whale/Whole representing the chaotic, evil, undifferentiated dwelling of the Leviathan. From my experience, Thanksgiving seems to celebrate gratitude in a way that confirms a titanic grandiosity—instead of gratitude as a form of restitution for something that has been lost. In Thanksgiving, there should be an atonement with the Native Americans without hurrying to feel better until a real political stand has been taken vis à vis the Puritans' and Pioneers' historical responsibilities. But this would contradict the archetypal fabric for which they are the shadow, whereas the white men and women were manifestly destined to be saved.

Halloween, on the other hand, is a peculiar archetypal carnival, in which the dead (the repressed shadows of evil, otherness, and impurity) come back to haunt and excite the living. Halloween is not enough, however. Instead of compensating for the conscious unilateral "Good ego," by symbolically appeasing the repressed Impure Others, the spirit of Halloween has now taken over the American political world, led by one of those Others: Donald Trump. Such an ego/shadow split—or "schizo-paranoid" complex—combines the three archetypes of the Puer, Senex, and Father, which I mentioned earlier.

Nourished by the infinite availability of physical space, the Puritans/Pioneers felt themselves to be the kings of an immense territory for which they were predestined. The infinite availability of space became a symbol of the infinite potential resources to which the Puritans/Pioneers were wholly entitled by God. In other words, everything was theirs because they would turn everything into something Good (Puritan), or because they would aggressively take everything for themselves and consume it (Pioneer). In fact, this is a disquieting picture of a grandiose Puer who will develop an infinite greed precisely because he sees in front of himself infinite possibilities. In this situation, the conjunction of such a Puer with capitalism created a deadly mix that is now literally devouring the whole planet, just like the greedy Kleinian child avidly empties and destroys his "Good Breast."[15] This is an ethos based on endless greed: always wanting something more, something bigger, something better, immediately, yet without envy.[16]

Perhaps, Melanie Klein did not take into consideration the possibility that a real (non-phantasmatic) infinite Breast—the limitless Mother-space of America—could actually exist.[17] Such an actual Breast promises the total absence of scarcity and unfulfilled desire. It furthers the belief that one can take whatever one wants from the Earth by divine right without causing either depletion or encountering competition. The way such a Puer deals with his object-world is quite destructive. As opposed to the reverence for nature of an Emerson[1] or Thoreau, the Puritan/Pioneer experienced the wilderness space either as empty or as evil, inhabited only by "partial objects"—beings with no rights of their own. These partial objects included everything from the forests and rivers to the American Indians themselves. Such an archaic relationship was a destructive one in the case of both the Puritan and Pioneer. For the Puritan it was destructive because it disavowed and annihilated any other culture in the name of the Glory of God; for the Pioneer, it was destructive because it turned everything into a commodity to be consumed.

The object-world of the Puer is based on hatred. As Freud wrote in *Instincts and Their Vicissitudes*, the Puer must destroy the partial non-self-object:

> Under the dominance of the pleasure principle a further development now takes place in the ego. In so far as the objects which are presented to it are sources of pleasure, it takes them into itself, "introjects" them ...; and, on the other hand, it expels whatever within itself becomes a cause of unpleasure.... The original "reality-ego," which distinguished internal and external by means of a sound objective criterion, changes into a purified "pleasure-ego," which places the characteristic of pleasure above all others. For the pleasure-ego the external world is divided into a part that is pleasurable, which it has incorporated into itself, and a remainder that is extraneous to it. It has separated off a part of its own self, which it projects into the external world and feels as hostile. After this new arrangement, the two polarities coincide once more: the ego-subject coincides with pleasure, and the external world with unpleasure (with what was earlier indifference).[18]
>
> The ego hates, abhors and pursues with intent to destroy all objects which are a source of unpleasurable feeling for it.[19]

The grandiose, manic ego tries to negate its fragility by projecting its shadow onto the object that it seeks to control or possess. The failure to ask what the cost may be of endless and accelerating technological and economic "development for the purpose of gaining 'wealth'" is a function of the Puer's delight in soaring, a flight that will inevitably lead to the depletion of Earth and a crash landing on the hard ground.[20]

The Puer's hatred of the object-world may also take the form of the neutralization of space, in which space itself becomes a sort of empty tabula rasa. This legitimizes the abusive use of the term *America* for the United States and *Americans* for its citizens, as if there are no other countries nor non-US Americans on the American continents—North, Central, and South. A second result of this mechanism of the neutralization of space is the almost total disinterest in geography within the American educational system. It is as if the location of space doesn't matter. This couples with a similar disinterest in history as a function of the abolishment of the Senex that carries an interest in time and history.

This picture is based on an inflated manic state in which everything seems possible, a state in which the Puer dominates the Senex by unilaterally celebrating youth, future, growth, rights, materialism, novelty, stimulation, rapidity, and immediacy (that is, immediate gratification and the destruction of time). This Puer domination obliterates the realm of the Senex who presides over ageing, past, slowness, melancholy, silence, memory, and spirituality. In the world of the Puer, Senex values become either incomprehensible or meaningless. The Puer tends toward mania, whereas the Senex bends toward depression.

Anger Games

During the 19th century the Pioneer cultural archetype took over and the Puritan one assumed a rationalizing function to justify its greedy ruthless actions. But, eventually, the material space was declared exhausted in the 1890 Census. Although this statement is not factually true (there was still an abundance of empty spaces), this is the first example of an ontological change in how the United States saw itself, which leads to the present time.

As the power of the archetype of unlimited material space through Westward expansion began to lose its hold on the American psyche by the end of the 20th century, a different form of expansion into space for God's glory began to emerge in the form of "spreading democracy" around the world. And John F. Kennedy's doctrine of the "New Frontier" extended that unlimited space even farther into outer space with travel to the moon. For Kennedy (a Catholic) the conquest was no longer over and against the "Red Devils," who had actually welcomed both Columbus and the Pilgrims. The Native Americans had become assimilated into the paranoid Puritan complex by becoming the dangerous incarnation of evil in a world that was divided into Good and Bad. Now, the New Frontier, the new space to conquer, was the space that the Soviets first claimed with the launch of Sputnik.

Americans' shock at Russia's launching of Sputnik hit at the foundational core of America having been built on the three cultural archetypes of unlimited space, the Puritan ethos, and the Pioneer spirit. Always in search of an empty wild space in which to project the Archetype of the shadow, the history of this threefold interplay of cultural archetypes has forever sought to invent a new virtual space to invade and conquer— whether through films, the internet, social media, or skillfully manipulated information, which has given shape to something similar to what William Gibson called "Disneyland with the Death Penalty."[21] Nevertheless, the end of unexplored physical space on the American continent made it impossible to split and project the shadow as before. At this point, the repressed shadow began to infest the American psyche. The only constant in this shifting screen of projections is that the shadow remains projected onto the African American community as before. Even with a dramatic shift in American outer space, the inner space still contains a scapegoated subject: the Black. It is through its deeply engrained racism—perhaps the greatest issue for the integrity of the American soul—that the American spirit tries to safeguard its manic defenses.

A second effect of the end of available unlimited physical and psychic space on American soil has been the increase in the very American trait of imagining secret plots—a typical paranoid trait. This also reflects the constant activity of the repressed shadow. Even if they cannot clearly individuate their impure, evil object, they sense that, if there is any disturbance within the idealized city, there must be someone plotting against them. Someone evil.

In the limited space of this chapter, what I am trying to show is the beginning of a deep crisis in the archetypal fabric of US mentality at the moment when infinite space ended. One effect of the infinity of space was the neutralization of any inferiority, such as poverty, which was basically excluded from the social scene.[22] This situation was unique in the Western competitive world, in which all political developments sprang from social conflicts. Not in the United States, however, where the Puritan/Pioneer was not trying to cope and resolve poverty, but to look and realize success through the realization of the Manifest Destiny for which the Puritan/Pioneer was predestined. Marx himself, in the first book of *Das Kapital*, recognized that the only society in which socialism would not apply was the United States, precisely because in cases of social conflict Americans could just move farther West, funding their own new communities. Now this possibility has become more and more rare, if not impossible.

The infinity of space and its ability to neutralize social conflict made it possible to build the nation and write a constitution without any of the fierce social conflicts that every other nation had to face. For Hannah Arendt, the American Constitution was a lofty philosophical product, an ideal object, a declaration of principles that still holds after almost 250 years because it was neither an expression, nor was it bound to actual historical social conflicts, but to the design of the beautiful "City upon the Hill."[23]

The Marxist idea of the structural engine of economic class conflict simply did not exist in the United States in the same way as it did in most other countries. The shadow could be projected into infinite space and the ego could always imagine a success soon-to-come. If it didn't, one could at least find refuge in the idea that just being an American meant being a member of a superior, chosen people. In this sense, the Puritan/Pioneer cultural archetypes, connected to that of infinite space, created a formidable, unique anthropological device to transform (assimilate) any immigrant into an American with an alluring, inflated, and titanic self-image. And the next Pioneer did not need to come from a Puritan background to quickly become American.

With the end of infinite space and the closing of the frontier, however, inner conflicts and split, repressed shadow images began circulating within the "City upon the Hill." Prisons became more crowded with shadow bearers (mostly African Americans or social underdogs), and American society began to face some critical attacks on its grandiose, aggressive optimism. The first shock was the Great Depression of 1929. The second was the realization that the Soviets, in the midst of a full Cold War, had invaded outer space with Sputnik, their first satellite, on October 4, 1957. The third blow was the Vietnam War and the images of American soldiers unable to conquer outer space anymore (and then be brought back home right afterward); those young soldiers were actually stuck in the jungle as the United States experienced its first defeat. The fourth shock might well have been the lasting trauma of the attack and destruction of the Twin Towers on September 11, 2001—the very symbol in some ways of America's conquest of unlimited space. It was a horrible act of terrorism, a terrible massacre that seemed to come from a wholly other universe.

The lack of empty space, as it had existed from the very beginning of the nation's history, contributed to a major shift in the relationship between the ego and the shadow at the collective level of the American psyche. First of all, the lack of space in which to project and to penetrate made it more difficult to sustain the grandiose Puer mentality. The room for projections of evil into unlimited space diminished, and the shadow began to return to American society in two ways. When the frontier was open, the future was full of opportunities and promises. The three foundational cultural archetypes as organizers of meaning made it possible for virtually any American, no matter how disadvantaged, to share in the common Puritan myth in which the predestined would be saved and prized with success and admiration. In fact, part of the Puritan myth is the conviction that "anyone can become president." This is much more true than in many other countries (for sure in Italy), but it still remains a huge statistical improbability. Almost like winning the lottery, someone sometimes wins a big prize; some others win moderate ones; many win small ones; whereas a huge majority just spend and lose an immense amount of money financing the whole system—the archetypal myth.

With the loss of space all of this is short-circuited. Gone are the others over whom to triumph manically; gone are the others who are supposed to envy American purity and grandiosity. And, in a compensatory move, the sense of needing to triumph over others intensifies. When the Puritan structures supporting the projection of guilt onto others collapses, shame and anger emerge in the social arena in a new series of heightened emotions that organize and give meaning to what is happening. The predestination to share in the basic good of America gives way to a sense of inferiority. The loss of shared participation in the grandiosity of the American identity further polarizes the poorer and less educated in the United States, for whom shame and anger now more fully enter into the social arena as fuel for a growing sense of inferiority, the feeling of being losers.[24] Unable to participate in the more grandiose notion of being an American, the "losers" move toward the political right in an alliance with the ultrarich who represent the inflated ideal—the real owners of the lottery. This moving to the right is mythically based on the "losers'" desperate, paradoxical attempts to keep the radical Puritan differences and distinctions alive—even if, at this point the real "winners" are those who inhabit a "wholly other" world made of exclusive neighborhoods, immense financial possibilities, and hyper-expensive universities.

Within the now limited space, the proximity of the shadow increases scapegoating and, with it, the rising risk of feeling ashamed of one's inferiority. Therefore, shame lurks just beneath the threshold of consciousness among the poorer members of the population. Any image that reflects back to them their inferiority does not produce knowledge and consciousness, but rage and polarization. Unfortunately, this is what has happened many times with progressives (politically the Democrats) and "intellectuals," the last example being Hillary Clinton's comment from a presidential election campaign speech delivered on September 9, 2016, about the nature of the right-wing electorate, which she referred to as a "basket of deplorables."

The more such comments about the ignorance, blindness, racism, and even the stupidity of others come close to their mark, the more polarized Americans become. Neumann explains this by saying that the "old ethics" is based on rigid polarization of Good and Evil, which can include in its web the difference between those "personalities who are actually superior" and those who aren't.[25] I would add: And of those who act as if they are superior. We are not dealing with rational analyses and choices, but with powerful unconscious affects mobilized from the archetypal, numinous depths of a schizoid-historical illusion, namely that of the original purity, certainty, and grandiosity of the Puritan/Pioneer mind held together by the notion of Atonement with God.[26]

Another phenomenon that results from the limiting of space can be termed the "blackening" of society, that is the infiltration of the shadow into mainstream society. A powerful symbol of this moment in history occurred when Elvis Presley first appeared, singing and dancing, on the nationally televised *Ed Sullivan Show* on January 6, 1957. The subtle infiltration of the shadow into society is not the same as its integration, which would involve a true disidentification from the cultural Puritan archetype.

Another interesting example of the infiltration of the shadow is the revolutionary video *Thriller*, by Michael Jackson, in which the dead of Halloween, the repressed impure shadow, hunts and enters the pure world.[27] Along the same lines, Philip Roth's *American Pastoral* explores how the pure certainties of Swede—the protagonist of the novel—are shattered from within.[28] Another example is Cormac McCarthy's *The Road*, in which the archetypal image of the infinity of space and of traveling through it has radically changed into a voyage through a devastated universe inhabited by cannibals.[29] This is a world far, far removed from the dream of the "Pursuit of Happiness," indeed. A last example from a multitude of possibilities is one of Stanley Kubrick's masterpieces—*The Shining*—in which the whole repressed unconscious shadow erupts on 4 July in a hotel (a collective house on the hill of everyone and no one) built on a Native American graveyard.[30] The image is

that of a whole world tilting under the menace of the breaking of the archetypes that have organized it thus far.

The United States is Ahab's ship, the Pequod, sinking into the same
negative, undifferentiated ocean of split off evil that has haunted the
American soul. Such an infiltration of the shadowy ghosts culminates in
the last historical attempt to revive the old archetypal world. Paradoxically,
the attempt was by none other than the first African American president
of the United States.

After Kennedy's New Frontier, after Reagan's successful triumph over the
Empire of Evil, after Bush's permanent war and the creation of a paranoid
climate in the whole country with his fake "Mission Accomplished," it came
time for Barack Obama to attempt a double miracle: to redeem the Blacks
from the shadow of the Whites and to revive the "Old World" through his
motto: "Yes you can!" This motto resonated with the memory of the infinite
potential territory of the archetypal America. And it was the disillusionment
of a country that was waiting for a miracle that could restore a mythical situation of manic omnipotence that created the most interesting and dangerous
president in US history: the great, dark archetypal Trickster—Donald Trump.

Here's Johnny!

We have finally arrived at the end of our historical journey, which unfolded
under the operative numinous forces of the cultural archetypes of infinite
space, the Puritan ethos, and the Pioneer spirit. As might be clear at this
point, I have approached history in a way that is similar to Herodotus or
Nietzsche—like a myth unfolding through time.

I did not "believe" that Donald Trump could really become president,
yet, almost half of those who voted, if they did not believe it, they surely
hoped for it. But he did become the president of the United States, and
the question now is: what does Trump represent within the unfolding
mythical history that I have described?

In my opinion, Trump is the perfect symbol, artfully crafted by this historical mythology, of the ultimate stage in which the cultural archetypes
that had given an orderly psychological and social shape to the American
spirit collapsed, letting the dark waters of Ahab's ocean flood the "City
upon the Hill." In alchemy this is called *putrefatio*, the excruciating chaotic
mix of life and death, of values and antivalues. Trump is the living icon of
the dark Trickster who embodies the chaotic mixture of all those oppositional forces and values that were once organized and tamed.[31] Once
again, many Americans in search of rejuvenation of the old manic spirit
chose their best candidate. Yet the times have changed, and the shadow
can no longer be cast outside the United States. Rather it has grown
within a polarized political system while, at the same time, it was gradually
infiltrating the American ethos.

The Trickster is an important feature of the elusive god Hermes/Mercurius, a hypercomplex symbol of the paradoxical processes of the collective unconscious, based on the constant polarization of potential unity into opposites.[32] In fact, as an image of the complexity of Self, Hermes/Mercurius is related to the Holy Trinity and, paradoxically, to the devil, which Jung believed:

> His positive aspect relates him not only to the Holy Spirit, but in the form of the lapis, also to Christ, as a triad, even to the Trinity.... In comparison with the purity and unity of the Christ symbol, Mercurius-lapis is ambiguous, dark, paradoxical and thoroughly pagan. ... The paradoxical nature of Mercurius reflects an important aspect of the self—the fact, namely, that it is essentially a complexion oppositorum, and indeed can be nothing else if it is to represent any kind of totality.[33]

In this way, the Trickster, in the form of the alchemical Mercurius, may be said to contain the totality of the psyche and, hence, in a collective domain, the totality of the collective spirit. When the opposites of such a totality dissociate, the archetypal Trickster constellates again within the collective unconscious of the individual or into the unconscious of the collective psyche.

> It is not surprising that the spirit of Mercurius has, to say the least, a great many connections with the dark side. One of his aspects is the female serpent-daemon, Lilith or Melusina, who lives in the philosophical tree. At the same time, he not only partakes of the Holy Spirit, but, according to alchemy, is actually identical with it. We have no choice but to accept this shocking paradox after all we have learnt about the ambivalence of the spirit archetype. Our ambiguous Mercurius simply confirms the rule.[34]

The Trickster steps in and points things out, asking a culture to look at its own folly.[35] This is because, as Paul Radin explains, the Trickster is a liminal Archetype that lurks on the edges of transitional processes in order to foster new symbolic (psychological and cultural) forms.[36] On the contrary, Kerényi's view of the Trickster is that of being always outside laws and customs.[37]

In his book *Thresholds of Initiation*, Joseph Henderson describes the state of the "uninitiated ego" as existing in an archetypal Trickster cycle, a transitory state between youth and maturity.[38] According to Henderson, identification with the Puer often manifests itself as the Trickster archetype. It is the adult (or a culture) who has somehow failed to "grow up"—an immature yet tremendously powerful individual.[39]

Trump looks very much like such an archetypal figure who, similar to the medieval king of Carnival, appears around the winter solstice when darkness triumphs and the sun is at its lowest point.[40] This time marks the liminal time of death and, God willing, rebirth. It is a universal midnight, a nadir when everything may turn into shadow, a ghost. It is a time opposite from noon, the zenith when time is suspended and there are no shadows anymore in the world.

The passage from the lowering to the raising is marked by feasts and rituals, like the Roman Saturnalia, the medieval Carnival, or, in America, Halloween, in which the underworld, the dead, the shadow, the antivalues, infiltrate the upper world and create a seemingly chaotic situation. This is what the alchemists called a *massa confusa*. The goal was to appease these darker forces and eventually allow them to be contained in their own world.

During Carnival the fool is made king, and the donkey celebrates mass. Men and women cross-dress. The thief is set free, and the just imprisoned, until the end, when the reestablishment of proper order marks the rejuvenation of cultural time.[41] Elementary drives take over the more developed, spiritualized cultural symbols, and, in a somehow phallocentric emergence of this archetype, Hermes's nature as the archetypal phallus acquires a central position.

In my opinion, Trump is the perfect king of such a Carnival, as he symbolically embodies all possible features of such a mad, mixed-up, upside-down world of antivalues, expressed through a unilateral phallic/machoistic way, starting from the frequent references to his penis to the use of women as pure, debased prey.[42] It is interesting to note that the deep, violent discrimination against women and their use as social partial objects exploded into increased consciousness at the same time, as if the "quality of the moment" (what the Chinese refer as the Tao), is presenting both mixed, oppositional sides of this issue.

As it happens with the upside-down king of medieval Carnival, who was chosen for his social, that is, sacred inferiorities and wounds (which in normal times would outcast him), this president projects an omnipotent image of himself, while being seemingly "mentally wounded." In the sexually Puritan America, the king is a "pussy-grabber." In the land of the self-made man, he inherited his patrimony from the Father, although he went to great pains to conceal that. In the land of opportunity created by immigrants, Trump confirms the archetypal idea that every other country may be a "shithole," and that every non-American is dangerous. Yet he is married to an immigrant. In an American world, in which the Puritan/Pioneer was in a constant state of war against the (demonized) enemy, the King has befriended the United States' traditionally most dangerous and obvious enemy—the Russians. In a culture in which a politician once could not be caught lying without serious consequences, the King is a dark, hermetic figure who spins the truth in almost every sentence he utters.[43] This last point is particularly important, as it is connected with a systematic use of information to manipulate, distort, and confuse reality in order to create a regressed *massa confusa*, in which everything becomes unconscious—or nondiscriminated.

Yet, the king of antivalues delusionally still seems to defend the old archetypal organizing values: paranoid, he wants to build a huge wall to contain the (lost) infinite space of impurity. For this king, America is "first"— a grandiose, titanic, manic pretense, constantly paraded in order to deny reality. By creating a delusional claim of a menace from the space Without, Trump tries to re-create the old feeling of inflated identity in which everyone else is inferior and guilty or, at best, irrelevant. In fact, within this exalted Manichaean differentiation, one of Trump's mottos against Hillary Clinton was "Lock her up." This implied a definition of the Other as ontologically negative, impure, inferior, *female*, and guilty—therefore someone to expel into space (in this case, the outside in the inside: the prison). We are the pure ones, destined to paradise; the Other is destined to nothingness.

In such a situation the denial of catastrophic global climate change, confirmed by every scientist on the planet, is quite understandable, as admitting it would imply the recognition that the United States is part of the "outside."

Seen from the old archetypal vantage point, who would have ever imagined that someone like Trump could sit where Jefferson did? Yet this King is a "necessary" product of an archetypal development, in which the "Old World" is undoing itself into a chaotic carnival of antivalues mixed with the old ones. We should not underestimate the danger, as it is not certain that after a putrefatio there will be a real rebirth of a conscious ego. Such a dark character raised from the American cultural unconscious has been anticipated by many symbolic products in art, literature, and films. The title of this section recalls just one of them that I have already mentioned—Kubrick's *Shining*. This work is a true, prophetic anticipation of these present times, in which Jack Nicholson, possessed by the flooding of the archetypal bloody shadow upon which the American dream has been built, is transformed into an anti-Johnny Carson. The dark, repressed other-me erupts from the depths and psychotically mixes familiarity with uncanny *unheimlich*.[44] Identity is lost and the American dream becomes a nightmare. H. L. Mencken also anticipated the current American situation 100 years ago when he wrote with biting satire:

> As democracy is perfected, the office represents, more and more closely, the inner soul of the people. We move toward a lofty ideal. On some great and glorious day the plain folks of the land will reach their heart's desire at last, and the White House will be adorned by a downright moron.[45]

Therefore, the final questions are: What should be done? What psychological stand should "we" develop? "We" are those who, as Christopher Bollas writes, did not "vote for Trump and therefore represent the 'losers.'"[46]

In this new, dystopic dark Carnival, the absolutely worst mistake that "we"—the losers—could make is to be assimilated by the same "old ethics" that Neumann convincingly describes and look at Trump as someone fundamentally Bad, someone who should not have existed.[47] On the contrary, it is precisely us, the losers, who must discover the reasons why he was meant to be, as the most radical challenge in the world—at this point not just the United States, but the whole capitalistic world—is that we must quickly learn how to deflate and elaborate our losses and our limits.

In fact, in the new, possible era the challenge will be to develop precisely that capacity to depressively withstand being partially impure, to be a loser sometimes—this may transform America and Americans—and with them the whole capitalistic world. In such a new era, the Senex may finally be able to compensate for the excesses of the Puer. In such a new era, a new human reality may emerge that permits the integration of the shadow, which allows for the creative blending of hopes and regrets. This would be a new transitional space Within/Without, in which the shadow may become a different resource for the ego, as it may finally carry in itself the humanizing marks of limitation and finitude, without which the reality of the world turns into a thin representation of unilateral desires or persecutory, angry regrets.

The only possible viable future belongs to those who may withstand the depressive, deflating feeling of being wounded losers. They, us, must bear the task to extract care, sympathy, and gratitude from the mourning of the very loss of our titanic grandiosity. Instead of projecting the shadow and its impurity "outside," the radical challenge that the American spirit is facing, more radical than any other nation due to its archetypal fabric, is ultimately that of caring for the object, Within and Without. In other words, caring for the Other as contained within the limited space of its true possibilities and bound to the passing of time. This would be a true revolution for "our" whole little planet—our real city—and for all its living and nonliving creatures.

Notes

1 Edmond S. Ions, Speech by John F. Kennedy, Washington D.C., January 1, 1960, in *The Politics of John F. Kennedy* (London: Routledge, 1967/2010), 34.
2 Cultural archetypes are to be distinguished from two other constructs: *cultural complexes* and *Archetypes* (with a capital *A*). When I mention the *cultural archetypes*, I refer to what seemingly are stable and pervasive social, cultural, and ideological—hence, psychological—organizers that operate in what Fernand Braudel called the *longue durée* history. Therefore, the term *cultural*

archetype will not necessarily imply a relationship with the *Archetype*, which refers to C. G. Jung's theory and involves the potential activity of presymbolic formal organizers connected with cosmological and biological evolution, hence not necessarily with symbolic historical and cultural contents and development. I will mention both forms of archetypal organizers, but this distinction allows me to disentangle the *cultural archetype* from the *Archetype*, as I believe that a discussion that refers to the cultural archetypes could hold even if the concept of Archetype was not considered valid or necessary. On the other hand, the construct of *cultural complexes* refers to the activity of the *cultural archetypes* when, unfolding through historical time, they take different shapes that will nevertheless express an essential sameness. Fernand Braudel, *The Mediterranean and the Mediterranean World in the Age of Philip II* (Berkeley: University of California Press, 1949/1996); Richard E. Lee, *The Long Durée and World-Systems Analysis* (Albany: State University of New York Press, 2012).

3 Frederick Jackson Turner, *The Frontier in American History* (London: Penguin Books, 1893); Perry Miller, *The New England Mind: The Seventeenth Century* (Cambridge, MA: The Belknap Press of Harvard University Press, 1939/1983); *Errand Into the Wilderness* (Cambridge, MA: The Belknap Press of Harvard University Press, 1939/1956); or Sacvan Bercovitch, *The Puritan Origins of the American Self* (London: Yale University Press, 1977).

4 The tradition of the President swearing on the Bible is an example of the curious kind of illuminism of the American spirit. Looking down to society, the constant literal quoting of the Bible is striking (as if a 500-years hermeneutic tradition had never existed), as is the reference to "God" (Which one? Whose?) by every politician and a multitude of sects, each one with its followers. In a totally opposite way from the British (and the French), the American spirit is soaked with a collective numinous influence that tends to take some aspects and shapes that are often theologically plainly ridiculous, when they are not wholly perverted, as in the frequent cases in which the "pastor" acts like a money-collecting machine (for his or her personal materialistic greed).

5 Bercovitch, *The Puritan Origins of the American Self.*

6 Turner, *The Frontier in American History.*

7 The following quotes from John F. Kennedy, Ronald Reagan, and Barack Obama are from Wikipedia, s.v., City Upon a Hill, last modified July 3, 2019, https://en.wikipedia.org/wiki/City_upon_a_Hill.

8 Francesco Dragosei, *Lo Squalo e il Gattacielo. Miti e Fantasni dell'Immaginario Americano* (Bologna: Il Mulino, 2002).

9 Fabio Tarzia and Emiliano Ilardi, *Spazi (S)Confinati* (Castel San Pietro Romano: Manifestolibri, 2015), 42.

10 Cotton Mather, *Humiliations follow'd with Deliverances* (Boston: B. Green & F. Allen for Samuel Phillips at the brick shop, 1696); Charles Brockden Brown, *Edgar Huntly or, Memoirs of a Sleep-Walker* (Philadelphia: H. Maxwell, 1799); *Saving Private Ryan*, directed by Steven Spielberg, screenplay by Robert Rodat (DreamWorks Distribution, 1998).

11 Tarzia and Ilardi, *Spazi (S)Confinati*; Miller, *The New England Mind* and *Errand into the Wilderness.*

12 René Girard, *Violence and the Sacred* (Baltimore: Johns Hopkins University Press, 1977).

13 Tobie Nathan, *La folie des autres: Traité d'ethnopsychiatrie clinique* (Paris: Dunod, 2013).

14 C. G. Jung, *The Collected Works of C.G. Jung*, vol. 9, *The Archetypes of the Collective Unconscious* (Princeton: Princeton University Press, 1969); James

Hillman, *Senex and Puer: Uniform Edition of the Writings of James Hillman*, vol. 3 (Thompson, CT: Spring Publications, 2015); Marie-Louise von Franz, *The Problem of the Puer Aeternus* (Toronto: Inner City Books, 2000).

15 Melanie Klein, *Envy and Gratitude* (London: Vintage, 1975).

16 This made it possible, at least to a certain extent, for a competitive society and mentality such as the American one to be transcended by the Puritan myth, which affirms that those who prevail fulfill the general plan of destiny. This myth includes those who lose by being positioned as *scapegoats*. African Americans have fulfilled this role within the United States as do the Others to be conquered outside the US.

17 Not anymore. The situation has now changed.

18 Sigmund Freud, *The Standard Edition of the Complete Psychological Works of Sigmund Freud*, Volume XIV, *Instincts and their Vicissitudes* (London: Hogarth Press, 1915), 133–134.

19 Ibid., 136.

20 Wealth refers to the original fulfilling relationship with the Great Mother (in reductive terms with the Milk-Mother). It may be useful to recall that for the Romans money was under the Great Mother Juno's domain—*Juno Moneta*.

21 William Gibson, "Disneyland with the Death Penalty," *Wired*, September/October 1993, https://www.wired.com/1993/04/gibson-2/.

22 R. Zorzi, Introduction to *Sulla rivoluzione*, by Hannah Arendt (Torino: Edizioni di Comunità, 1999).

23 Hannah Arendt, *Sulla rivoluzione* (Torino: Edizioni di Comunità, 1999).

24 Larissa MacFarquhar, "Trumptown: How a West Virginia County Turned Deep Red," *The New Yorker*, October 3, 2016, 56–67.

25 Erich Neumann, *Depth Psychology and a New Ethic* (Boston: Shambhala, 1990), 54.

26 Once again, I want to make clear that this is and cannot be a wholly satisfactory explanation. It is just the explanation that pertains to the level of analysis that I have decided to tackle. Specific economic, "racial," and gender issues, as well as many others are involved in the highly complex picture of the American spirit.

27 Michael Jackson, *Thriller*, directed by John Landis (Quincy Jones Productions, 1982), Official Music Video, https://www.youtube.com/watch?v=sOnqjkJTMaA.

28 Philip Roth, *American Pastoral* (New York: Vintage International, 1998).

29 Cormac McCarthy, *The Road* (New York: Vintage International, 2006).

30 *The Shining*, directed by Stanley Kubrick (Warner Brothers, 1980). Based on the novel by Stephen King, *The Shining* (New York: Doubleday, 1977).

31 In passing, I would like to point to a somehow uncanny aspect of what seems like a literal embodiment of the *Puer* in Trump's appearance, which makes him look like a grown-up baby. Although it may seem farfetched, so-called *Puer* personalities tend to look physically younger than their age. In Trump's case, this has been brought to quite extreme consequences.

32 C. G. Jung, "The Spirit Mercurius" (1943/1948), in *The Collected Works of C. G. Jung*, vol. 13, *Psychology and Alchemy* (Princeton: Princeton University Press, 1967), 288.

33 Ibid., 288–289.

34 Ibid., 288.

35 Kimberly A. Christen Withey and Sam D. Gill, *Clowns and Tricksters: An Encyclopedia of Tradition and Culture* (Santa Barbara: ABC-CLIO, 1998); Lewis Hyde, *Trickster Makes This World: Mischief, Myth and Art* (New York: Farrar, Straus & Giroux, 2010).

36 Paul Radin, *The Trickster: A Study in American Indian Mythology* (Oxford, England: Philosophical Library, 1956).
37 Karl Kerényi, "The Trickster in Relation to Greek mythology," in Paul Radin, *The Trickster: A Study in American Indian Mythology* (Oxford, England: Philosophical Library, 1956).
38 Joseph Henderson, *Thresholds of Initiation* (Wilmette, Ill.: Chiron Publications, 1967).
39 Ibid., 20.
40 The etymology of "carnival" is dubious: it may be *Carmen levare* (to sing prayers) or *carnem levare* (to strip the flesh away). Both are clearly religious etymologies, and the second directly refers to the underworld. The world upside down.
41 Radin, *The Trickster*; Michail Bachtin, *L'opera di Rabelais e la cultura popolare* (Torino: Einaudi, 2012); Vittoria Lanternari, *La Grande Festa: Storia del Capodanno nelle Civiltà Primitive* (Torino: Il Saggiatore, 1959).
42 Even the peculiar, unilaterally phallic nature of this specific form of the Trickster archetype denounces the need to reintegrate the split opposites (in this case, the "masculine" and the "feminine") through a liminal, chaotic, dangerous rite of initiation. There may well be different cultural forms in which the Trickster appears as a feminine figure. See Ricki Stefani Tannen, *The Female Trickster: The Mask That Reveals: Post-Jungian and Postmodern Psychological Perspectives on Women in Contemporary Culture* (London: Routledge, 2014).
43 Glenn Kessler, Salvador Rizzo, and Meg Kelley, "President Trump Has Made 10,796 False or Misleading Claims over 869 Days," *The Washington Post*, June 10, 2019, https://www.washingtonpost.com/politics/2019/06/10/president-trump-has-made-false-or-misleading-claims-over-days/?utm_term=.20f0dcc78e29.
44 Sigmund Freud, *The Standard Edition of the Complete Psychological Works of Sigmund Freud*, vol. XVII, *The Uncanny* (London: Hogarth Press, 1919).
45 H. L. Mencken, "Bayard vs. Lionheart," *Baltimore Evening Sun*, July 26, 1920.
46 Christopher Bollas, *Meaning and Melancholia: Life in the Age of Bewilderment* (London, New York: Routledge, 2018).
47 Neumann, *Depth Psychology and a New Ethic*.

Chapter 2

The Purity Complex

Betty Sue Flowers

Giovanni, a young student who has just arrived in Padua, looks down from his apartment window and sees a beautiful woman tending plants in a garden built around an old Italian fountain. After days of watching her, Giovanni falls in love—but begins to notice that although the young woman seems pure of heart, the bouquet he throws down to her wilts, and the lizard that has come near her immediately dies, as if poisoned. In fact, every plant in the garden is poisonous—and so is the breath of the beautiful maiden whose father has raised her as the subject of a scientific experiment in which she has become immune to the effects of poisonous plants.

"Rappaccini's Daughter," Hawthorne's 1844 short story, dramatizes not only the struggle of good versus evil and scientific objectivity versus desire, but also how we can *know* what is good and what is evil.[1] Is it through reason? Or through empathy? Is Beatrice, the young woman, a guide to the good, as Dante's Beatrice was? Or is she more like Eve, a force in the garden that leads to sin and death?

This story has fascinated generations of American readers because it springs from Hawthorne's deep engagement with one of the most powerful of American cultural complexes: the purity complex.[2] Because of the way the United States was founded and the context in which its government was constructed, the purity complex still exerts a magnetic pull over the inner life of the nation.

What is the purity complex and how was it formed? Why is the United States uniquely susceptible to it? And why, ironically, in the age of Trump, might it finally be rising up into our national consciousness?

Purity is "freedom from adulteration or contamination" or "freedom from immorality, especially of a sexual nature."[3] It is often represented by white, as in a bridal gown. Purity is without stain or blemish. The language of purity permeates the practice of Protestant Christianity in the United States, as many hymns attest—"Oh Precious is the flow/that makes me white as snow" or "What can heal a wounded soul/What can make us white as snow."[4]

Or consider this hymn from 1878:

Are you washed in the blood
In the soul-cleansing blood of the lamb?
Are your garments spotless? Are they white as snow?
Are you washed in the blood of the lamb?[5]

One of the earliest rivals to Christianity was Manichaeism, a religion originating in Persia and very popular from the 3rd to 7th centuries CE. Manicheans believed that the world was divided between good and evil, with the forces of light in a cosmic struggle with the forces of darkness. St. Augustine was a Manichean before he converted to Christianity, and good versus evil, purity versus sin, sex versus chastity, and other dualities permeated his thinking and the centuries of Christian theology he so influenced through his writings.

If animism is the natural religion of primal societies, then Manichaeism is the default religious position of primal rationality. Humans learn what *dark* is because of *light*. We know *up* only in relation to *down*. *Male* and *female* are also primal opposites, as are *thinking* and *feeling* and *left* and *right*. At a young age, we divide the world into opposites as a basic category of thought.

But then we tend to move, without awareness, from creating opposites to ranking them. Any group of students, if given a list of opposites, can agree on which is "higher and lower" or "better and worse" or "superior and subordinate": *intellect* is higher than *emotion*; *light* is better than *dark*; *right* is better than the *left* (*sinister* in Latin); *male* is superior to *female*.[6] It's not that the students believe this to be the case; it's that they know this to be the unconscious structure of cultural reality. They have no hesitation in deciding where to place the opposites in a table like Table 2.1.

Lower/Worse	Higher/Better
Low	High
Moon	Sun
Emotion	Intellect
Left	Right
Down	Up
Black	White
Unstable	Stable
Dark	Light
Female	Male
Irrational	Rational
Child	Adult
Unclean	Clean

A further human mental habit kicks in next—all the elements in the left column are associated with each other, so that female is dark, emotional, associated with the moon, unstable, close to the earth (low). Male is stable and intellectual and associated with the sun and higher things, like the light of reason.

What happens, then, when the human habit of understanding the world through opposites and then valuing one member of a pair over the other is amalgamated into a system in which the "higher" half of a pair is good and the lower evil? Anything of a mixed nature is impure and therefore on the side of evil. In the pair of opposites male-female, male is ranked above female, so the female becomes associated with evil. In Milton's *Paradise Lost*, paradise was lost when Eve (emotional, evil) tempted Adam (rational, good). But the mistake happened before the act when Eve's weak intellect succumbed to the rational but flawed argument of the snake and when Adam left the realm of reason, where he belonged, because of his desire to be with Eve. His reason was overcome by emotion.

The original sin of disobedience was the result of Adam succumbing to Eve. "In Adam's fall, we fall all." Sex is the archetypal coming together of the opposites, the paradoxical "coming down" of the male to the female, the original impurity, the mortal taint, the fount and origin of sin. Many of the rules pertaining to women's behavior and dress throughout the world are designed to protect men from contact with the impure, including their own "impure" desires.

The stark dualism underlying much of Christianity was ameliorated over the centuries by the Catholic Church. Like most institutions, it made accommodations to power; and being powerful itself, it became adept in the nuances of in-between spaces and gray areas—popes fathering children, or practices like confession, or the selling of penances that made living as a fallible human being more bearable.

But with the Protestant Reformation, a "purification" of the church led to a schism in Christianity and a diaspora of "Puritan" dissenters to New England. Many early founders created covenants among themselves and outlawed "impure" pagan practices that had been incorporated into Christian culture, such as Maypoles and Christmas trees.

The threat of evil became personified in the figure of the devil who possessed a number of young girls in Salem, Massachusetts, in the spring of 1692—or so the girls claimed, pointing out the "witches" who had caused their symptoms. During the next year and a half, more than 200 people were accused of witchcraft. Nineteen were hanged; one was crushed to death; and five died in prison. Only those who confessed they were witches had a chance of being saved. Most of the accused were women, who were considered to be more vulnerable to the wiles of the devil. John Hathorne, Hawthorne's ancestor, was the only judge in the Salem witch trials who never expressed remorse for his judgments.

The theme of purity occurred not only during the Salem witch trials, but also in another form during the pamphlet wars that formed part of the background leading to the American Revolution. The colonists initially argued that they weren't trying to break away from King and Mother Country but were simply trying to enjoy their full rights as Englishmen. Later, however, they began to talk in terms of "purifying" the English system (which they admired) in the hope that as they formed a more perfect union, the new American system would, in turn, inspire the English to purify and improve their own constitutional system:

> America "ere long will build an empire upon the ruins of Great Britain; will adopt its constitution purged of its impurities, and from an experience of its defects will guard against those evils which have wasted its vigor and brought it to an untimely end."[7]

"Wasting vigor" was a commonly repeated theme, for the American thinkers had in mind the fall of the Roman Empire, which they attributed to dissolution, immorality, and effeminacy (from the manly Julius Caesar to the degenerate Caligula, for example). The 18th-century courts, both French and English, with their excesses of luxury and immorality, shocked many American visitors:

> Like Rome in its decline, England, "from being the nursery of heroes, became the residence of musicians, pimps, panders, and catamites." The swift decline of her empire, which, it was observed, had reached its peak only between 1758 and the Stamp Act, resulted from the same poison that had proved so fatal to free states in classical antiquity: the corruption, effeminacy, and languor that came from "the riches and luxuries of the East" and led to a calamitous "decay of virtue" and the collapse of the constitution.[8]

The classic "virtues" of the Romans consisted of a long list of attributes, including gravity, dutifulness, truthfulness, and prudence—the opposite of "corruption, effeminacy, and languor." The Roman virtues were "manly" virtues, leading the mythical hero Aeneas to leave behind the soft enticements of Dido, the Queen of Carthage, and her court in order to fulfill his duty of founding Rome. Indeed, the word *virtue* itself comes from the Latin root *vir*, "man." (When applied to a woman, of course, *virtue* meant "virginity" or "chastity.")

In addition to the Puritan religious influence and the desire to purify the English constitution, there was a third key element in the early formation of the purity complex in American life: slavery, America's original sin. In the Manichean world of opposites, a black *man* might theoretically be superior to a woman, but a *black* man was inferior to anything that was white. Just a drop of "black blood" was enough to "stain" the purity of someone whose skin color could "pass" as white.

Black slots into the inferior side of the dualities, along with *child* and *emotion* and *irrational* and *unclean*. The unconscious association of *black* with *unclean* and *irrational* was manifest in then Senator Joe Biden's gaffe in 2007, when he praised Senator Obama, his rival in the Presidential race, as an "African-American who is articulate and bright and clean."[9] Unlike Trump, Biden has never been seen as particularly racist—but as studies of implicit bias are showing more and more clearly, even those of us who do not hold racist beliefs can be unconsciously biased. "My tribe" and "other tribe" seem to be built into the human dualistic structures of thinking.

If racism is a bias built on dualistic ways of thinking, these ways of thinking in themselves help to hold racism in place, in spite of our founding value that "All men are created equal." When the Civil War finally affirmed this value and black men legally got the vote, women were still left behind in the category of *child* and *irrational*—not fit to vote. And black men were still associated with the "lower/worse" side of the pairs of opposites that needed to be kept apart.

America has traveled a long way from its initial racist past—but not all the way, in spite of having elected an African American president. Perhaps the most chilling depiction of the American purity complex can be found in the 1916 film *The Birth of a Nation* (originally called *The Clansman*), which shows white-robed Ku Klux Klansmen as the potential saviors of helpless white women who otherwise are threatened by the prospect of rape from the now uncontrolled—and apparently demented—black men. The movie elicits disbelief these days. And yet 40 years after it was made, a 14-year-old African American boy, Emmett Till, was brutally murdered for allegedly whistling at a white woman in a grocery store.

The American purity complex leads to the pursuit of the good in Manichean terms—the complete absence of evil. It means we often seek to root out imperfection rather than to pursue the truth or strive for harmony. Truth and beauty as expressed in science and art tend to be complex and nuanced—we Americans are notoriously anti-intellectual in spirit and anti-art in principle, musicians originally being listed along with "pimps, panders, and catamites" as evidence of how far from being the nursery of heroes our mother country had fallen.[10] Unlike other Western nations, for example, we find it difficult to accept the preponderance of evidence for climate change because "some" scientists disagree or the scientific theory of evolution because details keep changing. We look for 100 percent evidence or something we can hold firm to as an eternal belief rather than what science offers—short-term theory, which, by design, is open to change.

The purity complex gained such a strong foothold in America not only because of the specific historical circumstances of our Puritan past and the daily challenge of justifying slavery but also because we are a "made-up" nation, founded during the Enlightenment through decades of philosophical argument. Anti-intellectual though we are, our political system is based on mental constructs. We did not grow organically from tribes rooted in prehistorical times. And unlike every nation up to that time, we separated church and state, religion and political power. Without a powerful religious institution to judge between right and wrong, more literal-minded judgments took over, allowing a black-and-white version of the struggle of opposites to flourish. The purity complex means that the nuanced gray of most human experience is difficult to tolerate in a public context.

One of the many examples of our purity complex is the image of the innocent American as compared to sophisticated Europeans, perhaps best illustrated by the novels of Edith Wharton (*The Age of Innocence*) and Henry James (*The American*, among others). Mark Twain, too, wrote a book called *The Innocents Abroad*, which was a travel-book best-seller—but which offered a rather nuanced view of the Holy Land, designed to shatter certain "innocent" American expectations.

Another example of our purity complex, in the political rather than the literary world, is the abortion "debate." In most other advanced nations, abortion is not the cause of the bombing of clinics, the murder of doctors, the heart of political campaigns, or the reason for religious fundamentalists to vote for someone with whom they share no values except a commitment to abolish abortion. And whatever one's opinion about when a fetus should become a human being with legal rights, the nature of the debate often exposes an underlying purity complex that is almost universal—the identification of women having sex as intrinsically sinful, evil, dark—especially if they enjoyed it. In 2012 Missouri Congressman Todd Akin argued against abortion even in cases of rape because victims of "legitimate rape" rarely get pregnant. "If it's a legitimate rape, the female body has ways to try to shut that whole thing down."[11] In 2017, Texas state representative Tony Tinderholt introduced a bill that would criminalize abortion without exception, declaring it a homicide and therefore worthy of the death penalty. He said that the measure was necessary to "force" women to be "more personally responsible" with sex.[12]

For having a child out of wedlock, Hawthorne's 17th-century Puritan character Hester Prynne has to stand on a scaffold for three hours and wear a scarlet *A* (presumably for "Adulteress") for the rest of her life. The father of the child, the Reverend Dimmesdale, whom she refuses to name, develops empathy through dealing with his secret guilt. Hawthorne shows Hester questioning the harsh dualities of religion and becoming wise in the process.

Ironically, in the age of Trump, the American purity complex might finally be rising up into our national consciousness. In an almost perverse reversal of the purity complex, the most powerful man in the world, rather than displaying the Roman virtues of a George Washington, appears to flaunt many of the characteristics of the "inferior" side of the pair of opposites—*emotional, unstable, irrational, child*—and to exhibit the love of luxury and "languor" that so shocked our 18th-century founders.

Trump's "pussy" tape not only brought a denigrating term in relation to a woman's body into presidential politics but also actually brought it out of the shadows into the light, when hundreds of thousands of women wore "pussy hats" in the Women's March on January 21, 2017, the day after Trump's inauguration. A term of shame became a symbol of resistance. A pussy hat was even placed on the head of a statue of Eleanor Roosevelt. The symbolic allusion to a term of degradation was transformed—just as Hester Prynne in *The Scarlet Letter* transformed the scarlet *A* she had to wear through adorning it with eye-catching golden embroidery.[13]

The inspiration of the Women's March, with its worldwide solidarity of women, led to expansion of the Me Too movement, which brought behaviors formerly tolerated by women (for fear of being blamed or punished) into the light—and turned blame onto the perpetrators. Overnight, it seemed, the old questions asked of rape victims—"What were you wearing?" or "How hard did you fight back?"—seemed ludicrous. The comedian Tracey Ullman did a skit during which a man in an expensive business suit is complaining to a police officer about having been mugged, and the police officer says, in effect, "Well, you were asking for it, weren't you? Look what you're wearing."

At the end of "Rappaccini's Daughter," Giovanni addresses Beatrice with "fiendish scorn" as "the pure daughter of Rappaccini." He gives her an antidote to the poison, which kills her. And as she dies, she says, "Oh, was there not, from the first, more poison in thy nature than in mine?"

In both this story and *The Scarlet Letter*, Hawthorne implicitly questions the American purity complex by situating good in something other than unspotted virtue and "poison" in the "spotless" judge. According to society, Hester is a sinner; because of the way she has been raised, Beatrice is poisonous; Dimmesdale is both a sinner and a hypocrite. And yet both Hester and Beatrice are pure of heart, and Hester's daughter Pearl is presented as wholly innocent in spite of her being conceived in sin. As a result of years of grappling with his failures, Dimmesdale is an empathetic minister who serves his community. Yet all are condemned by a society in the grips of a purity complex. Was there not more poison in Judge Hathorne than in the Salem witches he condemned to death? Is not goodness located in empathy rather than in the "right" side of any dualism?

The purity complex is a human complex, not a uniquely American one. After all, ethnic *cleansing* was—and is—practiced worldwide, not just against Native Americans. The plot of "Rappaccini's Daughter" came from an ancient Indian tale about a poisonous maiden—or, one could argue, from one of the most ancient tales of all, the story of Adam and Eve in the garden. But the American history of Puritanism, slavery, and a mental

rather than organic founding has made the purity complex particularly powerful in this country. The election of President Trump has activated this complex
so that compromise is difficult, discussion is polarized, and opposite points of
view are demonized.

Just as the abortion debate triggers the purity complex on the right,
extreme forms of "political correctness" activate it on the left. Groups on
the left often do not want to include those who have been tainted by
expressing right-wing opinions in the past, even if these opinions are no
longer held. Presidential candidate Joe Biden was strongly criticized by the
left for having collaborated with racist colleagues in the Senate to work out
compromises on contentious issues. Literature professors have been asked
to issue "trigger" warnings and content warnings before the discussion of
a novel that includes violence or death or any other subject that might
upset someone. When right-wing speakers are disinvited from appearing on
a college campus, purity of opinion is being valued above the kind of vig-
orous debate that might change someone's mind.

In the midst of the bitterly polarized discussions we see every day, in which
political positions are held with the self-righteousness of sides taken in
a religious war, we can find a kind of perverse hope in a curious factoid: parents would rather their children find a mate from another race or religion
than from the opposite party. Indeed, interracial or interreligious marriage is
now so common in the United States that some effects of the purity complex
are already dissolving.[14] Gay marriage used to be unthinkable. And the trans-
gender bathroom issue challenges the very basis of the purity complex in questioning one of its foundational dualisms—male-female. If these fundamental
dualities can be blurred or no longer judged as "good" and "evil," perhaps we
can begin to question duality itself as nothing but a structure of thought that
our beautiful, complex, multifaceted world does its best to contradict.

Pied Beauty

Glory be to God for dappled things—
   For skies of couple-colour as a brinded cow;
      For rose-moles all in stipple upon trout that swim;
Fresh-firecoal chestnut-falls; finches' wings;
   Landscape plotted and pieced—fold, fallow, and plough;
      And all trades, their gear and tackle and trim.

All things counter, original, spare, strange;
   Whatever is fickle, freckled (who knows how?)
      With swift, slow; sweet, sour; adazzle, dim;
He fathers-forth whose beauty is past change:
      Praise him.
                 Gerard Manley Hopkins[15]

Notes

1 Nathanial Hawthorne, "Rappaccini's Daughter," *Hawthorne's Short Stories* (New York: Vintage Classics Edition, 2011); Nathanial Hawthorne, "Rappaccini's Daughter," *Moses from an Old Manse, and Other Stories* (Adelaide, Australia: ebooks for Adelaide, 2014), https://ebooks.adelaide.edu.au/h/hawthorne/nathaniel/mosses/index.html.

2 The classic anthropological exploration of purity is the 1966 book by Mary Douglass, *Purity and Danger: An Analysis of Concepts of Pollution and Taboo,* which traces the concepts of clean and unclean in different cultures (London: Routledge and Keegan Paul).

3 Dictionary, Google, s.v. "purity," accessed June 24, 2019, https://tinyurl.com/y3tj7qpo.

4 "What Can Wash Away My Sin?" Lyrics by Robert Lowry, 1876.

5 "Have You Been to Jesus for the Cleaning Pow'r?" Lyrics and music by Elisha Albright Hoffman, 1878.

6 I tried this for many years with each class of undergraduate students just to see if my theory held up.

7 William Hooper to James Iredell, April 26, 1774, in W. L. Saunders, ed., *Colonial Records of North Carolina,* vol. 9 (Raleigh, NC, 1886–1890), 985–986; quoted in Bernard Bailyn, *The Ideological Origins of the American Revolution: Fiftieth Anniversary Edition* (Cambridge: Harvard University Press, 2017), 140–141.

8 Bailyn, *The Ideological Origins of the American Revolution,* 136.

9 Adam Nagourney, "Biden Unwraps '08 Bid with an Oops!," *The New York Times,* February 1, 2007, https://www.nytimes.com/2007/02/01/us/politics/01biden.html.

10 Bailyn, *The Ideological Origins of the American Revolution,* 136.

11 Todd Akin, local news interview August 19, 2012, airing on St. Louis television station KTVI.

12 Lyanne A. Guarecuco, "Lawmaker: Criminalizing Abortion Would Force Women to Be 'More Personally Responsible,'" *Texas Observer,* January 23, 2017.

13 Nathanial Hawthorne, *The Scarlet Letter* (1850) (New York: W. W. Norton & Company, 1988), 39.

14 Ten percent of marriages are interracial. See Kristen Bialik, "Key Facts about Race and Marriage: 50 Years after *Loving v. Virginia,*" *FactTank,* Pew Research Center, June 12, 2017, https://www.pewresearch.org/fact-tank/2017/06/12/key-facts-about-race-and-marriage-50-years-after-loving-v-virginia/. Of those married since 2010, 39 percent have a spouse in a different religious group compared with 19 percent of those wed before 1960. See Carlye Murphy, "Interfaith Marriage Is Common in U.S., Particularly Among the Recently Wed," *FactTank,* Pew Research Center, June 2, 2015, https://www.pewresearch.org/fact-tank/2015/06/02/interfaith-marriage/.

15 Gerard Manley Hopkins, "Pied Beauty," in *Poems of Gerard Manley Hopkins,* ed. Robert Bridges (London: Humphrey Milford, 1918). Retrieved from Wikisource, https://en.wikisource.org/wiki/Poems_of_Gerard_Manley_Hopkins.

Chapter 3

The Cultural Complex and Addiction to Dominion
Psychic Evolution Cannot Be Thwarted

Jerome Bernstein

I have asserted in previous publications and talks that I see President Trump as an agent of the collective unconscious. Trump himself is unaware of his role in this regard. His job description in that role has been: (1) to hasten the collapse of the no-longer-viable 20th-century psychic paradigm of American primacy and dominance as the leader of the Western world economically, scientifically, technically, politically, and militarily; (2) to thrust the nose of the American collective firmly up its shadow; and (3) to force a confrontation between our species and Nature to see if we can learn to live together in a life-sustaining reciprocal balance, and if not, who will be the survivor. All three are essential if our species is to survive. Regarding the first two, I would say that Mr. Trump has done his part of the job and has done it exceptionally well. We can no longer stick our collective heads in the sand without incurring serious kicks to the butt or even to head, heart, and soul. It is the third part of his job description that worries me the most, however. And as far as he is concerned, he is far from done.

My emphasis here is neither on Trump the man nor on Trump the politician, nor, in one sense, on Trump at all. In the long run, he is an agent—a psychic *impersonal* tool to carry out the three-point job description I just outlined. Mr. Jones, or Ms. Clark, or a backhoe would do just as well if they had Trump's intuitive skills as a reality TV performer and his irretrievably broken capacity for empathy toward other human beings.

The split between mind and body ushered in by the Cartesian Enlightenment and the age of reason was an essential dynamic step in moving what was to become Western civilization and Western culture out of the Dark Ages (and subsequently the Middle Ages and Renaissance). But it did leave us with a sense of a "group spirit" that came to see evolution over time as a phenomenon applied to biology and not to psyche.[1]

C. G. Jung's theory of the unconscious included a new and broader idea that he called the *collective unconscious*.[2] Among other characteristics, the collective unconscious was not only a container of forgotten or repressed cultural history but also an inherent drive to become conscious.[3] Jung's concept took the theory of evolution beyond Darwin's idea of "the survival of the fittest" and pointed toward a notion of evolution that had a *transrational* source and agenda of its own.[4] This transrational notion is evident in the development of such concepts as complex adaptive systems, self-organizing systems, complexity theory, and others, within the field of physics. This broader concept of evolution has been resisted by science and psychology in terms of being applied to *evolution of the psyche*, both individually and collectively.[5] Although that resistance has somewhat lessened in the 21st century, there is still little mention of "psychic evolution" as such in the science and psychology literature. The idea of psychic evolution as a phenomenon in and of itself, the *source* of which is other than the human brain, and one that is transrational in nature, is still almost universally resisted in Western culture.

All of this is crucially important if our species is to survive into the 22nd century. The current period is sometimes referred to as the *sixth extinction.*[6] Life on Earth has survived five previous "great extinctions" and likely will survive this sixth great extinction. The survival of species *Homo sapiens* is another story. Many if not most of the climate scientists engaged in the climate change crisis are pessimistic on that score. And, indeed, we may well end up going the way of the dinosaur.

Every culture, past and present, carries a defining story deep in its psychohistorical roots that not only reflects the history of that culture and its roots, but also its evolutionary *telos* as well as a roadmap into its future. The French and American Revolutions in the 18th century, for example, not only told the story of the imminence and eminence of the demise of monarchical rule, but also made conscious an archetypal dynamic that was *inherent* in each recognized-as-legitimate *individual.*[7] The American Revolution, in particular, with its written and attested Declaration of Independence, made this dynamic conscious. Prior to those monumental upheavals, all rights were granted by the monarch; if rights were not granted the individual had none. A primary function of psychic evolution is to make liminal heretofore unconscious—and very often unimaginable—archetypal dynamics, concepts, and images. They may then be made manifest in the immediate future of the collective in both people and their culture. And, very often, the new archetypal manifestation, once it has forced its way into collective consciousness and is received as such, becomes idealized by the collective.[8] Thus was the case with the Declaration of Independence. And any challenge to that ideal *as perceived* by the individual or group was and is fiercely resisted. This is what Singer is referring to when he says, "When this part of the collective psyche is activated, the most primitive psychological forces come alive for the purpose of defending the group and its collective spirit or Self."[9] These forces can be of psychotic, even murderous proportions, as we are witnessing in today's world.

In the Age of Trump, we are living through a massive attack not only on American ideals, but also on the prevailing archetypal paradigm that has been responsible for maintaining them. As a culture we seem to be engaging in slippery and often artful dodging and obfuscation and refusal to take responsibility for our shadow of genocide, slavery, racism, misogyny, and greed. We are *all* exposed—naked[10]—and our nakedness is seen by others and, most importantly—as it is provoked by Trump—is increasingly seen by ourselves.[11]

Where to hide? There is no going back to "unseen-ness" or to the psychic *status quo ante*. Existential reality has changed, and we are being forced by the global climate change crisis to know it and, increasingly, to feel it. And if the existential reality has changed, survival requires that we recognize it and learn to think differently, to act differently—profoundly so, at our peril, and more quickly than at any other time in the history of our species. In Singer's terms, do the laws of nature grant us sufficient time to learn how to adapt and move beyond the culture's archetypal defenses of its group spirit, that is, its "cultural complex," and learn to adapt to the emergent psychic reality of Borderland consciousness?[12] That question is where we are today. The survival of our species fully depends on how we respond to that question with our *actions* more than with our good intentions and rhetoric[13]—all of which takes me to the Hebrew Bible and specifically the Garden of Eden story in the Book of Genesis.

Garden of Eden Story

In the opening of the Garden of Eden story, Adam and Eve are in the Garden, naked and unconscious in the human sense that not being naked would differentiate them from all the other animals in the Garden.[14] Their nakedness is a defining detail since it leaves them essentially *un*differentiated from all the other animals. Pre-expulsion, everything, including humans, is of Nature. There is no "human world" in the sense of modern-day references to the human and other-than-human worlds.

It is clear in scripture that *they do not know* that they are naked, and thus nakedness itself has no meaning. Their recognition of their nakedness, *and that it made a difference* (that is, *differentiation*), is when "God" confronts them for having chosen to taste the fruit of the tree of knowledge (*self-reflective consciousness*) and shames them for doing so.[15] Shame is the spark that sets off the evolutionary quest and development of a highly evolved capacity for self-reflective consciousness over the 2,500 years since the writing down of the Genesis story. We, the post-expulsion humans, experience nakedness because it was the psychic evolution triggered by our species' expulsion that has led to a dimension of consciousness that is characteristic of our species alone.[16] I call that consciousness "self-reflective consciousness." It is self-reflective consciousness, ordained by the Creator in the wake of the "creation" of Adam, that is essential for carrying out His mandate of Dominion.[17]

Rather than get into circular arguments over the biblical meaning of *Dominion* (some versions of the Bible use the word *mastery*), for our purposes here, I would suggest that *Dominion* connotes "power over" or "authority to decide." All life forms, animate and inanimate, are subject to the authority of humans in terms of what is done to and with them.[18]

Until the 21st century, Dominion meant *rational* power over Nature. The definition of *rational*, however, has become more and more distorted in proportion to the degree that ego inflation, addiction to power, and mind-less acquisition have become primary defenses for preserving the "group spirit" of a prevailing paradigm that is no longer viable.[19] Rational power has meant in service to only human needs and wants and has thus carried narrow meaning and absolute authority, since it was God Himself, according to scripture, that granted the power—the highest authority rationally conceivable. The non-human world had no rights and no spirit. Thus, our own perception that our species' Dominion over the non-human world was absolute—beyond question. Then consider the advances made over the short period beginning with the advent of the Scientific Revolution and later the Industrial Revolution in the 1880s and the explosion of techno-logical genius in their wake. Along with awesome advances in modern medicine, leading to the discovery of life-saving antibiotics and even life-extending organ transplants, humans have landed on the moon and now are analyzing earth/rock samples on planets and asteroids millions of miles distant. All of these advances in less than a hundred years not only boggles the mind—at least it used to—it can also lead to the delusion that our spe-cies and its primary tools of science and technology can remediate any and all problems that threaten the idealized group spirit. It also has so inflated the collective human ego that it has had the emotional and behavioral impact of replacing any concept of deity or transpersonal power outside the genius of the human mind itself.[20] This inflation, coupled with modern capitalism and the legal concept of "corporate personhood," which led toward the Citizens United ruling by the US Supreme Court in 2010, has brought us to the pinnacle of the super-rich being the tail that wags the well-being and soul of Western culture and, even more importantly, to a disregard for the value of life in all its forms, human and non-human, animate and inanimate.[21] Practically speaking, spirit is dead, and all of this is replaced by staggering wealth and greed. This is the pathological state of greed—"the tragedy of the commons."[22] And there is plenty of historical evidence to support such a fantasy.[23]

But the age of global climate change has brought a new kind of chal-lenge; the *laws* of Nature threaten to take that certainty out of the hands of humans. Civilization and our species have never faced such a threat.

Dominion unchecked will kill us. It is no longer rational. Its primary characteristics increasingly reveal symptoms of a collective psychotic process. Dominion in dynamic balance with the psychic principle of Reciprocity is not only in keeping with the laws of nature, it also suggests a new kind of reality of which we have only the faintest of glimmers today. Daunting!

At the same time, we need Dominion to remediate the global climate change crisis. It is indispensable. The issue is to redress its one-sidedness and its addiction to having power over others, not to banish it, which wouldn't be possible anyway.[24]

Reciprocity

The primary characteristic of Reciprocity as a given psychic force is a deep spiritual knowing that all of life is sacred and, given that tenet, that a healthy life force requires respect for all species and living in balance with all its forms. "Living in balance" refers to both physical acts and spiritual connection. To be clear, I am not talking about chosen belief. I am speaking of a "knowing" from within the self and between humans and non-human life forms. That balance and respect is predetermined and inherent in all species. When the creative force ordained that the human species would have Dominion over all others, that tenet was disrupted and replaced with an imposed thrust on our species to explore and evolve self-reflective as well as other forms of consciousness—known and unknown—above all other goals.[25] Thus was set into motion what ultimately has become a suicidal addiction to power, a mindless acquisition, "the tragedy of the commons," and a phobic archetypal defense of the group spirit—a domineering cultural complex—that has led to a massive collective dissociation in the name of that defense.

At the same time, Indigenous peoples and, particularly for this chapter, Native American tribes who have always lived through a different psychic orientation based on an oral traditional psychic reality—more quantum than Newtonian in nature and dynamic *structure*—have lived in greater harmony with all of life. When Native Americans encountered Euro-American cultural forms they were not interested in them, and those following traditional ways still do not respect these forms.

Mythologically and psychically, oral traditional cultures never were kicked out of the Garden of Eden to seek Dominion over the rest of life. The vestiges of these indigenous forms of Reciprocity can be seen in the practices of elders and traditional families, most of whom reside on Indian reservations. This perspective is important because there is still available a manifest source of Reciprocity in its archetypal form to learn from, both in practice and in spirit, that Western culture ignores and denigrates as "primitive." These archetypal forms *are* "primitive" in the sense of being *original* and the closest remaining approximation of the Reciprocity dynamic that has become indispensable to the survival of Western culture and those who populate it.[26]

Reciprocity, in the form of a deeply felt spiritual balance and spiritual connection that holds that all life, animate and inanimate, is sacred, was not just left behind in the Garden of Eden. *Our species still carries that psychic dynamic deep in our collective unconscious.* We lived there once upon a time.

Human survival going forward requires an articulated goal of re-introducing the psychic principle of Reciprocity, conceptually and operationally, into the formulae necessary to remediate global climate change under crisis conditions —*in less than ten years.* Because the global climate change crisis has been caused by humans, it is vital to remember that the essential problem is human psychology—to reignite the dormant spark of humility and respect toward Nature and all of life. Unconsciously we have all relied on science and technology to provide the tools with which to "fix" *what we have caused and continue to cause.* Scientists and the IPCC are screaming at the world that our species has less than ten years before the laws of nature will overrule that option and our entire species will be on a trajectory toward probable extinction.[27] Reciprocity is deemed indispensable in the formulae to penetrate collective defenses and to reconnect Dominion and Reciprocity in dialogue in time to redress the imbalance we have caused and to save our species from collective suicide.

I have been writing here about the "Western world," as Jung referred to us in his last essay "Healing the Split," and about our need to respect all of life. But at bottom, it seems to me, if we sufficiently respected our own lives as sacred, individually and collectively, we would have been able to avoid the magnitude and imminence of this crisis. That is what we keep being told by Greta Thunberg.[28] Most other species and inanimate life forms have and do intrinsically behave in a manner that reflects the sanctity of all life based on a principle of balance *and respect for life itself,* as opposed to "authority to decide," and for the doing have survived—granted with five great extinctions preceding this one. *They* are still here.[29]

So do we respect and appreciate the sanctity of our own species and lives enough to undertake, on an emergency basis, the kind of massive mission that would dwarf the Marshall Plan and the space program combined? I'm far from sure at this point in time. It may be time to think about what we will tell our children and grandchildren when they ask.

And they *will ask.*

Notes

1 Thomas Singer, "Unconscious Forces Shaping International Conflicts: Archetypal Defenses of the Group Spirit from Revolutionary America to Confrontation in the Middle East," *Psychotherapy and Politics International* 5, no. 1 (2007): 45–61.

2 "*Collective unconscious,* a term introduced by psychiatrist Carl Jung to represent a form of the unconscious (that part of the mind containing memories and

impulses of which the individual is not aware) common to mankind as a whole and *originating in the inherited structure of the brain*. It is distinct from the personal unconscious, which arises from the experience of the individual. According to Jung, the collective unconscious contains archetypes, or universal primordial images and ideas [italics added for emphasis]." *Encyclopedia Britannica Online*, s.v. "collective unconscious" accessed June 6, 2019, https://www.britannica.com/science/collective-unconscious. At best I would say that Jung's assertion about this dynamic *originating* in the structure of the brain is a speculation or a theory, but not a fact supported by any known data or research. In fact, in his essay "Archaic Man," Jung powerfully questions the idea that the psyche originates *in* man. He says, "Does the psychic in general—that is, the spirit or the unconscious—arise in us; or is the psyche, in the early stages of consciousness, actually outside us in the form of arbitrary powers with intentions of their own, and does it gradually come to take its place within us in the course of psychic development?" C. G. Jung, "Archaic Man," in *Modern Man in Search of a Soul* (New York: Houghton Mifflin Harcourt Publishing, 1933), 147–148.

3 C. G. Jung, "Answer to Job" (1952), in *The Collected Works of C. G. Jung*, vol. 11, *Psychology and Religion: East and West* (Princeton: Princeton University Press, 1969).

4 *Transrational* is a term I have coined. It represents an objective nonpersonal, nonrational state, encompassing phenomena and experiences that do not fit into linear structures of cause and effect. For more information, see my book *Living in the Borderland: The Evolution of Consciousness and the Challenge of Healing Trauma* (Hove, East Sussex: Routledge, 2005); as well as my article "Nonshamanic Native American Healing," in *Psychological Perspectives* 57, no. 2 (2014): 129–146.

5 This is the case since science and many schools in psychology are chiefly concerned with what is observable, falsifiable, testable, and replicable.

6 The term comes from Richard Leakey and Roger Lewin, *The Sixth Extinction: Patterns of Life and the Future of Humankind* (New York: Anchor Books, 1996); and from Elizabeth Kolbert's Pulitzer Prize-winning *The Sixth Extinction: An Unnatural History* (New York: Henry Holt and Company, 2014).

7 Voting rights were largely restricted to white landowning males. Native Americans and slaves were denied basic citizenship.

8 Speaking to this powerful idealization, in 1974 Ronald Reagan famously said (referencing Puritan John Winthrop's essay "A Model of Christian Charity" from 1630), "*America* is a shining *city upon a hill* whose beacon of *light* guides freedom-loving people everywhere." Or, as the Declaration of Independence states, "We hold these Truths to be self-evident, that all men are created equal, that they are endowed by their Creator with certain unalienable Rights, that among these are Life, Liberty, and the pursuit of Happiness." Notwithstanding the fact that non-landowners were excluded and women were excluded. Many of the signers, including George Washington and Thomas Jefferson, held slaves at the time of adding their names to the Declaration of Independence.

9 Singer, "Unconscious Forces Shaping International Conflicts," 45.

10 The nature of our nakedness is akin to that of the emperor in Hans Christian Andersen's "The Emperor's New Clothes."

11 Thus, one of my names for Trump, "the consciousness-raiser-in-Chief." And I am not speaking tongue-in-cheek.

12 Singer, "Unconscious Forces Shaping International Conflicts."

13 Greta Thunberg is a Swedish high-school student who is taking action; she created the "School Strike for the Climate." I urge you to watch her powerful 11-minute

TED Talk, "The Disarming Case to Act Right Now on Climate Change," November 2018, at https://www.ted.com/talks/greta_thunberg_the_disarming_case_ to_act_right_now_on_climate?language=en.

14 It is emphasized that I am using "scripture," that is, the Garden of Eden story as written in the Hebrew Bible, which is the origin story for all three Abrahamic/monotheistic religions. Later interpretations of that original version of the story do not suffice in terms of archetypal integrity.

15 Many Jungians use the word *Self* as an equivalent term in order to avoid the unanswerable question of what God is, whether they are agnostic or atheist, or so on. However, Jung's concept of the Self goes beyond the meaning attached to the word *God* by most people.

16 A number of scholars cite Milton's *Paradise Lost* as the best and classic statement of expulsion from the Garden as necessary to the evolutionary development of consciousness.

17 For further information on this point, see my book *Living in the Borderland* as well as my chapter "Border*land* Consciousness: Re-establishing Dialogue between the Western Psyche and the Psyche-Left-Behind," in *Jungian Perspectives on Rebirth and Renewal: Phoenix Rising*, eds. Elizabeth Broderson and Michael Glock, 29–42 (London: Routledge, 2017).

18 Although *inanimate* is defined as lacking in life (from the Latin, meaning "not having anima, or soul"), this definition and understanding is characteristic of the *Logos*/Western mind. Our defining it as lifeless is a major reason for the trouble we are in with regard to global climate change. In Indigenous/Native cosmology and language, the distinction between animate and inanimate remains, but all of life is infused with spirit. Everything—we and "it" (*rocks, earth, air, water, and so on*)—is sacred life. The assumed contradiction is a product of the Western point of view, which comes from a Dominion psyche that is stuck in an increasingly archaic dimension of reality. There is another view: *Reciprocity*, characteristic of the Indigenous/Native psyche wherein the distinction between animate and inanimate remains valid, and yet the words, syntax, and psychic reality associated with these terms go beyond the idea of contradiction. I would estimate that more than 90 percent of the translation of Native *religion* (a term that does not exist naturally in Native languages) and myth were performed by Western white scholars and missionaries using ethno-European *Logos* alphabetic languages, which are significantly and often radically different in linguistic structure and which distort the Native oral traditional culture, history, and psyche. One dramatic example is the Hopi language structure because it has no tenses. My point is that the contradiction between animate and inanimate held by the *Logos*/Western mind is now being mirrored externally in the destructiveness of global climate change, owing to a rogue Dominion psyche that experiences itself as a superior, if not the *only* life form.

19 Singer, "Unconscious Forces Shaping International Conflicts."

20 For more on this concept see *Living in the Borderland*, Chapter 2; Singer, "Unconscious Forces Shaping International Conflicts."

21 In the wake of the 2010 Citizens United decision, opposition groups have focused on the ruling in terms of its ramifications for "corporate personhood," but the issue itself was not the object of the case.

22 Thank you to Jason Hickey, PhD, for pointing out this concept.

23 The 2014 study "Testing Theories of American Politics: Elites, Interest Groups, and Average Citizens" by political scientists Martin Gilens and Benjamin Page, concludes "that economic elites and organized groups representing business interests have substantial independent impacts on U.S. government policy, while

average citizens and mass-based interest groups have little or no independent influence. The results provide substantial support for theories of Economic-Elite Domination and for theories of Biased Pluralism, but not for theories of Majoritarian Electoral Democracy or Majoritarian Pluralism." This article appears in *Perspectives on Politics* 12, no. 3 (2014): 564–581, https://doi.org/10.1017/S1537592714001595. In "Who Rules America," Allan J. Lichtman cites the study, "A shattering new study by two political science professors has found that ordinary Americans have virtually no impact whatsoever on the making of national policy in our country. The analysts found that rich individuals and business-controlled interest groups largely shape policy outcomes in the United States." Allan J. Lichtman, "Who Rules America," *The Hill*, August 12, 2014, https://the hill.com/blogs/pundits-blog/civil-rights/214857-who-rules-america.

24 We do have a vivid picture of what it will be like if we fail. See the article "The Uninhabitable Earth," by David Wallace-Wells, in *New York Magazine*, July 9, 2017, http://nymag.com/intelligencer/2017/07/climate-change-earth-too-hot-for-humans.html.

25 The Sioux term for this is *The Great Mysterious*. For others, it might be referred to as the *Big Bang* or *God*. From my perspective, whatever the name, they all refer to the same creative force that seems determined to perpetuate life in all its forms.

26 I am not unaware of the relevance of Eastern cultures to this discourse. And there are some major differences and exceptions within those cultures. But that is too long a subject to engage here in this chapter. I will say here only that given the fact that Western culture in most of its forms has permeated most parts of the world I doubt that the peoples of Eastern cultures will fare better in the end than will Euro-Americans, specifically when it comes to the global climate change crisis. For more on this point, see Vine Deloria Jr., *C. G. Jung and the Sioux Traditions: Dreams, Visions, Nature, and the Primitive* (New Orleans: Spring Journal Books, 2009).

27 It is estimated that it will take 84 *months* if one takes into consideration the time it will take to undo the wholesale and deliberate dismantling and destruction of the global climate change remediation infrastructure built up over decades. See The Intergovernmental Panel on Climate Change (IPCC) Special Report, "Global Warming of 1.5 °C," October 2018, https://www.ipcc.ch/sr15/.

28 Thunberg, "The Disarming Case to Act Right Now on Climate Change."

29 An example of such is seen when a lion who is king of the pride fells a young wildebeest for food and then feasts on the catch while the rest of the herd and the lions engage in grazing less than 20 feet from one another.

Chapter 4

Wrestling with Our Angels

Inner and Outer Democracy in America Under the Shadow of Donald Trump

Donald E. Kalsched

Part I: Angelic Powers and the "System"

Near the end of his long and fruitful life, C. G. Jung left us with a challenge and a warning. We should study human nature, he said, because the psyche is the "great danger" now, and "we are the origin of all coming evil."[1] As a practicing psychoanalyst, I am daily involved in the study of human nature, and for many years, have been trying to understand how the psyche itself constitutes the "great danger" that Jung describes. This study has involved me in the exploration of mysterious and invisible *powers* resident in the dark recesses of the human personality—elemental emotional powers of *primitive hate* and *primitive love*—that Freud and Jung located in the *unconscious* realm of the mind. These archetypal powers, sometimes appearing in our dreams as *angels* or *demons*, represent primitive forces from deep within the psyche/soma. They are mostly invisible—just like the fundamental particles of physics that comprise all material reality (quarks, neutrinos, bosons ...). They can only be seen as they manifest in the "detectors" offered by human life—both inner symbolic detectors and outer behavioral ones. In personal psychology, we see them in the powerful binary emotions that get aroused when *personal complexes* are activated, or in the terrifying or exciting dramas of our dreams. In the outer collective we find them in what Tom Singer has described as our "cultural complexes," where normal human emotions are amplified by the group psyche and lead to extreme behavior in the culture—from the horrors of the Holocaust to the election of Donald Trump.[2]

I have discovered these elemental powers ("angels") in my work with a particular subgroup of patients—namely those who have suffered from catastrophic early childhood trauma. The inner world of such patients is riven by fear and constructed around a *system* of dissociative defenses that employ the "powers" to help regulate an otherwise emotionally dysregulated psyche and to protect an exquisite vulnerability at the core of the traumatized self. The result is a very controlling *totalitarian*—even *fascistic*—defensive structure made up of archetypal powers that take over the inner "government" of the personality where a healthy democratic ego should be. This system (described in my earlier writing as the *Self-Care System*[3]) is full of *violence* and *illusion*, built around a core of *vulnerability* and *innocence*, that is obsessively protected by tyrannical controlling forces. It is a *fortress psychology* designed (through dissociation) to keep things "out," as contrasted to a *democratic psychology*, which is permeable and tends toward inclusivity. When a dissociative psychology takes control, the daunting complexities of the real world are simplified and reduced to polarized opposites driven by extreme emotions and primitive defenses. A fear-driven, victim/perpetrator narrative takes over, and according to the implicit assumptions of this narrative, painful negative feelings and "bad" influences from outside are always threatening to intrude, corrupt, or humiliate the goodness and innocence inside the self.

In America today this polarizing us-them narrative has taken over much of our common culture. We see it on both the left and the right of the political spectrum. It is more prominent on the right—for example the alt-right's conviction that our essential American "innocence" and "goodness" is threatened at our borders (immigrants!), or by government regulation (the "deep state"), or by cynical negative reporting by the media (fake news!), or by a secretive power elite with a globalist agenda that is conspiring to take away our guns! But it is present on the political left as well—in the apocalyptic sky-is-falling hysteria and scandal-mongering obsessions that are conspicuous in some liberal news outlets, or in the equally bizarre sensitivities to trauma on some of our liberal college campuses where trigger warnings are required for upsetting content and so-called safe zones are needed for the protection of student-psyches too tender to bear the impact of "dangerous" negative material.[4] A recent survey revealed that a majority of college students think it is acceptable to shout down a speaker with whom they disagree, and 20 percent think violence is warranted in such a situation.[5] When the German philosopher and psychologist Theodore Adorno developed his Fascism scale in 1950 and administered it to a large post-war population, he discovered that authoritarianism and dogmatism were features of a fear-driven psychology found *on both the left and the right*.[6]

Whether on the left or right, the particular dissociative psychology I am describing thrives in times of great existential anxiety or instability, such as we live in today. It imposes order on a fearful chaos and thus creates safety and promotes survival, but at a great cost—the individual's solid relationship to reality. It is organized around *extremes* of every kind—extreme emotions, extreme opinions, extreme interpretations of history; polarized positions on every issue; and a reversion to all-or-none totalistic thinking. These extremes permit the discharge of angry emotions and are designed to defend against the painful, vulnerable feelings resulting from a trauma history and to give the dysregulated psyche coherence. Relying on powerful defenses (angels), such a psychology has an apocalyptic and absolutist mindset and nurtures wild conspiratorial fears. Often it gives one a megalomaniacal view of oneself and one's tribe as special or elect. It is dogmatic, intolerant of ambiguity, and mistrusts *otherness*. It thrives on suspicion of others, attributes ill will to one's opponent, and sees enemies and traitors everywhere. It represents what Theodore Adorno described as the "authoritarian personality," or what Richard Hofstadter called "the paranoid style" in American politics,[7] or what Christopher Bollas calls the "fascistic state of mind."[8]

As a mental structure, this autocratic dissociative psychology exists in all of us, living side by side with its healthier democratic twin. In psychoanalytic theory, we know inner democracy as a *conflict psychology*, and it is something toward which we, who practice psychotherapy, are continually striving—both in ourselves and our patients. The psyche exists in parts, and these parts must be integrated if the organism is to function as a whole. Speaking personally, I am always trying to help my patients transform a dissociative psychology into a conflict psychology.[9] Hence I am working for inner tolerance and for a democracy of the psyche, with all parts of the self allowed to exist in a representative central governance that we call the ego. This means wrestling with the absolutist powers—the "angels" of the dissociative system—in order to transform them—just like the Biblical Jacob did at the River Jabbok in the Old Testament (Genesis 32:22–32).

In psychotherapy, this process means wrestling with extreme emotions and absolutist attitudes, thereby slowly developing emotional literacy, so that conflicting emotions and attitudes can be entertained at the same time without splitting. By holding conflict inwardly and humanizing the archetypal forces of the psyche, we struggle daily to make a third space between the curse and blessing of the polarized and polarizing tendencies of the Self-Care System. In this third space, diversity, plurality, and inclusiveness are welcomed. Even the most vulnerable and disaffected parts of ourselves get represented in a central "government" of the ego (*e-pluribus unum*). This requires a certain kind of resilient consciousness that can only develop in emotionally safe and educationally informed environments—a consciousness that permits and encourages differences and opens to vulnerable human feelings.

The autocratic angels of the dissociative system do not like democracy. They do not like to be dragged down from their extreme positions onto the human plane of the embodied ego where painful feelings and inner conflicts are experienced. Because they were born in trauma, it is difficult for them to bear the pain of such humiliating co-presence—so they must split and project and expel from consciousness those contents that are too conflictual. That's what dissociation "does." It creates a tyranny of "divine" (archetypal) structures (angels) that assert their power over their limited human subjects. So the work of creating a conflict psychology and a true democracy of the psyche is a continual work of *incarnation*. It involves coaxing or inviting or bribing the angels to give up some of their celestial power, forcing them down to "middle earth," where they must take on more embodied, modulated, and vulnerable human qualities. In the psychotherapy relationship this can be a very stormy process, but it is the only way to wholeness.

In the pages that follow I will try to articulate and describe how these two psychologies—a democratic psychology on the one hand and a dissociative psychology on the other—are in a struggle for our national psyche, with a dissociative psychology lately getting the upper hand. In order to recognize the effects of a dissociative psychology on our personal and collective life, we must learn to identify the archetypal powers that take over in a traumatized life or culture. *The fact that these angelic powers are invisible—that is, unconscious—inclines us to underestimate them.* In the United States, many commentators on the current cultural scene have acknowledged the growing destructive polarization and incivility in American political life, attributing these trends to sociopolitical, technological, or economic factors such as lack of jobs, income inequality, lack of health care, and so on. Very few speak of the underlying psychological factors. Yet if Jung is right and the "psyche is the great danger now" then we must look deeper than the usual outer explanations. So, we must ask, what are these underlying powers or angels? Why are their destructive energies on the rampage in our troubled times? And how might a better understanding of how they operate in the *individual* psyche help us understand how they operate *collectively*? Finally what might we do in our common life to lessen their impact—or maybe even transform them?

Archetypal Affects and Our Angels

Readers of this book will know that C. G. Jung was dissatisfied with Freud's model of the *personal unconscious* and felt obliged to add a deeper *impersonal* and *mythic* layer underneath it that he called by various names—the *collective unconscious*, the *ground plan*, the *original mind*, the *hereditary psyche*, or the *objective psyche*. Moreover, for Jung there was an *implicate order* to this ground plan—it wasn't just a seething cauldron as Freud called the Id. This implicate order, according to Jung, was structured in *affect-images* that were archetypal in nature and tended to be personified as daimonic beings—devils or angels, and other preternatural presences and powers. Moreover, each archetype had an emotional side resident in the body and an image side resident in the mind.

On the one hand, archetypal affects form the emotional basis of the personality, and according to Louis Stewart there are seven such affects, ranging along a spectrum from positive (Interest/Curiosity, Joy, Surprise) to negative (Fear, Sadness, Anger, and Shame/Contempt).[10] These powerful affects are experienced by the immature ego as overwhelming, titanic, angelic, and they always occur in antinomies—extremes, totalistic or binary categories. They arrive in the child's psyche like 880 volts of electricity from the power grid, which is analogous to the primitive brain stem of the nervous system. The voltage is overwhelming and unusable (it will blow the circuits) until it is transformed—from 880 to 440 to 220 to 110 where it becomes usable electricity. A child overcome by hate is channeling its Dark Angel—completely possessed by rage. A child in love is equally possessed by a blissful Bright Angel and unable to tolerate the love-threatening limits of reality. In both cases, archetypal affects will have to be transformed into feelings. In the electrical grid, such transformation occurs in a device called a *transformer*, which sits on the telephone pole outside our houses. In child development the transformational containers will be relationships within the family and, then later, as the child enters the wider world, in friendships and sometimes even in the psychoanalytic transference relationship.

In the course of human development the powerful ambivalent affects from the body accrue images from the mind, and they too are binary. They appear as personified "great beings," *angels and demons* with superhuman powers. There's the great good mother and the great bad mother, the malevolent monster-demon and the benevolent guardian angel, Christ and the Anti-Christ, and so on. These images represent spiritual extremes—mythological absolutes—and opposites, totally one thing or the other. Such powerful images represent the spiritual and emotional fundaments of the primitive psyche (light and dark). They live "underneath" (in the somatic unconscious) or "above" (in the celestial unconscious of the mind), separated from the kingdom of middle earth where we live and the personal ego develops.

If we want to grow up to be mature, emotionally literate adults, we will have to learn to tame and harness the extreme powers of the archetypal psyche—to humanize them. If we are successful at this, we will end up with a secure sense of self, a flexible and a resilient ego-identity, made up of diverse emotional parts of the self, represented in a democracy of the psyche. We will have actualized our own personal vision of wholeness. If we are unsuccessful, we will find ourselves living amid autocratic and tyrannical emotional forces that will alternately inflate and deflate us, leaving us compartmentalized, emotionally unstable, lacking in secure self-esteem, full of unconscious fear and shame, and surrounded by raw, unprocessed emotions and rigid defenses.

The Traumatic Origins of the Powers

Extraordinary injuries to the psyche give birth to extraordinary defenses. Most "normal" defenses, such as suppression, repression, or denial, help us to manage painful experiences within what trauma psychologists call a "window of tolerance." But when unbearably painful injuries occur, we are suddenly "off the charts" of bearable pain or conflict and the psyche calls in its heavy artillery—the angels. Angels dissociate the psyche.

Let's imagine a small girl who is being sexually violated by a beloved and idealized parent. This child is suddenly flooded by overwhelming and unbearable emotion. Love is suddenly mixed with pain and horror, shame and anxiety. Hatred toward the needed object may flood the child with impossible conflict. At this point something remarkable happens. Suddenly the child is "on the ceiling" in a corner of the room, looking down at her little body being abused—understanding everything and feeling nothing. We call this attack on the integrity of experience *dissociation*, which means to split or separate. Dissociation is a severe and powerful defense that resolves the unbearable conflict within the child's feelings by disconnecting her from the pain of these feelings and leaving the scene altogether, through a mental trick. This trick involves an "escape when there is no escape."[11] The child is no longer screaming and crying but strangely numb, compliant, frozen, and "gone." She may even cooperate with her own abuse. And after the traumatic moment is over, the child will forget that the abuse ever happened. Not only the feelings, but the actual memory of the experience will often be forgotten, dissociated—fogged out in a kind of trauma trance. Life goes on as if the event never happened. Later it may return as a flashback, as frequently occurs in PTSD.

This defense (dissociation) is adaptive for the moment because it allows life to go on with vulnerable parts of the person's experience sequestered in an inner sanctum and separated from consciousness. The psyche is Balkanized, and conflict among the parts is walled off. But there is a price to be paid for this "security." Angels are put in charge of self-regulation instead of the ego. Angels are extremely powerful defenses. They can cast spells. They can catapult a child out of her body. They can throw an invisibility cloak over a painful memory so that it is forgotten. They can "kill" consciousness of an event and make the child numb to her feelings. Psychoanalysts call these defenses "primitive." Primitive defenses create systems of protection also known as *pathological structures*, and trauma survivors live inside such pathological structures. I believe that in the second decade of the 21st century in the United States, we are all trauma survivors and find ourselves inside such a pathological structure. Here is an image of such a structure.

The Self Care System and Its Tyranny

The accompanying illustration by William Blake is called *The Good and Evil Angels Struggling for Possession of a Child*. It's a good image for various parts of the divided self that make up what I call the Self-Care System.

Figure 4.1 William Blake (1757–1827). *The Good and Evil Angels Struggling for Possession of a Child.* 1795–? c.1805. Colour print, ink and watercolour on paper, 445 × 594 mm. Presented by W. Graham Robertson 1939. Tate Gallery.
Source: © Tate, London/Art Resource, NY.

On the left is the Dark Angel, represented as Satan or the Devil, shackled to the flames of Hell, eyes glazed over in a trauma trance, groping for the child. Archetypally speaking, the Dark Angel would represent pure evil or pure rage, pure hatred or pure negation—the death-drive, the Adversary, the Anti-Christ, the Terrorist, the Tyrant, the Accuser, the Critic. That's his "theology" and those are his mythic characteristics.[12] Dante's name for him in the *Divine Comedy* is "Dis" (from which we get the word *dissociation*). In the unconscious psyche of the trauma survivor, the figure of Dis, or Satan, is a conspicuous and ever-present threat. He is the persecutor, the inner critic, the shaming voice that attacks and denigrates every act of self-expression on the part of the trauma-surviving child. He is mean and malevolent toward the wounded child in the system because this child is a constant threat to him. The child's neediness and misery—his wailing and crying—fills the corridors of Hell with a sound he cannot tolerate! And he fears that the child's agony might be heard outside the system, making him look weak.

On the right, with the terrified child in its arms is a Bright Angel, standing on a cloud, connected to the celestial world of light and love. While the Dark Angel attacks the links with consciousness in an effort to *kill* the child's awareness of trauma, the Bright Angel casts spells. The Bright Angel is a specialist in altered states, such as psychic numbing, states of oblivion, forgetting, spacing out. The Bright Angel can spread the veil of illusion over the injured child and rescue it with fantasy-thinking and images of bliss or oblivion. This angel specializes in addictions—to alcohol, drugs, food, anything that makes the pain go away. Whereas the Dark Angel is a violent persecutor, the Bright Angel specializes in protective illusions.

"Fake news!" says the Bright Angel to the inner and outer child. "It never happened! The News media is lying! Stay with Me! I will save you!" Such are the ego-sustaining illusions and delusions that the Bright Angel specializes in. Troubled citizens in our nation who are confused by all the suffering and moral complexity of modern life, may long for rescue by such an "angel." Unconsciously they search for someone upon whom to project this powerful psychological factor. And Donald Trump, with his blonde hair, Midas-like wealth, and golden tower in the sky makes an easy target for such projections. There are also indications that Trump himself identifies with the Bright Angel, claiming he's the only one who can fix anything. Identification with archetypal powers is one definition of pathological narcissism.

So both the Dark and Bright Angels are personifications of defensive powers that serve as a dissociative self-regulatory system. The system's first goal (as I have come to understand it) is to keep the ego of the host personality from being overwhelmed, or even annihilated, by the radioactive intensity of unbearably painful traumatic memories—memories resident in the "child" in their care. Its second goal is to "save" a core of innocent aliveness associated with this injured child, which is crucial to all future development of the personality.

This child, visible in the Blake illustration, is therefore a kind of duality, just like the Bright and Dark Angels that are *spirit-beings* in human form. On the one hand, this child stands for the wounded, orphaned empirical child of the trauma survivor, carrying the historical injuries of traumatic abuse or neglect in his or her small body. On the other hand, this child represents the trauma-survivor's innocence—the pretraumatic core of the personality, carrying the divine spark of vitality and the instinct for life— now menaced by the great powers of the Bright and Dark Angels. Both angels are dedicated to the proposition that this child *must never be violated by reality again—its innocence must be preserved at all costs—and not allowed to leave the system.* But because of this encapsulation, the reality ego loses its capacity to tolerate feeling-experience and is weakened accordingly. Progressively the child becomes what James Grotstein calls an "Orphan of the Real."[13]

Once this system has taken over an individual, an autocratic and tyran-nical psychology is the result. Instead of representative governance, we have a dictatorship of the angels—a tyranny of the extremes—a system that thrives only by excluding (killing or encapsulating) parts of the self that are perceived as a threat. If the trauma survivor wants to heal his or her dissociation and reintegrate the lost parts of the childhood self, it will mean reexperiencing some of the unbearable pain that led to dissociation in the first place. It will mean *redemocratizing the psyche*—inviting the ban-ished parts back to the "table." But the dominant powers of the defensive system resist this process of inclusion and reintegration at all costs. These powers operate, like the Jewish Defense League after the Holocaust, on the principle of "Never Again!" The problem is that if innocence *never again* risks experience, the personality does not grow.

Clinical Example of the Dark Angel: Slaughter of the Innocents

Perhaps the most dramatic example of my encounter with "Dis," the Dark Angel in the Self-Care System, occurred many years ago in my work with an outwardly successful but inwardly depressed woman in her 60s. She had grown up in material luxury, but emotionally she had been catastrophically neglected and abused as a child. We didn't know how bleak her childhood had been—she had virtually no memories prior to age 11—until, fortuit-ously, she was cleaning out her mother's basement and found an old 8 mm (millimeter) movie taken by her father of her two-year-old self and her siblings at a wedding. We watched the movie together, and there we saw her as a toddler, desperately wandering among the tree-trunk-sized legs of adults at a cocktail party trying, with mounting anxiety, to get someone to notice her distress and pick her up. Finally, she fell to the ground, banging her little fists into the gravel, sobbing and screaming, in what appeared to be a seizure of grief. Undisturbed by his daughter's distress, the father apparently just kept filming!

As my patient and I watched this scene together, she burst into tears of compassion for her tiny self. I was also deeply moved, and as we sat in silence together, she noticed that I also had tears in my eyes, and there followed a shared moment of genuine felt intimacy between us. She left the session with intense feelings of gratitude and back at her home, stayed up most of the night writing poetry and reflecting on our "moment of meeting"—alternately crying with joy for this new opening to her feelings. "You affected him!" she wrote to herself. "You affected him." "He cares about you!" That night, still feeling tearfully open, she went to sleep and had the following dream:

Two sisters, long since separated, are anticipating a joyful reunion that is to take place on the upper balcony of a large curved double staircase shaped like a uterus. Full of excited anticipation, the patient is watching from below. One sister is waiting on the balcony as the other ascends the right-hand staircase. As she ascends, suddenly a curtain parts, and a man with a shotgun steps out and BLAM! blows her face away. She falls, bleeding and dying, rolling down the staircase as her sister, above, is overcome with grief and vomits over the bannister.

The patient was stunned by this dream, especially on the eve of the remarkable opening to her compassionate feelings from the night before and so was I. It reminded her of Rubens' painting *The Slaughter of the Innocents*, which had always disturbed her. To fully understand this dream the reader is referred to *The Inner World of Trauma* (1996, pages 19–28). For purposes of this chapter, we might summarize this understanding briefly as follows.

The pain of this woman's traumatically neglected childhood had been under strict and *authoritarian* banishment by tyrannical defenses for many years (dissociation). This inner tyranny was the source of her depression. When this childhood pain became conscious in our film session, the vulnerable child who had been split off and insulated by her defenses began to emerge into our relationship, and the terrible split between her inner and outer life began to heal. Her tearful gratitude was the sign of this healing. In her dream, the healing moment was pictured as a joyful anticipated reunion of two sisters (parts of her feminine wholeness) who had been separated for many years, now coming together as a kind of "new birth" on a uterine-shaped staircase. One might say that she was becoming whole; the split-off parts of her were coming together and actualizing a kind of "democracy" of her psyche. But there was another part of the psyche (the gunman) who was dead-set against this reunion, and dead-set against her consciousness of the terrible childhood pain that was now coming up in the form of her embodied tears and sadness—together with feelings of attachment toward an outer person, myself.

This dark killing part of the psyche (I have come to realize) is an important figure in the inner world, and although he often looks like pure evil, he did not start out as the deadly figure shown here. His original goal was to prevent consciousness of the unbearably painful feelings that have led to the trauma-survivor's defenses in the first place. But in the process, he ends up killing the loving, dependent parts of the self and elevating the destructive, superior, and invulnerable parts—with which the patient's ego tends to identify. He is a tyrant, and his inner narrative of fear and danger is very convincing to the terror-ridden patient. My patient became vigilant at scanning for danger in the world. Painful experiences in reality now seemed like proof that the killer's fearful story was true. There were dangers everywhere. She now lived inside a pathological narrative of fear, spending many hours obsessing about the dangers all around her. These distracted her from the genuine sadness and grief underneath—grief that (eventually, and after many years of work) would lead to greater consciousness of her true biography and to the eventual integration of the wounded and innocent child inside herself.

The day after her dream, my patient arrived at her next session numb, confused, and in a kind of trauma trance, feeling ashamed of her "sick" dream with its violence and death. "Who else has dreams like this?" she asked cynically. She had also "forgotten" how she felt the night of last week's session. In other words, her inner assassin had successfully dissociated her from any tender feelings. The orphaned child who had so joyfully come out of its imprisonment when we saw the film together, had retreated back into its inner sanctum and become hopeless once again about life in the real world. It was as though my patient had tasted the freedom and opening of a kind of Arab Spring, such as happened in Egypt in 2011, only to have the oppressive powers of authoritarianism clamp down again.

Clinical Example of the Bright Angel

A dramatic example of the Bright Angel in the Self-Care System came to my attention many years ago in a story told by Esther Harding, the well-known Jungian analyst from New York. It occurred in England and involved a little girl, aged four or five, who was asked by her mother to take an important note to her father who was reading in his den. The child came back a few moments later in tears and said "Mommy, the angel won't let me go in." Whereupon her mother, knowing her daughter's highly imaginative inner world, encouraged her to return again to the father's den and let the angel know that her mission was important! Soon afterward, the child reappeared in the kitchen, now sobbing uncontrollably and again saying, "Mommy the angel won't let me go in!" At this point the girl's mother, exasperated, took her by the hand and marched her down the hall to the father's room. As she entered the room, she stopped in horror as she witnessed her husband, slumped in his chair, drink spilled on the floor, dead from a massive heart attack.

This story demonstrates how the Bright Angel in the Self-Care System, just like her dark counterpart, is involved in the regulation of how much the hard edges of reality are allowed to intrude upon the ego—how much of reality is allowed to become conscious. Although not attacking or "killing" the child's consciousness like the gunman in the previous patient's dream, this angel nonetheless is involved in the process of dissociation. She helps create an alternative reality—a "necessary illusion" to help this child over this impossible situation.

In both these cases—where Bright and Dark Angels rescue the trauma survivor from a reality that is too much—there is a danger that the angels will take over the ego's functioning. This means that if a painful reality is to be rescued from annihilation (in the first case) or illusion (in the second), the possessing angels will have to be wrestled with and transformed. The outcome of this struggle will depend entirely on the relational resources in the patient's environment. In the first case, my patient had a relationship with me in the transference to help her humanize her inner killer. In the second case, we don't know whether the mother took over the angel's mediating role or not. If she failed in this task, then the light and dark powers would have moved in as a defense and child's removal from reality would have begun.

So to summarize: The Self-Care System gives us a picture of how the psyche dissociates under stressful or traumatic circumstances, splitting into different parts in order to tolerate otherwise unbearable experience. The preternatural powers of this system represent primitive untransformed affects and operate on an all-or-none principle such as good/evil, right/wrong, kill or be killed, do or be done to. The fragile ego, desperately needing identity and coherence, tends to *identify* with these powers—channels them as it were— and becomes narcissistically inflated—larger than life—either righteously aggressive and intolerant or puffed up and invulnerable.

None of us escapes these powers. They are active in all of us, especially under traumatic circumstances. And none of us escapes the responsibility of struggling to transform them. They lie hidden under the surface of our conscious lives, threatening to erupt and sweep away everything we have built up in our painstaking efforts to channel them into containing personal relationships on the one hand or, on the other, into the cultural forms, social institutions, or binding laws and legal restraints that preserve the fragile human values that make life worth living in the United States. *The "powers" are indifferent to these fragile accomplishments.* They are *daimonic*, amoral, chillingly disinterested in human affairs. They pursue their own blind intentions as indifferently as the Olympian gods and goddesses that so menaced the ancient Greeks with their power-mongering arrogance, their narcissistic infatuations, and their envious caprices. It is up to us to *humanize* them if we can. Everything depends on consciousness and the willingness to struggle in our human relationships, and within our cultural and legal institutions, to relate to and *transform* the indifferent destructive powers that menace us.[14]

Walter Wink and the Powers in the Social Order

The Bright and Dark Angels of what I call the Self-Care System are not just intrapsychic powers. According to 20th-century Protestant theologian Walter Wink, they have always existed and have always threatened the establishment of democratic human communities throughout history. Wink makes clear, for example, that the elemental powers were especially menacing to the early Christians as they tried to establish small centers of worship around the Middle East. The Apostle Paul wrote the following warning to the Ephesians

(6:12): "For we are not contending against flesh and blood, but against the principalities (archas), against the powers (exousias), against the world rulers (kosmokratoras) of this present darkness, against the spiritual hosts (pneumatika) of wickedness in the heavenly places."[15]

Wink's writings are useful for our purposes, because he makes clear that the elemental powers are beyond personal. They are archetypal, spiritual, cosmic, and they find their way into social and institutional life. In other words, they exist in the culture all around us, and, while invisible, they have profound unseen impact everywhere. In a telling description, Wink says:

> Every institution has its angel, i.e., its own unique spirit and this spirit is every bit as important as the physical [historical, economic, or social] ... aspects of institutions. If someone violates this spirit, though he keeps all the laws and precepts of the system, the system will condemn him ... *Conversely, if someone submits to this spirituality, he will be able to live in spite of violating all its laws and flouting all its institutions.*[16]

I think this statement is relevant to the dark spirit (angel) that has moved into our American national psyche—a dark spirit of which Donald Trump is only the most conspicuous avatar. Before the 2016 election at a campaign stop in Sioux City, Iowa, Trump said, "The polls, you know, they say I have the most loyal people. Did you ever see that? Where I could stand in the middle of Fifth Avenue and shoot somebody and I wouldn't lose any voters, okay? It's like incredible!"[17]

Here, Trump recognizes the dark spiritual wave he is riding and the fact that his "base" is mesmerized by its angel. As has become painfully clear during the first three years of his presidency, once this spirituality is in place, Trump continues to live, in spite of violating all the nation's laws and flouting all its institutions. And no one can understand how he gets away with it. He, like all the rest of us, is living inside a pathology—riding the dark spiritual energy that infuses a dissociative psychology with its violence, contempt, and corruption on the one hand and its illusion of American innocence and magical "greatness" on the other (Make America Great Again!).

Struggles to Transform the Powers

In this section, I propose to look at two examples from our national life of men who were possessed by hatred from their Dark Angels and how this archetypal affect was transformed into usable aggression—or not. The stories of these two men illustrate the difference between a healthy conflict psychology (Eisenhower) and an unhealthy dissociative psychology (Trump). Both men shared a childhood and adolescence full of powerful violent emotion. The first story about Dwight D. Eisenhower is reported by David Brooks in his recent book *The Road to Character*.[18]

Conflict Psychology—Dwight D. Eisenhower

Dwight Eisenhower was one of five boys raised by Ida and David Eisenhower in relative poverty in Abilene, Texas. David was a rigid man and strict disciplinarian whereas Ida had a warm, vibrant personality. Dwight would later call her "the finest person I've ever known."[19] One of the things Ida did for Dwight was to help him with his hate. Like Donald Trump, he had an innately aggressive and rebellious disposition that he would have to temper and discipline all his life to become the great general and later president that he was. Here is the story.

> One Halloween evening, when he was about ten, Eisenhower's older brothers received permission to go out trick-or-treating, a more adventurous activity in those days than it is now. Ike wanted to go with them, but his parents told him he was too young. He pleaded with them, watched his brothers go, and then became engulfed by uncontrolled rage. He turned red. His hair bristled. Weeping and screaming, he rushed out into the front yard and began pounding his fists against the trunk of an apple tree, scraping the skin off and leaving his hands bloody and torn.
>
> His father shook him, lashed him with a hickory switch, and sent him up to bed. About an hour later, with Ike sobbing into his pillow, his mother came up and sat silently rocking in the chair next to his bed. Eventually she quoted a verse from the Bible: "He that conquereth his own soul is greater than he who taketh a city."
>
> As she began to salve and bandage his wounds, Ida Eisenhower told her son to beware the anger and hatred that burned inside. Hatred is a futile thing, she told him which only injures the person who harbors it. Of all her boys, she told him, he had the most to learn about controlling his passions.[20]

Much later, when he was 76, Eisenhower wrote, "I have always looked back on that conversation as one of the most valuable moments of my life." His mother had never shamed him and had helped him hold his raging conflict in a compassionate and loving way. At the end of the conversation, Eisenhower admitted to his mother that he was wrong and felt sufficiently reconciled in his mind to fall off to sleep.

In this case the young Eisenhower's avenging angel erupted in rage, but was later held in a loving relationship and transformed into both inner conflict ("I was wrong") and usable anger—eventually, even gratitude. A person who has accomplished this can witness, and accept, his own personal complicity with evil—his own episodic identification with the Dark Angel and its raging tantrums, and take responsibility for the harm he has done or would like to do. Such a person can be in conflict with himself—can eventually see both sides of an issue without being triggered into defensive rage again. This, in turn, leads to an enhanced capacity for empathy with others—a growing moral center, deeper friendships—and greater resilience in the face of life's inevitable hurts, disappointments, and painful limitations.

These hard-won achievements of a conflict psychology and inner democracy lead further to a quickening of the human soul and a grasp of what we might call the *tragic nature of human life*. By the "tragic nature of human life" I am thinking about Heinz Kohut's sympathetic portrayal of "Tragic Man" as distinguished from Freud's "Guilty Man." For Kohut, the mature individual has gone beyond the conflict between his instinctual demands (angels) and the prohibitions of civilization to the larger, more existential conflict between his child-like aspirations and their innocent hopes, on the one hand, and his poignant, sad awareness of the limitations imposed by privations and misfortunes, including our mortality and death, on the other. This leads, for Kohut, not to sadness, pessimism, or despair, but rather to the deep joy that attends our capacity to integrate the tragic aspects of life and accept ourselves, along with others, "as transient participants in the ongoing stream of life."[21] We embrace what William Wordsworth described in *Tintern Abbey* as the universally human and profoundly beautiful "still, sad music of humanity."[22]

Dwight Eisenhower was lucky to have had the kind of compassionate containment that his mother provided him on this occasion—and probably on many others. It gave him choices about how much of his rage and anger to unleash on the world later. He became one of the most effective generals in all of history, directing massive amounts of aggression against the Nazi enemy in the European theater. But his aggressive use of this power was no longer motivated by primitive hatred or identification with his avenging angel. He had mastered and neutralized his high-voltage hatred and converted it into anger he could talk about and use. He had wrestled with his Dark Angel and received its blessing. It was he who warned us later of the dangers of the military-industrial complex.

Dissociative Psychology—Donald Trump

It was different with Donald Trump. One of Trump's moments of rage was captured by a PBS *Frontline* documentary called "The Choice 2016" about Donald Trump's life.[23]

A partial transcript of the documentary describes how in the late 1980s, Trump—now a self-proclaimed 40-year-old billionaire—inserted himself into presidential politics, relishing the publicity and involving himself in controversial issues in New York City like the Central Park "jogger case." Five young black men—ages 14 to 17—had been accused of raping and almost beating to death a young woman jogging in Central Park. Their alleged crime had caused widespread outrage in the city and Donald Trump was especially angered by it. He lashed out with a full-page ad in the New York papers that read: "*Bring Back the Death Penalty, Bring*

Back Our Police." The young black suspects accused of this crime should be executed, he said.

"They're beasts ... they're animals ..."
    "You better believe that I HATE the people that took this girl and raped her brutally. You better believe it! And it's more than anger. It's HATRED! And I want society to hate 'em."

The documentary continues to describe how for Trump the five minority kids who were accused of this brutal crime were less than human and should be exterminated. The accused young men spent years in prison but were later completely exonerated when the actual rapist admitted to the crime. But no apology was ever forthcoming from Donald Trump. He couldn't admit he was wrong and has not apologized for his violent reaction since. Nevertheless, Trump's rage had worked. It made him an overnight celebrity and talk of "President Trump" began.

To me this television documentary is a good illustration of the co-presence of innocence and violence in the psyche of Donald Trump—the invisible child in the system and its protective and persecutory angels, especially the violent angel known as Dis. Some part of Trump was unconsciously *identified* with the violated young girl's innocence. He himself felt violated. We don't begrudge him this reaction—his outrage—about the crime that violated an innocent girl. But notice what happened next. Trump wasn't satisfied with expressing his feelings and leaving the rest to law enforcement. He was filled with ultra-human passion—inflated hatred—off the spectrum of potentially constructive aggression, identified with his avenging angel. He needed to ACT on these feelings in order to discharge them. This is characteristic of a dissociative psychology. Action discharges affect. Conflict is avoided. To promote this discharge, Trump vilified the black youths who were suspects in the case, calling them beasts and animals, destroying in his mind any innocent humanity they may have possessed—reducing them to the totalistic category of evil and thereby justifying more hate, demanding their deaths.

Let us imagine he had been in a position to execute these five men like he recommended—and that they were then exonerated later after their deaths. One can hardly imagine the outrage and hatred this would have triggered—especially in the black community! This is how the unmediated binary structures and all-or-none stereotyping of the primitive neurological system and its angels promotes precipitous action and leads to the destructive chain-reaction we have seen so often in our country.

It is frightening to realize how much of US foreign policy has been based on such binary thinking, vilification, and precipitous action in defense of innocence. George W. Bush made Saddam Hussein into an evil man in his mind, claiming he was about to use weapons of mass destruction against innocent people, and this justified a "shock and awe" bombing campaign in which tens of thousands of *actual innocent people* died. When it was discovered that there were no such weapons ... well, oops, sorry ... but there was no acknowledgment, no apology, no genuine regret. And we wonder why extremists in the Muslim world hate us and blow up our buildings!

Hateful action from one dissociative psychology breeds more hateful action from another. The result is the vicious cycle known as the *retributive justice cycle*, leading from one violent action to another *ad infinitum*. There is no room for a struggle with avenging angels—no taming of the powers—in this madness. Which is why some of our greatest social justice leaders (Lincoln, King, Gandhi) have recommended nonviolent resistance in an effort to break this retributive cycle. Such nonviolent resistance is in the democratic tradition of the New Testament prophet who said (Matthew 5:37–39):[24] "Simply let your 'Yes' be 'Yes,' and your 'No,' 'No.' *Anything more comes from the evil one*" (italics mine).

In the discipline of nonviolence, a conflict must be taken "in"—and not acted "out." This is a form of suffering and sacrifice required by a democracy of the psyche. "*Anything more comes from the evil one*," says Jesus—that is, from the avenging angel "Dis" in the defensive system whose seductive powers seduce us into action.

In Part I of Goethe's *Faust*, the poet laments, "alas, two souls dwell within my breast." This is the ultimate lament of a conflict psychology—of an inner democracy. Alas! ... we are divided within ourselves. We love and we hate—angelically!—and we have a core of innocence and "divine entitlement" that paradoxically justifies either love or hate, but not the two in conflict, together. So we need to be constantly reminded "*Simply let your Yes be 'Yes,' and your No, 'No.' Anything more comes from the evil one.*" Democracy grounds the angels in our human-all-too-human limitations. But it requires suffering of the opposites (wrestling with our angels), and we would rather do almost anything to avoid this! A dissociative psychology always lets us off the hook of suffering the "two souls that dwell within our breast."

Part II: Applications to Our Culture

When I was a child, there was a special object in my grandfather's study that fascinated me, and that I played with for hours. I didn't know what it was then, but since discovered that it was called a *Stereopticon*, or "magic lantern." Its "magic" was that it used two images to create a three-dimensional effect. In the remainder of this chapter, I want to do the same thing. Specifically, I would like to review three issues in our current culture, side by side with the two psychologies I have outlined, in hopes that our collective experience might come into focus in a deeper, more three-dimensional way. The three issues are (1) conspiracy theory and one of its major advocates, Alex Jones;

(2) immigration and exclusion versus inclusion; and (3) the American gun culture and the psychology of mass murder.

But first, a brief description of how collective trauma has taken over the American psyche.

A Traumatized American People and Defenses Against Reality

Trauma is universal in human life and always has been. It has to do with the fact that *we are all given more to experience in this life than we can bear to experience consciously.* This "inability to bear what we are given" within an open ego-structure is the root of all psychological difficulty because it generates anxiety, which in turn generates dissociative defenses; these defenses are made up of the great powers I have been exploring.

Is it possible, then, that we, as American citizens, are facing "more" in our contemporary world situation than we can bear to experience consciously? In other words, have we inadvertently fallen into the violence and illusion of a dissociative system in our national life? Are we confronted by terrors and incomprehensible problems on our globalized world stage that simply cannot be understood or metabolized—overwhelming our integrative capacities as a people? Leading us to fall back on the *fundaments* of the totalitarian inner system—making us *fundamentalists*?

I believe these are reasonable questions and that the answer to them, from my perspective, is a definite "Yes!" Many of my patients are afraid, these days (and I along with them), to turn on the news. We are afraid of the trauma-generating images we will be exposed to—the children starving in war-torn African nations, images of dead immigrants washed up on the shore, stories of mass killings of innocents in our schools by armed teenagers shooting fellow students with high-powered rifles, journalists beheaded by ISIS fighters or radical government thugs, devastation by wild fires caused by out-of-control global warming, destruction of rainforests and wildlife habitat, ushering in a "Sixth Extinction," with the mass die-off of life-forms occurring all around us.

These *realities* are bad enough. Worse still is the fact that they come to us embedded in a news cycle full of willful ignorance, corruption, dishonesty, and greed, where our leaders spend their energy blaming others instead of offering constructive solutions. Meanwhile the news media, instead of educating us on the complexities of the issues that face us, obsessively covers every story of corruption and outrage to satisfy our seemingly endless appetite for scandal, lies, and malicious gossip. Never have the dire warnings of the poet been more prescient—"the best lack all conviction while the worst are full of passionate intensity."[25]

Robert J. Lifton has written a remarkable book called *The Climate Swerve: Reflections on Mind, Hope, and Survival.* In it, he examines the psychological reaction to the threat of nuclear annihilation on the one hand, and the creeping threat of climate change (and what Tom Singer calls "extinction anxiety") on the other. Both, he says, call forth the dissociative defense of psychic numbing.

> Such numbing … has to do with the mind's resistance to the unmanageable extremity of the catastrophe, to the infinite reaches of death and pain. … We find ourselves continuously searching for—and also resisting—images that might help us to take in what is an unprecedented phenomenon. With both nuclear and climate threats, we have trouble "imagining the real." No wonder we tend to see each of them as beyond description or comprehension, as driven by otherworldly forces that render us tiny and helpless, rather than as lethal mechanisms we ourselves have created and are quite capable of understanding. Both call forth the unmanageable imagery of extinction … and lead to psychic numbing, the human equivalent to the way animals "freeze" (sometimes called "playing dead") when threatened and lacking a path of either resistance or escape. The widespread numbing created by nuclear and climate imagery of extinction can be understood as playing dead on the part of the majority of people on earth.[26]

Psychic numbing and "playing dead" are dissociative defenses. They come into being when we need an "escape when there is no escape."[27] The angels in the Self Care System know how to facilitate the illusion of such an escape. That's what they "do."

"Fake News" and Defenses Against Reality

As we have seen, trauma survivors often become "Orphan[s] of the Real."[28] Reality has assaulted them with *too much—too soon*. Fear floods their fragile egos and soon archetypal defenses grow up around their vulnerabilities to avenge the wrongs of their unfair treatment and protect them from further feelings of humiliation and shame. Soon they are living in an altered reality.

Our current president is a master of such illusionism, identified as he is with the Bright Angel in the Self-Care System. It started very early in Trump's presidency, at his inauguration. In William Davies's recent book *Nervous States: Democracy and the Decline of Reason*, he reminds us of Donald Trump's skirmish with the press over the size of his inauguration crowd.[29] *The New York Times* had published an estimate, suggesting that the size of the crowd was only one-third the size of Obama's inauguration, which had been estimated at 1.8 million. Comparative overhead photos supported the *Times*'s estimate. But Sean Spicer, the White House press secretary, accused the press of trying to "minimize the enormous support" that Trump had attracted, claiming that the crowd was, in fact, "the largest audience ever to witness an inauguration, period."[30] When he was accused of lying, Trump advisor Kelly-Anne Conway told the public that Spicer had simply offered "alternative facts" to the ones believed by the journalists.[31] Later Trump accused the press of persecuting and insulting him, complaining to a reporter "they demean me unfairly." He then pointed to a photograph of the crowd that he claimed was from a better angle: "I call it a sea of love," he said.[32]

For Davies, this is an example of *how polarized emotion smothers rational discourse* (italics mine): "For Trump this was no mere disagreement over 'facts.' It was an opposition between two emotions: the arrogant sneer of his critics and the love of his supporters."[33] In the light of the analysis I am pursuing in this chapter, these polarized emotions are none other than the two angels in the dissociative system with which Trump alternately identifies—violence on the one hand, illusion on the other.

Thus, for Donald Trump and his allies, climate change and global warming are a "Chinese hoax," and other facts that make him look bad, like paying off sexual playmates to protect his campaign, are "fake news." The appearance of Trump's personal lawyer, Michael Cohen, before the House Judiciary Committee contained such humiliating testimony that the President pronounced it a "fake hearing." This is how our President negotiates a painful reality—by denying its existence. Disagreeable facts are not allowed to penetrate the fragile boundary of his fortress-self, defended by the light and dark angels. If he were to accept these negative reports and allow himself to feel something other than defensive outrage about them (that is, grief, guilt, remorse, sadness, shame), he would suddenly be in conflict with himself. This would make him a tragic figure like the rest of us—and one we might be inclined to cut some slack. Instead he refuses to join the human struggle and sits alone in his tower, untouchable, "victimized" by the press, surrounded by his illusions of innocence, tweeting dictation from his possessing angels. He is a modern-day Nero, fiddling while Democracy burns.

Conspiracy Theories

Recently I went for a walk in the nearby arroyo here in Santa Fe. Along the winding sandy river-bottom I remember pausing for a moment to watch a flock of beautiful Steller's jays feeding in the trees above. An elderly couple happened by, walking their large German shepherd dog and, seeing me looking skyward, said sympathetically, "looking at those chemtrails are you?" Perplexed, I explained I was looking at the birds and then, looking higher, noticed the contrails from jet planes crisscrossing the sky. "Do you mean those?" I asked. "Jet contrails?" "Yea," the man said, and we began a conversation. I soon realized I was going down the rabbit hole into a completely alternate reality. "You should know about those chemtrails!" the woman warned ominously. There's lots of evidence showing how the government is trying to alter the weather around here—or worse! You can Google it if you want."

So I did Google it and found several links that led inevitably along the path of the "chemtrail conspiracy theory," an apparently very active subject on the web—to which more and more people are turning for their "news" these days. The whole phantasmal scheme is based on the skewed belief that the contrails of jet-engine exhaust are really "chemtrails" consisting of chemical or biological agents sprayed by the government in a secret scheme to test weapons, change the weather, or mitigate climate change. Here was a little window into the American psyche that was really quite disturbing.

Apparently for these likeable folks, out walking their dog on a sunny afternoon, a conspiracy theory made sense of a world that was otherwise overwhelming and, apparently, very frightening. Undifferentiated anxiety is much worse than fear. With their conspiracy theory, at least they had something to fear. They knew who the *enemy* was. If reality was too much to bear, or too complicated to comprehend, or just not to their liking, then "chemtrails" offered them a simple explanation for the incomprehensible and ever-changing things that they saw around them. And there were enough sites on the internet that *looked like* news for them to be convinced. Apparently the posts of conspiracy crackpots on Google had become their source for news about reality, so it was with complete confidence that they could tell me to "Google it!"

As I left the scene and continued my walk, I wondered how many more of my wealthy neighbors in Santa Fe had drunk this particular Kool-Aid. Sadly, it turns out that the answer is apparently many!

Kurt Anderson's best-selling book *Fantasyland: How America Went Haywire—a 500-Year History* chronicles some of the remarkable illusions/delusions that seem to have taken over our American consciousness.[34] Anderson points out that we Americans have always been wide-eyed idealists, true believers, and passionate dreamers, but that lately, various cultural and technological developments have taken us "over the edge" and "down the rabbit hole." Among these developments, he highlights the substitution of opinions for facts that emerged with the repeal of the Federal Fairness Doctrine in the 1980s and how the subsequent vacuum was filled by right-wing radio talk shows—Rush Limbaugh, then Fox News, MSNBC ... Now, instead of receiving a single standard version of the news on one of the three major broadcast networks (CBS, ABC, NBC), Americans were locked into their silos, listening to their own private, partisan, and emotion-driven versions of the truth. In addition, says Anderson, the internet amplifies the problem with crackpot opinions, broadcast all over the airwaves—looking like real news. The result is what he calls the "fantasy-industrial complex." It promotes pure subjectivity over objectivity—so that people now think and act *as if opinions and feelings were just as true as facts.*

Anderson's statistics are frightening: Roughly 25 percent of Americans, he says, believe that the government and its co-conspirators are hiding all sorts of monstrous truths from us—concerning assassinations, extraterrestrials, the genesis of AIDS, how vaccines cause autism, and so on. A similar quarter of the population believe that Barack Obama is the Anti-Christ and was born in Kenya, that Donald Trump really won the popular vote in 2016, that US officials were complicit in the 9/11 attacks, and that "the media or the government adds secret mind-controlling technology to television broadcast signals."[35] Anderson estimates that roughly a 100 million Americans have strongly conspiracist predispositions and ideas, while a small but significant fraction of that—perhaps several million—"are committed to beliefs that seem symptomatic of mental illness."[36]

The Education of Alex Jones

Alex Jones is a case in point. Jones began his career in the 1990s and has thousands upon thousands of followers as well as an annual income of at least 20 million dollars. In 1995, he accused the US government of planning the Oklahoma City bombing. Then six years later, he made a similar claim about the September 11th attack on the World Trade Center. He sees climate change as a hoax perpetrated by a "New World Order" of financial elites who profit by fueling exploitable hysteria. Evil lurks everywhere for Alex Jones.

But the most flagrant of his delusions—and one that he has promulgated over the airwaves and the internet for 7 years now—is that the massacre of 20 innocent children by Adam Lanza at the Sandy Hook Elementary School in Newtown, Connecticut, in 2012 .... *never happened!* It was a "false flag" operation, he says, engineered by gun-control advocates to drum up support for "taking our guns away." In Jones's language "no-one died." It was "a synthetic completely fake event with actors."[37]

Jones might be easily dismissed as a complete crackpot—a minor fringe figure on the radical right—were it not for the fact that he has the ear of the president of the United States! The "fringe" has now been folded into the center. Trump appeared as a candidate on Alex Jones's show in 2016 and after the election phoned him with effusive praise and gratitude for his role in the campaign.[38]

Alex Jones is a significant case study for our purposes in this chapter, because he has just fallen out of his Self-Care System and into a reality that he finds intolerable. His case graphically illustrates the dissociative psychology we have been exploring and how the culture has colluded to keep it in place. The story emerged in a recent *New York Times* article by Charlie Warzel published on March 31, 2019, and entitled "Why Courtrooms Are Kryptonite for Alex Jones."[39] The article described a three-hour deposition under oath as Jones was questioned by attorneys for ten families who had sued him in a defamation lawsuit for his role in spreading conspiracy theories that had caused survivors of the massacre to be harassed, stalked, and threatened. These families had won a series of court rulings that required Jones to testify. Attorneys then posted his deposition online for everyone to see. Tens of thousands of viewers apparently did.

Warzel describes Jones's heavy sighing and wincing under aggressive questioning from the attorneys—totally out of control—suddenly forced to admit that his *"confidential sources" were really nothing more than message-board trolls and cranks.* The attorneys made him read from a disturbing police report, chronicling the testimony of emergency medical workers, and then immediately watch footage of his past broadcasts denying the violence was real. As he squirmed and tried to revert to his meandering soliloquies and belligerent verbal outbursts from his broadcast persona, attorneys cut him off and dismissed his answers as "nonresponsive." For the first time, his anger was caged. He blamed "the media," suggesting that he was the victim of an unfair smear campaign, tried to cast doubt on the film clips that were shown to him, claiming they were altered or heavily edited ... "fake news, all of it!" he said. But Jones's efforts to flood every topic with confusion and doubt did not work with the lawyers doing his deposition.

His tactics fell flat, and finally, he fell apart—and fell into reality. Near the end of the deposition he admitted that the killing at Sandy Hook was real. Then he suggested that his claims about the massacre being fake were the result of a mental disorder! "I almost had like a form of psychosis back in the past where I basically thought everything was staged, even though I'm now learning a lot of times things aren't staged," he said.

Alex Jones was, indeed, learning. He was learning from reality, and the lessons were painful. He began to face the fact that some things in the outer world are so horrific that we can't metabolize them. They are unthinkable. We have to dissociate them ... or deny that they ever happened. Alex Jones discovered that he had been living in a system of complete denial. Powerful forces (Dark Angels) were helping him to "kill" his consciousness of reality and then to weave comforting delusions around his pain (Bright Angel). His *feelings* and the opinions they generated had become his *facts.* Now he saw that his "evidence" was an echo-chamber consisting of the postings of trolls and cranks. When he finally broke down under the insistent questioning of the attorneys, there was a moment when Alex Jones entered a conflict psychology. He was forced by the legal system itself to finally wrestle with his angels instead of just channeling them. He was asked to embrace his own *democracy of the psyche.* Suddenly, he had to face his own complicity with evil—his own lying, his own dissociative defenses, and to look directly into the eyes of his own duplicity. It was not a sight he tolerated easily. He became almost human. He started to cry. This lasted for only a moment. Then quickly he returned to his victim/perpetrator story. He blamed his mental illness—another way to keep his innocence from suffering experience—to keep it enshrined in amber—another way for him to avoid responsibility.

Immigration, the Wall, and a Personal Lesson in Inclusiveness

Recently, at a local restaurant, I had a brief struggle with my own intolerance at the "border" of my own identity. On a small scale, this experience put me in touch with the issues of inclusion versus exclusion that define a spectrum of opinions on the immigration crisis at our southern border.

My wife Robin and I were having a birthday dinner, tucked into a small table in the corner near the end of a long bank of tables pushed together apparently to accommodate a large party expected at the restaurant. Halfway through the meal a huge gentleman—perhaps 6'4" and 300 pounds sat down at the assembled tables and motioned the waiter over. I overheard the conversation. "Could we move some chairs around a bit, because we have some very large folks joining us?" he asked. Soon an obese woman waddled in—she must have been 400 pounds—followed by what looked like her sister—equally large. One of them sat on two chairs pushed together ... the other in the window seat. Two others soon joined them. Then after a few minutes, each of these large individuals got up and walked to the bathroom, pushing their way through the other tables, in one case pulling the tablecloth off a nearby table and creating a moment of chaos and irritation among the diners.

I could feel my *disapproval* rising (recall that Dante's name for the Dark Angel in the Self-Care System is "Dis") and my negative judgments. "Thank God," I thought, "I'm not on an airplane with someone like *that* sitting next to me." I began to feel that these people were pushing into my boundaries in some way, and I was building internal walls against them to preserve some implicit "superiority" in myself. They constituted my own private "caravan" from Guatemala! I began to wrestle with my angels. "How difficult it must be for them," I thought. "They must be shunned and denigrated on a regular basis ... it's a shame." "But then," I wondered,

> why don't they lose weight? They have a choice after all, don't they? On the other hand, maybe they don't have a choice ... maybe it's glandular or inherited. Or perhaps they are addicted ... maybe all trauma survivors with intractable defenses.

Back and forth went my inner argument. At one moment I was open—even sympathetic—to these women, and at another, contemptuous toward them. And for this contempt I felt ashamed of myself. Then, to complicate matters, I began to feel an inner resentment for the scolding I was giving myself about my bigoted, exclusive, elitist attitudes. I could imagine what a relief it would be *not to feel ashamed* of these negative reactions—not to be so politically "correct" for once. I could feel my inner Donald Trump and it disturbed me. In short, I was struggling to stay *within* a conflict psychology.

In retrospect I realized that this conflict within myself was—quintessentially—a democratic negotiation among the various parts of my feelings and reactions, and that I was clearly in a wrestling match with my Dark Angel— and maybe my Bright Angel too, hiding in the idealized "shoulds" behind my negative judgments. I was in a major conflict with my feelings—a readiness to love and a readiness to hate. I also realized how much *guilt* I had to suffer to stay inside this conflict and how much I wanted to get *rid* of this guilt—almost as much as I wanted to get rid of these people!

This moment, for me, was a lesson in our national obsession with immigration and the "Wall" that Donald Trump wants to build. Democracy is *inclusive*, with complicated solutions to complicated problems, whereas totalitarianism is *exclusive* with easy simple answers. In this restaurant I was clearly both. A democratic psychology requires a lot of mental/psychological struggle and the capacity to hold conflicted feelings (to suffer them), whereas a dissociative psychology doesn't hold conflict. It builds walls. It is phobic about conflict and intolerant of the mixed feelings that must be held while conflict is resolved. It simply projects the *bad* and gets rid of it with an avenging angel. In order to justify his "Wall," Trump must make immigrants bad, so he calls them terrorists and rapists and says they bring drugs and disease, and must be kept *out*. In this way he fans the fires of anxiety in the people and then purports to put these fires out with a simple solution—the "Wall."

At one time in our history it was different. In 1886 the Statue of Liberty was given to the people of the United States by the people of France to honor the American-French alliance that won the Revolutionary War and to celebrate the open-hearted welcome that our nation had given to displaced European refugees who had flooded by the thousands through New York Harbor and found refuge and a new home on American soil. "God's Crucible" is what the playwright Israel Zangwill called the new nation in his 1908 play *The Melting Pot*. In that play, the main character—a Russian immigrant—rhapsodized about the new American inclusiveness:

> Ah, what a stirring and a seething! Celt and Latin, Slav and Teuton, Greek and Syrian ... black and yellow ... how the great Alchemist melts and fuses them with his purging flame! Here shall they all unite to build the Republic of Man and the Kingdom of God. .... What is the glory of Rome and Jerusalem where all nations and races come to worship and look back, compared with the glory of America, where all races and nations come to labor and look forward![40]

This was a remarkable testimony to the equality and potential openness of the young democracy and to the spirit of democracy everywhere! And inscribed on the base of The Statue of Liberty is a moving poem by Emma Lazarus that expresses the essence of this inclusive attitude. In fact, Lady Liberty may be the best representation we have of what Abraham Lincoln, in his Second Inaugural Address, meant by the "better angels of our nature"—not the two angels of violence and illusion we have been exploring as part of a dissociative psychology, but a third angel, the angel of democracy herself:

> Give me your tired, your poor,
> Your huddled masses, yearning to breathe free.
> The wretched refuse of your teeming shore,
> Send these, the homeless, tempest tossed to me.
> I lift my lamp beside the golden door.

Democracy makes room for the "wretched" and the "homeless"—for "*les misérables*," the miserable ones. They too are to be included. The light held high in the lamp of Lady Liberty is a stirring symbol for the wholeness that democratic diversity and inclusiveness signify. And the "Wall" is a perfect symbol for its opposite—a dissociative psychology that excludes. Inclusiveness versus Exclusiveness. These are not a pair of opposites but competing psychologies, competing politics. Both are necessary for the proper regulation of what gets "in" and what stays "out" of the United States. There would be no possibility for inclusiveness if we didn't have firm boundaries. Walls are necessary, including on our southern border, especially today when immigrants are flooding in from failed states in South America. When Nancy Pelosi pronounces that "the Wall is an immorality," she is flirting with extremism and coming dangerously close to a dissociative psychology. Walls are necessary. Walls, as Robert Frost said, make good neighbors. But they need windows and doors and apertures through which we can embrace otherness when we want to. They need to be supported by an *immigration policy* that is informed by the better angels of our nature—the angels of democracy—not the angels of fear and exclusion.

Guns as Angel-Weapons: Mass Murder in America

I grew up with guns in a family of outdoorsmen. My father, grandfather, and uncles, all hunted. I know the heady power of shooting guns—the explosive power when you pull the trigger, the speed and impact of the bullets or shot charges, the thrill of hitting a moving target at a distance, the power to kill an animal or bird and the ritual of cleaning and eating wild game. Having a gun in your hands is having immediate access to archetypal power—power that amplifies the limited power of the body—the powers of great warriors, heroes, and gods. Guns make you strong and powerful. Knowing how to use a gun makes you special in the eyes of others. Guns make others afraid. Guns are powerful defenses—880 volts of untransformed power. *Guns are angel weapons!*

I know these things because my loving father, who was a talented professional man with a big local reputation and many creative abilities, was also angry and afraid. Afraid of blacks, afraid of communists, afraid of "anti-gun liberals" who might "take our guns away." My father grew up in a neighborhood in Detroit where he was bullied and picked on. He was a skinny, weak kid with asthma, but he built himself up by boxing and weightlifting and then he bought guns. Teddy Roosevelt was his hero. He would regale me with stories of the Wild West and how the colt revolver was the "great equalizer" on the frontier, making even weak men strong. And how an armed militia was the best defense against a possible takeover of the country by communists. He kept a colt revolver in his bedside table and practiced "dry-firing" at Indians riding horses around the wagon trains in TV Westerns. Once he accidentally shot out the television set after reloading his gun, falling asleep, and waking to the sound of a cavalry charge! My mother thought he had killed himself, but he was only defending the household against menacing Indians!

I inherited my guns from my father, but I have now given them up ... sold them all ten years ago after a significant spiritual crisis, following my viewing of the movie *War Horse* with my wife Robin. That's another story.[41] But one reason I gave up my guns is because of the dissociative psychology of the gun culture in America—especially the fear-mongering, paranoid psychology sponsored by the National Rifle Association (NRA). Over the course of my lifetime, the terrified, tormented, and violently defended psychology of the NRA has become a malignant cancer in the American psyche and a true threat to the democratic values that I hold dear.

The psychology at the center of the NRA is built around *fear* and *defense.* It is a perfect, collective national out-picturing of the Self-Care System with its violent and sentimental illusions (Bright and Dark Angels) and the fragile, weak, and innocent child in their care. For the NRA the "child" is America's innocence, goodness, and exceptionalism—the shining city on a hill. And the threats against this fragile center are perceived to be everywhere. During the Cold War, it used to be communists but with the collapse of the Soviet Union and the fall of the Berlin Wall, the threats have metastasized to include criminal gangs, jihadist Islamic terrorists, Antifa leftists, and even what Wayne LaPierre called "jackbooted government thugs coming to harass and intimidate law-abiding citizens" and take away everyone's guns. The main threat, at the center of NRA paranoia is the government itself, threatening to take away our constitutional rights to self-defense.

There is no awareness in this psychology of the extreme distortions emanating from the heroic angels of the NRA's system—especially the dark one named "Dis." The whole organization lives in terror. As fears mount in the national psyche, the only thing the gun lobby is able to imagine is giving the good guys more guns! And not just more guns, but bigger guns—AK 47s, assault rifles, machine guns—more archetypal power to defeat our human fears, to keep our unconscious vulnerabilities at bay, to "kill" them if we can. This is a fascist state of mind, and the apotheosis of the dissociative psychology we have been exploring. Seeing evil everywhere, it sets the stage for our own possession by evil, and there is no better example of this than the mass shootings of innocent people occurring with increasing frequency in our schools, churches, mosques, and synagogues.

Adolph Hitler

To understand the psychology of evil that enters our collective American experience through mass shootings such as occurred in Newtown, Connecticut, or Parkland, Florida, we must understand how the demon of destructive rage finds its way into the dissociated *individual* psyche and what it wants to "kill" there. Almost always, the host personality who houses such a killer has a personal history in which his own vulnerability was brutally violated, humiliated, and shamed, so that he has become hateful of the tender aspects of his own experience.

Adolph Hitler provides a prime example. Here is Alice Miller's description:[42]

> Hitler was brutally beaten by his father during his early life—sometimes to the point of unconsciousness. He became hardened, "counter-dependent" and shut off his feelings by counting the blows on his body—once there were 32 of them that he bragged about taking without a tear. Feeling utterly humiliated, shamed and weak, but unable to cry, Hitler went on to write: "My pedagogy is hard. What is weak must be hammered away. In my fortresses of the Teutonic Order a young generation will grow up before which the world will tremble. I want the young to be violent, domineering, undismayed, cruel. The young must be all these things. They must be able to bear pain. There must be nothing weak or gentle about them. The free, splendid beast of prey must once again flash from their eyes. I want my young people strong and beautiful. That way I can create something new."[43]

This quote from *Mein Kampf* illustrates the dissociation of childhood parts of the psyche that carry painful memories split off from destructive narcissistic parts of the self that provide a sense of invulnerability, superiority, and inflated self-esteem. The tension between these parts is resolved by "killing" the vulnerable dependent parts in identification with the avenging angel in the system—just like my patient's gunman murdered the young girl in her dream. In his identification with this Dark Angel, Hitler prepares to wreak vengeance on whole nations and peoples as a way of getting even for the cruelty he experienced as a child.

Nikolas Cruz and the Psychology of Mass Murder

Hitler's psychology is alive and well in the United States of the 21st century. On Valentine's day in 2018, a young man named Nikolas Cruz,[44] who had been expelled from high school the year before because of angry behavior, took an AR-15-style semiautomatic rifle with many magazines of ammunition and walked into his former school in Parkland, Florida. He then went on a six-minute rampage, shooting into locked classrooms and through windows and walls and blasting people in the hallways. He killed 17 people, 14 of them students. Then, wearing an old high-school polo shirt, he threw away his rifle and fled the building along with panic-stricken students, escaping the school before police entered. He was caught while walking on the street.

Cruz, who was adopted along with his brother, had been a troubled child much of his life. His adoptive father died in 2004, and his mother, to whom he was very close, died in November 2017. After this he made two suicide attempts with drugs and alcohol. His behavior became erratic after his father died, and he was sent for therapy. Although he showed signs of improvement, his rages continued. He started wearing military clothing, killing animals, and became obsessed with violent online video games and with guns. Frequently he would blow up in a rage if he lost a video game—once destroying the family TV set. He punched holes in walls. A neighbor found him hitting his head and covering his ears, as if tormented from within. Kids had been picking on him and bullying him. He complained of intense loneliness and lack of friends and said he scared girls away.

It turns out that for years Nikolas Cruz had been wrestling with a Dark Angel—but the angel was getting the upper hand. In a confession released by Broward County, he told detective John Curcio that he had long been hearing a voice in his head. The voice started around the time his father died and worsened after Cruz's mother died of pneumonia, just months before the rampage. "It's my bad side," Cruz told the detective. "It's my demon." The voice told him to cut himself, to kill himself, to hurt others, to buy guns, to "Burn! Kill! Destroy!" It also told him to buy the rifle he used in the massacre. Sometimes, Cruz would buy guns to protect himself from the voice, and he kept the guns locked up to keep the voice from getting them. The voice in his head kept him from being lonely, he said—like a friend—"I just wanted to have somebody."

Nikolas Cruz's avenging angel wanted to kill his pain and the people who had caused it, just like the gunman in my patient's dream. It had tried twice to kill the pain by killing Cruz himself in two unsuccessful suicide attempts. Then, in his increasing alienation, loneliness, and isolation Nikolas Cruz began to fill with rage. He got no help in his struggle with his demon. His parents were both gone and no one seemed to care. He started buying guns. He played violent video games obsessively. He had just been shunned by an old girlfriend and had gotten into a fight over her. Finally Valentine's day arrived—the day of love ... and death. Cruz heard the voice of his avenging angel again—louder this time. We don't know what it said. And then there was nothing but the blood of children drenching the carpets and spattered on the walls.

As a nation, we were traumatized ... again. An assault rifle in the hands of a troubled teenager shooting innocent kids at close range. It is too much to bear. It shatters us and makes us numb and it makes us angry and it makes us want to act instead of understand. Our fear and terror leads to primitive defenses. We turn things over to our angels, and so we find ourselves thinking in the stereotypical patterns of the primitive archetypal mind. We become fundamentalists again—extremists. Nikolas Cruz, we say was insane—a mental case—a predator, possessed by evil. Give him the death penalty. Lock him up. And then (we imagine) we can put armed guards in our classrooms or arm our teachers themselves so we can kill someone like him before he kills others. That's what our President has suggested on several occasions, and the NRA loves it. And while Donald Trump showed some initial signs—right after the shooting at Parkland school—of being open to a few minor regulations on the sale of guns, he rapidly fell in line with the NRA's cynical mantra "guns don't kill people, people kill people." Or as the NRA said after Newtown, "An armed society is a polite society. To stop a bad guy with a gun it takes a good guy with a gun!"

Readers of this chapter will have no trouble identifying this response as a *dissociative response* to collective trauma. This psychology is completely identified with the archetypal powers of the defense system—the Bright and Dark Angels. Such a psychology holds itself "above the fray" of our broken world and our broken hearts. It will not let these feelings "in." It splits the world into powerful good guys and weak or disturbed bad guys, vilifies or discounts the bad guys, keeps innocence over here on "our side," and resolves the complexity of a multifaceted psychological and sociological issue with simplified partisan answers and actions. It is conflict-avoidant and therefore phobic about democracy.

W. E. B. Du Bois once said, "Back of the writhing, yelling, cruel-eyed demons who break, destroy, maim and lynch and burn at the stake, is a knot, large or small, of normal human beings, and these human beings at heart are desperately *afraid* of something."[45] He goes on to say that their fear is of many things, but mostly of being dehumanized, marginalized, degraded, disgraced, and of losing their hopes and their futures. All these despairing realities had come true for Nikolas Cruz.

Behind the heinous acts of Cruz's avenging angel there was a human story. He was a young man in terrible conflict with powers that he had no help in dealing with. Terrified, alienated, and friendless, he acted out and brought more rejection upon himself. He got thrown out of school. He was bullied, picked on, pushed around, and beaten up. Soon he felt like he no longer belonged to the human community. So he retreated to his inner angels and found similar outraged angelic and demonic voices on the internet to amplify his own. His human anger turned into archetypal rage, then possessed him. He identified with it. When he turned his demon loose it simply did what rage-demons do. It killed and killed and killed.

If we are to have any chance of understanding kids like Nikolas Cruz or shaping a collective response to traumas allegedly "caused" by them, then we must struggle to understand the common ground of humanity that we share. This is difficult work, because their crimes are so monstrous—so heinous—that it is easy to cast them *out* instead of taking them *in*. We get some help in this struggle from C. G. Jung who often quoted the maxim of the Roman playwright Terence: *Homosum; humani nil a me alienum puto* ("I am a human; therefore I count nothing human alien to me").[46]

Applied to ourselves, this means—among other things—that there's a avenging Dark Angel in all of us—a heartless killer who wants to obliterate our awareness of feeling when feeling has become "too much." We need to remind ourselves that behind the mask of that killer there's a story—a human story like ours—even if we're too angry or numb or traumatically dissociated these days to look into it. As citizens of a democracy, we must look into it because this is our work—finding the humanity in the "enemy," even if the enemy has been possessed by evil. We don't do this because we are bleeding-heart liberals and want to rehabilitate everyone, but because we need to understand what human circumstances—what human weakness or misfortune—allowed this possession in the first place. We need to wrestle with our angels so that we can help them wrestle with theirs. We are all survivors of trauma, and now people like Nikolas Cruz threaten to create in us the same raging anger, the same wretchedness, the same avenging angels that led to their crimes. We must be careful not to repeat the defensive pattern of killing consciousness by splitting *their* human stories off from *ours*. As citizens in the American experiment and "trust holders of democracy," we must make this effort to listen and to understand.

Final Thoughts on Democracy

In depth psychology, it is well known that the human personality exists in parts and not originally as a whole. The ego develops as a kind of volcanic archipelago of conscious islands slowly rising out of a sea of unconsciousness. These islands represent different experiences and are not always compatible with each other or with the ego-ideal or the aspiring identity of a person. And so they exist initially as "part-selves" or separate "self-states" (Bromberg) in conflict with each other.[47] In a safe and healthy "democratic" inner environment, the separate part-selves get to know each other and even benefit from the struggle with their differences. Slowly, a dynamic and resilient ego develops and a wholeness that contains *more* than just the sum of the parts comes into being (*e-pluribus unum*). This wholeness contains a mystery and has been called various things in psycho-analytic theory: "the transcendent function" (Jung[48]), the "analytic third" (Ogden[49]), the "potential or paradoxical space" for open-hearted living (Winnicott[50]).

By contrast, in a traumatic environment, some of the "islands" of experience are so painful or alien that they cannot be included in the whole and fear of their inclusion floods the spaces between them. Dissociative defenses become necessary and "angels" are called in to both kill (Dark Angel) and encapsulate (Bright Angel) those painful injuries and childhood memories that cannot afford to be consciously associated with the central ego, lest the personality be broken or annihilated. The ego identifies with these heroic angels, and narcissistic survival is exchanged for real living from a core of selfhood that includes our woundedness and vulnerability. The heart is frozen and closed and has forgotten how to open. Life goes on, but at the cost of intimacy and creative living. The result is a dissociative psychology, and we have seen several of the monstrous and distorted forms this takes when it gets hold of our collective life.

Terry Tempest Williams once wrote that "*The human heart is the first home of democracy*," and I think she is right about this. She goes on to say that the heart is "the house of empathy for the pain of others." It is "where the bravery lives ... that allows us to stand in the center of uncertainty with strength." It embodies a wisdom that "dares to be vulnerable in the presence of power."[51]

All this is true, but in this chapter I've been suggesting that, as the "first home of democracy," the human heart is something more. It's also an arena for a battle—a battle between conflicting emotions. It's the place where we wrestle with our angels—all day and all night if necessary, like Jacob did—until they bless us. It's the place where we struggle with our loves and our hates in order to transform them into something workable—into feelings we can use to deepen our relationships in communion with others.

Such an *Agon*—from the Greek "struggle or contest"—is what Jung appears to mean by the perennial and universal struggle to unite "the opposites" in the individuation process.

> When you say "Yes" you say at the same time "No." This principle may seem a hard one, but as a matter of fact there must be this split in the libido or nothing works and we remain inert. Life is never so beautiful as when surrounded by death. Once I had a very wealthy patient who on coming to me said, "I don't know what you're going to do with me, but I hope you are going to give me something that isn't grey." And that is exactly what life would be if there were no

opposites in it; therefore the pairs of opposites are not to be understood as mistakes but as the origin of life.[52]

The struggle with the opposites—to bring them together in a *coniunctio oppositorum*—is for Jung what gives life its dynamic vitality. It is also what makes life *meaningful* because consciousness is born from the experience of this struggle between opposites. And the creation of greater consciousness was, for Jung, the true "telos" of a meaningful life. "As far as we can discern, the sole purpose of human existence is to kindle a light in the darkness of mere being."[53] It follows from this, as Edward Edinger says, that "Experiences of inner and outer conflict which are resolved creatively and are accompanied by a sense of satisfaction and life enhancement are examples of the creation of consciousness."[54]

This only happens in a democracy of the psyche. Inner and outer democracies are always breaking down fundamentalistic, totalistic, and absolutist categories into relativistic, provisional, and contingent ones— always transmuting 880 volts into usable electricity—always generating conflict and then resolving it. Democracies, in this sense, are to the collective polity what healthy families are for bringing up civilized, emotionally literate children. They are transformational containers. They are projection-eating machines. They take in evil, digest it, and give it back as hate and finally as civil disagreement. This struggle increases consciousness.

So in its struggle with the opposing powers of a dissociative psychology, democracy—both inner and outer—*is effectively an engine of consciousness-creation*. Democracy is a way of both opening the heart and increasing the light of consciousness.

For these reasons, democracy, within and without, is precious and worth fighting for. As an engine of consciousness-creation, it is unique among all the polities in the world in its ability to transform and humanize the primitive powers that menace us with their absolutism, their extremity, and their seductive simplifications. Nonetheless, like the psyche itself, democracies can be weakened by trauma and the defensives that grow up around it. The biggest threats to our democratic traditions at this time in the United States are the trauma-generated fears that foreclose honest conflict among the feelings and opinions that generate the energy that gives us light—like hydrogen burning at the center of a star. If this inner struggle between opposing factions dies out or is displaced by disputatious wrangling, so too does the light of democracy and the hope for greater consciousness and meaning that it offers the world. This is our challenge, because as we speak at this time in American history, the light is dimming. Because we speak—and because we *can* speak—the light brightens once again.

Notes

1 C. G. Jung, "Face to Face Interview," in *C. G. Jung Speaking*, eds. William McGuire and R. F. C. Hull (Princeton: Princeton University Press), 436.
2 Thomas Singer and Samuel Kimbles, eds. *The Cultural Complex: Contemporary Jungian Perspectives on Psyche and Society* (New York: Brunner/Routledge, 2004).
3 Donald Kalsched, *The Inner World of Trauma: Archetypal Defenses of the Personal Spirit* (London: Routledge, 1996); and *Trauma and the Soul: A Psycho-Spiritual Approach to Human Development and Its Interruption* (London: Routledge, 2013).
4 See Greg Lukianoff and Jonathan Haidt, *The Coddling of the American Mind* (New York, Penguin Press, 2018).
5 See Natan Sharansky with Rachel Friedman, "The Centrality of Dissent," in *Fight for Liberty: Defending Democracy in the Age of Trump*, ed. Mark Lasswell (New York: Public Affairs, 2018).
6 Theodore Adorno, Else Frenkel-Brunswik, Daniel Levensin, and Nevitt Sanford, *The Authoritarian Personality* (New York: Harper and Brothers, 1950).
7 Ibid.; Richard Hofstadter, *The Paranoid Style in American Politics* (New York: Random House, 1952/2008).
8 Christopher Bollas, *Being a Character: Psychoanalysis and Self Experience* (New York: Farrar, Straus & Giroux, 1992), Chapter 9.
9 Philip M. Bromberg has written extensively about this struggle in the clinical situation. See especially *Awakening the Dreamer: Clinical Journeys* (Mahwah, NJ: The Analytic Press, 2006). For example: "In a growth-facilitating treatment, there develops an increased ability to surrender the safety afforded by dissociation, and a simultaneous increase in the capacity to bear and process internal conflict" (69).
10 Louis H. Stewart, (1987) "A Brief Report: Affect and Archetype," *Journal of Analytical Psychology* 32, no. 1 (1987): 35–46, https://doi.org/10.1111/j.1465-5922.1987.00035.x.
11 Bromberg, *Awakening the Dreamer*.
12 Blake's image borrows from the Judeo-Christian tradition and portrays the opposing divine powers as "angels," one of whom (Lucifer) has "fallen" from Heaven. Other mythologies demonstrate the same tripartite structure. For example, in ancient Egypt we find (1) a source of violent dismembering energy threatening the cosmos (Seth); (2) a principle of goodness, harmony, and civilization, which is constantly threatened by Seth (Osiris); and (3) a child born from Osiris (and his wife/sister Isis) who is part human and part divine. Ultimately it is the dual "child" who establishes his kingdom on earth and defeats the dark forces of dissociation (Seth). The psychological meaning is the same in both mythologies.
13 James S. Grotstein, *Who Is the Dreamer Who Dreams the Dream? A Study of Psychic Presences* (Hillsdale, NJ: The Analytic Press, 2000).
14 This will involve us allowing ourselves to "feel" them: Edinger's suggestion of how to experience the opposites is to figure out what you love and hate. See Edward F. Edinger, *The Mysterium Lectures: A Journey Through C. G. Jung's Mysterium Coniunctionis* (Toronto: Inner City Books, 1995), 323.
15 Quoted in Walter Wink, *Naming the Powers: The Language of Power in the New Testament*, vol. 1 (Minneapolis, MN: Fortress Press, 1984), 84.
16 Ibid., 108. Italics mine.
17 Katie Reilly, "Donald Trump Says He Could Shoot Someone and Not Lose Voters, *Time*, January 23, 2016, https://time.com/4191598/donald-trump-says-he-could-shoot-somebody-and-not-lose-voters/.

18 David Brooks, *The Road To Character* (New York: Random House, New York, 2015), 52ff.
19 Ibid., 50.
20 Ibid., 52.
21 Heinz Kohut, *The Restoration of the Self* (Chicago: University of Chicago Press, 1977), 237.
22 William Wordsworth, "Lines Composed a Few Miles Above Tintern Abbey," Lines 88–93. From the Project Gutenberg ebook of *Lyrical Ballads, 1798*, by William Wordsworth and Samuel Taylor Coleridge, https://www.gutenberg.org/files/9622/9622-h/9622-h.htm.
23 "The Choice 2016," *Frontline*, directed by Michael Kirk (PBS, 2016), minutes 57:28–60:15, https://www.pbs.org/wgbh/frontline/film/the-choice-2016/transcript/. The full episode can be found on PBS.org: https://www.pbs.org/wgbh/frontline/film/the-choice-2016/.
24 Berean Study Bible, https://bereanbible.com.
25 William Butler Yeats, "The Second Coming," https://poets.org/poem/second-coming. Poem is in the public domain.
26 Robert J. Lifton, *The Climate Swerve: Reflections on Mind, Hope, and Survival* (New York: The New Press, 2017), 36–37.
27 Frank W. Putnam, "Discussion: Are Alter Personalities Fragments or Figments?" *Psychoanalytic Inquiry* 12, no. 1 (1992): 95–111, 104.
28 Grotstein, *Who Is the Dreamer Who Dreams the Dream?*, 215.
29 William Davies, *Nervous States: Democracy and the Decline of Reason* (New York: W. W. Norton & Co., 2018).
30 Harry Cockburn, "Donald Trump Again Claims to Have the largest Presidential Inauguration Audience in History," *The Independent*, January 26, 2017.
31 Ibid.
32 Ibid.
33 Davies, *Nervous States*, 4.
34 Kurt Anderson, *Fantasyland: How America Went Haywire* (New York: Random House, 2017).
35 Ibid., 6–7.
36 Ibid., 359.
37 Ibid., 358.
38 Ibid., 360.
39 Charlie Warzel, "Why Courtrooms Are Kryptonite for Alex Jones," *The New York Times*, March 31, 2019, https://www.nytimes.com/2019/03/31/opinion/alex-jones-sandy-hook.html.
40 As reported in Jon Meacham's *The Soul of America: The Battle for our Better Angels* (New York: Random House, 2018), 74.
41 The interested reader can read that story in Donald E. Kalsched, "Getting Your Own Pain: A Personal Account of Healing Dissociation with Help from the Film *War Horse*," in *The Routledge International Handbook of Jungian Film Studies*, ed. Luke Hockley, 303–314 (London: Routledge, 2018).
42 Alice Miller, *For Your Own Good: Hidden Cruelty in Childrearing and the Roots of Violence* (New York: Farrar, Straus, & Giroux, 1983). In the *Preface of The Truth Will Set You Free*, Miller says: "In the childhoods of the worst tyrants in history I discovered a recurring pattern: extreme cruelty, idealization of the parents, glorification of violence, denial of pain, and revenge wreaked on whole nations and peoples as a way of getting even for the cruelty they had once experienced and then denied." See *The Truth Will Set You Free: Overcoming*

Emotional Blindness and Finding Your True Adult Self (New York: Basic Books, 2001), xiii–xiv.

43 Adolf Hitler, *Mein Kampf* (Munich: Eher Verlag, 1925); quoted in Miller, *For Your Own Good*, 18.

44 Details from Richard Fausset and Serge F. Kovaleski, "Nikolas Cruz, Florida Shooting Suspect, Showed 'Every Red Flag,'" *The New York Times*, February 15, 2018, https://www.nytimes.com/2018/02/15/us/nikolas-cruz-florida-shooting.html.

45 W.E.B. Du Bois, *Black Reconstruction in America*, 1935; quoted in Jon Meacham, *The Soul of America* (New York: Random House, 2018), 3.

46 Terence, *Heauton Timorumenos*, 1.1.25; quoted in C. G. Jung, "The Tavistock Lectures," *The Collected Works of C. G. Jung, vol 18, The Symbolic Life* (Princeton: Princeton University Press, 1976), 91n.

47 Bromberg, *Awakening the Dreamer*.

48 C. G. Jung, "The Transcendent Function," (1916), *The Collected Works of C. G. Jung*, vol. 8, *The Structure and Dynamics of the Psyche* (Princeton: Princeton University Press).

49 Thomas Ogden, *Subjects of Analysis* (Northvale, NJ: Jason Aronson, 1994).

50 Donald W. Winnicott, "Transitional Objects and Transitional Phenomena," in *Playing and Reality* (New York: Basic Books, 1971), 1–26.

51 Terry Tempest Williams, "Engagement," *Orion*, July–August 2004, http://www.orionmagazine.org/index.php/articles/article/143/.

52 C. G. Jung, *Analytical Psychology: Notes on the Seminar Given in 1925*, ed. William McGuire (London: Routledge), 78.

53 C. G. Jung, *Memories, Dreams, Reflections* (New York: Random House, 1961), 326.

54 Edward F. Edinger, *The Creation of Consciousness: Jung's Myth for Modern Man* (Toronto: Inner City Books, 1984), 18.

Chapter 5

America Exists!

Reflections on My American Cultural Complex

Joerg Rasche

This chapter is a circumambulation. I am German, born in 1950. My *American cultural complex* will, of course, mirror my *German culture complexes*, which include being proud of my German culture's achievements with Bach, Beethoven, Goethe, and Einstein. I am also aware of our secret German grandiosity, inferiority, guilt, grudges, and our longing for home. America, however, played an ever-present role in my life, like background music on a loop. My childhood memories go back to the ruins of World War II in the city of my birth—Würzburg in Bavaria—to the kind US soldiers in the 1950s (Würzburg was in the US zone), to a famous "uncle" from Palm Springs, California, and finally to the adventures of the characters in *Winnetou*, *Leatherstocking*, and *Uncle Tom's Cabin*.

My American saga actually began with an amazing painting that I first saw when I was eight years old. I was struck by the featherheaded "America" in Giovanni Battista Tiepolo's famous fresco *Apollo and the Four Continents* in the Würzburg Residence. This baroque palace was bombed by the allied British and US forces on March 16, 1945, but the Tiepolo painting survived the fire and was later rescued by an American officer who in the chaotic first post-war months cared for a provisional roof that protected the famous stair hall from rain. As a boy I was fascinated by this painting. For me, America became a dream of a land of miracles. An opposite image of the United States emerged later when, as a student, Vietnam and the massacre at My Lai opened my eyes to a darker America. Shadows began to varnish the image. Hannah Arendt explained the contradictions in the big continent overseas, tracing them back to the heritage of the strict Puritan Pilgrim Fathers, the slave economy, and the idealistic US Constitution.[1] The fate of the extinct Winnetou, a fictional Native American hero of a popular German series by Karl May, was like a fatal foreboding of countless contradictions in the immense country held together by a dream. Today I would say this dream is not limited to *God's own country*; it is a projection of the cultural complex of freedom and liberty, of wilderness, of unlimited possibilities, and of individuation as a cultural project. The United States was the projection screen. Today, during these times of climate change and solipsistic politics, my fascination with the United States is over, as it is for countless others. Europe has lost its *American Dream* and has been thrown back onto itself. "America" now shall be realized here in Europe, not with Coca-Cola®, but within the European mind. There it exists and shall be realized, not in narcissistic heroism but in mutual cooperation, inspired fortitude, and self-confidence.

What a Dream!

My childhood America was a dream of a wonderful, free world. Certainly one trigger for this positive complex was my father's plans to emigrate from Europe. He was forced to serve as a soldier in the German army in World War II, and his family suffered under the Nazis' hostility. My American cultural complex was basically a kind of escapism, an attempted flight from our still traumatized family and national psyche after the end of the Nazi era. There was also the fear of a possible new World War between the West and the USSR. With their plans to immigrate to the United States, my parents visited California when I was six. We children stayed at home in Germany with a nanny. My father, a medical doctor, worked in San Diego for six months, but finally he returned to Germany, having given up plans for the family to emigrate. He brought home with him a beautiful Native American feather headdress and told us children fantastic stories about the big mountains, deserts, forests, grizzly bears, skyscrapers, and the Indigenous population of Native Americans.

For me the feather headdress became a symbol of the big and fantastic continent overseas that was first born in my mind in the Würzburg Residence. In the great hall of the Residence, Giovanni Battista Tiepolo's Feather Crown was included in his massive fresco of the four continents, painted between 1751 and 1753. It included Europe, Africa, Asia, and America (Australia had not yet been explored). Many days after school I went there and became lost in amazement. The fresco included elephants, tigers, palm trees, dragons, the most beautiful and bizarre Rocaille ornaments, and white clouds opening to the clearest blue and sunny Italian sky. It was (and still is) heaven on earth. The Americans are shown as dangerous daredevils, adventurers with turbans and primitive musical instruments. In the center of the America section of the fresco is an impressive topless wild woman with a feather crown on her head. She is shown riding a monstrous crocodile or alligator. In front of her a shot antelope lies on the ground. Tiepolo didn't know much about America, but his fantasy stimulated my fantasy. How could this impressive naked lady ride the crocodile? And how did all these wild, dangerous people live together? There were not only Indigenous people but also Africans. I wondered, how would it feel to shoot an antelope? How would it feel to run and play in the free atmosphere of this wide land on this wonderful earth, far from here? My fantasy of America had been triggered.

Figure 5.1 Giovanni Battista Tiepolo (1696–1770). Residenz Würzburg, staircase, ceiling fresco, detail of the "America" allegory.

Source: Photo: Joerg Rasche. Courtesy of Staatliche Schösserverwaltung.

A few years later Winnetou and Old Shatterhand stepped onto my inner stage as characters from the wildly popular novels by the German writer Karl May (1842–1912), whose *Winnetou* series sold more than 200 million copies worldwide. The tales about the wise Winnetou and his brave Mohicans inspired many young European people over the decades, among them young Theodor W. Adorno, Thomas Mann, and Franz Werfel. Karl May's heroes became symbols of a heroic struggle for freedom and justice, and filled many young souls with images of adventure and the eternal battle of good versus bad. In my daydreams I often sat with Old Shatterhand and his friends around a camp fire on the prairie, talking about the heroic deeds we would undertake the next day. The more authentic adventures of trappers in the *Leatherstocking Tales* by James Fennimore Cooper followed May's books in good German translations. They stimulated not only heroic fantasies but also inner images of a great and untouched country with endless forests and lakes. A better future world existed without a doubt.

My America in the 1960s and the Hammond Organ

When I was about 12 one of my father's American acquaintances appeared in Würzburg. "Uncle Conrad" traveled once a year from Palm Springs, California, to Europe. Every year he bought a new Mercedes Benz in Germany for his European tour and sold the car after his return to the United States. He made enough money on these deals to pay for his holidays in Europe. "Uncle Conrad" showed us photos of all the prominent movie stars, which he had taken as a photographer in Palm Springs. He fulfilled all the projections of a "rich American uncle." He was a kind man in his sixties who treated us boys with a type of respect that was different from the more authoritarian German men.

When I was about 16 (in 1966) I began to play in a Beat band on my Hammond Organ. My father gave me this beautiful instrument (a Hammond A 100 with a Leslie cabinet) when I was 12. It, too, was an American icon. I played a lot, especially music by Bach. Playing in the Beat band my friends and I discovered the new world of British Beat (*Small Faces, The Animals* and "We've Gotta Get Out of This Place," *Eric Clapton, Ten Years After* ...) and American jazz. We played four nights a week in the US Army officer and GI clubs near Würzburg. We played Beat until midnight, and after midnight, jazz for our own delight. My favorite was, of course, Jimmy Smith at the Hammond Organ, followed by Wild Bill Davis. The GIs loved it, and when we played they dreamed of their homes in Georgia while "Sitting on the Dock of the Bay," ... The United States was a leading paradigm for a new culture. We were unaware of the shadow side of our American Dream. Jimmy Smith and most of the jazz artists we admired were black. Their music was that of people living in a state of racist segregation. Our beloved Animals song "We've Gotta Get Out of this Place" was popular, especially among the Marines during the most horrible times in Vietnam. We didn't know about this side of things at all. We had a very positive image of America. The Americans had rescued Germany and Europe from the Nazis, and they had even saved Tiepolo's wonderful fresco in Würzburg, which they had bombed before!

Darkening of the Bright Image

By the time I left Würzburg for West Berlin in 1970 at the age of 20 to join the student movement, my inner image of the United States had changed dramatically. In 1970 the United States attacked Cambodia, and the Vietnam War spread to other neutral Asian countries. The Vietnam War resulted in the killing of more than four million people; it was never "in truth a noble war," as President Johnson called it. The war also became a disaster for our naïve projections onto the United States. Strangely enough this disillusionment opened our eyes to the deeds of our parents during World War II. Obviously they had not done any better as humans. The horrors of the Holocaust and the deeds of the US Marines seemed to open a similar abyss regarding human mentality. Our protest against the Vietnam War and our German-guilt complex became mixed up. The entire world of our parents' generation, be it German or American, seemed to collapse in front of us. Stalin's empire was not an alternative either, since in West Berlin we were confronted by the Wall and Iron Curtain each day.

I began to protest the Vietnam bombings in front of the America House near Bahnhof Zoo in Berlin-Charlottenburg (https://www.co-berlin.org/en/amerika-haus). Simultaneously, we also became aware of the appeasement policies made by Western European countries with Hitler. We were told that the Treaty of Munich in 1938 between Germany, France, England, and Italy, which resulted in the abandonment and sacrifice of the Sudeten territory of then Czechoslovakia to the Nazis, stabilized Hitler's position and Germany's power against Stalin's communist empire. The capitalist West hoped that the Germans would fight Bolshevism, and for this they not only sacrificed their own official values but also risked the lives of millions of people. We German students came to realize that none of the Western powers had any truly positive orientation with which we could identify to help us work through our German guilt and guilt complex. We lost all sense of security and positive projections as exemplified by the story a companion told us about his dialogue with a member of the admired Black Panther Party.

"I am German, I am white—what shall I do?" He asked the member of the Black Panthers.
The answer: "Kill your parents."
"And then?" the German asked.
The answer: "Kill yourself!"

I am writing about this to underline the desperate dilemma and psychological collapse many of us experienced as young students awakening to the horrors of the world. It was a complex situation. For some, it meant joining with the suicidal acts of terrorist groups like the so-called Red Army Fraction (RAF) in the 1970s, a far-left militant organization in West Germany.

Sometimes positive projections and cultural complexes are essential for psychological survival! The breakdown of the positive American cultural complex was a disaster. Where are we today in Iraq, the near Middle East? What comes to mind is the news I saw after the defeat of Saddam Hussein. The Iraqi people wanted to see movies from the United States. The first movies shown in the cinemas in Baghdad were literally pornographic. The old bearded Muslims were shocked. Surely, they must have thought, "This is the culture of Satan!"

Seen from Outside

I am writing these lines in 2019. Other aspects of my American cultural complex come to mind. Writing in a foreign language—for me English—feels like slipping into a foreign skin that is not mine and never will be. It is just the opposite of a snake shedding its skin to permit new growth. I don't feel comfortable with this, and that is part of my American cultural complex. English is not my mother tongue. I know that there is a huge cultural complex about it, not only for me but also for many continental Europeans. Americans often know only one language—their own, English—and most of them don't care if a foreigner with another mother tongue understands their chewing-gum-like speech and pronunciation. This situation is quite different from that of continental Europe, where students are expected to learn a second (and often third) foreign language. Whether a tribute to the multi-cultural patchwork of the European continent or just part of the common culture, such multilingualism provides a feeling of belonging to a family with different histories and identities.

Another part of this problem comes with great sadness: the German language—and with it a large part of German pre-Nazi culture—has lost its value and international recognition. The rich German literature and science that existed before 1933 is known today to only a few and mostly in translation. Peter Watson wrote an amazing book about the forgotten "German Genius" before Hitler's rise to power.[2] Today a shallow kind of American English prevails in international science and business. Only the French language (and to some extent also Spanish) still plays an independent role.

The reason for the defeat of the German language lies, of course, in reaction to the perversion of many Germans' thinking during the Nazi era. And the winner of any conflict has the privilege of defining the future. After 1945, the victors were English speaking and thus the English-speaking countries projected an imperialistic attitude. My grandfather told me that Churchill hated German culture and, therefore, ordered the bombing and destruction of as much of Germany as possible, even in 1945 only weeks before the collapse of Hitler's empire. This imperialistic attitude toward the non-English-speaking world included both the written and oral word. During my lifetime, I have never met a British or American woman or man who reflected back to me just for a second the feeling of others possibly being humiliated by the post-war turn to American English as the universal tongue. Germans usually don't complain about this; they keep it inside as an unconscious grudge. Perhaps many people who live in other countries, such as Russia, Latin America, or the Asian countries, feel the same. The French are more outspoken about this grudge.

There is a positive side to this development as well: the globalized American language has an emancipative aspect. English uses a simple grammar. In English, nonnative speakers can think and write much more independently from their own cultural barriers to thinking and expressing ideas than when speaking in their mother tongues. Speaking and writing in English can provide a feeling of freedom, of uncensored imagination, somehow uprooted and flirting with irresponsibility.

If people use only a limited vocabulary in their speech, however, they will be more superficial, instrumental, and less modulated. With a limited means of expression, a person's level of thinking tends to become shallow and superficial. The English language itself pays a price for its global use as the international idiom. An English writer once told me how much she suffered when she had to read the shallow language of international papers. Sometimes she said she would return to a piece by *Shakespeare* to re-create her mind.

This language phenomenon also has an impact on the Europeans' American cultural complex in general. It would be easy to see the shallow discourse of Fox News as symptomatic of the entire American culture in decline. In these Trumpian times, we must be careful not to slip in simplistic prejudices like these. The fact is that US society is deeply split, and there are, in fact, many different "Americas." The shallow and racist discourse on Fox News is not paradigmatic for citizens living on the coasts such as in New York City or San Francisco.

C. G. Jung himself called Hitler "the voice of the Germans" in the catastrophic times of the 1930s, just as Trump celebrates himself as "the voice of the Americans."[3] Fortunately Trump is not as fanatical as Hitler was, and US democracy is much stronger than the political system in Germany after World War I. We say history repeats itself, but in history there is no simple repetition. Putin doesn't equal Stalin. Also the Russian population has learned its bitter lesson, I hope. But even after 1945 and the end of World War II, and 1989 and the fall of the Berlin Wall, there are still three nations that behave like empires: the United States, Russia, and China. *Empire* means (as the historian Timothy Snyder says) that your nation is better than the other, that it has the right to take other nations' land (as Russia took the Crimea and Eastern Ukraine), and that you claim the right to destroy other states, cultures, and people.[4] I think of China in Tibet or the United States in Chile (Allende!), other Latin-American states, or the Middle East. "Empire" has to do with space and resources. Hitler's attempt to build an empire at any costs was not the last example of this bloody error. Snyder says that today the European Union is the only region on the globe without imperialistic attitudes, a peace project and at least a glimpse of hope. Today we have, too, the digital empires, and we have to realize that the algorithms are stronger than we are. Silicon Valley, the origin of this newest technological revolution, is a result of a specific American liberty and the clever spirit of enterprise. Everything is possible if you are adventurous enough, even the project of a technologically created immortality. You can even live forever, if you live long enough to see the results of Mark Zuckerberg's technological quest for immortality. The question arises: what makes us still human in a technological world, or how do we become human?

Happy America

Wolfgang von Goethe (1749–1832), the German poet and scientist, showed in 1822 a fine intuition about the American psyche:

> *Amerika, du hast es besser als Europa, das alte,*
> *hast keine Burgen und Schlösser und keine Basalte.*

> America, you're better off
> than our Old Continent
> with its ruined castles
> and its old piles of basalts.
> You are not troubled inside
> in present days
> by useless memories and pointless fights.[5]

For Goethe the new continent was not burdened with the age-old heritage of European social structures and miseries. He thought that the happy American continent had no seismic problems, no volcanoes and earthquakes and, therefore, no basalt (*basalt* is a volcanic mineral)—a symbol for an undisturbed future without psychological and ecological problems. Goethe was already a witness to the French Revolution in 1789, a heroic attempt to put an end to the old system of exploitation and to humanize society. He was also a contemporary of the American War of Independence and the United States Constitution, signed in 1787. Much had happened in America in the 70 years since *Tiepolo*'s artistic vision painted in Würzburg (1751–1753) when Goethe wrote his poem about America in 1822. There had been waves of immigration, the extinction of millions of the original Indigenous inhabitants, the development of the slave economy, the War of Independence, and growing industrialization. The American Dream had already revealed its impressive positive and its disgusting sides. Goethe, in his late years, tried to keep alive the illusion of a possible American paradise overseas. He projected his optimism onto the New Continent.

These phantasms hold on. The United States offered shelter and home for many migrants after catastrophic European famines as well as for those suffering political, religious, and racial persecution. This has never been forgotten. For many, the United States was a kind of Noah's Ark, a living symbolic container able to protect both individuals and groups of people in the midst of crisis. I don't want to write here about the decline of

America today as a symbol of safety, freedom, and opportunity for so many people everywhere in the world; rather I want to focus on the idea of the uncivilized, free born, and wild human in its own country, forest, and steppe.

This leads us back to the woman in the feathered headdress in Tiepolo's fresco. What does this symbolic image mean today, of the Indigenous woman on her crocodile, as imagined by Tiepolo, and of the adventurous men around her? In fact, an archetypal image was at the heart of both Tiepolo's painting in 1751 and the dream of the young boy Joerg Rasche, in Würzburg. It shows the eternal longing for free space and development, for joy and for wilderness. Everybody needs a wild space inside where he or she can re-create. We all need space in which everything is possible, a space in which we live in accordance with the nature around and in us. The idea of the good-natured wild man, as in Rousseau's *Emile* or Voltaire's *Candide*, was born in times of pending revolution against the *Ancien Regime*. It seems to me that we face similar limits and fears today, such as those Thomas Singer writes about in "The Extinction Anxiety,"[6] or those that come directly from our age of climate change, technological grandiosity, and militaristic adventurism. Such deep distress all around us may evoke wistful images similar to those inspired by the new virgin continent that came to Tiepolo or Goethe at earlier times of revolution in the face of decay. This wild Indigenous woman, representing America to Tiepolo with her tremendous energy, may need to be reborn inside us—or perhaps it will never be again. If America exists somewhere, however, the ideals of it, we will survive. Then we may care for the crocodiles in us; we may even learn to ride them. Tiepolo's utopia is not a lost paradise if we save our dreams.

Notes

1 Hannah Arendt, *The Human Condition* (Chicago: The University of Chicago Press, 1958).
2 Peter Watson, *The German Genius: Europe's Third Renaissance, the Second Scientific Revolution, and the Twentieth Century* (New York: HarperCollins, 2010).
3 C. G. Jung, "After the Catastrophe (1945)," *The Collected Works of C. G. Jung,* vol. 10, *Civilization in Transition* (Princeton: Princeton University Press, 1968).
4 Timothy Snyder, "Judenplatz 1010: A Speech to Europe," (You Are More Than Your Myths), presented as part of the Tipping Points Talks 2019, ERSTE Foundation, Vienna, Austria, May 9, 2019, https://www.youtube.com/watch?v=7zs41CkIjRw.
5 Wolfgang von Goethe, "Amerika, Du hast es besser," *The Maxims and Reflections of Goethe.* Trans. Bailey Saunders (New York: The MacMillan Co., 1906). From Project Gutenberg, https://www.gutenberg.org/files/33670/33670-h/33670-h.htm. Retranslated by the author.
6 Thomas Singer, "Extinction Anxiety: Where the Spirit of the Depths Meets the Spirit of the Times, or Extinction Anxiety and the Yearning for Annihilation," in *Rocket Man: Nuclear Madness and the Mind of Donald Trump,* eds. John Gartner and Steven Buser, 205–212 (Asheville, NC: Chiron, 2018).

Chapter 6

The Second Goya

Craig San Roque

> *I am aware of the manner in which the world breathes,*
> *suspended always,*
> *a wicker basket on the Nile, floating on an outrush,*
> *gathered in with kindness, for a day, for a night.*
> *The ibis stalks among the reeds, gathering fish.*
> *The jackal eye is open.*
>
> Nicholas Rosen[1]

This chapter, written as a fiction, takes as a device a dream within a dream like Matryoshka Russian Dolls, enclosing a mother within a mother in a series. Intimate anxieties are revealed through conversations of the characters, Nicholas Rosen and the narrator. The theme is a psychic contagion actively spreading from turbulent America.

Phone from London

Nicholas Rosen called from London. For him it was night; for myself, on the east coast of Australia, the call came early in the morning. His warm English accent, hesitating, politely asking if he could tell me something, discuss something—a disturbing dream.

Rosen and I have known each other over many years, since the time I lived in London. Now and then we talk on matters that concern us. I send him something; he sends one of his books, *Broken Souls* being the first—case histories revealing the psychological consequences for individuals and their families who suffered European wars. *The Schizoid State* is on bureaucracies that punish. *Psychotic Revolutions* charts the course of political revolution, or rather, how people's hopes generate sweeping political change that then converts into regimes of cruelty and suppression. *The Fear of the Refugee* became a BBC documentary. His most recent book is *An End to Time*.

Nicholas writes to the heart of human suffering. His pen touches a blind silence in which the seed-core of the human mind is wrapped. He is attuned to the manner in which humans govern themselves—the continuous breakdown and restoration of the social contract, the generational consequences of war, paranoid autocracy, collective dissociation, doublethink. As a psychotherapist his practical concern is with what happens to individual souls who become damaged or driven mad when infected by a venomous disorder that is not of an individual's own making. Rosen's books describe disorders generated in the world in which we live. Disorders that flood and carry us along. Turbulent infections that we make and inflict upon each other. Unto oblivion.

When Rosen called, I was about to walk to the ferry that takes me to the city. If I took up his request at that moment, ten minutes to seven in the morning, would I make it to the city? Perhaps, perhaps not. For Nicholas I would rearrange the thread of the day.

The Dream Setup

The dream begins with Rosen seeing himself in a room. He is on the phone, arranging an appointment. He is standing on a red Bokhara carpet. He knows the house as being north of New York City. I asked him to be specific. He said, "It's a house in Westchester County, New York state. I stayed there once; I remember the carpet. It is a prayer carpet. I would not have been standing on it, but in the dream that is the position. Listen carefully," he said, "I don't know what I am seeing."

It is no surprise that Rosen's dream might locate him in New York state. He is known there.

He is familiar with people in the United States of America. His father, a physicist, was extricated from Prague at the outbreak of World War Two. Rosen's parents found refuge in the US, recruited into the development of the Manhattan Project nuclear program.[2] After Hiroshima and Nagasaki and the conclusion of the war, Professor Rosen resigned from that program, both he and his wife disagreeing with the continuing intentions of the US Chiefs of Staff and the then president. Professor Rosen moved in 1948 to London with his partner and their two-year-old son, Nicholas. He worked for British Intelligence. She taught Slavic languages.

The Dream Itself

Nicholas was saying, he in London, I in Sydney: "I am on the phone. I hear a woman's voice asking for a discreet and very confidential consultation. She gave her name as Ms. Rodham, from Chappaqua. 'You were recommended,' she says. I reply, 'I do not practice in the USA. I am not an American.' She responds, 'I am consulting you on this matter precisely because you are not an American. A dream is disturbing me—very disturbing ...' She is persuasive. I accept the meeting.

"She is at the door. I recognize her, but greet her by the name that she had offered on the phone, Ms. Rodham. I understood the need for discretion. There are two very attentive men in a black car waiting in the street. It is winter. She wears a winter coat. She is standing, poised in the room. She is uncertain, yet determined. We perform the courtship of the beginning of a session. She places on the table a large print of a painting. She says, 'In my dream I see this painting. I can taste the surface of the paint, the gloss of the oil. It's luminous. I am about to kiss the paint. It is Goya's paint. I am inside the events of Goya's painting. I am there. I am that man in the execution. The man in a white shirt, my hands in the air. I am there facing the soldiers. Their rifles raised. They are upon us. They cannot miss. My cohort are on the ground dead and wounded. I know what is coming. Nothing will stop the blow. The blood in my throat spurts; I feel the shock in my heart; I am falling ... Some of the men with the rifles, I know them. Some are men of my own party. Some are of the enemy.'"

Figure 6.1 Francisco de Goya y Lucientes (1746–1828). *The Third of May, 1808, in Madrid.* 1814. Oil on canvas. 2.68 × 3.47 m. Museo de Prado.

Source: Copyright of the image Museo Nacional del Prado/Art Resource, NY.

Nicholas paused, then continued. "She sits very still. She is lost in thought. Eventually I speak to her. 'This dream, when did it come?'

"'On November 7, 2016.' She stopped midsentence, her eyes open, gazing into mine, making sure I appreciated the significance. On November 7, 2016, she had been defeated in her bid for the presidency of the United States."

"Then she says, 'It was a recurring dream right through December 2016 and January the next year: the sound of the shots, the shock in my heart, the fall ... That same dream in variation, faces of the shooters shifting. Always the same ending. I was in a bad way through all that time.' She ceased to speak. She sat as though she were reviewing events. Perspiration glistening, a touch of tears rimming her eyes. In the dream it seemed that she had assumed the stillness of a portrait. Hillary Clinton after the storm. Then I heard the words, perhaps from herself, perhaps from me. 'How could we have misjudged Napoleon?'

"'Ms. Rodham,' I say, 'This painting by Goya, you know the circumstances?'

"'Yes, of course, these are the executions in the streets of Madrid on May 3, 1808.'"

On the phone, listening to Nicholas story, I was feeling at a loss. The details of the painting were not clear for me. I asked Nicholas for background on events in Spain in 1808. And why had she said, "How could we have misjudged Napoleon?" I could hear Rosen grunt, irritated perhaps, but I needed more information if I were to be of use.

Napoleon

He described the painting, then explained that in Goya's street scene the riflemen, the executioners, are French military. The men shot are Spanish. Townspeople, not soldiers. Why? Napoleon Bonaparte is on the rise. This, before he crowned himself Emperor. Napoleon had made a deal with King Carlos of Spain and his son, Prince Ferdinand, to jointly invade Portugal. In November 1807, Napoleon's army crossed over the French border into Spain by Spanish consent—or so it appeared. Once his troops were inside Spain, Napoleon reneged on the deal with King Carlos. He also reneged on his secret conspiracy with the mayor of Madrid and the prince to remove the old king. The young Ferdinand expected Napoleon to give him the throne—to set up a new deal to make Spain magnificent again. Rosen laughed, then continued.

"So here is the picture: Napoleon is inside Spain with his army in place. He doesn't follow the deal. He exiles the entire royal family, disbands the government, sets up his brother, Joseph Bonaparte, as king of Spain. A family coup. He had pulled off a remarkable power play at a time when conditions in Spain were ripe. The situation was confusing for the people. Many Spaniards, like Goya himself, were sympathetic to the French Revolution. Perhaps they hoped Napoleon would bring a change of the old order; perhaps no one could quite believe the audacity of the Bonaparte deception. (This was not a revolution; it was a takeover.) The Spanish, ambivalent or hopefully uncertain were compliant, perhaps waiting to see what Bonaparte would be like. However, by May 1808, the resistance had begun, first in Zaragoza, then in Madrid. Napoleon ordered swift, brutal reprisals; protestors on the streets were shot. That is the incident Goya paints in *The Third of May 1808*."

I said, "An American Secretary of State would understand that kind of scenario. Why would it trouble her?"

Rosen replied, "She said to me (or rather in the dream I knew what she was thinking)—'I saw that painting in Madrid. I studied Bonaparte, his tactics. I wanted that Goya in my office. The President was worried. Hillary, he said, Goya's *Third of May 1808* is like a sorcery image. You hang that painting in your office, you will invoke such a fate. He was right.'

"'Secretary …' I begin to say. She cuts me short—'I am no longer Secretary, Doctor.' I apologize. 'Madam, you seem to understand this dream. The situation is clear. You have the shock of it, true, but you are a seasoned woman of state. You know ambitious men. You know deception and reprisal. The events of November 2016 … Wikileaks, American hysteria. Napoleonic lies, Russian interventions. Let us accept that you were shot down as surely as if you had indeed been that man in a white shirt in Madrid. The sensations packed into your Goya dream are accurate. Your dream confirms what happened; and that you know. What is there for me to add?' And she replied—'I have not come to consult you on the executions of November. I know what happened. I have come to speak with you about the second Goya.'"

The Second Goya

"She said, 'November, 2017, a year later, I had the second dream.' She stopped speaking. She remained still; the tension enough to crack the furniture. She stood; she walked to the window; she walked to the door. She opened the door. I thought perhaps she was walking out. The two men in the car moved. She acknowledged them, hesitated, turned back into the room, saying—'I cannot bring myself to speak of it.' She drew from her bag a rolled poster. From the Prado. She set that upon the table. She spread it out. 'This is the second Goya. On the night of November 8, 2017, I dreamt I was back in Madrid. In the Prado. I was in the Black House.'"

Nicholas, as an aside, said, "She is talking about the special rooms in the Prado where Goya's famous Black Paintings are held; all 14 murals were reinstated from his house, *Quinto del Sordo*.[3] Saved from ruin, restored, his rooms reconstructed in the gallery with the original paintings. She has changed the name, but you can appreciate that, given the time she spent in the White House—and then didn't.

"She is saying, 'I am standing with Goya; no, not Goya himself but his paintings. There in the Black House in front of Saturn devouring …'

Figure 6.2 Francisco de Goya y Lucientes (1746–1828). *Saturn devouring one of his sons.* 1820–1823. Oil; Wall transferred to canvas. 1.435 × 0.814 m. Museo de Prado.

Source: Copyright of the image Museo Nacional del Prado/Art Resource, NY.

"She is gazing at the image, the creature, the eyes, the hands, the mouth, the body of a man, or a woman or a child … with the head torn. 'Struggling, choking,' she said, 'In this dream I am face to face with him standing there, ready to rape, to eat children.'[4]

"She began to retch, a terrible anguish pouring from her. 'I let him in. I let them all in. They came in over my dead body. I allowed this thing to happen. How could I have been so deaf. Where were my eyes. What kind of American am I that I allow such things to happen?'

"And then she began to dissolve, framed in the light of the windows in the Black House, her figure began melting into Goya's painting, becoming part of the figures in that terrible scene. She was gripped by him. She became transparent. I could see that titanic creature consuming her, absorbing her, its mouth swallowing the head … then the whole scene fell into bits, bits of Goya's wall and oil from the body of the creature, falling into rubble."

Rosen was coughing.

"He's eating America."

"What's that?"

"Nothing," I said. "Nothing."

"No, no, what did you say?"

"Nicholas I'm sorry. I said—'He is eating America.'"

Rosen was quiet. I think we were both looking at that face, that mouth, that body in the hand of Saturn.

After a while I said. "Nicholas, this is more a vision than a dream. Let's go back; I can't make sense of it all … this Saturn character? Go back to the body before it disintegrates. That happened too fast. I interrupted you. The shock. Replay the scene. Tell me what you feel in your own body."

After a while he spoke. "I am staring into the belly of Saturn, the Cronos."

"And what do you see?"

"The figure in his hand is Ms. Rodham, Hillary Clinton, just for a flash. All the events of November 2016 return. The frenzy, the brutal nightmare. And yes, you are right. American people are being eaten by this creature. This Cronos arising. This Saturn rising up from the guts of the country. It is bigger than all of them. It is not of one party or the other, it is something deeper, seething in the brain and blood of 326 million American bodies."

"What do I see? In his belly I see chewed-up particles. I see the chewed-up history of America. I see Portugal, Spain. 1492. I see Columbus's ships: *Santa Maria*, *La Niña*, *Pinta*. I see the *Mayflower*. I see indigenous Americans. I see New Amsterdam. New York. I see slaveholders, the eye of an African, the arm of a soldier. I see guns, chains. I see America. I see horses, flags of the South, flags of the North. I see division. I see broken ribs. I see riflemen. I see gold. I see the city of Chicago, I see the sun in New Mexico. I see Navaho women walking through smoke. I see Los Alamos. I see Oppenheimer; I see Fat Man and Nagasaki. I see Hiroshima in the morning. I see Oppenheimer drinking with my father, late at night in Los Alamos, 1945. The windows broken. I see the explosion. I see the

Joint Chiefs of Staff. I see midnight in Harlem. I see chewed-up veterans. I see Dallas, Texas. 1963. The Kennedy blood. I see Clint Eastwood. I see five million National Riflemen. I see every borderline disorder in the United States of America. I see the writing on the wall. I see Florida. I see blonde women toting red baseball caps. I see gray snow in Brooklyn, in Minnesota. I see the cold coming down. I see the face of every president who put me here. I see Nixon's finger, drunk, looking for that button to push. I see impeachment. I see mothers at the kitchen table crying—what is going on?"

I said to him, "I see all that."

The Navel

The phone was silent, I heard Rosen sigh. "I don't know. I don't know ...." I waited. Then Nicholas said, very quietly, "I see two men at a table, the broken window, and my father. I can see my father. Then my father alone. He is sitting at his desk. Alone. In the apartment. I remember that apartment. It was after we moved to London. After he gave up on the nuclear program. My father is writing equations. Fission, fusion? Patterns that may be DNA spirals; it must be after 1953 and Watson and Crick. I must be six or seven. 1954. He is staring into space. He has a glass. I know now it must be whisky. He has drawn three spirals. A triple helix. One for the holding. One for the making. One for the breaking. I can see his designs. They are very simple. My father is looking at the genome of destruction. He is writing the equation. After Nagasaki, safe in London, my father is comprehending the incredible energy in the genome of destruction. It coils around the code of life. To me, as a boy, it looks like a predatory eel. A moray. The sharp teeth, the glittering skin. It is coiled there in the belly of America, wrapped around the liver and intestines. In my vision that eel of a thing is sucking all of America in."

Rosen was silent.

"Nicholas, are you there?"

"No. I wish I was not. How many parents are there in the United States who go out to work to put more guns on the table?"

I could hear him breathing, then he said, "No one could make any sense of this."

"Nicholas, we haven't finished this yet. I have another question."

"Go on."

"How long is it since you had a medical checkup?"

"What do you mean?"

"You have had a very bad dream. One thing inside another breaking down. Disorder. What is eating you? In your own belly, what is there?"

A long silence from Rosen. "I'll think about it."

"Nicholas, call me back after you think about it."

"Thanks for listening." He was gone.

I put the phone away, starting to walk for the next ferry, feeling upset; maybe I shouldn't have asked him about himself just then, the whole story is too much to take in—the state of America, the mess of the narcissist, the fucked-up condition of the world, the death of species. The money, the fear, the anxiety, his childhood memories, his father's despair after Nagasaki. Nicholas seeing himself as a link in the chain of the damage done. The genome of destruction playing out. The "eel in the belly" of America is a strong enough metaphor of the cultural complex. That serpentine, knotted, nuclear kernel of repetitive energies, wrapped in slippery hard skin, a tumor of grief turning in on itself, eating itself, spreading contamination. Like a turbulent sea current, this inner force is too big for us to navigate, even if we do know it is there. That is the action of an unconscious collective complex, as I see it. It is neurologically imprinted. It seeps across countries and the sea like the plague. But something else is eating at Nicholas. Pray God tomorrow the tide will come in again. I am going for the ferry.

Leocadia

Suddenly he came back on the phone. "I forgot the end of the dream. She was leaving. She turned at the door, saying, 'There is another Goya. *Leocadia*, a woman, leaning against a rock, perhaps a tomb. Goya's consort, Leocadia. She'd know the state of mind he'd been in, painting that Saturn. She'd know the harrow of the times in Spain. Yet Goya paints Leocadia in composure; even if she is mourning, the composure remains. That is what I see. Will I ever find composure?'"

The House of the Deaf Men

A few months later, in February 2018, Nicholas called again. He said, "You were right."

"Right about what?"

"I had the medical, it had come back."

"What came back?"

"I've started treatment again. Cancer. That's what's eating me. I called you, remember, and you said that. I might have caught it in time. Thanks."

"What about the other stuff you were raving about—all that American shit?"

"That too, it's all there, like we said, it's a Russian Doll, one thing inside the other. When it comes down to the wire, people like me get cancer as well. It's a bad movie. You don't believe it. All of a sudden it happens."

I have turned up the music that accompanies the writing of this account. This account of our search for the identity of the thing that is eating America. The music is Gorecki's *Symphony of Sorrowful Songs*. The soprano,

Figure 6.3 Francisco de Goya y Lucientes (1746–1828). *A Manola: Dona Leocadia Zorrilla.* 1820–1823. Oil; Wall transferred to canvas. 1.457 × 1.294 m. Museo del Prado.
Source: Copyright of the image Museo Nacional del Prado/Art Resource, NY.

Zofia Kilanowicz, is singing the three lines inscribed on wall 3 of cell 3, the basement of Gestapo Headquarters, Zakapone, Poland—a prayer to Mary, the Mother of Jesus, for protection, imploring her not to cry. Beneath is the signature of Helena Wanda Blazusiakowna and the words "18 years old, imprisoned since 26 September 1944."[5]

How do we handle this? How do we acknowledge that country that gave solace and opportunity to so many people afloat on the incoming tide after so many lamentable European mistakes? And then solace to more people from more mistakes around the world. And now the tide shifts. I think about Leocadia and Ms. Rodham and Nicholas's vision and the illness that fired his vision. His own illness that now has claimed him. And the illness of our civilizations. I listen to that three-line lament on the fall of a young woman in the European war. A war that half the world feared and half the world believed could never happen.

I see a ring of Black Houses around the world. White Houses, Black Houses, Houses of the Deaf Men.

I see Goya's house, *Quinta del Sordo*, a place to paint the terrors of his time, the titanic greed that eats us all. And a place to show composure. Goya went on painting even if, for a time, his work was locked away. Goya and the Polish girl wrote on the wall of the Black House and we remember composure. Time stretches about the globe: we wake; we sleep at different hours. The monstrous eel in the belly of the second Goya never sleeps.

Final Note

In April 2019 I received a final note from Rosen. The cancer had him. His lungs giving out.

He wrote: *I am aware of the manner in which the world breathes, suspended always, a wicker basket on the Nile, so fragile, floating on an outrush, gathered in with kindness, for a day, for a night. The ibis stalks among the reeds, gathering fish. The jackal eye is open. The jackal stalks the ibis.*

Rosen's dream began on a prayer carpet and there I shall end. In this ruin of a world the first word and the last is "compassion." So be it.

Acknowledgments

With thanks to Francisco Goya and Museo del Prado, Madrid.

Rosen is a fictitious character, as is his father. Apologies and thanks to Ms. Rodham for the use of her dream apparition, for it came unbidden.

Thanks to Eric Rhode's *Psychotic Metaphysics* (London: Karnac Books, 1994), especially Chapter 12, "Disappearing Into Light," which supported the idea for this story.

Notes

1 These lines "... the ibis stalks ..." are attributed to Nicholas Rosen from his book *An End of Time*. Rosen and the titles of his books are a fiction.
2 The Manhattan Project was a US government research project (1942–1945) that produced the first atomic bombs and subsequently led to the US nuclear program. *Encyclopedia Britannica*, s.v. "Manhattan Project," accessed July 2, 2019, http://www.britannica.com/event#689283.
3 The house *Quinta del Sordo* (The House of the Deafman) is in Madrid, where Francisco Goya lived toward the end of his life between 1819–1824 and where he painted a series of 14 murals in oils, known as the *Black Paintings* (*Los Pinturas Negras*), of which the Saturn/Cronos figure is one. After Goya's death the paintings were eventually removed from the walls and reinstated in the Prado and can be seen there now in reconstructed rooms. See, for instance, the Prado/Goya section website at https://www.museodelprado.es/en/the-collection/art-work/the-drowning-dog/4ea6a3d1-00ee-49ee-b423-ab1c6969bca6.

4 Saturn in the Roman pantheon is derived from Cronos, a Titan who figures in the formative phase of the creation/destruction myth, according to Grecian stories. Titans are larger-than-life prehuman phenomenon, as described in Hesiod's *Theogony* and referenced, for example, in George Tripp's *Dictionary of Classical Mythology* (New York: HarperCollins, 1988). Cronos/Saturn is the youngest, most anarchic of the Titans. The name *Cronos* in original Greek is probably related to Crow (*corone*). See Robert Graves, *The Greek Myths* (London: The Penguin Group, 1992), especially page 38. In some versions, at the bidding of his mother Gaia/Rhea, Cronos castrates his volcanic father. Cronos then enters an incestuous liaison with his mother. She bears five offspring, all eaten by Cronos/ Saturn. The sixth cosmic "child," Zeus, hidden by his mother, returns, confronts his father, tricks him into vomiting up the five siblings who miraculously become reconstituted. Cronos is exiled. Such omnivorous mythic (satanic) creatures are often linked with messianic, heroic saviors of the people—Zeus, Beowulf, Boadicea, Perseus, Theseus, Jesus of Nazareth (and presidential candidates who capitalize on cultural anxiety).

5 From Henryk Gorecki, Song 2, *Symphony No 3, The Sorrowful Songs*, 1976. Recorded by Zofia Kilanowicz, Soprano, Polish State Philharmonic Orchestra, conducted by Jerzy Swoboda Philips. Decca Recording, 1990, 1993.

Part II

Specific Cultural Complexes

Race

Chapter 7

Every Voice, Every Vote Counts

Challenges to a Multicultural Democracy in the Shadow of American Political Economy and American Cultural Complexes

Alan G. Vaughan

I am certain my own complexes are discernable throughout this chapter. Since January 20, 2017, I have awakened each morning into the nightmare of contemporary American political theater, a daily reality show, where a vacuous morally and intellectually bankrupt person occupies the office of the US presidency. He lies obsessively, blurs the boundaries between fact and fiction, governs by tweets, devalues the media, assaults the US Congress and US Intelligence agencies, and attempts to appoint ideologues and incompetent jurists to the US judiciary to garner support for his executive orders. His ambivalent, impulsive decision-making style continues to cause great anxiety for the nation. In his grand narcissism, which he has visited upon the nation, he misunderstands executive privilege, employing it as a personal edict and absolute immunity for his loyalists. This is reflected in our transactional free market government, where political favor and congressional votes are for sale. The American governance structure is under threat and great duress. The cancer of narcissistic self-interest is personified in this shadow drama of capitalism and the American cultural complex of corruption, eating away at the protean ideals of Western democracy and the well-being of the collective body and spirit of humankind. The malignancy of today grows through the agency of the executive branch of American government that seeks to assert autocratic power over the citizenship and the tripartite constitutional governance structure, destroying the balance between the legislative, judicial, and executive branches of American government. These are the challenging, troubled times in which we find ourselves—and the historical ground for the experience of American cultural complexes.

I have written this chapter from my experience of these complexes as an African American male and Jungian analyst with doctorate degrees in clinical psychology and jurisprudence. Jung suggests that confession is good for the soul. So, at the outset, I confess my alarm, disappointment, and anger over injustice, racism, inequality, and other practices of inhumanity. This includes the conscious denial of climate science and the abuse and destruction of the planetary ecosystem.

I propose a multicultural democracy in which every voice is heard and every vote counts as a critical path forward to address the cancer at the core of a failing American democracy and the active dynamics in American cultural complexes. I discuss this theme and the challenges to multicultural democracy as shadow elements of the US political economy and American cultural complexes, which I define in the context of analytical psychology and post-Jungian theory and examine in the light of Eurocentric libertarian ideology, the myth of democracy, and the emergence of multicultural democracy. Challenges to multicultural democracy are seen in the covenant of whiteness at the core of Eurocentrism, the psychopathology of racism, and examples of the negative patterns or phenomenology of the trickster archetype. These patterns are embodied in the shadow of the US political economy as capitalization of electoral politics, partisan gerrymandering, racism, and voter suppression. I conclude with the assertion that the archetypal anima figure Maat can inform and guide us toward a new higher consciousness and balance in applying principles of truth, order, social justice, and cosmic and ecological harmony within the individual, the collective psyche, and the governance structures of the nation.

American Cultural Complex

Extending Jung's original ideas about complex theory in post-Jungian theory, Thomas Singer and Samuel Kimbles offer a list of characteristics thought to define a cultural complex.[1] These characteristics have a bipolarity of positive and negative effects on the individual and on different ethno-groups that comprise the American citizenry. I have come to recognize the source of these effects in the shadow culture of capitalism, racism, the predicate race fiction, and social-class structure.[2]

American cultural complexes operate in the shadow culture of capitalism as libertarian to far-right ideologies that threaten the fundamental constitutional principle of government for and by the majority, serving the interest of the collective good in a multicultural society. The myth of democracy is overshadowed by a Eurocentric libertarian ideology that argues for limited federal government and super-ordinate states' rights that operate in the interest of an elite minority of individuals and corporations seeking economic liberty, government deregulation, and unlimited wealth. The intent is a non-representative government by the few for the benefit of the few. This leverage of the existing governance structure is to be taken seriously as it has emerged from the shadow into the light of today's political processes.

The phenomenology, values, beliefs, and psychodynamics associated with American cultural complexes that are corrosive to our democracy and the realization of a multicultural democracy are as follows: a Eurocentric cultural orientation and perspectivism; control of political and economic power; privatization of common lands, goods, and services; rugged individualism, that is, every citizen for himself or herself; free market capitalism; no or low taxation on the wealthiest individuals in society; intergenerational protection and transmission of wealth; limited, deregulated government; absolute economic liberty; rule of the majority by the self-interested few; subversive manipulation of representative government outlined in the US Constitution; and the ongoing production of racist ideas and transgenerational practices of institutional racism. These American cultural complexes are energized by an ideology of "winner take all" and the practice of "divide to conquer" pitting the ethnic and social-class groups of the nation against one another. Each becomes "other" to the "other." The conscious intent of Eurocentric libertarianism is to undermine and counter any ideas of multiculturalism that adversely impact an elite minority that lays claim to political and economic power, white identities, white privilege, and white supremacy. The complexes are inflamed by fear of economic devastation among poor and working-class citizens who claim white identities. It is also inflamed by fear of reprisal and retribution for past wrongs, the unbridled pursuit of wealth by any and all means, and political actions that compromise the American judicial system. This compromise of the judiciary is seen in the partisan appointment of judges in municipal, state, and federal courts and at the US Supreme Court. We see partisan state legislatures caught in subversive acts of gerrymandering, rigging the outcome of local and state elections through coordination of the State Political Network and the Electoral College. And they manifest in voter suppression through renewed poll taxes, new laws requiring government-issued identification, and the increased practice of purging voting rosters. Union busting is another strategy to curtail, if not end, collective bargaining, leaving manufacturing employees without leverage to negotiate fair wages and labor conditions. This is another dynamic assault on the ideals of democracy, the American Dream, and its mythology of a fair and equitable representational government. Extreme wealth has infiltrated and infected electoral politics, leveraging the interest of well-funded individuals, corporations, and even foreign governments over the public interest and common good. These strategic initiatives advanced from the 1950s to the Bush administration (2000–2008) and from the 2010 US Supreme Court decision in *Citizens United v. Federal Election Commission*. In addition, privately funded conservative think tanks like the Cato Institute, Heritage Foundation, and Hoover Institute, among others, produce policy statements and recommend public policies to the partisan legislative branch of government that contravene the collective good. The policies and draft legislation are adopted, if not in fact commissioned, by partisan politicians whose campaigns are funded by these wealthy self-interested donor institutions.

Eurocentrism and Libertarian Ideology

In general, libertarians believe that public education post *Brown v. Board of Education* (1954) should be limited, privatized in a voucher system or charter schools, with higher education paid for by students who can afford it. They believe that healthcare is not a human right, and that social security for citizens should be limited and reduced. Further, they believe that funds collected in the social security system should be made available for privatization and investment in the free market.[3] These values, beliefs and enactments, which assault the citizenry, are shocking and untenable.

The negative expression of the trickster archetype manifests as energies, patterns of thought and behavior prevalent in libertarian ideology, and in political and economic practices that reflect American cultural complexes. Jung speaks of the trickster as a "collective shadow figure, a summation of all inferior traits of character in individuals."[4] He suggests that "the most rudimentary insight into the shadow sometimes causes the greatest difficulties for the modern European."[5] For example recent partisan tax-reform laws have resulted in billions of dollars of offshore corporate earnings being repatriated as untaxed income in America. These dollars are needed to support infrastructure development and a healthy efficient government that can advance the common good. Apple alone received $200 billion in new tax breaks with the passage of this Republican legislation. Amazon and Berkshire Hathaway received comparable tax advantages, in some instances paying zero corporate tax. As a result, Berkshire had a $110 billion cash surplus.[6]

Partisan support for such tax-reform legislation misrepresented that these repatriated dollars would be used to infuse fiscal health into the US economy, support infrastructure repair and development, and trickle down to workers. The theory was predicated on a pattern of falsehood and misrepresentations. In reality, much of the money was reinvested in stock buybacks to strengthen corporate ledgers and to increase executive salaries and bonuses. Flush with cash, American companies bought back $806 billion of their own stocks in 2018, rather than spend more on building businesses or raising wages. These dollars neither trickled down to employees nor funded government/private partnerships for infrastructure development. In 2017, the Republican Congress was put on notice by donors that if they did not pass this sweeping tax-reform legislation, campaign contributions would cease—a rallying cry from the elite that was heeded! In the dead of night, in closed chambers, the tax-reform legislation passed with no bipartisan debate or public hearings. A single party controlled this imbalanced, one-sided legislative process, arguably without integrity if not corruption. The same was true of Congress's less successful efforts to repeal the Affordable Health Care Act, which passed in 2010.

US Constitution: Democracy or Oligarchy?

The 7 articles and 27 amendments of the US Constitution provide the architecture and governance structure for the nation. They articulate the delicate system of checks and balances between the executive, legislative, and judicial branches of government necessary to achieve the mission, vision, and goals outlined in the document. These include forming a more perfect union, establishing justice, ensuring domestic tranquility, providing for the common defense, promoting the general welfare, and securing the blessings of liberty for ourselves and our posterity.[7]

The US Constitution seeks to perfect a *representative* democracy rather than a needed *direct* democracy that involves direct choices by individuals and the collective of an informed citizenry. This is at the heart of the document, governance structure, and the current myth of American democracy. *Representative democracy* has been severely compromised and subverted to serve the interest of capitalists and capitalism. The founding fathers themselves were under the influence of the negative expression of the trickster archetype as they shaped the nation's early colonial history. They were the immigrants! The Constitution was drafted by wealthy men with European identities and dominion over the emergent wealth of the nation, derived in major part from the appropriation of vast amounts of common lands inhabited and shared among Indigenous peoples of the Americas. These lands were then cultivated and developed by African peoples conscripted into an economic system of chattel slavery, designed to provide free labor— all in support of the growth of capitalism. The white shadow of capitalism is the American cultural complex of privatization and the relentless pursuit of excess capital. The pursuit of wealth is linked to psychological security and the exercise of power, dominion, and control of others and the environment. These are American cultural complexes endemic to capitalism. Although many features of capitalism have propelled ingenious development of the Western world, its shadow has caused the underdevelopment of the non-Western world, led to group ethnocide, impoverished individual psyche, and fostered a one-sided European perspectivism.

Has the ideal of American democracy devolved into a shadow oligarchy or aristocracy? *Democracy* is defined in *Black's Law Dictionary* as "a form of government in which the sovereign power resides in and is exercised by the whole body as free citizens, directly or indirectly, through the system of representation, as distinguished from a monarchy, aristocracy, or oligarchy."[8] It seems evident that the existing 45th president is under the narcissistic delusion that America should be a hybrid governance structure of monarchy, aristocracy, and oligarchy. The boundaries are blurred for him along with the rule of law. A *monarchy* is a form of government in which a single person holds supreme authority in ruling a country, a position that is usually inherited. An *aristocracy* consolidates strength in the hands of a small, privileged ruling class. The term derives from the Greek *aristokratia*, meaning "rule of the best-born." In an *oligarchy* a small group of people have control of a country, organizations, or institutions.[9] America is being governed by a small group that controls and or seeks to control the governance structure outlined in the US Constitution. They seek to manipulate, if not make personal advantageous changes to our Constitution. By what means have they obtained this level of influence and control? Seen through the looking glass of Alice, or Alex, in Wonderland, the call to "Make America Great Again" translates as "Back to the Future." This calculated statement from social media data mining, rings hollow; it reflects a regression in the development of the country and a disregard for the well-being of its citizens. This is the phenomenology and language of the trickster! It reflects the ideology and patterns of behavior that contravene the idea and goal of an inclusive, diverse multicultural democracy in favor of Eurocentrism. This is an American cultural complex rooted in the hybridity of a patriarchal oligarchy with an archetypal core of power; rule by fear, force and violence; and manipulation of nations, ethnic groups, and individual members.

Myth of Democracy

Robert Segal suggests that at least three significant questions can be asked of a myth: What is its subject matter? What is its origin? And what is its function?[10] Theories of myth differ not only on the answers they give to these questions but even more basically on which questions they ask. I believe that there are more relevant and pressing questions for us today as we consider the myth of democracy. Can there be an American democracy if the popular vote does not count in a representational system of electoral politics? Can we make a case for the viability of an American democracy if the popular vote does not outweigh other narrower source structures of the electorate with disproportionate power and influence? Can the architecture and the best ideals of American democracy survive in these challenging times of shadow capitalism and the cancer of narcissism, both negative aspects of American cultural complexes? Can the Constitution and governance structure envisioned by the framers withstand the assault from libertarian ideology and psychology? If there is another form of truly representative government that can emerge from the flames of our current American democratic system, what is it? How can the existing compromised system of representational government be reformed? Is this even possible?

Although these are questions for the citizenry to consider, I posit that from its inception American democracy was a myth. Citizens as a whole have neither formed the governing body of the nation, nor have their direct votes on governance and public policy issues resulted in the will of the people. The shadow dynamics of capitalism in representational democracy have made this impossible. Indigenous populations were excluded from citizenship status and voting on America's governance architecture and subsequent public policies. I reassert that the transcendent function informed by the Kemetic Egyptian deity of Maat and the principles of truth, justice, and balance, which if applied in American political economy, can mediate current divisions and tensions between representative democracy and a re-emergent oligarchy in this mythic American democracy.

African American historian John Hope Franklin said during World War II "that democracy is essentially an act of faith."[11] Echoing this truth in her recent book, Nancy MacLean traces how the American ideal of democracy is challenged at contemporary crossroads by this incipient oligarchy:

> The United States is at one of their historic forks in the road whose outcome will prove as fateful as those of the 1860s, the 1930s, and the 1960s. To value liberty for the wealthy minority above all else is to enshrine in the nation's governing rules, as Calhoun and Buchanan both called for and the Koch network is achieving, play-by-play, is to consent to an oligarchy in all but the outer husk of representative form.[12]

MacLean explains further:

> But nearly all else about the political economy of mid-century Virginia enacts their dream: the uncontested sway of the wealthiest citizens; the use of right to work laws and other ploys to keep working people powerless; the ability to fire dissenting public employees at will, targeting educators in particular; the use of voting rights restrictions to keep those unlikely to agree with the elite from the polls; the deployment of states' rights to deter the federal government from promoting equal treatment; the hostility to public education; the regressive tax system; the opposition to Social Security and Medicare; and the parsimonious response to public needs of all kinds—not just the decent schools sought by aspiring teenagers like Barbara Rose Johns and John Stokes but also the care and shelter of the elderly poor, the mentally ill and others in whose names Dr. Louise Wensel ran for in her 1959 senate campaign against Old Harry. Her core criticism, after all was that he worshiped "the golden calf": that he prized the accumulation of private wealth over the Golden rule and democracy "no matter what the cost."[13]

In closing her critical historical analysis, MacLean notes that the tools of this insidious oligarchy, generated in Virginia, are being grafted onto the governance of the nation and are part of the detrimental forces and psychology that counter and impede the achievement of a multicultural democracy.

This is the Eurocentric libertarian ideology and strategic action plan to safeguard ego-syntonic Eurocentric perspectivism in American life and the exclusion, subordination, devaluation, and manipulation of "others," as negative and defensive dynamics in these American cultural complexes. As a child, I was enrolled in a segregated Catholic elementary school when the Eurocentric libertarian cause first attracted wider support during the Southern resistance to the 1954 US Supreme Court decision in *Brown v. Board of Education* and the earlier predicate decision in higher education rendered in 1950 in *Sweat v. Painter* 339 U.S. 629.[14] The resistance of Southern whites to these decisions was violent, irrational, inhumane, and incomprehensible. It was frightening to watch this on television along with the assassinations of John F. Kennedy, Robert Kennedy, and Martin Luther King. These experiences influenced my decision to study law as an adult. The South viewed desegregation and equality in public education as a crisis that would have a detrimental effect on the American way of life. The resistance was never really about principles of equality and freedom, as most people would define it. It was about racism and the freedom to practice it in American cultural institutions.

The persona of freedom in Virginia and other states was in the advocacy of states' rights to determine their own system of education and all matters of commerce and governance without interference from the federal government. In the shadow culture, Virginia chose to close public schools, curtailing public education rather than integrating its public school system as ordered by the highest court in the land. In so doing, Virginia chose ignorance and inhumanity over humane actions serving the well-being of all of its citizens. It chose protection of the old Southern order of oligarchy and capital supremacy over transformative change for the common good of the state and the nation. Virginia chose privatization of education within the state and the deprivation of education for the children of color. The racism crippled multicultural intergenerational equity in relations among school-age children within the state. It weakened achievement of the collective educational potential for America. The ideology and behavioral patterns were duplicitous and promoted pathological division among American people for generations and today.

Eurocentric Libertarian leaders had no scruples about enlisting "white supremacy" to achieve "capital supremacy" to install advantage and systems of patronage or white privilege. Poor and working-class citizens with white identities, in fact and fiction, were promised real and illusory economic and political advantages over people of color. The fear that these privileges would be lost or even annihilated is at the heart of the racism and the violence in El Paso Texas and Dayton Ohio now encouraged by the executive branch of American government.[15] This fear of annihilation is at the core of white nationalism and hatred. It is reinforced by a secondary fear of retaliation and retribution for evil and malice done to all peoples of color in the Americas. Libertarians know that the majority of American citizens do not share their goals and would stop them if they understood the end game of the team of operatives who have been recruited, screened, and trained in the cause. They include academics operating within institutions like the Buchanan Center, part of the George Mason University department of economics, and think tanks like the Cato Institute, Heritage Foundation, the American Legislative Exchange (ALEC), and the Mont Pelerin Society, all supported and funded from the wealth amassed by the Koch brothers. Other conservative sources include political organizations like the State Policy Network and operatives in the judiciary, the Federalist Society, along with economists and captains of industry paid by Koch and others who seek to win by stealth. "Now as then, the leaders seek Calhoun-style liberty for the few—the liberty to concentrate vast wealth, so as to deny elementary fairness and freedom to the many."[16] MacLean underscores the point known to African Americans and other people of color: that white supremacy is an agency for capital supremacy, predicated on conditioned divisions between ethnic groups and social classes rather than the real division between capitalists and the general citizenry tethered and indentured to the free market.[17]

Multicultural Democracy

How do we define multiculturalism as a relational foundation for multicultural democracy? Revelations from MacLean's research on the insidiousness of the libertarian agenda make a clearly strong case for a multicultural democracy to remediate and evolve a compromised and failing American democracy.

Lillian Comas-Díaz offers relevant commentary on the origin of multiculturalism psychological theory.[18] She notes that it derived from the domestic social and political US civil rights movement in the 1950s, through the 1980s, and today.[19] I posit that multiculturalism also emerged from the synchronous confluences of the Pan-African liberation movement in Africa and the Caribbean and the African Diaspora that included the United States and Europe. This was a collective movement against Western cultural imperialism and hegemony in the inhumane forms of domestic apartheid and international colonialism. I underscore that the broader contextual historiography was the African Diaspora, the shared geopsychological and sociocultural spaces occupied by persons with ancestral origins in Africa dispersed around the globe. In the 21st century, a multicultural perspective and psychology promotes awareness of worldview, cultural contexts, domestic and global citizenship, and the pursuit of cultural competence as a lifelong learning process. Multiculturalism accommodates the integration of ancient ethnocultural history and healing wisdom traditions into contemporary theory, research, and clinical practice. It fosters equity of "other" and "otherness" relations among members of the human family, promoting consciousness, empowerment, change, and transformative dialogue on oppression and privilege.[20]

Anand Marri describes multicultural democracy as incorporating socioeconomic, cultural, and political diversity, going beyond current conceptions of democracy by asking these critical questions[21]: Who is and is not participating in democracy and on whose terms? How wide is the path to participation? I have further questions: Can a multicultural democracy better serve those who are disenfranchised from the benefits of an American democratic system and political economy even though, at its core, this system is constructed from myth? How can serving the needs and interests of the disenfranchised enrich the lives of the enfranchised beyond social philanthropy and tax breaks? How can serving the disenfranchised and enfranchised enhance the national psyche and intractable global economy? How can social equity and justice be achieved in the redistribution of national human and natural resources?

These important transformative questions should involve a national dialogue hosted by a progressive, evolutionary American leadership—leadership not steeped in capital supremacy, partisan manipulation of the public trust and corruption. Can we actively imagine a new governance structure for a reformed American democracy, a multicultural democracy that ensures every citizen has a vote, every voice is heard, and every vote counts? Can we envision a system of citizen-formed government where the governing body votes directly on issues, policies, and practices that promote its survival, well-being, and evolution? Can this dialogue and vision offer a counterpoint to the foundational and fundamental historical problems of our current failing representational American democratic system? Do our allies in Europe offer examples of successful direct governance models? Can international organizations like the United Nations host discussions on global governance reform and creation of new governance institutions that supersede its mission and vision as we move through the 21st century and beyond? How can it halt the protectionist global regression to nationalism?

I suggest that conscious recognition of an inclusive and diverse multicultural democracy with an educated, healthy, and economically secure population will make the United States stronger. The country cannot regress and evolve at the same time. We are in a serious regression that some seek to make permanent. A multicultural democracy offers the United States a solid platform for leadership in the global community, mindful of its own natural and human resource needs, and interests and those of our regional neighbors and the world community. The United States has the resources to aspire to creative evolution as a nation and to inspire the creation of effective global institutions necessary to safeguard the survival and evolution of planet Earth—if they are not wasted in the inhumanities of wars, weaponry, and other forms of self-destruction, destruction of others and the environment. We have access to active imagination and economic resources to advance a transformative agenda and institutions that serve the common good of the citizenry. To do so requires that the country encounter its white shadow and engage in the alchemical transformation of Eurocentrism into multiculturalism—symbolically, a rainbow nation synchronized with a rainbow world culture of cultures. This is one world with one human species.

The white privilege and white supremacy that constitute our most potent American cultural complex originated early in America's history, continue to exist today, and are key contributing factors to the decline of American democracy. The arc of American political and economic histories suggests that the draftsmen of the US Constitution, the founding fathers, were all men of European ancestry who acquired great wealth from substantial amounts of common land, in the millions of acres, appropriated from Native Americans. As noted, these lands were cultivated by free labor through the enslavement, commodification and sale of Africans, and the discounted indentured labor of poor Europeans working in the new world. With the doctrine of Manifest Destiny providing a rationale, white men of privilege wrote the framework for discrimination, oppression, and exclusion into state and federal laws. Today a few of these families own a disproportionate amount of land and wealth in America. White privilege, an artifact of the covenant of whiteness, was the basis for their participation in a scheme of priority consideration for the acquisition and redistribution of land, wealth, and subsequent economic opportunities that included employment, education, and healthcare. As a matter of fact, the myth of American democracy was founded on a Eurocentric experiment of incipient libertarianism in which private property and wealth were key requirements for participation in efforts to construct a democratic process—in stark opposition to multicultural democracy, which is based on equity and equal opportunity for all.

Fast forward to the 21st century and we find that the same Eurocentric libertarian ideology is held by an elite group in the numerical minority, a group that believes in the supremacy of capital and the unregulated pursuit of economic activities, and that private property interests should supersede the public interest of the majority. Further, they are committed to an active, heavily financed campaign to pursue an agenda that is regressive in character and detrimental to the well-being of the majority and the environment we all share. Aspects of the agenda include taking over the current American government with the intentions of disabling it, and encumbering it with debt so substantial as to severely limit its power, authority, and resources. These intentions as goals are being achieved by use of tricksterism, subversion, mendacity, and manipulation. The libertarian agenda continues to be a cancer of self-interest in the shadow of capitalism.

Direct Government: Each Voice, Each Vote Counts

In America, a representative democracy, in which citizens elect representatives from among themselves, has been highjacked and sacrificed to the self-interest of a few—compromised by the shadow of capitalism. Elected officials are for sale through the agency of campaign contributions, leaving us, in effect, with a transactional government. The Electoral College is currently under the influence of partisan state legislatures and private funds released into electoral politics by the 2010 US Supreme Court decision in *Citizens United v. Federal Election Commission*. This decision allows unlimited campaign contributions from named and unnamed corporate and union sources to heavily influence election outcomes.

Psychopathology of Racism: The Covenant of Whiteness

Racism is another cancer that eats away at America's democratic ideals, crippling its imagination and progressive development. Since the United States was founded, the covenant of whiteness has fueled the growth of racism in the shadow of American democracy. *Racism* is a set of discriminatory practices based on the fiction of race and racist ideas. Racism has to be confronted and addressed as a psychopathology that must be treated and healed for multicultural democracy to take deeper root, to grow, and thrive in the American collective conscience and consciousness.

Racism is certainly a core element of the American cultural complexes now being discussed in the post-Jungian literature as a particular "racialized complex" and "white shadow."[22] Beyond psychological complexes, there are bodies from "the Middle Passage" on the floor of the Atlantic Ocean and blood on the landscape and hands of American cultural history. We all suffer the trauma effects of this lived yet unspoken history. A confession is needed to unburden and lighten the heavy heart and soul of America.

Based on personal and professional experience, I have come to understand racism as a deeply rooted pathology in the American psyche, very much alive and yet to be fully interrogated and cured. The scholarship of modern historians such as Ibram Kendi offers refined, contemporary definitions of racism:

> My definition of a racist idea is a simple one: it is any concept that regards one racial group as inferior or superior to another racial group in any way.[23]
>
> Time and again, powerful and brilliant men and women have produced racist ideas in order to justify the racist policies of their era, in order to redirect the blame for their era's real disparities away from those policies and onto Black people.[24]

I define *racism* as psychopathology with the covenant of whiteness at its core. *White supremacy, white identity development,* and *white privilege* are recently named essential dynamics of this disease in the American psyche. Jung informs us that secrets are a source of incipient psychopathology.[25] People of color, especially those Americans with African ancestry, have been the objects of these negative projections and patterns of behavior. In 1946, Albert Einstein underscored this view in an invited talk at one of the historically black colleges (HBCU), Lincoln University: "There is separation of colored people from white people in the United States. That separation is not a disease of colored people. It is a disease of white people. I do not intend to be quiet about it."[26]

Racism is embedded in racist ideas of white privilege and white supremacy.[27] Frances Welsing underscores the reality that nine-tenths of the world's population are people of color. This generates a threat to survival in white folks that causes them to behave badly. Frederickson describes white supremacy as a system of beliefs, values, and practices elevating the interests, power, land hunger, and materiality of those laying claim to whiteness and white identities in American society and who have used the force of violence and the threat thereof to maintain a system of apartheid and subjugation that began with the founding fathers in their treatment of Native Americans.[28] This system of apartheid appropriated and converted their common land into private property, incarcerated Native Americans on reservations, separated families, miseducated their children, and simply killed them by various means.[29] Today, the continuation of these inhumane patterns of behavior continue in US immigration policies and practices toward Latinx populations.

The covenant of whiteness is at the center of racism suggested earlier by Albert Einstein. In defining this covenant and its core pathology existing among individuals and ethnic groups laying claim to white identities, Kendi quotes W. E. B. Du Bois, who argued

> that the Reconstruction era was the first and only time the United States had ever truly tasted democracy. After the Civil War, Black and White commoners came together to build democratic state governments providing public resources for the masses of southerners. White elites overthrew these governments by securing the loyalty of White commoners, a feat accomplished not only by offering them higher wages, but by holding up the rewards of the lucrative "public and psychological wage." From Du Bois, historians now term these rewards "the wages of whiteness": they were the privileges that would accrue to Whites through the application of racist ideas, discrimination, and segregation within the political economy. And to receive them, White laborers needed only to stand shoulder to shoulder with White elites on the lynched, raped, and exploited Black bodies.[30]

In the dimly lit shadow of the European American historical narrative, we see this system of American apartheid predicated upon constructed notions of race and rationalized in pseudo-science that emerged from the institutional intersections of the academy, geopolitics, and global labor economics and markets from the 15th through 20th centuries. Along with global European imperialism and cultural hegemony in the agency of colonialism, the social construction of the "race fiction" and production of racist ideas emerged as reasoned justification for institutional practices of inhumanity. This psychopathology is simply defined as a disorder in mental functioning that causes pathos, disease, or suffering of body and soul.[31]

In a previous publication I elaborated on how from America's inception extreme practices of inhumanity took root and were codified into the existing laws of the times, practices that continue today. I have discussed how slavery as an economic institution of free labor helped to develop appropriated rural lands and urban centers while it disenfranchised much of America's citizenry.[32] This extreme inhumanity occurred within the expanding framework of the existing laws. In addition to slavery, we have also witnessed racism in the removal and internment of Japanese Americans, upheld by the 1944 US Supreme Court decision in *Korematsu v. United States*, 323 US 214. We see the practices of racism then and now in current US immigration policies and behavior toward Latinx populations; babies and children are separated from their parents in overcrowded detention centers across the country as they immigrate to America from Central America through Mexico, seeking asylum and a better life. They have not been welcomed!

Jung offers guidance to us in his stages of psychotherapy for treatment of psychopathology: confession, elucidation, education, and transformation. Nelson Mandela, the heroic South African leader, also offers a path to cure the psychopathology of racism in the example of national efforts toward truth and reconciliation, to which I would add "repair—reparation" in order to make the nation whole. Active imagination needs to be brought to the task and challenges of this collective repair.

Shadow Culture: The Trickster Archetype in Eurocentric Libertarian Ideology and Practices in the US Political Economy

Jung's thinking about shadow phenomena in the archetypal energies of the trickster is a useful critical lens through which to view the failing ideal of American democracy today. Jung states:

> The trickster is a collective shadow figure, a summation of all the inferior traits of character in individuals. And since the individual shadow is never absent as a component of personality, the collective figure can construct itself out of it continually. Not always, of course,

as a mythological figure but in consequence of the increasing repression and neglect of the original mythologems, as a corresponding projection on other social groups and nations. ...

The most rudimentary insight into the shadow sometimes causes the greatest difficulties for the modern European.[33]

Jung noted that instead of repressing or denying the shadow, we may also project the shadow onto others, attributing to them those nasty, unsavory qualities that we would like to deny in ourselves. Shadow projections can result in paranoia, suspiciousness, and a lack of intimacy—all of which afflict individuals, groups, and even entire nations. Far from solving the problem, shadow projections only exacerbate the troublesome quality of this dark side of our soul, injecting a kind of poison into interpersonal relationships through self-righteous denial and distorted perceptions.[34]

The archetypal energies, phenomenology, and behavioral patterns of the trickster are recognizable in the political actions of the current Republican party, comprised of heterogeneous groups and individuals that lay claim to white identities and privileges, imagined or real. The conflated agenda of the leadership has embraced a Eurocentric libertarian ideology and political platform from the 1950s, rooted in the beliefs of economic liberty, limited government, states' rights, and self-determined individualism. We hear this refrain in congressional testimonies from the current US cabinet secretaries: Commerce, Treasury, Education, Housing and Urban Development, Environmental Protection Agency, and across the spectrum of government agencies filled with Republican political appointees. Many have limited or no qualifications to discharge the requisite duties of their agencies. Most have character disorders. Some have signed loyalty oaths and nondisclosure agreements. All have the intent to weaken the agencies placed in their charge. In keeping with the belief in limited government, the mandates for leadership in the core organizations and administration of the federal government are to dismantle the agency, eliminate vital functions, rollback progressive legislation of the previous Democratic administration, and subvert rulemaking in service of deregulation—and to do this by any means available or that can be created where they do not exist. Their belief is that these mandates sustain the portal to economic freedom.

The heterogeneous Republican party constituency includes capitalists from the top 1 percent to 10 percent of wealthy Americans, libertarian and conservative professionals (lawyers, economists, academics, businessmen and businesswomen, healthcare providers, scientists), Catholic anti-abortionists, Christian evangelicals, the indentured working class, the poor and extreme white ethno-nationalists—all bound together in the covenant of whiteness. Motivated, in part, by fears of losing economic well-being, white privilege, and fear of annihilation, they have engaged in extraordinary coordinated efforts to leverage the political process and American democracy to permanent advantage and control of libertarian Republicans, almost all of them with white identities and a Eurocentric cultural orientation.[35] Their systemic efforts, which have become most transparent since 2016, are unprecedented. Individual and group efforts are driven by the fact that those claiming white identities will become a numerical minority in the United States in the years between 2025 and 2045.

The following examples demonstrate how the phenomenology of the trickster archetype and negative patterns of thought, affect, and behavior have been constellated and operate in the shadow of American psychology and the political economy as American cultural complexes. We see the negative energies of the trickster in the 2010 legal case of *Citizens United v. Federal Election Commission*, national gerrymandering practices to ensure one-sided partisan party elections, voter suppression that contravenes the constitutional right of citizens to vote in US elections and the Voting Rights Act of 1965, and a consequentially subversive partisan libertarian political agenda.

Citizens United v. Federal Election Commission, 558 US 310

Citizens is a landmark US constitutional law case, involving campaign finance and regulation of political campaign spending by organizations, unions, and for-profit and nonprofit corporations. The US Supreme Court held (5 to 4) on January 21, 2010, that the free speech clause of the First Amendment to the US Constitution prohibits the government from restricting independent expenditures for communications by for-profit and nonprofit corporations, labor unions, and other associations (*Citizens United v. Federal Election Commission*, 558 US 310).

The conservative nonprofit organization *Citizens United* sought to air a film critical of Hillary Clinton and to advertise the film during television broadcasts shortly before the 2008 Democratic primary election in which Clinton was running for US president. Federal law (2 USC §441b), however, prohibited any corporation or labor union from using their general treasury funds for an "electioneering communication" (defined as a broadcast ad reaching over 50,000 people in the electorate) within 30 days of a primary or 60 days of an election or making any expenditure advocating the election or defeat of a candidate at any time. Limits on electioneering communications had been upheld in 2003 in *McConnell v. Federal Election Commission*, 540 US 93, 203–209. In 2010, however, the court found that these provisions of the law conflicted with the US Constitution. The court upheld requirements for public disclosure by sponsors of advertisements. The case did not affect the federal ban on direct contributions from corporations or unions to candidate campaigns or political parties. The decision was highly controversial and remains a subject of widespread public discussion.[36]

In a recent case, the court, in an unsigned order, declined to consider a challenge to a Massachusetts law barring for-profit corporations from donating to political campaigns. In doing so, the justices kept in place a key pillar of campaign finance law and rejected an opportunity to dramatically expand the court's impactful *Citizens United* ruling in 2010. This decision allowed corporations to spend unlimited sums of money on candidate elections, as along as the spending remained independent of candidates. This ruling, and a separate appellate court decision later that year, helped give rise to free-spending super PACs, which strengthened the success of the libertarian agenda.[37] This decision has infected electoral politics with capital supremacy, severely weakened American democracy, and is an intended barrier to a multicultural democracy.

The Gerrymander

The goal of gerrymandering is to draw political boundaries in ways that maximize a governing party's advantage. Drafters of such maps accomplish this mainly through two practices called *packing* and *cracking*. A *packed* district includes as many members of the opposition party as possible. This helps the governing party capture and hold surrounding districts in which the opposition's strength has been diluted. *Cracking* does the opposite: it splits up clusters of opposition voters among two or more districts so they will be outnumbered by backers of the governing party, in each district. An efficient gerrymandered map doles out just enough support to governing party candidates to let them win and hold seats safely, even in "wave" elections when their opponents do especially well. Gerrymander limits opposition to a minimum number of packed districts that it wins overwhelmingly.[38]

New York Times columnist Michael Wines reported on the current controversy involving gerrymandering and the impact of the 2020 citizenship census question, which again illustrate shadow phenomena and negative patterns of the trickster.[39] Attention to the controversy arose from the death of leading Republican strategist Thomas Hofeller, PhD, who died in August 2018. He is described as the "Michelangelo of gerrymandering" and the architect of partisan political maps that ensured the Republican party's national prominence in state and congressional contests. His digital records, discovered by his daughter, indicate that he played a central role in the 45th presidential administration's decision to add the citizenship question to the 2020 US census. The question itself would deter responses from minority groups and noncitizens, many of whom are immigrants, and keep them from being counted among the US population. It would advance Republican interests toward exclusion and aid efforts toward continuous gerrymandering, skewing political boundaries to their advantage when redistricting begins in 2021.

The maps are usually drawn by state legislatures and commissions appointed by the party in power. Hofeller recommended that census data be drawn only on American citizens of voting age, essentially disenfranchising and diluting the political power of the Latinx population, the fastest-growing ethnic group not only in Texas but also across the United States. Hofeller reasoned that no clear census data exists on this target group for drawing maps; adding the question to the upcoming 2020 census would provide this information. A relevant alternative source for this data has been the Department of Justice, which verifies that the Voting Rights Act (1965) ensures voting rights to people of color. Without inclusion of a citizenship question on the 2020 decennial census questionnaire, Hofeller believed that using the citizen voting age population was functionally unworkable. The trickster energy here is the misrepresentation that data from the new citizenship question in the 2020 census are necessary to enforce the Voting Rights Act of 1965, and to increase Latinx political representation when, in fact, it would have the opposite effect.[40] The trickster in the libertarian playbook obscures the truth or lies to establish self-serving objectives beneath crafted legal arguments and rationalizations. The same was true in the Citizens United case.

Experts say that adding a citizenship question would deter immigrants and subordinated residents of color from responding to the census, leading to an undercount, estimated at 630,000 households. Millions of residents in the predominantly Democratic areas where most of them live would be unrepresented. In addition, a census that reveals with precision where non-citizens live is crucial to plans by some conservatives to base political districts, not on total population but on the number of voting-age citizens. This, too, would benefit Republicans, especially in states like Texas and California with large numbers of foreign-born residents.

Under the stewardship of the current secretary of commerce, decisions have been made in secret, without testing the language of the question. This is in contrast to the years of surveys and consultations that have preceded every previous change in the census questionnaire. In a December 2017 letter to the Census Bureau, the Department of Justice requested that the citizenship question be added, arguing that the current population data fall short of the 1965 Voting Rights Act requirements. This matter was decided by the US Supreme Court on June 27, 2019. The decision effectively returned the matter to the federal courts for further evidentiary hearings. The reason was that the rationale for inclusion of this new census question offered by the secretary of commerce and the executive administration was not credible.[41] The US Supreme Court did not support inclusion of the citizenship question on the 2020 census because of pretextual incredibility. These manipulative political actions are part of the ongoing effort to leverage the political process in service of white supremacy and capital supremacy! In June 2019, the president sought to cloak in executive privilege the unethical, if not illegal, misconduct of his secretary of commerce (and attorney general), in whose jurisdiction the Census Bureau resides. This is his shield against investigation and oversight by the US Congress. The US House of Representatives issued contempt of Congress sanctions to both the secretary of commerce and the attorney general as coconspirators in this matter.

The US Supreme Court consolidated cases on partisan gerrymandering in Pennsylvania, Ohio, North Carolina, Texas, Wisconsin, Michigan, and Maryland. In Ohio, the federal district court had ordered that new election maps be drawn by June 14, 2019, for use in the 2020 election, when Democrats will fight to preserve the House majority. The ruling follows decisions by four other federal courts striking down partisan gerrymandering in Wisconsin, North Carolina, Maryland, and Michigan. All but Maryland were gerrymandered by Republicans.[42]

Gerrymandering has been a principal means by which the Republican party has gained control of 37 to 44 state legislatures and the US Congress since 2012. Owing to the results of the 2018 midterms and judicial interventions, the number of Republican-controlled legislatures has been reduced to 29. The political actions in Ohio ground the example of the negative aspects of the trickster. Ohio maps in effect since 2012 have solidified a congressional delegation that has remained unchanged in four elections—12 Republicans and 4 Democrats, or 75 percent for the one party in a swing state that has benefited Republicans in recent close presidential and state-wide elections.

In a 301-page decision, the Ohio court judge ruled: "We conclude that the 2012 map dilutes the votes of Democratic voters by packing and cracking them into districts that are so skewed toward one party that the electoral outcome is predetermined." In 2018, the Pennsylvania state Supreme Court ordered electoral maps to be redrawn, which resulted in less partisan districts in the midterm elections and helped Democrats net three seats formerly held by Republicans.

In the recent multistate cases on gerrymandering, decided by the US Supreme Court, a central issue was whether courts could draw a line between acceptable political maps and those state legislatures whose partisan goals overstep constitutional bounds, a question with which the justices have struggled for decades. I would add that these state legislatures dictate the presidential electorate and have collaboratively pushed hard the libertarian agenda to limit collective bargaining, place bans on abortion, and in some instances (for example, Wisconsin) limit the authority of governorships held by the Democratic party. This behavior also occurs in the Republican-held US Senate, whose agenda includes leveraging the judiciary to overturn *Roe v Wade*, 410 U.S. 113 (1973), the landmark "right for women to choose abortion." Caucasian women have 60 percent of all abortions in the United States, which is the percentage of Caucasian births believed needed to sustain the ethnic majority for those claiming white identities in America. Thus, male legislators claiming white identities believe that limiting abortion is critical to survival of political control. With the aid of the Federalist Society, the agenda also includes "stacking and packing" the judiciary with conservative judges, even when they are not qualified through the agency of the "old boy network."

On June 27, 2019, the US Supreme Court ruled that the federal courts should not have the power to hear legal challenges to extreme partisan gerrymandering within states. This means it is left to the states to determine policy and practices involving gerrymander. However, as noted, it did delay and effectively exclude the citizenship question from the 2020 census.[43] We shall see what this means for the demise of American democracy. Do we have a partisan judiciary in the agency of the US Supreme Court? Has the Federalist society been successful in achieving its strategic mission of placing conservative jurists in all American courts, with the aid of the current Republican Senate Majority Leader?

Voter Suppression

Voter suppression has a blood-stained history, from Reconstruction after the Civil War through Jim Crow, the US Civil Rights movement, and today.[44] Stacy Abrams, the African American female candidate for the 2018 governorship of Georgia, speaks to current practices of voter suppression in her unsuccessful bid for office. Her opponent was Georgia's secretary of state, under whose charge the election was conducted. Despite the ethical conflict of interest, he oversaw the electoral process while he campaigned for office. This was a clear violation of ethics, if not state or federal law, and certainly the playground for tricksterisms.

In *The New York Times*, Ms. Abrams outlined tactics of voter suppression that included purging registrants from the rolls if there were errors in data entry, instituting poll taxes, moving voting sites, closing polls early, using faulty voting machines, and enforcing a policy of "use it or lose it"—vote in the election or your name is removed from voting rolls.[45] Ms. Abrams stated, "Although exact match lacks the explicit racial animus of Jim Crow, its execution betrayed its true purpose was to disenfranchise voters of color in Georgia."[46] The Georgia secretary of state held 53,000 voter registrations hostage under the exact-match policy in 2018, 70 percent of which came from black voters who made up only 30 percent of Georgia's eligible voters. A missing hyphen or typo in government database entries formed the basis to withhold the right to vote.

Another example of the trickster as malfeasance in voter suppression was reported in a North Carolina congressional race. This involved absentee ballot collection for the state congressional representative. The candidate hired a third-party consultant to help with his campaign against the legal advice of his son, an assistant US attorney. The consultant and his employees collected absentee ballots and promised to mail or deliver them for rural voters, primarily African Americans. To ensure the votes were for the Republican candidate, the consultant changed or destroyed ballots that were for the Democratic candidate. The matter went to a formal hearing where the illegitimate favorable outcome for the Republican candidate was not certified by the state election commission.[47]

In yet another example, Texas purged voting rolls with the claim that there was voter fraud in which 95,000 noncitizens allegedly voted. Data was taken from the Department of Motor Vehicles, which does not track reliable citizenship information for naturalized citizens.

These are examples of the negative aspects of trickster energies manifest as negative aspects of American cultural complexes in partisan psychology, behavioral patterns and political actions in the American political economy. These illegal and unethical activities are ongoing in shadow American society. As contemporary political theater informs us, the American ethos is to win by any and all means necessary including corruption. If caught in a lie or criminal conduct, the trickster denies the truth as fake news or inconsequential fact, changes the subject and the narrative, becomes the expressive belligerent victim, and tries to cut a deal behind closed doors. If this pattern fails, the identified perpetrator submits a resignation with or without apology and attempts to avoid criminal or civil prosecution. This is the moral climate of the times in a rudderless transactional leadership. Capital supremacy and white supremacy are the impetus behind the furor over US immigration policy and the current irrational efforts to reduce immigration. The cheap labor is welcome, but not the workers and their families as citizens.[48]

Archetypal Perspective: Maat, the Kemetic Egyptian Deity of Truth, Justice, Order, Balance, and Cosmic Harmony

In this chapter, mindful of my own complexes, I have tried to make the case for a multicultural American democracy and the need for equity participation in the US political economy through the agency of analytical theory. While multicultural democracy emerges as a construct from the collective unconscious, I have employed theory about American cultural complexes, the challenges that reside not only in the individual and collective group shadow and in the liminal psyche space of the United States, but also in Western European shadow culture. Here, I would like to engage the light of higher consciousness—that of spirituality and transcendence offered by the archetypal perspective—in relation to American cultural complexes and the multiculturalism necessary to achieve equity and social justice in American democracy, and the political economy. To be clear, the necessary shift is from a European American cultural orientation and perspectivism to a multicultural plurality and democratic orientation.

Can analytical psychology help assess conflict, one-sidedness, and imbalance? Where can we find the scales on which to achieve the balance of social justice in the individual and collective psyche and in the US political economy? Calling on the transcendent function as the mediator of dialectical opposites, the archetypal perspective allows informed and enlightened ego consciousness to move across historiographies and cultures and to harness active imagination toward remedy and cure found in balance and new consciousness. We are in great need of leadership with active imagination, vision, a constructive agenda, and transformative changes that benefit the majority of the American population.

In analytical theory, archetypes represent and symbolize the essential and common elements of culture. Offering the wisdom of the ages, they provide guidance on what is necessary for the survival, maintenance, and evolution of individuals, groups, and relational civil societies of the world. Analytical psychology posits that reflection on common themes across comparative mythologies offers epistemologies, or ways of knowing, as proofs of the universal nature of commonalities and diversities found in the heart of organizational structures of human and even nonhuman societies. We have seen the multicultural mythological expressions of the trickster archetype in Coyote among Native Americans, Elegba among the Yoruba in the African Diaspora, and Hermes in Greek mythology and the West. Here we turn to Maat, an archetypal anima figure in Kemetic Egyptian mythology. She offers lessons on truth, balance, and weighing matters with the heart to achieve cosmic and ecological harmony, equity and social justice.

Maat in Myth

Much has been written by historians and Egyptologists about the goddess Maat.[49] In brief, Maat is the administratrix of the Hall of Judgment and closely connected to the god Thoth in deciding which souls upon death will enter the eternal Underworld, the realm of Osiris. In her capacity as regulator of the path of the Sun-god, Maat is said to be the "daughter of Ra," the "eye of Ra," the "lady of heaven, queen of the earth, mistress of the underworld," and "lady of the gods and goddesses."[50] As a moral power, Maat was the greatest of the goddesses, and in her dual form of Maati, goddess of the South and the North, she was the lady of the judgment hall. She became the personification of justice, who awarded every man or woman his or her due.

Maat's judgment involved weighing the heart of the deceased soul against the lightness of her feather on the scale of justice. A heart heavy with misdeeds and malfeasance was weighed against the truth, honesty, compassion, and good deeds symbolized by the lightness of her feather. If the heart is as light as her feather, the soul moves forward with admonitions to the jury of the 42 assessors and finally to Thoth, who speaks and records the name upon entry to the realm of Osiris. If the heart is too heavy from misdeeds, it is devoured by Ammut, who sits in readiness next to the scale of justice. Ammut is cute but lethal. She has the head of the crocodile, her neck mane and foreparts are those of a lion, and her rear quarters are those of a hippopotamus. She feeds on heavy hearts. Her composite form of land and water animals leaves the damned no place to escape from this goddess of wrath.[51]

In some vignettes, Maat represents the weighing of the heart, and at times she takes the form of the balance itself.[52] The hall in which Maat sits in her double form, Maati, to hear the "confession" of the dead is often depicted in connection with the Egyptian Book of the Dead. According to Budge, the word *Maat* means "'that which is straight'—a rule, law, or canon by which the lives and actions of men and women are kept straight and governed."[53] The Egyptians used the word in a physical and moral sense. It came to mean "right, true, truth, real, genuine, upright, righteous, just, steadfast, unalterable."[54] Maat is the personification of physical and moral law, order, and truth. She is balance and alignment of spirit and matter in law and conscience in morality.

Maat an Agency for Multicultural Democracy: Alignment of Spirit and Matter in Law

Psychologically, Maat is the relational path toward deep aspirations for universal principles of truth, honesty, social justice, orderly administration of justice, proper weighing of the heart, order, the balance of morality against immorality of the soul in this life and the afterlife, and a conjunction of spirit and matter in law. Maat embodies justice and administers the laws of the earliest recorded civil society in Kemet Egypt, which predates the modern European American cultural orientation to Greco Roman civilization. The Greeks and the Romans appropriated much of classical Egyptian civilization as their own before destroying the great libraries of Alexandria to conceal the theft. As a Western cultural complex, this is the negative historical pattern of appropriation of land, material, and natural and human resources that reached into the new world of America and continues today as Western practices of racism and colonialism in non-Western countries.[55]

For Cheryl Grills, a clinical and community psychologist and professor of psychology, the Ma'atan ideal is grounded in three critical elements: perpetual veneration, interconnectedness, and spiritual oneness.[56] *Perpetual veneration* is seeing oneself as a representative of a vital part of a supreme system that includes all life everywhere. Each person is an extension, a spark, of the divine. *Interconnectedness* means viewing life as a historical, dynamic, and ongoing interconnected process of causality. What I do today is a reflection of yesterday and the impetus for what I, and others, do tomorrow. *Spiritual oneness* is acknowledging the spiritual dimensions of human experience. All beings are an extension of the singular source of creation, so we are connected not only to the source but also to one another. The seven cardinal virtues of Maat (truth, justice, propriety/compassion, harmony, balance, reciprocity, order) and the 42 admonitions of the assessors are considered the keys to human perfectibility. The more they are recognized and practiced in life, the more developed the self becomes. Maat provides the guidelines for correct behavior and the standard against which the soul of the deceased is judged.[57]

Conclusion

For these modern times, and indeed all times, Maat embodies the principles of alignment and integration of spirit and matter in law, balance, right action, social justice, the common good, and interconnectivity of planet Earth. She offers the archetypal energy and embodied patterns of these principles in harmony, and the wisdom to neutralize the negative aspects of the trickster archetype seen in libertarian ideology and core patterns of self-indulgence, inhumanity, and the capital-supremacy-driven destruction of our planet. Maat advances relational instinct, kinship libido, and Ubuntu; a guide toward sociocultural equity and a bridge to consciousness of the necessary conjunction between spiritual and civil order needed to transcend the dialectic of inhumanity versus humanity.[58]

As an archetypal anima figure, Maat also offers a path to conscious action toward truth, reconciliation, and individuation of the judicial function of individual psyche in moral judgments and the collective ethics and laws of judicial systems. She mirrors, informs, and elevates ego consciousness of the persona and shadow of the American judiciary, under threat of compromise through the agency of the trickster archetype in the misuse of political power in judicial appointments of ideologues and incompetent partisan jurists and support of corruption. She invites a comparative inquiry of judicial systems across cultures and across the arch of time: past, present, and future—"then in now."

As enlightenment, the "eye of Ra," Maat can rebalance the scale of imbalances. She is the lived experience of balance, cosmic and ecological harmony, the weighing of the heart that aligns reason and the spirit and matter in law, the US Constitution, American cultural complexes, and a multicultural democracy.

My hope is for an emergent conscious and intentional multicultural democracy. We are in great need of broader creative vision and a matrix for the evolution of modern America. It must include strategic planning and implementation programs in the service of the collective good. This will need to include government reform. Also, it will require leadership transition that is driven by a diverse younger generation like the Democratic aspirants to the office of the US presidency in 2020. "Make America Great Again" is code, the simple and complex voice and language of the trickster. Translated, it means "back to the future," a future of the way things were in the past from the inception of America. Today, the spirit of Maat empowers us with enlightenment to address, remediate, heal, and transcend the ills and psychopathology within the body politic, the heart and soul of American democracy and American cultural complexes. Enlightened consciousness, elevated conscience, and critical theory offer lessons to correct the false narratives of American history, false constructs of American democracy, false notions of race and racism, and the covenant of whiteness in American cultural complexes. The recommendations that follow are offered to aid the conscious and necessary emergence of a multicultural democracy that takes America "forward into the future."

1. *Limits on campaign finance contributions and transparency in identified sources.* This requires a reversal of *Citizen United v. Federal Election Commission* and/or congressional legislation to limit the impact of capital and capitalism on electoral politics. If this imbalance is not changed, the nation will suffer from the consequence of capital supremacy.

2. *Government regulation of technology, social media platforms, and cybersecurity to deter foreign influence in US electoral politics.* Many of us were surprised by the intrusion of the Russian government and perhaps other nations into the US presidential election of 2016. Groups such as Cambridge Analytica and campaign operatives have used these platforms to spread disinformation and divide the nation on a grand scale. These intrusions are a form of propaganda and an attack on truth, honesty, and the well-being of collective citizenry. Cybersecurity is essential to support multicultural democracy in America and to safeguard the nation from external threats and attacks on vital communication and utility systems.[59]

3. *Limit gerrymandering.* Former Attorney General Eric Holder (2008–2015) is leading efforts to reform the illegalities involved in extreme partisan gerrymandering and cracking and packing among state legislatures. For example, the state of Ohio offers a formula to balance the negative impact of gerrymandering. Last year, Ohio voters resoundingly approved a legislative ballot initiative that will blunt partisan influence on redistricting starting in 2021, after the next census. The measure encourages compromise. New congressional maps must pass the state house and senate with at least 50 percent approval from the minority party. If they fail, a seven-member commission—made up of the governor, two other state officials, and two Democratic and two Republican lawmakers—will draw the maps. This represents legislative change in Ohio and reasonable efforts toward balance and alignment of the spirit and matter of the law. In late June 2019, the US Supreme Court ruled that the federal courts have no power to challenge state

partisan political gerrymandering. This is another states' right ruling. It will be up to the state legislatures and state supreme courts, political parties, commissions, and people to make needed corrections toward rebalancing voting maps and American politics. In her dissenting opinion on the two combined cases, *Rucho v. Common Cause* and *Lamone v. Benisek*, Justice Elena Kagan stated, "The practices challenged in these cases imperil our system of government. Part of the court's role in that system is to defend its foundations. None is more important than free and fair elections."[60] I submit that "each voice and each vote counts in a direct multicultural democracy." This is the journey to the future.

4. *Institute multicultural democratic reform.* The role of the Electoral College is an important consideration. Its purpose, history, and effectiveness are in question and should be revisited. A multicultural democracy requires government by the people for the people. Representative democracy appears to be in a crisis of paralysis, held hostage to capital supremacy, white rage, trickster(isms), malice, and forethought. It is failing and on the brink of death. Direct voting in which every voice and every vote counts is the viable alternative. To this end, 11 states are enacting legislation that requires state electors to follow the popular vote, closing the split between the popular vote and the weighted votes of electors. This, too, is the direction toward correcting and rebalancing US electoral politics. We need a strong federal government to oversee fair elections in light of changes to the Voting Rights Act of 1965 and foreign interventions in American elections.[61]

5. *Treatment of the psychopathology of racism requires truth, reconciliation, and reparations for slavery, Jim Crow segregation, and ongoing discrimination in the United States.* Journalist David Brook and senator Elizabeth Warren are recent public advocates for the importance of repair—the repair of the heart and soul of the United States with confession, truth, reconciliation, and reparations.[62] The psychological trauma and dissociation along with the political and economic imbalances created by these practices have been harmful to all—victims and perpetrators. The fears fueling the current white supremacy ideology and nationalist movements require treatment, and deconstruction of capitalist supremacy. Continued denial of the collective sins of the nation, the personal and collective dissociation from this inhumanity, and the transgenerational institutionalization of racism will continue as a cancer to destroy the humanity of the Western world and the common ecosystem. An active imagining of a multicultural social democracy is the path toward the future.

6. *Transcendent function.* In truth, we are a rainbow nation, a multicultural society in search of a multicultural democracy in which every voice and vote counts. There is one Earth, which now requires a planetary consciousness for our sustainability and equitable distribution of natural

and human resources. There is a need for reformed and new governance structures and institutions to mediate the impacts of deindustrialization and advancement of technology networks connecting all of us in the world. There is a call to envision the human species, other species, our future, and the future of the planet as one.

7. *Unbuntu, "I am because we are, we are because I am," harmony within, with each other and the universe.*[63]

Notes

1 Thomas Singer and Samuel Kimbles, *The Cultural Complex: Contemporary Perspectives on Psyche and Society* (Hove and New York: Brunner-Routledge, 2004). See also Thomas Singer and Joerge Rasche, eds., *Europe's Many Souls Exploring Cultural Complexes and Identities* (New Orleans: Spring Journal Books, 2016).

2 See "Cultural Complexes" in the Introduction by Thomas Singer for a description of the characteristics of the cultural complex.

3 Nancy MacLean, *Democracy in Chains: The Deep History of the Radical Right's Stealth Plan for America* (New York: Viking, 2017).

4 C. G. Jung, "On the Psychology of the Trickster Figure" (1954), in *The Collected Works of C. G. Jung*, vol. 9i, *The Archetypes and the Collective Unconscious* (Princeton: Princeton University Press, 1968), 484.

5 Ibid., 486.

6 Scott Morgan, Opinion, *The New York Times*, May 4, 2019.

7 Henry Campbell Black, *Black's Law Dictionary* (St. Paul, MN: West Publishing Co, 1979), 1491; Paul Krugman, "The Great Republican Abdication," *The New York Times*, April 22, 2019.

8 Black, *Black's Law Dictionary*, 389.

9 Michael Tomasky, "Is America Becoming an Oligarchy? Growing Inequality Threatens Our Most Basic Democratic Principles," *The New York Times*, April 15, 2019, Opinion.

10 Robert E. Segal, *Jung on Mythology* (London and New York: Routledge, 1998).

11 MacLean, *Democracy in Chains*, 232; John Hope Franklin and Alfred A. Moss, *From Slavery to Freedom: A History of African Americans*, 7th Ed. (New York: Alfred A. Knopf, 2000).

12 MacLean, *Democracy in Chains*, 233.

13 Ibid., 234. In 1959, Louise Wensel challenged Harry Byrd for his Virginia senate seat and his obstructionist policies toward desegregation of American public education ordered by the US Supreme Court in *Brown v. Board of Education* (1954). The Byrd oligarchy/dynasty had defied the US Supreme Court order and closed all of the public schools rather than integrate them. They argued states' rights to determine education policies within each state. Privatization of education grew out of this resistance movement, segregated academies for students with white identities flourished and the prescient voucher system, using public tax dollars to pay for private school tuition became the new policy for adoption. African American children and children of color received no public education within the state of Virginia for a decade or more. Barbara Rose Johns and John Stokes were African American students in Prince Georges County Virginia instrumental in challenging the state segregation practices in public education.

14 Derrick Bell, *Race, Racism and American Law* (Boston and Toronto: Little Brown and Company, 1980); Derrick Bell, ed., *Civil Rights: Leading Cases* (Boston and Toronto: Little Brown and Company, 1980).

15 Frances Cress Welsing, *Isis Papers: The Keys to the Colors* (Chicago, IL: Third World Press, 1991); Alan Vaughan, "Humanity and Inhumanity: Relational Themes in Humanistic–Existential Psychology and Multiculturalism Reflected in the United States Constitution, U.S. Constitutional Jurisprudence and the United Nations Universal Declaration of Human Rights," in *Humanistic Approaches to Multiculturalism and Diversity*, eds. Louis Hoffman, Heatherlyn Cleare-Hoffman, Nathanial Granger, and David St. John (London and New York: Routledge, 2019).

16 MacLean, *Democracy in Chains*, 234.

17 Ibid., 234.

18 Lillian Comas-Díaz, "Multicultural Theories of Psychotherapies," in *Current Psychotherapies*, 10th Ed., eds. Danny Wedding and Raymond J. Corsini, 533–564 (Belmont, CA: Brooks/Cole, 2014).

19 Ibid., 563.

20 Ibid., 544; Vaughan, "Humanity and Inhumanity"; Derald Wing Sue and David Sue, *Counseling the Culturally Diverse: Theory and Practice*, 4th Ed. (Canada: John Wiley & Sons, Inc., 2003).

21 Anand R. Marri, "Multicultural Democracy: Toward a Better Democracy," *International Education* 14, no. 3 (2003): 263–277, https://doi.org/10.1080/1467598032000117060.

22 Fanny Brewster, *African Americans and Jungian Psychology* (London and New York: Routledge, 2017); Thomas Singer, "Playing the Race Card," in *Sacral Revolutions: Reflecting on the Work of Andrew Samuels*, ed. Gottfried Heuer, 252–260 (London: Routledge, 2010); Thomas Singer, "Snapshots of the Obamacare Cultural Complex," in *Analysis and Activism: Social and Political Contributions of Jungian Psychology*, eds. Emilija Kiehl, Mark Saban, and Andrew Samuels, 147–156 (London: Routledge 2016); Karen Naifeh, "Encountering the Other: The White Shadow," *Jung Journal Culture & Psyche* 13, no. 2 (2018): 7–20, https://doi.org/10.1080/19342039.2019.1600976.

23 Ibram Kendi, *Stamped from the Beginning: The Definitive History of Racist Ideas in America* (New York: Nation Books, 2016), 5.

24 Ibid., 9.

25 C. G. Jung, *The Collected Works of C. G. Jung*, vol. 16, *The Practice of Psychotherapy* (Princeton: Princeton University Press, 1954).

26 The Albert Einstein quote comes from a speech given on May 3, 1946, at Lincoln University, where he received an honorary degree, as reported in the *Baltimore Afro-American*, May 11, 1946.

27 Welsing, *Isis Papers*.

28 George M. Fredrickson, *White Supremacy: A Comparative Study in America and South Africa* (New York and Oxford: Oxford University Press, 1981).

29 Ibid., 4–5.

30 W. E. B. Du Bois, quoted in Kendi, *Stamped from the Beginning*, 331.

31 Franklin and Moss, *From Slavery to Freedom*; Alan Vaughan, "African American Jungian Analysts on Culture, Clinical Training/Practice and Racism," *Journal of Analytical Psychology* 64, no. 3 (2019): 320–348.

32 Alan Vaughan, "African American Cultural History and Reflections on Jung in the African Diaspora," *Journal of Analytical Psychology* 64, no, 3 (2019): 320–348.

33 Jung, "On the Psychology of the Trickster Figure," 484, 486.

34 Joseph Henderson, *Shadow and Self-Selective Papers in Analytical Psychology* (Wilmette, IL: Chiron Publications, 1990). Robert H. Hopcke, *A Guided Tour of the Collected Works of C. G. Jung* (Boston: Shambhala Publications, 1989), 82.
35 Sabrina Tavernise, "Why the Announcement of a Looming White Minority Makes Demographers Nervous," *The New York Times*, November 22, 2018, Opinion; Joseph E. Stiglitz, *People, Power, and Profits Progressive Capitalism for an Age of Discontent* (New York and London: W.W. Norton & Company, 2019).
36 Jeffrey Toobin, "Money Unlimited: How Justice Roberts Orchestrated Citizens United," *The New Yorker*, May 14, 2012, https://www.newyorker.com/magazine/2012/05/21/money-unlimited.
37 Toobin, "Money Unlimited"; Zephyr Teachout, "The Anti-Corruption Principle," *Cornell Law Review* 94, no. 2 (2009): 341–408.
38 Black, *Black's Law Dictionary*, 618; Michael Wines "What Is Gerrymandering? What If the Supreme Court Bans It?" *The New York Times*, March 26, 2019, https://www.nytimes.com/2019/03/26/us/what-is-gerrymandering.html.
39 Michael Wines, "Deceased GOP Strategist's Hard Drives Reveal New Details on Census Citizenship Question," *The New York Times*, May 30, 2019, https://www.nytimes.com/2019/05/30/us/census-citizenship-question-hofeller.html.
40 Michael Wines, "Fight Over Census Documents Centers on Motive for Citizenship Question," *The New York Times*, June 12, 2019, https://www.nytimes.com/2019/06/12/us/census-citizenship-question-motives.html.
41 Wines, "Fight Over Census Documents Centers on Motive for Citizenship Question."
42 Trip Gabriel and Michael Wines, "Ohio Congressional Map is Illegal Gerrymander, Federal Court Rules," *The New York Times*, May 3, 2019, https://www.nytimes.com/2019/05/03/us/politics/ohio-gerrymander-ruling.html.
43 Adam Liptak, "Supreme Court Green-Lights Gerrymandering and Blocks Census Citizenship Question," *The New York Times*, June 27, 2019, Opinion.
44 Tera W. Hunter, "When Slave Holders Got Reparations," *The New York Times*, April 16, 2019, https://www.nytimes.com/2019/04/16/opinion/when-slaveowners-got-reparations.html.
45 Stacy Abrams, "We Cannot Resign Ourselves to Dismay and Disenfranchisement," *The New York Times*, May 15, 2019, Opinion, https://www.nytimes.com/2019/05/15/opinion/stacey-abrams-voting.html.
46 Ibid.
47 Carol Anderson, "Our Democracy Is Being Stolen. Guess Who the Thieves Are." *The New York Times*, March 14, 2019, https://www.nytimes.com/2019/03/14/opinion/voting-fraud-north-carolina.html.
48 U.S. Census Bureau, World Population Prospects 2017, https://population.un.org/wpp/. Elaboration data by the United Nations, Department of Economic and Social Affairs, Population Division, www.worldometers.info.
49 Muata Ashby, *Egyptian Mysteries*, vol. 1 (Miami, FL: Cruzian Mystic Books, 2004); Ernest Alfred Wallis Budge, *The Gods of the Egyptians: Or, Studies in Egyptian Mythology* (New York: Dover Publications, 1969); Anthony T. Browder, *Nile Valley Contributions to Civilization* (Washington, DC: The Institute of Karmic Guidance, 1992); Theodor Abt and Erik Hornung, *Knowledge for the Afterlife: The Egyptian Amduat—A Quest for Immortality* (Zurich: Living Human Heritage Publication, 2003); Maulana Karenga, *Maat, the Moral Ideal in Ancient Egypt* (London: Routledge 2004); Anna Mancini, *Maat Revealed: Philosophy of Justice in Ancient Egypt* (Buenos Books America, 2004); Michael Rice, *Egypt's Making: The Origins of Ancient Egypt 5000–2000 BC* (London and New York: Routledge, 1990).

50   Budge, *The Gods of the Egyptians*, 418.
51   Richard H. Wilkinson, *The Complete Gods and Goddesses of Ancient Egypt* (London: Thames & Hudson, Ltd., 2003), 218.
52   Budge, *The Gods of the Egyptians*, 418.
53   Budge, *The Gods of the Egyptians*, 417.
54   Ibid.
55   Niall Ferguson, *Civilization: The West and the Rest* (New York: Penguin Press, 2011).
56   Cheryl Grills, "African Psychology," in *Black Psychology*, ed. Reginald Jones (Hampton, VA: Cobb & Henry Publishers, 2004).
57   Reginald Jones, ed., *Black Psychology*, 4th Ed (Hampton, VA: Cobb & Henry Publisher, 2004), 175–176.
58   Vaughan, "African American Cultural History and Reflections on Jung in the African Diaspora."
59   Matthew Rosenberg, Nicholas Confessore, and Carole Cadwalladr, "How Trump Consultants Exploited the Facebook Data of Millions," *The New York Times*, March 17, 2018. Christopher Wylie, who helped found the data firm Cambridge Analytica and worked there until 2014, has described the company as an "arsenal of weapons" in a culture war.
60   Liptak, "Supreme Court Green-Lights Gerrymandering and Blocks Census Citizenship Question."
61   See Akhil Reed Amar, "Actually the Electoral College Was a Proslavery Ploy." *The New York Times*, April 6, 2019, Opinion; Sean Wilentz, "The Electoral College Was Not a Pro-Slavery Ploy," *The New York Times*, April 4, 2019, Opinion.
62   David Brooks, "The Case for Reparations: a Slow Convert to the Cause," *The New York Times*, March 7, 2019; Kriston Capps, "Elizabeth Warren's Housing Crisis Plan Hints at Reparations," *The New York Times*, January 4, 2019.
63   Vaughan, "African American Cultural History and Reflections on Jung in the African Diaspora."

Chapter 8

The Racial Complex

Fanny Brewster

I was first drawn to Jung's mention of what I have termed the *racial complex* through his comment in volume 10 of *The Collected Works*, in which he said the following:

> Just as the coloured man lives in your cities and even within your houses, so also he lives under your skin, subconsciously. Naturally it works both ways. Just as every Jew has a Christ complex, so every Negro has a white complex and every American (white) a Negro complex. As a rule the coloured man would give anything to change his skin, and the white man hates to admit that he has been touched by the black.[1]

At the time of these words Jung had begun writing about America's ethnic situation—what he believed were the problematic racial differences between white people and black people and the causes of such differences. Though he did not say very much in this particular paper, *The Complications of American Psychology* (1930), he emphasized the negative "fall-out" from the influence of the "primitive"—African and Native Americans—on white American society.[2] It seems important to expand on Jung's initial writing about the racial complex, Negro and American, because in referring to African Americans he only identified their desire to become white—to change ethnicity.

Embedded in Jung's minimalist comment is so very much that speaks to our unconscious processes of "race" and racism in the United States. As with much of Jung's work from decades ago, it rests with others who have an interest to deconstruct, refine, and examine for applicability his theories to our 21st-century lives. I believe that within us and at times holding us are psychological complexes. I also believe that a complex that is devoted to raciality, racism, and ethnicity does exist. At the time of Jung's bare reference to what I have termed a *racial complex*, he could only identify an Africanist wish to be white and white "hate" at touching the skin of African Americans.

His focus was initially on skin-color differences as a determining factor for defining intellectual functioning, spiritual beliefs, and interpersonal behaviors. I believe that many in our American Jungian community have been uncomfortable with Jung's words from the 1930s—these words with their negative racial commentaries generally about African Americans and specifically about those of Africanist lineage. As a result, I believe that we have, like the larger collective, cultural racial complexes.

As an Africanist individual I do not have a white complex as Jung stated because I wish to be white. I have a *cultural racial complex* that embodies all that I have inherited due to this life—personal associations, the lives of my ancestors, and archetypal patterns of all that has come before. In discussing how Freud became the modern-day discoverer of the unconscious, Jung addresses the issue of complexes:

> The via regia to the unconscious, however is not the dream, as he thought, but the complex which is the architect of dreams and of symptoms. Nor is this via so very "royal," either, since the way pointed out by the complex is more like a rough and uncommonly devious footpath that often loses itself in the undergrowth and generally leads not into the heart of the unconscious but past it.[3]

I can appreciate Jung's idea and image of the complex as a devious footpath because it suits one of my ideas regarding a racial complex. I would like to return to shadow for a moment—the place where we hide in the "undergrowth" all the things we cannot tolerate seeing, feeling, and experiencing. I think our racial complexes often live in that dark place of shadow. They can also become that rough footpath that keeps knocking us down and leading us astray. African Americans, I believe, have known more on a conscious level regarding this fact because they have been on the negative symptomatic end of the racial complex.

Although American society's complicated racial relationship has been well documented, there is still so much more to tell. Within the last 150 years we have begun to open Pandora's box regarding ethnic issues and racism in the United States. Today I believe we have more of a dialogue than ever before. But if we are to believe Jung, these conversations will not eliminate our racial complexes.

I agree with Jung. Complexes, as psychic material from the unconscious, develop and have a free will of their own.

I think the only control we can exercise—through free will—on these autonomous split-off parts of psychic material is to first learn about them, further unveiling them through shadow work and seeing into our cultural individual and group defenses. By then engaging in ego strengthening, we support the discovering of places where we project our weaknesses and shadow onto an Other.

Our Racial Cultural Complexes

What exactly are our racial complexes? As an African American I have a white American complex—or so Jung believed. How does it haunt me? How am I *hag*-ridden?

When I was a child, my grandmother used to talk about haunts or hags riding people and the things you needed to do to not incur the wrath of haunts or spirits. She also used to speak about the healing remedy for getting rid of haunts. Let's say my racial complex with its white complex haunting me lives in my unconscious self—lowercase *s*. How might I be uncomfortable in my own skin, certainly with my identity? How does my ethnicity cause me a repetitive experience of the psychological trauma of identity tied to race as an individual as well as tied to an American group identity?

Growing up African American meant that I learned racial lessons at a very young age. The lesson of skin-color differences brought with it sociological and psychological wounds and the trauma of racism. This is a fact of living in the United States. It is a personal experience as well as a known part of our American societal history. It is certainly my own cultural collective group experience.

The suppression, repression, and amnesia of racial complexes has contributed to the wounding of the American psyche. Over centuries Americans have continued to inflict physical and psychological pain because of a constructed idea regarding differences due to ethnicity. Collective cultural trauma shows itself as having a cultural racial complex that was formed and nurtured, first by slavery and then through the following decades by the racist aspects of American life. Jung's theory of opposites has done much in probably an unintended way to promote American racism. Samuel Kimbles has spoken eloquently regarding the racial issues inherent in groups that have their own cultural rituals and rites of passage.[4] One of the landmark traumatic rites was the passage of Africans to the Americas as slaves. This event remains an extremely uncomfortable discussion topic for many Americans, even though we have not even begun to see deeply into the psychological trauma still being experienced by the descendants of slaves. The horror of American slavery lasted for centuries. Unfortunately, in our unconscious amnesia, we continue to live out our fears through racial complexes often expressed through racist actions. Jung says, "Complexes are something so unpleasant that nobody in his right senses can be persuaded that the motive forces which maintain them could betoken anything good."[5]

No wonder we have avoided, even within the Jungian community, an in-depth discussion of racial complexes.

Dissociation in the s/Self Relationship

Identity is crucial to psychological health and well-being. From the beginning of our biological, and I would also say psychic, lives, which include the DNA of the archetypes, we need recognition in the form of identity. Because of racial relations in the United States, we are taught early on about ethnic differences. Jung pointed to something that was present in our shadowed collective unconscious that was, and continues to be, acted out through negative racial acts.

When we cannot recognize or see ourselves because of a complex taking over ego consciousness, then we are limited in developing a connection between our ego selves and the archetypal Self. This dissociation in the s/Self relationship belongs to the traumatic event of slavery and all the racial identity problems that have followed as part of a racial complex in the United States. We have seen the struggle to "find" the "right" identity for African Americans—within African Americans themselves as well as in the collective at large. First we were called black African, then colored, then nigger emerged and has reemerged, black—the negative one and the one of beauty in the 1960s—finally we have arrived at African American, again. Our American collective has struggled with finding its identity in terms of how we will and must be treated because of skin-color differences and the cultural meaning of such a circumstance.

The psychological trauma of being Other impacts people of color. We can be Other, but a part of our consciousness makes the Other—the white person— also an Other. One of the aspects of white privilege and its cultural white racial complex is that it perceives itself as the only thing that can confer qualities such as "Otherness." In the case of African Americans, these qualities, both consciously and unconsciously in the shadow, would have us be "primitive," not rational-minded or reasonable human beings. We would be unintelligent and slow to learn. These beliefs come from racial complexes that have lived unexplored within the shadow for many centuries since the arrival of slaves in the Americas in the 1600s.

The cultural collective that is African American has, as a group, been bound, not only by the act of physically being bound for centuries, but also by the psychological suffering of being individuals held within a racist societal structure. This structure has controlled and promoted through conscious habits the educational, financial, and emotional deprivation of this cultural collective. This external imposition of a negative racial construct has supported the deepening of a negative racial complex within individuals and in group psychic consciousness. Lynchings and the rise of groups such as the Ku Klux Klan are examples of this type of negative group consciousness—a cultural complex that erupted into American society. Jung stated that complexes are split-off parts of psychic material originally caused by trauma. I have considered a specific complex, that of the racial complex, partly because it has not been discussed in any manner within historic Jungian psychology circles, with the exception of Jung's reference to it in 1934 and American psychiatrist John Lind in 1913 with the publication of his article in the first volume of *Psychoanalytic Review*.[6]

I look to Jungian practitioners to open a dialogue on one of Jung's theories that emerged from his work on the Word Association Experiment. The racial complex is one such underdeveloped theory. I have considered a written discussion of the racial complex because I believe we are caught in this complex, in a constant struggle with it, while attempting to forget about its existence. The pain of such a complex, as Jung noted, has left us without any peace. The very real suffering of racial discrimination, which has led to physical death because of one's identity, can cause severe emotional trauma. It feels like the never-ending waves of a tsunami. The days of mass lynchings of African Americans have passed. However, the terms *alt-right, states' rights, voter suppression*, and *white nationalists* all date back to a time when psychological and physical trauma were daily events for Africanist people. African Americans carry not only the collective fear of such events held in their Africanist psyche but also the individual anxiety at the continuous possibility of being physically harmed due to their skin color.

There has been a reluctance to discuss racial complexes in our Jungian collective. Jung himself predicted that this could happen due to the very "devilish" nature of complexes—they appear to be adequately suppressed by the ego only to come back stronger. Jung identified the Germanic group cultural complex that could be seen in the rise of Nazism leading to World War II.

This rise of a group of people who participated in the murder of millions showed the distinct manner in which complexes can take hold of us. Individuals made up the armies, medical staff, and administrators that formed Hitler's Nazi party. The victims of the trauma of this persecution were also individuals. We can lose sight of the importance of the individual—not only in terms of a process of individuation, which the Self promotes, but also when dealing with complexes and with the suffering that can occur. The untold millions who have been tortured and/or murdered are so great that it is difficult to comprehend and stay within our own ego's psychological place of comfort.

When complexes haunt us, we lack peace of mind. The trauma of racism and its affects has not disappeared; it accompanies each of us on a daily basis. I propose that any racial complex of African Americans will be closely "identified" with this type of trauma. I want to stress what Jung knew: *complexes do not disappear.* They are uncovered. They are considered and worked with until we can learn how to live with them in some way that creates less continuous psychic and emotional pain.

Healing Intergenerational Trauma

How can we do this? How can we create less pain when that pain was originally caused by an initial traumatic event such as the African Holocaust? We must first open ourselves to conversations about historical collective trauma and intergenerational psychic pain lived out in everyday contemporary life. Silence only harms us. The reoccurring trauma experienced as a racial complex moves in relationship with the self and the shadow. This relationship creates anxiety and a fear specific to the trauma that initially caused such a complex to develop and becomes repeatedly realized through the generations.

The tension and anticipatory anxiety caused by issues of racial identity, discrimination, and fear of physical harm only intensifies psychic pain and a separation or dissonance with the Self. Of course psychological work to reconcile the s/Self would be complicated—as Jung said of American psychology when addressing the issue of ethnic differences in America. In the final paragraph of his essay on complexes, he says, "As can be seen, I have contented myself with describing only the essential features of the complex theory."[7] He does not provide the solutions that are created by the complexes but does say "Three important problems would have to be dealt with: the therapeutic, the philosophical, and the moral. All three still await discussion."[8]

This discussion of an African American cultural racial complex, brought about by the trauma of the African Holocaust and racism, is one avenue for looking at our deeply complicated American collective as well as individual problems in all three of these areas that Jung has posited—the therapeutic, the philosophical, and the moral.

Complexes do not go away. We bring them into consciousness out of the shadow. We make the unconscious conscious. As we delve further into Jungian theories and concepts, it is incumbent upon us to explore, discuss, and examine those things that continue to haunt us. This the true work of being aligned with depth psychological work. When we pick up the slender threads of the beautifully woven tapestry of consciousness and begin to create a different pattern with this familiar fabric, we follow a depth psychological way. I believe the development of ideas regarding cultural racial complexes are in alignment with this proposition.

Two aspects of racial complexes that are exposed through racism are emotional suffering and the pain of invisibility. These aspects combined with the struggle for identity are only a part of what needs healing within the parameters of negative racial complexes. I recognize these aspects because I have seen them played out in my own life, in my family, and in my cultural collective. I have seen the results of negative racial complexes exhibited in the broader American collective.

How do we begin to think about healing these places of psychic pain—of longstanding psychological suffering? Most of us wish for and strongly desire a state of inner peace, a harmonic connection between our ego and our unconscious, in this case our archetypal Self. But Jung gives us a warning in regard to our complexes as we seek harmony. He discusses this in *A Review of the Complex Theory*:

> We are only too ready to make anything unpleasant *unreal*—long as we possibly can. The outbreak of neurosis signalizes the moment when this can no longer be done ... from this moment the complex establishes

itself on the conscious surface; it can no longer be circumvented and proceeds to assimilate the ego-consciousness step by step, just as previously, the ego-consciousness tried to assimilate it. This eventually leads to a neurotic dissociation.[9]

The beauty of analytical psychology is that it can oftentimes provide the answer to our suffering. The remedy is in the poison. Jungian psychology is a psychology of discovery. The path will usually be in the form of a labyrinth—it will, of course, *not* be easy. The acceptance of this fact and the actual experience of both the suffering and joy of life—both the pain of the complex and the numinosity of the divine Self—*can* continue to offer us hope.

Acknowledgment

An earlier version of this essay first appeared in *The Racial Complex: A Jungian Perspective on Culture and Race* (Routledge, 2019).

Notes

1 C. G. Jung, "The Complications of American Psychology" (1930), in *The Collected Works of C. G. Jung*, vol. 10, *Civilization in Transition* (Princeton: Princeton University Press, 1968), 963.
2 Ibid.
3 C. G. Jung, "A Review of the Complex Theory" (1934), in *The Collected Works of C. G. Jung*, vol. 8, *The Structure and Dynamics of the Psyche* (Princeton: Princeton University Press, 1969), 210.
4 Samuel Kimbles, *Phantom Narratives: The Unseen Contributions of Culture to Psyche* (London: Rowman & Littlefield, 2014).
5 Jung, "A Review of the Complex Theory," 211.
6 Ibid.; John Lind, "The Color Complex in the Negro," *Psychoanalytic Review* 1, no. 4 (1913): 404–414.
7 Jung, "A Review of the Complex Theory," 219.
8 Ibid.
9 Ibid., 211.

Chapter 9

Crime and Punishment in America

A Cultural Black Hole

Ronald Schenk

In 2016, a young woman, Karina Vetrano, was savagely murdered while jogging in a Queens park in New York City. The entire city was appalled and over 100 detectives were assigned to the case, but little headway was made in finding the killer. Months after the murder, a police lieutenant played out a hunch. Twice, months before the murder, he had spotted a black man, Chanel Lewis, in the predominately white neighborhood where the crime took place. Mr. Lewis lived with his mother, three miles away in Brooklyn, having graduated from a school for the learning disabled. In the subsequent investigation Mr. Lewis was accused of the murder after DNA samples and a confession were obtained. In the trial that followed, the defense asserted that the DNA evidence was tainted and video showed the defendant confused during the confession in which he stated he had conducted the attack because he had been angry at the loud music of a neighbor. The trial ended with a hung jury and a new trial was called. The entire incident with its issues of racial profiling, forced confessions, and mishandling of evidence was reminiscent of the beating and rape of a jogger in Central Park in 1989 when five young men of color were wrongly convicted.[1]

In 1990 Tyrone Brown, a black teenager, was sentenced to life for smoking marijuana while on probation. After 17 years in prison, he was released to lifetime probation.

In 2007 Emma Stewart, a single African American mother of two living in Texas, was arrested on a drug sweep occasioned by what turned out to be false testimony to the prosecution. Although her court-appointed attorney urged a plea bargain, she maintained she was innocent of all charges. After a month in jail she decided to plead guilty to receive probation and avoid years in prison. Out of prison she found herself branded a drug felon and, therefore, evicted from public housing, homeless, without custody of her children, ineligible for food stamps, and dispossessed of voting privileges. Another black woman under similar circumstances as a convicted felon in the same state who did vote received five years in prison as punishment.

Richard Boyer has spent 34 years on death row in San Quentin Prison with no sign of execution or release.

These individuals represent exemplary cases of a condition in the psyche of the country, mass incarceration, that has become manifest in the last several decades but has its roots going back hundreds of years to the country's settling. Although its emergence indirectly adversely affects the entire country, it directly affects only a relatively small community within the whole, that of urban African Americans, most particularly young male adults. Its concealment from the main body of the culture at the immense cost of financial resources and drainage of psychological energy indicates the split-off, yet powerful underlying gravitational pull of a cultural complex. A psychological agency of this kind has a life of its own, the roots of which are there to be teased out and analyzed in its interactions with other psychological systems.

Prison and Race in America

Imprisonment and slavery have always been associated either directly or indirectly in American cultural practice from its beginnings. Both slaves and convicts were seen as property, shipped and held in the same quarters, and sold in the same manner. Means and equipment for punishment and torture in jails were borrowed from those used with slaves. As with the lifetime control of slaves, the control of criminal offenders went beyond their jail sentences as they were barred from rights to maintain marriages, obtain jobs, and enter contracts. At the time of the country's founding, slaves were considered property. The Northwest Ordinance of 1787 passed by the Confederation Congress forbade slavery and involuntary servitude in the Northwest Territory *except as a form of punishment for crime* (a stipulation repeated in the 13th Amendment to the Constitution). They also determined that runaway slaves were to be returned to their owners. People of color were singled out in the North for possible conviction for several reasons, most prominently that they could be fugitive slaves. The United States Constitution, written by men of social status, was structured to protect land and slaveowners, and as James Madison wrote, the goal of government was to "protect the minority of the opulent against the majority."[2] The Constitution directly contradicted the Declaration of Independence in that people of color were not considered citizens, and it proportioned electoral votes by counting slaves as 3/5 of an individual, when determining a state's population, an appeasement not only to plantation owners but also to poor whites to maintain their support in that they could derive some consolation from not being enslaved.

In 1829 the first person to be held in a US penitentiary was black, "one who was born of a degraded and depressed race."[3] In 1831 Gustave de Beaumont and Alexis de Tocqueville noted higher proportions of black to whites prisoners in the Northern states—1 out of 4 in prison versus 1 out of 30 in the general population, an indication that jails served as a substitute for slavery. In 1857, Chief Justice of the Supreme Court Roger Taney wrote the following in the Dred Scott Case:

> people of African descent are not and cannot be citizens of the United States. ... the black man has no rights which the white man is bound to respect ... [and] the enslaved African race were not meant to be included in the Declaration of Independence.[4]

This attitude prefigured Supreme Court decisions in the decades to come, as the court upheld segregation in direct opposition to the 14th Amendment of 1868 granting citizenship to all persons born in the United States and equal protection to all citizens. The early decades of the nation set the tone of bias and discrimination against people of color using the criminal justice system in conjunction with slavery to maintain control on the basis of race. Although slavery was abolished per se by the 13th Amendment, the conditions of slavery were maintained in one form or another over the ensuing decades.

After the Civil War and even during Reconstruction, Southern African Americans were essentially abandoned by the North, leaving them without a means for satisfying basic needs for housing, employment, and education. A new form of slavery evolved, the "Second Slavery," wherein the only available work for freed slaves was under inhumane conditions for pittance as wages, leaving them living in impoverished conditions, indentured to landowners for life. W. E. B. Du Bois summed up the development: "the slave went free, stood a brief moment in the sun; and then moved back again toward slavery," a situation that was "a paradox too tragic to explain."[5] The slave-like working conditions for black men and women led directly to the deaths of many; others bore the marks on their bodies "of the most inhuman and brutal treatment ... so poor and emaciated that their bones almost come through their skin."[6] Lynchings of black men became endemic, more than 4,000 over a matter of six decades, a reprisal of the archetypal spectacle of public execution as punishment of centuries past, and lynchings were then replaced with a rise in the number of death sentences.[7] "Black Code" laws aimed at black people, delineating "offences" such as "vagrancy" that were essentially meant to humiliate any person of color that did not conform to social expectations based on white superiority, were upheld by the Supreme Court.[8] In addition, racially biased legislation and attitudes popularly known as "Jim Crow," which were *imported from Northern states* where segregation had been experimented with, provided a plentitude of prisoners who lived and worked under harsh conditions, with their labor contracted out for the profit and benefit of the state. (As a side note: at this time the blossoming temperance movement against saloons was reinforced by a racist mentality that feared the black man under the influence of alcohol, prefiguring the paranoia regarding black people and drugs in the 1970s–1990s.) The custom of using prisons as a means of surveillance and as a way to control people of color can be seen in the fact that in 1880 black people made up about one-tenth of the population nationally, but approximately one-third of the nation's prison population.[9]

The two World Wars brought about the massive migration of black people to Northern urban centers where they were systematically funneled into ghettoes, keeping them separate from whites and, at the same time, under the surveillance and control of white people. "Ghettoization" forced black people to live under prison-like, overcrowded, underserved conditions with little chance for socioeconomic advancement due to engrained white bias against black people in the areas of housing, education, and jobs, thus creating a self-perpetuating cycle of marginality. Seven out of eight inhabitants of high poverty urban areas were of minority races.[10] Unhealthy and dangerous conditions in black ghettoes have shortened life expectancy and have made life precarious due to interracial violence from which the black community is unprotected.[11] The disparity in living conditions between ghetto and suburban life goes largely unnoticed until violent civil strife breaks out—as it did after World War I, during the 1960s, and in more recent riots responding to police brutality, such as in Fergusson, Missouri, in 2014. In 1968 the Kerner Commission on civil unrest stated bluntly,

> what white Americans have never fully understood—but what the Negro can never forget—is that white society is deeply implicated in the ghetto. White institutions created it, white institutions maintain it, and white society condones it. ... Our nation is moving toward two societies—one black, one white—separate and unequal.[12]

When Justice Anthony Scalia questioned a young black woman regarding affirmative action, stating point blank that he did not see why black people needed a college education given their diminished capacity to learn, he was echoing a sentiment held by leaders of the United States since its founding. Frederick Douglass described this condition to the National Colored Convention in 1853:

> A heavy and cruel hand has been laid upon us. As a people, we feel ourselves to be not only deeply injured, but grossly misunderstood. Our white countrymen do not know us. They are strangers to our character, ignorant of our capacity, oblivious to our history and progress, and are misinformed as to the principles and ideas that guide us as a people. American citizens estimate us as being a characterless and purposeless people; and hence we hold up our heads, if at all, against the withering influence of a nation's scorn and contempt.[13]

The Kerner Commission got only one thing wrong—the United States has always been a divided society, separate and unequal. Racism is a deep character agency in American culture. Beginning in the 1970s a cultural complex was discharged with full force, stemming from its racist traditions of strict penal corrections in the North and slavery in the South—the mass incarceration of people of color, particularly young black men.

Mass Incarceration

I will start with brutal facts:

- For several years up until the early 1970s approximately 100 of every 100,000 American adults were imprisoned. By the 1980s the number had reached 700 of every 100,000 adults, by far the highest incarceration rate of any country.[14] By 2003, 1,000 of every 100,000 adults was in prison for a total of 2.1 million incarcerated adults, and by 2007 more than 7 million Americans were involved in the correctional system.[15] In 2016 the numbers were 450 out of every 100,000 adults were incarcerated; there were 6,741,400 individuals in the correctional system, with 2,173,800 incarcerated and 4,650,900 under correctional supervision.[16] Currently, America makes up one-fifth of the world's population, but holds 25 percent of the world's prison population.
- Whereas African Americans made up 12 percent of the total population in 1995, they made up 53 percent of the prison population that year and 70 percent in 2009. African Americans were eight times more likely than white people to be imprisoned. Sixty percent of black high-school dropouts could expect to be imprisoned at some point in their lives as well as 1 in 3 black males overall as compared to 1 in 400 white males.[17]
- From 1980 to the mid-1990s, although drug use did not increase, the rate of arrest for drug use increased by 250 percent.[18]
- Seventy-five percent of those incarcerated for nonviolent drug offenses are black, despite the fact that white people use drugs more than people of color.[19]

Background factors: In the 1960s the deplorable living conditions of black urban ghettoes along with unfavorable economic conditions of the time gave rise to several urban riots. In addition, the civil rights movement, the anti-Vietnam War movement, and the reemergence of the feminist movement, generated unrest in the establishment white patriarchal culture. Playing on endemic cultural fear, politicians responded by creating the rhetoric of "the breakdown of law and order," describing a perceived surge of criminality that it equated with movements for social change. Richard Nixon insisted that increasing crime "can be traced directly to the spread of the corrosive doctrine that every citizen possess an inherent right to decide for himself which laws to obey ...."[20] In his 1964 campaign, Barry Goldwater admonished, "Choose the way of the (Johnson) Administration and you have the way of the mob in the street."[21]

Inevitably, crime became associated with race by segregationists and, more covertly, by the general public. The face of the threatening criminal came to be a black face, something to be feared and from which white society needed protection. The genuflecting phraseology that came into vogue, "crack down on crime," meant an increase in focus on "crime in the streets" with black urban ghettoes as the chief targets. Central to the reemergence of Nixon and the Republican party was an underlying racism. H. R. Haldeman revealed that as president, Nixon "emphasized that you have to face the fact that the whole problem is really the blacks. The key is to devise a system that recognizes this while not appearing to."[22] What could be interpreted as the cultural failings of a system that failed a marginalized population was instead put forth as being caused by the moral failings of that same population in light of the professed American values of individual responsibility and independence. In 1968, 81 percent of respondents to a Gallup poll thought that "law and order had broken down" with the majority blaming "Negroes who start riots."[23] Simultaneous with the economic breakdown of urban ghettoes and urban unrest, an epidemic of crack cocaine spread throughout urban America. The underlying cultural conflation of crime, poverty, substance abuse, and race, inherent in the American psyche since Colonial times, thus gained a new foothold in the wake of a newly aroused generalized fear, resulting in a "war" on crime and drugs aimed at the urban ghetto.

In addition to targeting drug use, the racially biased criminalization of poverty also found a second front in an assault on welfare. Whereas the black male came to be imagined in the form of a drug-using "human predator," the black female was associated with "welfare fraud," resulting in rigid control of the "welfare queen" and the diminishment of benefits, adding to the culture of poverty that gave rise to drug use in the first place. All of this occurred while corporate America gained billions of dollars in government "welfare" through tax loopholes.

Ronald Reagan, the master of the "sound bite," was expert at implying racial association with social problems without using explicitly racist terms. Reagan's super-masculinized spectacle of gesticulation regarding law and order led to the defection of 20 percent of Democratic voters, most of them poor whites. In 1982 Reagan announced a War on Drugs that turned half of the Justice Department specialists in white-collar crime into marshals of street crime and increased the budget of federal antidrug law enforcement agencies by as much as 3,000 percent. In 1988 a new Anti-Drug Abuse Act was put into effect expanding penalties for drug offenders, eliminating benefits regarding housing and education for those convicted of drug offenses, including a five-year minimum sentence for drug possession. Later that year George H. W. Bush ran his infamous campaign ad depicting the black rapist Willie Horton as the face of crime that threatened the nation. The next year, as president, Bush referred to drug use as "the most pressing problem facing the nation."[24] In 1994, in an attempt by the Democratic party under President Clinton to wrest control of the "tough on crime" issue from Republicans, Clinton introduced his "three strikes and you're out" policy and put into action a bill that created dozens of federal capital crimes, mandated life sentences, and allocated billions of dollars for spending on expanding prisons and local law enforcement agencies, resulting in the largest increase in federal and state imprisonment under any president. Tellingly, whereas the budget for federal housing was cut by $17 billion under Clinton, at the same time excluding anyone with a criminal history, the budget for prison construction was increased by $19 billion. President Obama did release several minor offenders from federal prison, but he also continued the policy of criminalizing the poor through penalizing drug use, vastly increasing federal funds for antidrug law enforcement in the Economic Recovery Act of 2009. Joe Biden, "liberal" 2020 Democratic presidential candidate, was a champion of militarized police action against drug offenders (just as he was a proponent of the war in Iraq). President Trump, through his first Justice Department Secretary, Jeff Sessions, advocated maximum sentences for federal prosecutions, and then turned an about face, backing a proposal for reducing the incarcerated population in the wake of conservative focus upon the extreme financial cost previous sentencing policies had entailed.

There has never been any conclusive evidence that the War on Drugs has diminished drug use or that mass incarceration has reduced crime. In the face of its fear, fear that might be described as fear of dispossession by the Other in whatever form that might take, the nation has resorted to a simplistic exhibition of overly masculinized muscle flexing through the theater of violent control by the penal state. This has cost billions of dollars and involved the wholesale hypervigilance and warehousing of a portion of the population through the mass incarceration of males from the black community as well as diminished benefits for thousands of households. This particular phenomenon is part of a lifelong cultural tradition of throwing money and militaristic power, heedless of the complexity of factors at work and void of imagination and insight, at whatever appears threatening to the white, patriarchal, corporate establishment both domestically and internationally, resulting in a perpetual cycle of impoverishment and marginalization of the disenfranchised. It has also given rise to the very behaviors of delinquency and drug use it is meant to diminish. In short, the mass incarceration of black people, under the control and vigilant eye of a predominately white, elitist patriarchy and in service to a fearful culture obsessed with the fantasy of protection, is one of many instances that gives lie to the received fantasy that the culture operates bravely out of a ground of freedom, equality, and democratic values. Loïc Wacquant lays it out:

> [T]he law-and-order merry-go-round is to criminality what pornography is to amorous relations: a mirror deforming reality to the point of the grotesque that artificially extracts delinquent behavior from the fabric of social relations in which they take root and make sense, deliberately ignores their causes and their meanings and reduces their treatment to

a series of conspicuous position-takings ... rather than the pragmatic attention to the real, ... (and) simultaneously appeases and feeds the fantasies of order of the electorate, reasserts the authority of the state through its virile language and mimics, and erects the prison as the ultimate rampart against the disorders which, erupting out of its underworld, are alleged to threaten the very foundations of society.[25]

Esteemed forensic psychiatrist Karl Menninger has stated unequivocally: "The inescapable conclusion is that society secretly wants crime, needs crime, and gains definite satisfactions from the present mishandling of it."[26]

The Multiple Forms of Racial Bias in the Criminal Justice System

The staggering depth and breadth of bias in American criminal justice is evident in the multiple levels and forms of its process. An exploration of the complexity of these multiplicities starts with the political system. Laws reflect moralities that are subject to relative factors. A society may consider it a crime for an individual to consume a certain substance, but corporations polluting the air, adversely affecting millions of people; maintaining dangerous working conditions in mines or factories; knowingly manufacturing and promoting an addictive tobacco or opioid and then the subsequent marketing of an antidote to that addiction; operating a business (more than 50 in the US) knowing that the customer database has been hacked by foreign operatives and then impeding any government intervention for fear of losing business—none of these is a crime. Legislators create those laws they believe reflect the emotional tone of their electorate. More fundamentally they will make laws that reflect the desires of those lobbyists and corporations that will keep them in power; therefore, they subject themselves to interests that support them financially. In the 1960s and 1970s cultural disorders manifesting in various social movements and urban violence led to the enactment of laws that both reflected and created an image of threat that was simply renewed in a different way—the impoverished, black, urban male under the influence of a substance. Once this image was instilled in the public imagination, spectacularly punitive laws were passed, exempt from critical or rational analysis, involving extreme prison terms, mandatory sentencing, and abolition of parole—all echoes of the severely racist values of Puritan and slave cultures.

Law enforcement has then become the arena of spectacle. Again, how laws are enforced is very much a matter of collective values as well as material benefit. Ghettoes are easy targets for totalitarian drug raids, "round ups," and "sweeps" in service to antidrug laws funded by federal dollars. In America, twice as many black people as white people are stopped and searched, even though incriminating evidence is found only 10 percent of the time. In the past several decades the Supreme Court has, in service to the War on Drugs, basically nullified the 4th Amendment, which calls for probable cause and a warrant to search and reasonable individualized cause for seizure. Although drug use by white people is greater than that of black people, black people are arrested four times as much on drug-related charges, and a hundred times as much for use of crack than white people for the more expensive cocaine powder.[27] Police often have a stake in the arrest through the illegal seizure of property as well as the need to reach a certain quota of arrests. Finally, the militarized nomenclature of "war" on drugs and crime has been carried over into the policies of police forces who employ extreme violence during arrests and "shakedowns" of black people. As a result, 40 percent of police shootings involve black victims, even though they comprise only 13.4 percent of the population.

Antidrug laws have made prosecutors the most powerful agents in the criminal justice system. They have wide discretion in determining the probability of guilt. The fate of the accused, usually too poor to afford bail or an adequate defense attorney let alone a trial by jury, is in the hands of prosecutors. In some cases confessions are forced without the presence of any legal representation for the accused. In cases in which the accused is poor, he or she is represented by a public defender who, even if barely competent, is most often overworked and able to spend only a few minutes with the accused before a hearing. The vast majority of cases end up as plea bargains, with prosecutors essentially deciding how much time in prison the accused will receive. The result is that 95 percent of those charged plead guilty simply to avoid a mandatory sentence.[28] In 2004 the American Bar Association declared, "All too often, defendants plead guilty even if they are innocent, without really understanding their legal rights or what is occurring," in spite of the fact that there is a known link between childhood trauma, mental illness, poverty, and ultimate incarceration.[29] The prosecutor is armed with the full police report, eyewitness interviews, grand jury testimony, test reports, and follow-up investigations, all of which may be slanted, misleading, or just plain false. Often the accused is "loaded up" with charges to give the prosecutor leverage in sentencing and to obtain the testimony of the accused for related cases. If the case does make it to a jury, the prosecutor has unlimited discretion in eliminating potential jurors of color through preemptive challenges. Prosecutorial misconduct has been found to be deliberate—perjury, withholding evidence, coercive interrogation, which has been found in three out of four exonerations that have come to light with DNA testing.[30] Finally, there is egregious disparity in the sentencing of the accused who are rich and white versus the accused who are poor and black. When Trump campaign director Paul Manafort, who had virtually stolen millions, was given less than a five-year sentence with the likelihood of probation in a shorter time, it was noted that a poor black man who had stolen several quarters from a vending machine was given the same amount of time without a chance for probation and a first-time offender was given a mandatory sentence of over 40 years for illegal drug use. This event was reminiscent of the deliberately reckless and fraudulent Wall Street management of banking assets for the purposes of increasing the wealth of managers, as happened in 2008, resulting in the loss of life savings and the financial ruin of millions, when not a single individual was prosecuted.

The prosecutor is the one to decide if a case is to be brought up to a judge for sentencing, and with mandatory minimum-sentencing laws that don't allow parole for nonviolent crimes, the judge has little leeway or discretionary power. In 1982, a man received 40 years for possession and attempting to sell 9 ounces of marijuana. Years later, a man was given a life sentence for a first-time conviction for attempting to sell 23 ounces of crack cocaine. In 2003 an individual was given 25 years for stealing three clubs from a golf shop and another man was given 50 years for stealing children's video tapes, both without a chance for parole. These sentences were all upheld by the Supreme Court against assertions of grossly disproportionate sentencing in violation of the 8th Amendment that protects citizens from cruel and unusual punishment. In 1987 the Supreme Court conceded that racial disparities in sentencing "are an inevitable part of our criminal justice system," due to the supposed difficulty in proving direct intent; thus the courts are, in effect, a source of discriminating practices.[31]

Nor is consignment to America's prisons considered to be cruel and unusual, in spite of the situations in many state and local prisons that are often described by prisoners and outsiders as "hell on earth"[32] and "soul crushing."[33] Once in jail, convicts are subjected to years of punitive conditions designed to break the individual spirit. A long-time prisoner commented that rather than rehabilitation, the goal of prison was vengeance, making the inmates feel "unredeemable." Jails are overcrowded to the point that some accused are forced to wait for days in buses even before their case is brought before the authorities, and then once in jail, they are forced to sleep on a mattress on the floor with poor protection from cold or heat in extreme weather. Personal possessions are taken, movement is controlled, and little attempt is made toward, nor are there resources for, rehabilitation or education. Lockdowns, in which all prisoners are confined to their cells for long periods of time, are common, as is physical, emotional, and sexual abuse by prison guards as well as fellow prisoners. Solitary confinement—24 hours/day for months at a time in an 8×10 cell—awaits anyone acting out, and up to 100,000 prisoners may be in solitary at any one time in the country. Staff are poorly trained and supervised, and in reality, gangs often take over day-to-day control of the prison. Medical and psychiatric services are minimal, and convicts often leave prison with diagnosable mental and physical illness. Depression in prisoners has been described as manifesting in a look of "lostness" and the experience of a kind of death that can lead to suicide.[34] Little attention is paid to differentiating prisoners according to violation nor to the smuggling of contraband. There are recreational facilities and jobs, but prisoners still spend much of their time watching television and playing cards, anything to keep from being bored. In short, prisons are a form of warehouse for a certain segment of the population that has been stigmatized and swept out of sight. As one prisoner put it, the most hellish part of prison is that it is a place of perpetually waiting, waiting for nothing.[35]

Once out of jail, the black ex-convict finds a life of barriers in a community broken by the deprivation of one-third of its males, slim employment opportunities, substandard housing, ravaged educational facilities, and depleted social service benefits such as aid for mothers with dependent children, most of whom are working. In fact, prison is seen by sociologists as a developmental stage in its own right for young black men, and what is accomplished is the proclivity toward further delinquency once outside. For the ex-convict conditions are worse than when he went in. Family life is likely to have been shattered, as 50 percent of black children who live in urban ghettos can expect to have at least one parent in the correctional system.[36] Prison substantially reduces the chances for black men to get married and have a family, and those who have been married have a substantially greater chance of being divorced. Getting a job is doubly difficult. "Being black in America today is essentially like having a felony conviction in terms of finding employment," writes sociologist Devah Pager.[37] A return to crime presents an inviting alternative to young black men, as to be black and a felon makes gainful employment even more difficult. When they are employed, their prison record renders their income up to 40 percent lower than for those who have not been imprisoned. Finally, felons have their right to citizenship taken away in the form of the right to vote or serve on juries. In summary, the black male felon out of prison finds himself alienated, socially and culturally isolated, a proverbial stranger in a strange land, his chances for recidivism greatly increased by a lack of resources and support systems, and the punishment of Sisyphus, forced by Zeus to forever roll a huge boulder up a hill, begins all over.

Conclusion

> The society sets up the crime; the criminal commits it.
>> Ancient Chinese proverb

The black comedian Richard Pryor had a joke in which he visits a jail in Phoenix and finds only black prisoners there. He is taken aback because in the city of Phoenix itself, he had seen no black people. A visit to the city jail in a large metropolitan area has been described as touring a lower rung of Dante's Inferno with naked black men behind bars swarming as close to the visitor as possible with various beseeching appeals. If we take these two images as exemplary given the history and condition of mass incarceration in the United States, some broad questions present themselves. What *necessity* does the criminal as black man and the extravagant extent of his punishment fulfill for white, patriarchal, corporate-run American culture? The obvious is the economic factor: prisons, public and private, directly and indirectly, are the third largest employer in the country. In spite of there being no evidence that mass incarceration reduces crime or drug use, each year $200 billion is invested in the criminal justice system as a whole, money that could otherwise be spent on alleviating conditions that give rise to crime.[38] From a deeper perspective, we would have to say that mass incarceration serves as a way to control the perceived threat to white patriarchal privilege. Mass incarceration both conceals this "threat" and maintains the means of surveillance to exert the power of control over it ... but then we are faced with more vexing questions: Is there a psychological necessity that drives black culture to take on and maintain the role of the oppressed within white culture? What is the underlying source of the cruelty of this dynamic in a culture that rests its foundational identity on fantasies of courage, equality, and freedom?[39]

In his essay, "Guilt," from *On the Genealogy of Morals*, Friedrich Nietzsche locates the origins of selfhood and society in guilt stemming from the forbearance of aggression, which is turned back upon the self. Guilt, in turn, creates memory through a kind of "burning in" to the will, ultimately giving rise to the creation of systems of crime and punishment. The establishment of penal order can then be imagined in economic terms of creditor and debtor. The doing of injury (crime) can be associated with a taking on of credit for which one owes a debt or penance to be paid in any of various ways, most primally through bodily pain. Criminals inflict injuries for which they, in turn, suffer pain in accordance with their crimes and in doing so become psychological subjects. The ability to take on a credit required the development of memory, and the development of memory occurred through pain, leading to guilt, giving birth to the subject "I."

> Man could never do without blood, torture, and sacrifices when he felt the need to create a memory for himself ... all this has its origin in the instinct that realized that pain is the most powerful aid to mnemonics.[40]

Through memory the "I" who made a promise or inflicted an injury is the same "I" who now owes a debt or incurs a punishment. "I" am now "calculable," in my existence, through my payment, the suffering of punishment and the establishment of guilt.

On the other side of the dynamic, the injured or the creditor represented by the state becomes a subject through the pleasure or sense of power and well-being that accompanies the infliction of pain. Carrying out the penalty, bloody in its origins, is an event of "voluptuous pleasure ... a genuine festival, something that ... *was prized the more highly, the more violently it contrasted with the rank and social standing of the creditor.*"[41] At the same time, punishment of the criminal serves society as a sacrificial payment of its debt to the ancestors or gods, thus serving the dual role of working toward relieving the society of its guilt while giving it the pleasure of punishment.

To summarize, pain leads to memory leads to guilt, giving rise to the evolution of society through the notions of crime and penal law. Every injury or crime has its economic equivalent and can be paid back through an exchange of pain and pleasure, providing identity on each side of the dynamic between debtor and creditor. This exchange rests on a pool of blood, which, in turn, is sublimated into sensibilities that create a credible, calculable self through memory. "I" am the perpetrator, suffering the penalty; "I" am the injured, enjoying the punishing. Self is created and sustained as the suffering and enjoyment of punishment becomes more internalized in a perpetual cycle as the debt can never be paid off and the restitution never achieved. Structures of crime and punishment are now achieved through a dynamic and society has achieved an aspect of soul.

The French philosopher Jacques Derrida sees in this idea a precursor to Freud's notion of the death drive from *Beyond the Pleasure Principle* that presents an alternative to the notion that pleasure is the central principle of psychic life.[42] Neither pleasure nor death are originary in that each is entangled with the other. Society is ever creating and destroying in the fluidity of its evolving emergence. Criminal and state both suffer *and* enjoy pleasure. The criminal suffers as debtor never able to fulfill the debt, whereas the society as creditor suffers the initial injury as well as the perpetual guilt of debt owed to the ancestors or gods through sacrifice. At the same time, each gains pleasure, the prisoner (criminal) from the stolen credit as well as the pleasure inherent in suffering, the jailor (society) from the cruelty in inflicting punishment. Each side both suffers and takes pleasure in conjunction with the other. The society needs the expulsion of the bloody scapegoat, just as the scapegoat needs to be cast away by society; each take their place in a larger picture of evolution of the soul of culture.

We might then reimagine the myth of Prometheus as the underlying archetypal core of contemporary mass incarceration. When Zeus decided that humans should present a portion of each animal sacrificed to the gods, Prometheus made two bags from the skin of a cow. In one he put the bones of the sacrificed animal and covered them with a layer of fat. In the other, he placed the meat and concealed it beneath the stomach. Zeus, seeing the fat and assuming it to be accompanied by the meat, chose the former bag. When he discovered he had been tricked into choosing the bones, he went into a rage and denied humans fire, declaring, "Let them eat their flesh raw." But Prometheus stole the fire and gave it to the humans anyway. Society deceitfully offers the gods the bones of mass incarceration in place of meat. The black male becomes the Promethean hero/criminal bringing the stolen fire of guilt to burn memory into the soul of society. For honoring humans over the gods, Prometheus was chained to a rock where Zeus's eagle came every day to eat at his liver and then every night his liver was regenerated. The punishment of this figure can then be imaged in a cultural perspective as the daily consumption and nightly reemergence of the Promethean liver (soul) at work in the larger project of racial oppression.

One final image: Mass incarceration of predominately African American men is the emergent phenomenon or cultural complex that results from the congruence of a perfect storm of inherent factors in the American psyche, namely, fear, of the "Other" based on a fundamental Puritan identity as the Latter Day Children of Israel; racism, most prominently against African Americans not only as a legacy of slavery, but also as a derivative of the association of racial superiority that accompanies the European patriarchy of the Age of Reason and the Enlightenment; capitalism, which carries its own dynamics of competitive aggression of the upper against the lower classes; misogyny, in which inferiority is attributed to the domestic realm, making it the target of budgetary cutbacks. This swirling complex of forces, converging around African American culture and the African American male, in particular, can be imagined to form the gravitational pull of an astronomical black hole from which nothing, not even light, can escape. In space, matter in the form of extremely compacted gas and dust forms an intense gravitational pull that results in an infinite hole. Anything going near the black hole becomes a kind of spiraling wafer that is heated to the point of creating its own strange swirling light before eventually "feeding" the hole by slowly sliding into its maw. The emergence of mass incarceration in the ongoing, autonomous life of a nation can be imagined as a contemporary form of this grotesque, darkened light, perpetually sinking into the oblivion of the inherent fear and aggression underlying American culture.

Author's Addendum

According to Ellen DeWitt, as of May 23, 2019,

- There are 2.3 million adults incarcerated in the United States.
- Whereas black people make up 13 percent of the population, the incarcerated population is 40 percent black.
- Over one-half of the total incarcerated population are classified as having come from living conditions below the poverty level.
- Of those confined one-third have not been convicted of a crime but are too poor to pay bail.[43]

Notes

1 Jan Ransom, "He Confessed to a Deadly Beating, But It Isn't that Simple," *The New York Times*, March 25, 2019, A24.
2 Michelle Alexander, *The New Jim Crow: Mass Incarceration in the Age of Colorblindness* (New York: The New Press, 2012), 25.
3 Ibid., 187.
4 Scott Christianson, *With Liberty for Some: 500 Years of Imprisonment in America* (Boston: Northeastern University Press, 1998), 161.

5 Alexander, *The New Jim Crow*, 22; Adam Gopnik, "The Takeback," *The New Yorker*, April 8, 2019, 78.
6 Bryan Stephenson, "A Presumption of Guilt," *The New York Review of Books*, July 13, 2017, 8.
7 Stephenson, "A Presumption of Guilt," 8–9.
8 Louis Menaud, "In the Eye of the Law," *The New Yorker*, February 4, 2019, 18–22.
9 Christianson, *With Liberty for Some*, 190.
10 Alexander, *The New Jim Crow*, 196.
11 Issues of racism emerged during the water crisis in Flint, Michigan, in 2015, and the flooding crisis in New Orleans during Hurricane Katrina in 2004, while in Baltimore the gap between white and black life expectancy is 20 years, and the United States ranks 43rd in the world in maternal mortality largely due to conditions in urban ghettoes.
12 Fred Harris and Alan Curtis, *The New York Times, Op-Ed*, March 11, 2018, A27.
13 Alexander, *The New Jim Crow*, 140.
14 Ibid.
15 Bruce Western, *Punishment and Inequality in America* (New York: Russell Sage Foundation, 2006), 13; Alexander, *The New Jim Crow*, 60.
16 Zhen Zing, "Jail Inmates in 2016," Bureau of Justice Statistics, February 22, 2018, NCJ 251210, https://www.bjs.gov/index.cfm?ty=pbdetail&iid=6186.
17 Loïc Wacquant, *Punishing the Poor: The Neoliberal Government of Social Insecurity* (Durham: Duke University Press, 2009), 65.
18 Western, *Punishment and Inequality in America*, 58.
19 Eric Schlosser, "America Busted," *The New Yorker*, February 24, 1997, 49.
20 Alexander, *The New Jim Crow*, 41.
21 Ibid., 42.
22 Ibid., 44.
23 Ibid., 46. Similarly, in 1970, 75 percent of the country believed that unarmed students protesting the Vietnam War at Kent State College in Ohio deserved to have been shot by state troopers.
24 Alexander, *The New Jim Crow*, 55.
25 Wacquant, *Punishing the Poor*, xii–xiii.
26 Karl Menninger, *The Crime of Punishment* (New York: Viking, 1968), 84.
27 Western, *Punishment and Inequality in America*, 41.
28 Kate Summerscale, "On the Sofa," *London Review of Books*, January 5, 2017, 32; Jed S. Rakoff, "Why Innocent People Plead Guilty," *New York Review of Books*, November 20, 2014, 16.
29 Alexander, *The New Jim Crow*, 86.
30 The Editorial Board, "Prisoners Exonerated, Prosecutors Exposed," *The New York Times*, Editorial, February 16, 2016, A20.
31 Stephenson, "A Presumption of Guilt," 10.
32 Evans D. Hopkins, "Letter from Prison: Lockdown," *The New Yorker*, February 24 and March 3, 1997, 71.
33 Nick Paumgarten, "Getting a Shot," *The New Yorker*, January 29, 2018, 35.
34 Ibid., 40.
35 Ibid., 45.
36 Schlosser, "America Busted," 49.
37 Katherine Seelye, "Devah Pager Dies at 46: Exposed Shocking Race Bias in Job Market," *The New York Times*, Obituary, November 11, 2018, B12.
38 Alexander, *The New Jim Crow*, 287.

39 See also the chapter "The Soul of Race/The Heart of Color" in my *Dark Light: The Appearance of Death in Everyday Life* (Albany: The State University of New York Press, 2001).
40 Friedrich Nietzsche, *On the Genealogy of Morals*, trans. Walter Kaufmann and R. J. Hollingdale (New York: Vintage, 1969), 61.
41 Ibid., 65. Italics mine.
42 Jacques Derrida, *The Postcard: From Socrates to Freud and Beyond*, trans. Alan Bass (Chicago, The University of Chicago Press, 1987).
43 Ellen DeWitt, "Mass Incarceration by the Numbers," *Stacker*, May 23, 2019.

Gender

The Body Blow of Trumpism

Shame and Fear as a Cultural Complex

Sharon Heath

Cultural complex theory offers a particularly viable lens through which to observe powerful and primitive feelings activated by and within the body politic. And it is the body itself as a repository and agent of social and political attitudes that I'm moved to reflect on here.

In his groundbreaking book *Between the World and Me*, Ta-Nehisi Coates locates the site of racism's most insidious impact in the body of the black person. He fashions his tale as a letter to his young son and begins it with a metaphor that is also quite literal: "Son, Last Sunday the host of a popular news show asked me what it meant to lose my body."[1] Coates blasts though all the noise of our nation's sordid racial history to redefine racism as the creator, not the consequence, of race and to make painfully palpable the existential terror and shame permeating the cells and self-identities of people of color from the beginnings of American slavery up to the present.

In considering the cultural complexes feeding into the phenomenon of Trumpism, my own imagination keeps drawing me to the roles of the void, dissociation from the sacredness of the Earth, and shame and fear experienced in the body in America's current political crisis.

On November 9, 2016, I woke from whatever fitful sleep I'd managed to get with a physical sensation that nearly all of my patients likewise reported in the following days: I felt as if I'd been punched in the gut, a visceral evidence of a cultural complex having been activated. The sensation persisted for some time and was partnered with all the emotions that I imagine would accompany that literal experience: shock, difficulty in catching my breath, a sense of being violated and robbed, not dissimilar to what I'd felt years ago when my home was broken into in the middle of the night less than an hour after my young son had toddled into my bedroom to ask for a glass of water.

Since then, the experience of the "blunt force trauma" of Donald Trump's election has been articulated by many, including David Sedaris in an excruciatingly funny piece in *The Paris Review*, titled "A Number of Reasons I've Been Depressed Lately."[2]

So why was I so surprised several weeks later to read on an acquaintance's social media page a thread of comments responding to a remark by

Valerie Jarrett, senior advisor to President Barack Obama, that Donald Trump's election was a "soul-crushing punch to the stomach"? The comments on the thread were vicious and violent, calling her a bitch, suggesting variously that she needed a "skull crushing shovel to the back of the head" and a literal punch to the stomach; reportedly, the thread of brutal comments made one respondent's face "hurt from smiling."

These comments nearly drove me out of my mind. I shot off a response to my acquaintance telling him I was ashamed of him. Which was rather ironic—at least on one level—coming as it did from a woman who was at that point only able to fall asleep at night after fantasizing about Melania Trump throwing a dinner party for her husband and his cabinet and poisoning the lot of them. It was also cowardly, as the shaming itself was a defense against what I was really feeling, which was terror.

That terror brings me to what Thomas Singer has so aptly imaged as the *teratoma*—or malignant cluster—of personal and cultural complexes to which we are each as vulnerable as we are to those unconscious personal knots of affect (or personal complexes) so fully elucidated by Jung. One of the most tensile threads in my own teratoma was woven in response to my birth as a "red diaper baby." My parents were Jewish communists whose political views were truly their religion until they became aware of Stalin's crimes. My earliest memories are rooted in profound feelings of fear and shame for being connected to the collective devil of that era. When I was in kindergarten, my mother and father were outed on the front page of the *Los Angeles Times* after being named in hearings by the House Un-American Activities Committee (HUAC). My older brother lost school friends overnight. Whereas my father's first childhood memory was of hiding in the rushes by a Ukrainian river from the scythes of Cossacks on horseback seeking the necks of Jews, in the 1950s his siblings with legal immigrant status had to fight deportation from "the beacon of democracy" back to Russia, based on the McCarran-Walter Act's scapegoating of immigrants based on their political beliefs. When Ethel and Julius Rosenberg were executed for espionage, I was given a piggy bank bearing a poignant photo of their children, so that I could contribute my saved pennies and nickels to the orphans' survival and care. I was terrified that my own mother, whose name was also Ethel, would be put to death, too, for her political beliefs. I regressed to wetting the bed at that time.

Additionally, I was an olive-skinned girl, tanned to a deep brown, in my Hermosa Beach home town—in those days what felt like the world capital of Dust Bowl refugees. Those immigrants from Oklahoma were Bible-thumping Baptists whose blue-eyed, tow-headed, pale-skinned children had the habit of throwing the epithet "Nigger" at me when they weren't teaching this child of Jewish communists to pray to the Baby Jesus. That particular epithet was even more confusing to me, as my parents were active in the civil rights movement and used to joke that the darkness of my skin was because my real father was one of their heroes, Paul Robeson. People of all races and cultural origins met and partied at my home, and the communal feeling tone was warm, passionate, and inclusive. But the world outside was perceived—quite rightly, I concluded—as dangerous. When I was four, two of the older neighborhood boys who were the most consistent name callers threw me to the ground in the alley behind my house and forced ashes from an incinerator into my mouth.

I began to detest my skin color, hide my parents' politics, distrust and fear the mainstream, identify with the underdog, and find solace in the natural world. I had a numinous experience of transcending my chronic worry and shame while standing outside on a gloriously sunny day. I reached out to touch a particularly aromatic bush and became intensely aware of the sun-shining-down-on-me-touching-the-bush. Looking back, I can see how that moment seeded the emergence, decades later, of my fictional protagonist Fleur Robins in *The History of My Body*.[3]

I became an activist myself in the peace and freedom movement of the 1960s. But my youthful optimism received a series of body blows when a succession of our most inspiring leaders were assassinated. The violent underbelly of the American story continued to weave itself more thickly into my teratoma. Woven in, too, was the shabby treatment of women within the protest movement, merely one aspect of the rather lengthy shadow of the left, which included large portions of self-righteousness, my own very much included.

I still struggle with that tendency to self-righteousness, and it popped right up, handy-dandy, as an inflating defense when I read those vicious Facebook comments about Valerie Jarrett. The fact is, self-righteousness is popping up right and left each day we're subjected to the latest "shock and awe" of this unusual presidency: starting with Trump's campaign comments that he could murder someone in the middle of Times Square and his supporters would still vote for him and that if Ivanka weren't his daughter, he'd be dating her. Such comments play on epigenetic, as well as personal trauma, and activate alternating states of avoidance and rage.

These days, I'm both a profoundly distressed citizen and that terrified four-year-old girl all over again. And it's not just about Trump and his regime. As Jung wrote in my own year of birth, 1946, in an epilogue to his *Essays on Comparative Events*:

> The conflagration that broke out in Germany was the outcome of psychic conditions that are universal. The real danger signal is not the fiery sign that hung over Germany, but the unleashing of atomic energy, which has given the human race the power to annihilate itself completely. The situation is about the same as if a small boy of six had been given a bag of dynamite for a birthday present ... How can we save the child from the dynamite which no one can take away from him?[4]

What might Jung have said—what do *we* say now—when the threat of species extinction via climate crisis perches like a buzzard side by side on the tree of life with our potential for nuclear catastrophe? How do we understand and respond to the shamefulness of potentially throwing away so lightly the sacrifice, courage, and hopes of over 7,000 generations of *Homo sapiens* who came before us?

The companion pieces to shame are pride and contempt. How many times have we all heard the phrase, "I'm proud to be an American"? Patients I work with who suffer from inordinate shame often come into analysis with the very American hope that I can help them feel absolutely self-confident and powerful. They've starved their bodies, avoided intimacy, shrunk from self-expression, and punished themselves in penitence for not coming anywhere close to their internalization of the American ego ideal of control.

My colleague Constance Crosby first alerted me to the fact that, when one member of a family behaves shamelessly, his or her shame is inevitably unconsciously carried by others in the family. So when we consider a shame complex in its larger context, it must inevitably include shamelessness. Which is where Trump struts in. It's easy to feel shame about Trump. He's crude, thrives on flattery, falls asleep tweeting *covfefe*. Many liberals were ashamed of George W. Bush, made fun of him as the village idiot, but *who* expressed *shame* about Dick Cheney? Liberals may have vilified him as an evil scoundrel, but his vulnerabilities were impeccably hidden behind the armor of intellect and arrogance. He was a master of self-discipline, whereas Trump, with his silly hair and lewd comments and nonsensical tweets, is more the clown. A painfully dangerous and shameless one in his hubris and impulsivity, but a clown nonetheless. Considered as a figure in our waking dream, he could be seen as the psyche's attempt to call attention to the shamelessness of a culture whose dominant cultural complexes sanctify money, power, violence, and individual advancement over the grounding awareness that the survival of our species rides on our soulful interconnection with each other and our shared biosphere. As an Iraqi-born Lyft driver put it to me during a recent ride: "Paradise without others is not paradise."

In 1982, Godfrey Reggio released his film *Koyaanisqatsi*, the first of a series of films in a similar vein whose title was taken from the Hopi word for "life out of balance." It was a wordless tone poem of images portraying the stark intrusion of human technology into the natural world, set to music composed by Phillip Glass. Reggio once commented in an interview that these films have no words because language itself is in such a state of degradation that it can no longer convey the world in which we find ourselves.[5]

There are certain places where I truly live: writing is one of them. It's where the spirit of my own depths speaks to me and where I can allow myself to listen. Some people advise fiction writers to "write what you know"; I've realized that I write what I need to learn. The novel of mine that has so far taught me the most is *The History of My Body*, whose title came to me courtesy of a big dream during analytic training, in which I was told it was my task to serve the Church of Her Body, as opposed to His Story. The novel begins with these words, spoken by a particularly perceptive young girl:

> The Bible says that in the beginning was the void, and it hasn't escaped me how fast the Lord moved to take care of His own particular vacuum—dividing day from night, spitting out vast oceans, carving out competing continents that could one day have the power to blow each other up. What an inspired series of creations to keep the devil of boredom at bay. No wonder God kept seeing that it *was* good.[6]

Later, she comments, "I figure any species lacking fangs and claws had a powerful incentive to evolve an active sort of mind."[7]

Prior to the emergence of that idiosyncratic young protagonist in my psyche, I had insufficient respect for the kind of void to which the human psyche is prone. In virtually every creation myth, the void is the source of all innovation, creation, and discovery, but it's the source of great mischief, too.

Whenever I observe Donald Trump speaking, I see what strikes me as a person suffering from an immense inner void. His comments and actions suggest a man absolutely desperate for mirroring and profoundly unsure that he actually exists at all. That's what makes him so dangerous, for if you don't know that you exist, what is there to lose in allowing or initiating species annihilation?

Another danger of this particular man with his particular dog and pony show is that the trivializations by and about Trump can so easily distract us from the systematic dismantling of our governmental institutions perpetrated, not just by the man who's been described by Australian journalist Chris Uhlmann as "uneasy, lonely, and awkward," but by those staid, suited men in Congress who seek to gut every semblance of beneficial and reasonable care for our common life.[8] The contempt for our democratic institutions and lack of concern for such staples of the collective good as affordable health care, clean air, safe water, and the integrity of the voting process has been, again, quite literally breathtaking.

Post-mortems of Nazi Germany, including Jung's, have asked what makes a large number of people susceptible to such tragic folly. Alas, we in the United States are compelled to ask it now. Since the November election, there have been many insightful analyses of the cultural and class divides in the United States, including Joan C. Williams' *White Working Class: Overcoming Class Cluelessness in America*.[9] Ms. Thompson makes the point that white working-class people can easily resent the elitism and condescension of professionals who serve them, whereas the super wealthy are sufficiently removed from any contact, which allows them to be idealized. The richer they are, the more mystical their aura. Don't forget: the Kardashian family are gods and goddesses for millions of Americans. If voting for the all-too-flawed Donald Trump compensates their experience of shame and fear of economic and social marginalization by taking them closer to those rarefied heights of great riches, then dishonesty and incivility become mere road bumps on the road to the promise of entering America's Holy Land.

But the worship of money in America would not be nearly so pernicious without our tenacious attachment to growth, the shadow side to decades of progress. Growth is an appropriate image for the young. My grandkids respond with delight when I line them up against my service porch door and make a mark to indicate how much they've grown. Growth and expansion are essential driving forces for a child, a young species, and a young nation. In greater numbers, we have a better shot at survival. The drumbeat of world power has pretty much been that the more we use those fine human minds of ours to subdue, domesticate, and essentially conquer other creatures and nature herself, the safer, more stimulated, and prouder we feel.

Alas, the more we conquer others, the more unconsciously ashamed we become. As Jung so aptly commented in *Symbols of Transformation*:

> The fact that an incredibly large proportion of the people languished in the black misery of slavery is no doubt one of the main causes of the singular melancholy that reigned all through the time of the Caesars. It was not in the long run possible for those who wallowed in pleasure not to be infected, through the mysterious workings of the unconscious, by the deep sadness and still deeper wretchedness of their brothers.[10]

As a companion piece we might consider Ta-Nehisi Coates's articulation of the projection of the white conquerers' shamefulness onto people of color. That mechanism of managing the shame and fear of our own violence by projecting it onto others was visible writ large in Nazi Germany, And alas, we're witnessing it in relation to people of color and immigrants today.

As for conquering nature, the more we do so unconsciously, the more dissociated from her we become, which leads not only to destructive technologies, but also to spiritual emptiness, which lends itself to the vicious cycle of pursuing more growth to fill our voids. Which is where that Hopi notion of life out of balance comes in. Jung learned through his own suffering and observation what happens when the principle of perfection overshadows its necessary partner, wholeness. Neither the perpetual seeking of money nor the cultural complex of growth supports the soul's longing for wholeness. The true opposite of shame—and the real antidote to the dark side of the void—is humility: the realization of ourselves as small elements within a significantly larger whole that, in turn, carries and nourishes us.

What would we do without twenty different types of toilet paper to wipe our behinds or the latest iPhone to keep our eyes glued to screens while we walk down the street? The collective exploitation of our voids for profit has been described by Naomi Klein in *This Changes Everything: Capitalism vs. the Climate* as an unchecked, rapacious turn in the evolution of capitalism that reduces the subjectivity and interconnectivity of incarnated life into "thing-ism," where people become brands or demographics and corporations are treated legally as persons.[11] But to my mind, her greatest contribution is her characterization of our situation in the face of climate change: "Time's up."

As Peter Victor, Professor in Environmental Studies at York University and author of *Managing Without Growth*, has said, "What we're seeing is mounting evidence that the planet can't cope with all this extraction of materials and disposal of waste and occupancy of land by humans that we're imposing on it."[12] We are delivering a potentially fatal body blow to the planet that supports and feeds us.

If we take the backlash of Trump voters a little less concretely, what needs re-examining isn't just dividing up the pie more equitably: it's recognizing that the pie, like life itself, is actually limited.

I became a grandmother a few years ago, and from that moment everything mattered even more deeply than before. What most shames and terrifies me these days is how our species' inability to contend with our boredom, our spiritual emptiness, our constant consumption, and our literal enactment of the cultural complex of growth is fast killing off our grandchildren's very future. It's not the Hitlers or Trumps that Jung was talking about, but us. Each of us. *We* are the six-year-olds Jung was warning us about.

So how to hold the tension of opposites between inquiring into what cultural complexes are at play in our national crisis and in ourselves and the moral imperative to take sides when danger and decency require it? I feel that Palestinian-American writer Suheir Hammad offers some wise guidance in her "First Writing Since: Poem on Crisis of Terror," composed after 9/11, which ends with a powerful exhortation to affirm life by carrying one another. It's a poignant entreaty to humanize rather than polarize.[13]

At the core of the complex and the archetypal defenses is the Self, with a teleology that—to paraphrase Jung—represents mere being's longing to fill its void by knowing itself. What I owe my friend in response to his Facebook post is telling him about my fear—not from a place of shrinking, but with respect for that fear, honoring it as I honor my anguish over the prospect of species extinction. It is sacred fear. It comes from the intermix of my history and the history of my family with the story of the Earth Herself, from new generations of children longing to be born, and from the Church of Her Body. It comes from the very blood of the feminine that Trump and his cohorts seem to be so frightened of and repulsed by.

If I can acknowledge my own fears, I might make a bit of space for my Facebook friend to articulate his own fears. I've had a chance to do just this with a politically conservative analysand of mine with whom I've worked for over 15 years. Because, at one point in our work together, I was moved to share with her my political roots, she's come to feel safe articulating her own feelings of fear and isolation as a teacher at a private school that avowedly, and loudly, leans liberal. If she dares voice her own perspective in the staff room, she's ridiculed and derided. Frankly, her voting for Trump and her terror of a Muslim takeover of our country has strained my capacity to sit with her in openness and equanimity, but my own deep fondness for her as a human being and hers for me seems to be allowing us to tenuously but steadily create something of a bridge to explore her teratoma and my own with curiosity and tenderness.

Recently, she described to me a horrifying video she'd seen of a group of black kids torturing a disabled white boy, and I commiserated with the agony that it caused her, particularly since she herself is the mother of a disabled child, but I also shared with her my own distress over the increase in violent attacks on Muslims, Jews, African Americans, and Latinos, as well as the large placard that had been placed at a bus stop near my home, emblazoned with the words, "No niggers." She was shocked, and we were able to acknowledge that we are being exposed to entirely different material via our chosen news sources.

I found myself wondering aloud, "Is what we're doing right now analysis?" And she replied, "It's very meaningful to me. I have no one else I can talk with in this way." I believe such moments might be described as a creative hybrid of personal and cultural analysis, forged in the flames of a perilous time. It does feel like our mutual attempt to carry each other and to affirm life. Who knows where it will take us?

Notes

1 Ti-Nehisi Coates, *Between the World and Me* (New York: Spiegel & Grau, 2015), 5.
2 David Sedaris, "A Number of Reasons I've Been Depressed Lately," *The Paris Review*, June 5, 2017, http://tinyurl.com/y9tzy5u3.
3 Sharon Heath, *The History of My Body, The Fleur Trilogy, Book 1*, 2nd Ed. (Deltona, FL: Thomas-Jacob Publishing, LLC, 2016). All quotations from *The History of My Body* are by permission of the publisher.
4 C. G. Jung, *Essays on Contemporary Events: The Psychology of Nazism* (Princeton: Princeton University Press, 2014).
5 *Essence of Life*, directed by Greg Carson (MGM Home Entertainment, 2002). DVD. In this short documentary Godfrey Reggio and Phillip Glass talk about Reggio's film *Koyaanisqatsi* See *World Future Fund*, http://tinyurl.com/y7qky3eg.
6 Heath, *The History of My Body*, 1.
7 Ibid.
8 Chris Uhlmann, "President Donald Trump Skewered as 'Friendless' and 'Awkward' in Viral Take-Down," *News.com.au*, July 10, 2017, http://tinyurl.com/y9v6rbml.
9 Joan C. Williams, *White Working Class: Overcoming Class Cluelessness in America* (Watertown, MA.: Harvard Business Review, 2017).

10 C. G. Jung, *The Collected Works of C.G. Jung*, vol. 5, *Symbols of Transformation* (1952) (Princeton: Pantheon/Bollingen Press, 1967), 104, fn 59.

11 Naomi Klein, *This Changes Everything: Capitalism vs. The Climate* (New York: Simon & Schuster, 2014).

12 Peter Victor, *Managing Without Growth* (Cheltenham, UK: Edward Elgar Publishing, 2008).

13 Suheir Hammad, "First Writing Since: Poem on Crisis of Terror," *Motion Magazine,* November 7, 2001, http://tinyurl.com/y8m3glf2.

Chapter 11

Walt Whitman on Religious Liberty

Marriage Equality and the American Cultural Complex

Steven Herrmann

The breakdown of organized religions and need for new unifying myths to give coherence to changes that are taking place in the world today present us with an urgent psychological task. Our religious texts are lagging behind worldwide political events, and we are badly in need of new myths. One of the political issues challenging our nation is the rightness or wrongness of *marriage equality*. America's most comprehensive poet, Walt Whitman (1819–1892), not only tapped into the archetype of marriage equality, but also may have foreseen its emergence in a prospective and teleological way in the American polis and around the world. Whitman provided a vision of marriage equality that was as far-seeing as it was protective of our religious freedoms. His answer was found in his vision of *Religious Liberty*, or Spiritual Democracy.[1]

As I'll show in this chapter, Whitman placed images of same-sex marriage alongside the rights of the well-married husband and wife in his poetry. His visions appear to have anticipated a movement commemorating national recognition of marriage equality, now legal in all 50 states. This major civil rights victory came after a landmark Supreme Court decision on June 26, 2015.

Any new truth that changes the old Judeo-Christian-Islamic notions of marriage must be based, at least in part, on a firm foundation of science. Therefore, in order to examine a new archetype of transformation from the core of the cultural complex of marriage in America, I have to look at it from a point of view outside any limited and biased culture; I have to examine it cross-culturally, which is to say *transreligiously* and *transnationally*.

Many of the biases in disputations surrounding marriage equality seem to be based on overly rigid religious beliefs. These conflicts in the United States, from the point of view of the religious right, for instance, appear to be centered on an old-time biblical injunction that wedlock shall be exclusively between a man and a woman. The controversy appears, therefore, to be at least partially based on the Bible.

When religious freedoms are encroached upon by big government, however, the freedoms of citizens and their mental health are at risk, and it becomes an ethical and political concern, a matter of conscience for depth psychology to weigh in upon, in current world affairs and clinical practice. To address this concern, I will first turn to the US Constitution. The First Amendment to the US Constitution, in the Religion Clauses, reads: "Congress shall make no law respecting an establishment of religion, or prohibiting the free exercise thereof." In these noble words, "the framers' central purpose ... was to protect religious liberty—to prohibit the coercion of religious practice or conscience, a goal that remains paramount today."[2] It was the appearance of the Religious Clauses in the First Continental Congress, on June 8, 1789, that marked the birth of the United States as "Liberty's nation." The Religious Clauses were an attempt to solve a problem that originally led the colonists to leave Europe in quest of religious freedom in the first place.[3] Yet contradictions have persisted since the First Amendment was sanctioned.

Understood psychologically, what we have witnessed over the past two decades in the political debates over the issue of marriage equality is a *bipolar cultural complex*, by which I mean a splitting-complex, one with a tendency to polarize the conscience of an entire nation along two opposing axes.[4] Such a polarizing complex is rife with conflict, infighting, and division, and those who choose to continue to fight against marriage equality, post-2015, misuse outgrown religious opinions to promote their personal and prejudiced views and are caught in a cultural complex without their knowing it.

Addressing the inherent contradictions in marriage equality disputes is not only a political or legal issue to be solved by legislators, but more importantly, I feel, it is a religious or spiritual matter. Whitman offers some words of wisdom that cannot be found in any of the newsflashes of the day: "Do I contradict myself?" Whitman asked rhetorically about his own progressive spiritual views in 1855:

> Very well then I contradict myself,
> (I am large, I contain multitudes.)"![5]

The question of how to discuss a political issue such as marriage equality, without being captured by one pole of the cultural complex in its *bipolarity*, was answered affirmatively by Whitman; by holding both sides of it in consciousness, without being possessed by merely one side of it, he found a solution. Whitman answered a conundrum inherent in the Religious Clauses by presenting an autochthonous view of poetry from an ecstatic and transcendent attitude informed by the newest developments in modern science. Such a vision was presented in the most comprehensive way possible after Whitman's reading of the Prussian botanist, geologist, and world-traveler Alexander von Humboldt, who in 1844 published the first of his comprehensive five-volume set *Cosmos*.[6] Ralph Waldo Emerson read Humboldt's first volume in the original German (*Kosmos*) and penned his famous essay "The Poet" the same year. Yet, what Emerson could only hope for by appealing to the American people for a poet of national promise, Whitman gave conscious answer to, in an unprecedented 95-page book, handprinted and self-published on July 4th, America's Independence Day, 1855. He called it *Leaves of Grass*.

This initial volume consisted of a 10-page prose Preface followed by 12 poems of 85 pages. By the third 1860 edition, only five years later, Whitman dropped the Preface and added many new poems. This impressive volume, totally 446 pages, contained two important clusters—"Enfant d' Adam" or "Children of Adam," and "Calamus"—in which his love poems to women and to men were placed side-by-side in what I've called a *bi-erotic* grouping. By bi-erotic, I do not mean what is commonly referred to today as bisexual. Whitman's sexual leanings were definitely toward men, and the poems to women were more imagined than based on any real sexual experiences verified by literary historians. I've analyzed these two clusters carefully in my psychobiography of Whitman in two books.[7] Whitman worked on *Leaves of Grass* and revised it numerous times throughout his lifetime and it contained over 400 poems by the time of his final "Deathbed Edition" in 1891–1892.

The inspiration that gave Whitman wings to transcend all nations and arrive at a quality of universal consciousness, latent in all human beings, came from the religious currents set in motion by the New England Transcendentalists. It was out of the spiritual currents set in motion by Emerson that Whitman was enabled to transit to a state of transnationality above the world's religions, where he could view them all from a Vista. The word *Vista*, which I capitalize here, comes from Whitman's magnificent prose essay, written in September 1870, "Democratic Vistas." Whitman refers frequently throughout this essay to Vistas of Democracy with a capital *V*. By this he means *Vistas of a third spiritual stage of Democracy* in which the United States might fulfill its destiny through the publication of its "archetypal poems."[8]

Humboldtian science made possible the vision for Whitman to behold the unity of all religions for the first time in human history, from an astronomical angle, that is, at an altitude in space outside religious nationalism. While reading *Cosmos*, Whitman realized that science was indispensable for empirical and metaphysical truth-telling. Whitman saw himself as an exemplar of a new dream of Religious Liberty. He saw there were no Absolutes regarding marriage. He saw his subjective experience of the Divine was just as legitimate as anyone else's. He believed his vision of marriage equality was an equally binding experience of the Self, a new kind of revelation of its very own.

In *Leaves of Grass* Whitman included an untitled prose "Preface," which was omitted from the second edition in 1856. As an undergraduate student at the University of California, Santa Cruz, I had an opportunity to read parts of Whitman's "Preface" in a beautiful fine-printed book titled *American Bard*. Arranged in verse with woodcuts by the California poet William Everson, it was handsomely handprinted on rich handmade paper, measuring a full foot by a foot and a half. Captivated by the text, I read,

THE AMERICANS, of all nations at any time upon the earth,
Have probably the fullest poetical nature. The United States themselves
Are essentially the greatest poem.[9]

A bit further on I read some more interesting lines:

OF ALL NATIONS the United States with veins full of poetical stuff
Most need poets and will doubtless have the greatest and use them the
greatest.
Their Presidents shall not be their common referee so much as their
poets shall.

I read further:

The American poet is to be transcendent and new.[10]

Although I did not know it then, I realized later that Whitman had
found a technique to get above the cultural complexes of religion, slavery
and race, sexism and homophobia, by constellating what C. G. Jung called
the *transcendent function*.[11] Let me unpack what I have come to understand about Whitman's masterpiece since I first beheld the "Preface" in the
magnificent folio pages of *American Bard*.

The Fierce Wrestler

In Whitman's 1847 ("Fierce Wrestler!") *Notebook* he personifies a nuclear
dynamic within the American Self:

Without core
Loose in the knees,
Clutch fast to me, my ungrown brother,
That I infuse you with grit and jets of life
I am not to be denied—I compel;
It is quite indifferent to me who you are.
I have stores plenty and to spare
And whatsoever I have I bestow upon you
And first I bestow my love.[12]

The preceding lines contain the hidden meanings of Whitman's same-sex
marriage symbolism in its seedbed. "Without core" implies lack of compelling
force, enthusiasm, or "core" of personality. "Loose in the knees" implies lack
of physical strength or stamina. Thus, the "ungrown brother" is the puerile
28-year-old Walter Whitman. "Jets .... not to be denied" are an instinctive
influx of masculine vigor, essential for personal and cultural transformation.

They are jets of an instinctive-energetic impulse, a source of wild masculine energy from the center of the cultural complex. The Voice speaking through Whitman is not the personal "I" in the poem; it addresses Whitman as a "you." The emergent Voice in the poem is an incarnation of a psychological God-image, in its chthonic-spiritual form. Later, the Voice becomes an aspect of Whitman's mature poetic voice, as he reaches his rhythmical stride. It's part of his creative muse, or *daimon*, and is therefore archetypal and impersonal. This is the masculine portion of the American Self speaking objectively through him. It intends to incarnate itself in him through a *marriage of sames.*

Thus, Whitman becomes the initiate to the bipolar cultural complex of love, which is an impersonal archetypal force, an impregnating power in all nations. It has the capacity to impregnate him indifferently with lyrical words. The energy bottled up in the cultural complex of male sexuality is filled with the potent word power to transform nations. It is not to be denied and compels him to write. Rather than frightening Whitman's visioning ego, the Voice reassures: "And first I bestow my love."

Now we turn to the next sequence in his experiment with active visioning:

> Unloose me touch you are taking the breath from my throat
> Unbar your gates—you are too much for me.—
> Fierce Wrestler! do you keep the heaviest grip for the last?
> Will you sting me most even at parting?
> Will you struggle even at the threshold with spasms more delicious than
>   all before? ...
> I did not think I was big enough for so much ecstasy
> Or that a touch could take it all out of me ....
> I am lurid with rage!
> I invoke Revenge to assist me.—[13]

Note the accent Whitman places here on *ecstasy.* The impersonal energies of the bipolar complex of marriage equality have now become wedded to Whitman's ego-consciousness. There appears to have been some kind of sting during the fierce grapple, a loss of breath in the poet's throat, followed by delicious spasms of some kind. Homoerotic imagery is evident here. The pain at parting is followed by intense *anger*: "I am lurid with rage!"

Whitman's vision of the syzygy is presaged by a fierce grappling with the opposites of ecstasy and violence, pleasure and pain, in the throes of a love-grip. Whether this was a portrait he painted of a physical act, or purely imaginal, has puzzled many Whitman scholars for over a century. Opinions have varied on a continuum from "yes" to "maybe" to "no." To my mind, it sounds like homoerotic longing for a union with the touch, breath, and heat of the male body.

Whitman's expression of protest after his visioning ego has been overpowered by the impersonal force is affectively charged, and we can only hypothesize, therefore, that he was in a complex. The Wrestler seized him as its victim, he submitted to interpenetration, and then he reacted with strong bipolar emotions: ecstasy followed by anger. The archetype with which he was wrestling was the positive side of the bipolar organization (marriage equality is right), which he integrated into his own self-experience and then responded to with an intention to invoke "Revenge" in order to assist him. Revenge would ignite a bi-erotic revolution, which Whitman would launch in 1860 in an effort to heal the bipolar split complex in his nation and the world.

Whitman gives voice here to the power we feel when we are gripped by a cultural complex; then, with energy fueled by his emerging sense of Selfhood as a poet, he gives words to the complex itself. Assuming the standpoint of the "I," Whitman's visioning ego is initially receptive; then he speaks back to the Voice with his own inner authority as the future American Bard. Both voices (the impersonal Voice and personal voice) are parts of his individual and cultural identity. This is also how the cultural complex, with all the demonic force of an emerging counter-will to the conventional heterosexual marriage institution momentarily possesses him with a calling to live by.

In 1855, seven years later, his initiation experience by the "Fierce Wrestler!" finds fuller expression in the evocative lines:

> Thruster holding me tight and that I hold tight!
> We hurt each other as the bridegroom and the bride hurt each other![14]

Here the same-sex marriage symbolism is clearly revealed: Whitman and the "Fierce Wrestler!" are now in a marriage bed together.

The "New Bible"

By 1857, Whitman had become preoccupied with a "spinal idea" for a lecture "Founding a New American Religion (? No Religion)."[15] What did he mean by "religion" and why might his idea of "founding" a "No Religion" be pivotal for the United States of America? In June 1857, Whitman wrote further: "The Great Construction of the *New Bible*," the "main life work—the Three Hundred & Sixty five—(it ought to be ready in 1859.—(June '57)."[16]

Scholars do not generally recognize that Whitman placed same-sex marriage as the cornerstone of *Leaves of Grass*, yet it cannot be denied that same-sex marriage is the rock, the foundation of his book. It is the stone the builders of the world's religions rejected. For Whitman, the foundation stone was to become the head of the corner to cure the nation of its illness.

The New Bible was paradoxically meant to include all religions. His insights seemed to come from a remarkable kind of spiritual experience, a new kind of relatedness and human love, which he called *Amative love*, and *Adhesive love*. He used these two terms before the words *heterosexuality* and *homosexuality* were coined. What he meant was a "perfect equality of the female with the male."[17] Thus, by 1857, Whitman had lain a cornerstone for a new American epic that would be published in his 1860 "Children of Adam" and "Calamus" clusters. Reverberations of this edition of *Leaves* were heard in the far western state of California a century later.

In 1955, Alan Ginsberg, who openly claimed Whitman as his ancestor, published a controversial poem called "Howl," which landed him in a heated legal trial in a San Francisco Superior Courthouse about its overt sexual content. What Ginsberg did as an openly gay man in "Howl" was to liberate heterosexuality and homosexuality and naturalize sex in a bisexual rendering of the human libido. Yet we must acknowledge that Ginsberg got his main inspiration from Whitman. Ginsburg's trial eventually proved him right, and his victorious trial was marked by a series of synchronicities, which would vindicate Whitman. For it was in the far western United States, Whitman had proclaimed, that the "spine-character of the States" would eventually emerge into the consciousness of the nation. This is what actually happened as a fact of modern Democracy.[18]

Calamus

The 1860 edition of *Leaves of Grass* contains illustrations of three butterflies, in three similar drawings, and they are all placed strategically by Whitman in pivotal sections of his book. The three butterflies are perched on a human index finger on a left hand and they are ready to take wing. They connote some hidden yet emergent meaning. The butterfly at the beginning of the volume points upward, toward words that announce the prefatory poem, "Proto-Leaf," and reveal the book's thematic program. The second butterfly is placed just before "Enfant d' Adam" and "Calamus," which contains the spine of the volume. Sexual imagery is revealed in the first cluster and concealed in the second. A third butterfly is placed after the concluding poem, "So Long!" What might these three butterfly illustrations mean psychologically? Why did Whitman place them there? How do they relate to his ideas on Religious Liberty? How might they relate to deliberations in our world today about religion, marriage equality, and the rights of LGBTQ people?

The symbolism of the three butterflies is central to the book's theme, which centers on personal and cultural transformation in a globalized world. Whitman announces his aim in "Chants of the Many In One."[19] He vows in this opening section to sing songs of a new "Spirituality" that he names "the translatress, the openly-avowed"; these songs all emanate from the "satisfier," the "mistress, the Soul."[20] So right at the beginning of the new edition of his book Whitman assumes the form of a singer of a new series of songs from the Feminine principle, the American Soul. This *translatress* is the international Butterfly-Soul, Liberty, speaking through him with a Feminine voice, the voice of a transformed Love. He aims for this transformed American Soul to take wing and soar through his words to all nations of the world. The book's central theme then emerges, the *cornerstone*: the "song of companionship" and the "ideal of manly love," which is his medicine of *homoaffection* and *homospirit*.

In "Calamus," Whitman seeks to dissolve the walls of homophobia dividing homosexual and heterosexual men by establishing an unforgettable portrait of the bi-erotic nature of human Love.[21] In the "New Bible" two primary voices speak through the poet—one heterosexual, another homosexual. Together these two voices represent the basic bisexuality of all human beings. Through the two clusters of chants the bi-erotic energies of the human body and the soul are in transit toward a higher form of spiritualized Love through which the bipolarity of the cultural complex will be fully integrated.

Homoerotic love is a burning fire at play within Whitman's body, soul, and spirit, a flame of passion that threatens to consume him. This flame of Love (burning from the core of the cultural complex) he gladly gives himself up to: "I will write the evangel-poem of comrades and of love."[22] By "comrades," Whitman means male friends, companions, or soul-husbands. Then comes a series of lines that repeat the word *Religion* seven times; these seven words are all spelled with a capital *R*. Why seven times? Seven, of course, is a biblical number. It is also the most common number in shamanic societies worldwide and a primary number for initiation.

Understanding that the problems in the American psyche are religious at their core, Whitman does not choose to argue. He announces:

IF THE GREATNESSES are in conjunction in a man or woman it is
    enough,
The fact will prevail through the universe.[23]

Whitman addresses his male comrade in an image of a male-male *conjunction* as "Mon cher!" (a French word for *dear*, or *beloved*). He concludes "Proto-Leaf" by saying finally that it is Religion that "makes the whole coincide" and his poems were merely to "drop in the earth the germs of a greater Religion":

My comrade!/For you, to share with me, two greatnesses—
And a third one, rising inclusive and more resplendent,
The greatness of Love and Democracy—and the greatness of Religion.[24]

These announcements in "Proto-Leaf" reach their climax in the emphatic lines:

O my comrade!
You and me at last—and us two only;
O power, liberty, eternity at last![25]

Whitman speaks personally and affectionately here to the man he loves about power and liberty and eternity; through this one man—whose love was apparently not returned—he declares an international Love to all women and men. The poems emphasize a personal address to a divine "You," a perfect lover and equal, a Comrade, latent in all men. It is a call for a higher understanding of the meaning of Religious Liberty and its sociopolitical and spiritual aims in history.

Whitman's answer to the contradictions in the current marriage debates seem to lie, paradoxically, in the "Calamus" cluster. It is in this seminal cluster of 43 poems that the contradictions in the bipolar complex are redeemed through Love. We know from Whitman's *Notebooks* that homosexuality was a part of his spirituality and his spirituality a part of his sexuality: it was non-dual. It is precisely the spiritual dimension, however, that is so sadly lacking in news relating to marriage equality, or Religious Liberty, that Whitman provides access to.

Whitman instructs us affirmatively to unloosen ourselves as the Self emerges into the nation's cultural identity:

> I announce adhesiveness,
> I say it shall be limitless, unloosened.[26]

"Adhesiveness" is another name in Whitman's lexicon for "Comradeship," "manly love," or "robust American love."[27] In chant 5 of the "Calamus" cluster, he addresses the "States!":

> Were you looking to be held together by the lawyers?
> By an agreement on a paper? Or by arms?/Away!

Whitman comes as a "new bridegroom," bringing "Calamus" leaves to the American people "beyond all the forces of courts and arms."[28]

What Whitman brought to each of the United States and the globalized world at this pivotal time, on the eve of the Civil War, was the "old breath of life, ever new." Whitman predicted a supreme "new friendship" would circulate through the states and shall be called after his name and by all nations "victorious." All nations, he says, will want to claim him as their own. Adhesiveness will solve every one of the problems of Freedom and Liberty, and comrades who love each other shall be "invincible" to the attacks of the rest of the world.

> The most dauntless and rude shall touch face to face lightly,
> The dependence of Liberty shall be lovers,
> The continuance of Equality shall be comrades.

As a "new husband" of the states, Whitman says, in ecstasy: "I extatic, O partners! O lands! Henceforth with the love of lovers tie you." He ends this chant by saying that he is trilling his songs of Liberty to the Divine Mother, the Mother of All, who he refers to endearingly again as "ma femme!"[29] As the consort of women and men alike, he espouses Liberty as his spiritual wife in soul or psyche.

Whitman is not trying to destroy monotheistic institutions in such poems. He is announcing a new vision of Religious Liberty that touches on truths that previous religious dispensations and the founding fathers of the United States left out. It is becoming ever clearer to a great number of people in the United States, and in other parts of the world, that the judgments of conservative or fundamentalist rabbis, priests, or imams can no longer be considered Absolute, however important the contributions of the Hebrew-Christian Bible and Koran may be to the world's religions. Former religious values, laws, and institutions are in need of revolution and repair. We need new myths to further advance toward marriage equality worldwide, particularly those that originate from the deeper layers of psyche: the levels at which cultural complexes are *affectively* active. Whitman's voice is a call to action. As poet and "referee" of people, Whitman opens doors to affection's source; and by swinging them wide open, he announces himself as one of America's greatest Lovers.

Thanks to the first principle of equality, vouchsafed in our Bill of Rights, we are at a major turning point in the way we have traditionally viewed marriage: "Of all mankind the poet is the equable man."[30] The image of the calamus root, growing plant-like from Whitman's breast, at the level of his heart, appears to have been born out of the tension he felt in the American cultural complex that had been splitting him in two. Whitman knew the potentially explosive nature of the poetic ideas he was unleashing in 1855. Although he announced Adhesiveness in 1860, he had to be cautious, for he knew he was carrying same-sex love as his seed-child, in an age when to come out with the truth about who he was, or what his true beliefs about America were, was exceedingly dangerous.

Whitman does not evangelize or preach Comradeship; he is Comradeship; he speaks from the Comrade's source, which is affection's source, Love's source. Whitman stands for Love, plain and simple, every bit as much as Krishna, or Christ, or Buddha. The source is the same in everyone, he claims; it is the source of compassion and Love. By announcing Adhesiveness in "Calamus," Whitman means to send "immortal reverberations" throughout the United States. Whitman offers this "medicine" of homoaffection for the unification of the world:

> Only I will establish in the Mannahatta and in every city of these States
>   inland and seaboard, ...
> The institution of the dear love of comrades.[31]

To Whitman, marriage is an archetypal reality, Love's empirical and metaphysical basis for a just and open society, which should be shared equally by all people. When he published the "New Bible" he made a promise to California to "teach robust American love," for he said he knew such love belonged on the "Western Sea" and "These States will tend inland also—and I will also."[32] All of the "Calamus" poems are translucent in their meaning and spiritual aims: They all point to the phenomenon of marriage equality, which is at the center of *Leaves of Grass*.

A New Myth for Our Times

Psychologically speaking, all religious symbols are what we might today call *myths* in modernity. Treated as such, they can help us take the facts of science forward toward new vistas of empirical understanding and spiritual seeing, through which we can include theological truths into our inventory of the psyche. I personally do not view Whitman's "New Bible" as a religion; I see it as a myth. On another, spiritual plane, however, what is revealed in Leaves may one day become a theological truth, if we can get out of the literalism in which the spirit of truth has been denied for over three millennia. The patriarchal truths of Judaism, Christianity, and Islam have been limited in terms of providing nonprejudiced metaphorical meanings of Love, yet Whitman arrived at a vision of marriage equality by reaching a psychological Vista, situated above all creeds and schools and theologies, in what he called the final "science of God."[33] Like his contemporaries, Herman Melville and Emily Dickinson, Whitman wrote much more than a personal philosophy.[34] His story is psychological. It speaks to certain universal concerns that are present in the conscience of our Global Village. Whitman's words attempt to encircle the world by appealing to "the genius of the United States," which is "not best or most in its executives or legislators," but "always and most in the common people."[35]

Whitman's aim was to call for an internationality of poems and poets across all nations, from a unitary quality of consciousness and conscience above infighting, at an altitude overhead the God-images of the world:

Here at last is something in the doings of man
That corresponds with the broadcast doings of the day and night.
Here is not merely a nation but a teeming nation of nations.[36]

Other nations had founded their national identities on the basis of certain religious creeds and ideologies in the past; Whitman came along as a transnational transformer of the cultural complexes of America—religion, slavery, homophobia, and sexism. In a democratically free society, Whitman revolutionized the field of poetry in a personal "bible" based on sound democratic principles. In "Democratic Vistas," published in 1871, Whitman said he would reconstruct and "democratize society."[37] He called for a new American poetry to "soar above others" in "its original styles in literature and art," and supply its own "intellectual and esthetic master-pieces, archetypal, and consistent with itself."[38]

Whitman's new notion of bi-erotic marriage provides a counter-narrative to those who fear marriage equality might destroy religion in our country. Whoever you are, Whitman gives his "kiss" especially to you. Equality is what Whitman teaches: marriage equality for all people. Writing for a multicultural, multispiritual, and internationally aware libertarian society in the United States, Whitman inserted into his new message of Love the seeds for a possible transnational institutionalization of marriage equality, worldwide, in the present and future. Today we're seeing the positive pole of the cultural complex of same-sex love assert its rights now, as an equivalent principle alongside the heterosexual marriage institution, like at no other time in human history.

Whitman wrote a poem recognizing such a possibility in 1871. He entitled it "The Base of all Metaphysics." In this philosophically informed poem, Whitman addressed an imaginary audience of learned "gentlemen," after specifically naming the great Greek and German philosophers, alongside Christ: Plato, Socrates, Kant, Fichte, Schelling, and Hegel. With words of American wisdom, he then claimed the "finale" of all metaphysics to be human compassion in all its bi-erotic forms: The well-married love of man and wife, parents and children, and man and man—physical, soulful, and spiritual Love.[39]

In the 1871 poem "Passage to India," moreover, Whitman arrived at the place where Love, and Love alone, achieves its goal in the mindful Self, the root of roots from which all religions flow. Whitman passed beyond all God-images in history by transiting imaginatively to the "Year" of the "marriage of continents" at whose "wide-flung door" he greeted new "brides and bridegrooms" of the blue-green planet earth.[40]

The symbolism of marriage in this poem unites people; at a marriage ceremony all are potentially one with bride and bridegroom, whatever gender they might be. Whitman claimed to have accomplished this with empirical facts of science and arrived thereby at "the new theology—heir of the West—." In similar prose statements he called it "the supreme and final science," or "science of God—what we call science being only its minister—as Democracy is, or shall be also."[41] Circumnavigating the globe, Whitman sailed on "waves of ecstasy" to "primal thought" and "realms of budding bibles."[42]

Whitman's point here was that there are no dualisms regarding marriage. Marriage is a unitary notion. Equality (nonduality) is what Whitman teaches:

> I will make cities and civilizations defer to me,
> This is what I have learnt from America—it is the amount, and I teach it again.[43]

His new myth gets down to the basic domain of the body and has the potential to impact world religions, world politics, and the world's social and legal institutions. For when our soul-concepts are changed, we may transcend old ideas about marriage as connoting only betrothal, wedding, or union between a man and a woman.

The changes taking place in our soul-concepts have the potential to inaugurate a paradigm shift that may reverse the axis of marriage from a hierarchal and patriarchal top-down perspective to a more matriarchal and horizontal plane of equality for all. Such a vision of marriage equality might be ushered in more rapidly if theology and psychology aim together at the same goal of collective transformation.

Of course, in our democracy, everyone is permitted to voice their own points of view, and there are many who persist, ignorantly, I dare say, in their creedal opinions. We are all in this bipolar cultural complex mix together, and we are all affected by it. My prediction is that the minority ethic in the marriage disputations will continue to baffle the religious right as their religiously driven beliefs are increasingly exposed as bigoted by a growing liberal majority. For in a transnational vision of gender equality, all religions are equalized in God.

In the Liberty of the American Soul, we may all be embraced in the global marriage dance, one day, without harm of religious, social, legal, or psychological misjudgments gripping us with their antiquated prejudices. We are all free to believe whatever we want and are free to worship whatever God, or no-God, we please—as this very religious freedom is built into the foundation of the US Constitution. Marriage equality is at the base of Whitman's vision of social justice.

The Third Butterfly: Bi-Erotic Marriage

I use the term *bi-erotic marriage* in this chapter to describe the two conjunction possibilities in all women and men. Whitman's poetry is bi-erotic in the sense that it inheres to an embodied instinctual and spiritual experience of both women and men, in both their heterosexual and homosexual iterations. I see Whitman's bi-eroticism in the two poetic clusters "Children of Adam" and "Calamus" as pivotal to his expansive vision of marriage equality, which does not leave out anyone. His poetry expresses the paradox of masculine and feminine opposites that has traditionally limited the fantasies of poets and adds something new. A basic principle in his vision of Religious Liberty appears to be the bi-erotic nature of the human soul. The third butterfly in my equation, therefore, refers to his tying and thus personally binding the knot of bi-erotic marriage, not to a woman and man alone, for that would indicate two marriage types only, but a third (butterfly) through himself, taking wing as an avatar of a more all-encompassing spiritual Nature.

As the New Adam, Whitman envisions potent mothers who are equal to men and who will even, eventually, surpass men in the spiritual domain. He cancels out not only homophobia in his poems to women, but also all phobic reactions to the body and sex, which he sees as completely Natural. Whitman does not address only particular women or female goddesses (Liberty) in his creativity, however; rather, he gives women and their bodies full recognition, as capable of the same pleasures he himself delights in. In Whitman's view, body and soul are one; there is no division, no higher and lower copulation imagery can be found in his poems; both are equally Divine. Only the head creates dualisms, whereas the awakened body and masculinized soul, yoked together with the spirit, create unions, heterosexual and homosexual unions, and they are equal—hence, his call to write the "New Bible."

He realized by 1855, when the poems were first published, that he was an individual and that his erotic identity as a man, who could love women and men the same, made him in that respect identical with the eternal principle of Androgyny in everyone. Whitman's attempts to speak out of the self-centeredness of the great Androgenic personality, the Self within him, and the American Soul, for all nations of the world, was a celebration, not of his separate personal and cultural identity only, but a loyalty to the inborn law of his being, an assertion of an "I" that he referred to simply as "Myself."

Whitman knew in the depths and heights of his soul that the World Soul was truly *Bi-erotic*. Standing up for the erotic and spiritual, in all their forms, was one of Whitman's main life tasks. Looking at the entire corpus of his writings and studying carefully where he put the homosexuality in and where he left it out, it is clear to me that he formulated a concept of marriage equality that would include everyone's bodily and spiritual experiences. He needed to include his own sexuality, enough to consider women's experience, too, and what he wrote is still as true today as it was when he was first read by women in his day, who really felt liberated by him—so much so in fact that Anne Gilchrist, a published writer across the Atlantic, moved to Philadelphia with her two children to court him! After Walt sent her his ring, Anne sailed with her children from England to offer the poet her hand in marriage. He kindly declined and became her intimate friend and a friend to her children instead.

Whitman also spoke up for the bi-erotic in his communication to John Addington Symonds that he had fathered six children. His statement to Symonds could be taken as a poetic metaphor for the fact that his work had been seminal and found fertile ground in which the homosexual liberation movement was only one of his "children" in a global culture of marriage equality. This is to say that there were many children in Whitman's calling. His poetic project was based on a Religious Liberty that included an amative and adhesive love for each of us.

Shortly after he sent his ring to Anne, moreover, Whitman gave a second ring to his young friend Harry Stafford. Stafford cherished this ring for the rest of his life. The two rings make up a bi-erotic pair, a union of the two conjunction-greatnesses, and they were each consummated in outer relationships. Both rings were complicated by Walt's affections, because he did not know what they meant fully, and his emotions sometimes got in the way, but they both were necessary for his betrothal to the World Soul at that time, even if he was not clear what they might mean to LGBTQ readers today. Walt loved Anne, and he was not heterophobic, but it was never the same as his love for the men he loved and posed with for four different wedding photos. In these four wedding photos Whitman got behind the phenomenal world to the underlying archetypal reality of marriage as a unitary experience that is both psychical and physical, material and spiritual, as four is the most common numerical value Jung assigns to wholeness.[44] Thus, Whitman inscribed on the cornerstone of American Religious Liberty an equivalent value for same-sex marriage and heterosexual marriage. He made them equal: he equalized them. He married them both in a great mandala symbol of an international marriage circle in "Passage to India."

Conclusion

What the bi-erotic imagination ultimately led Whitman to was a transcendent state of awareness and supreme happiness. The division in the cultural complex of marriage can continue to be healed by Whitman's life-long grappling with Eros, as an all-encompassing factor of human Love. His calamus leaves are not so much about sex, therefore, as they are about erotic and spiritual Love between men. By 1860, Whitman realized that it was *supreme emotionality*, not sex, which was the ultimate state of awakened Awareness. The erotic in all of its forms was Whitman's medicine in a culture of Religious Liberty divorced from the rich aroma of the human body. As a poet of Liberty, he claimed the immense landscape of America as his own and gave it its unique bi-erotic stamp. For this remarkable contribution to the evolution of world culture toward a more egalitarian attitude toward the body, sex, and the human spirit, we can only be grateful.

Acknowledgments

I would like to thank Jungian analysts John Beebe and Lori Goldrich for their assistance in helping me edit portions of this chapter.

Notes

1 Steven Herrmann, *Spiritual Democracy: The Wisdom of Early American Visionaries for the Journey Forward* (Berkeley, CA: North Atlantic Press, 2014).
2 Derek H. Davis, *Religion and the Continental Congress 1774–1776* (New York: Oxford University Press, 2000), 9.
3 Ibid., 137–149.

4 Steven Herrmann, "Emergence of the Bipolar Cultural Complex in Walt Whitman," *The Journal of Analytical Psychology* 52, no. 4 (2007): 463–478.

5 Walt Whitman, *The Project Gutenberg Ebook of Leaves of Grass*, available at https://www.gutenberg.org/files/1322/1322-h/1322-h.htm.

6 Alexander von Humboldt, *Cosmos: A Sketch of the Physical Description of the Universe*, Volume 1 (Baltimore: John Hopkins, 1997).

7 For a discussion on the bi-erotic imagination in Whitman's poetry, see Steven Herrmann, *Walt Whitman: Shamanism, Spiritual Democracy, and the World Soul* (Durham, NC: Eloquent Books, 2010); and Herrmann, *Spiritual Democracy.*

8 Walt Whitman, "Democratic Vistas" (1870), *Walt Whitman: Complete Poetry and Collected Prose* (New York: Library of America, 1982), 932. The reader may also refer to *Democratic Vistas, and Other Papers* (London: W. Scott, 1888), available at Internet Archive, https://archive.org/details/democraticvis tas00whitrich/page/n13.

9 Walt Whitman, *American Bard: The Original Preface to Leaves of Grass Arranged in Verse by William Everson* (New York: Viking, 1981), 9. All quotations from *American Bard* are by permission of Jude Everson.

10 Ibid., 13.

11 For a discussion of Whitman's cultural attitudes toward slavery and race in America, see Steven Herrmann, "The Cultural Complex in Walt Whitman," *The San Francisco Jung Institute Library Journal* 23, no. 4 (2004): 34–61. For a discussion of his attitudes toward homophobia, see Steven Herrmann, "Walt Whitman and the Homoerotic Imagination," *Jung Journal: Culture & Psyche* 1, no. 2 (2007): 16–47.

12 Walt Whitman, Notebook LC #80 | The Thomas Biggs Harned Collection of the Papers of Walt Whitman, 1842–1937, Library of Congress, Washington, D.C. Transcribed from digital images of the original, https://whitmanarchive.org/manu scripts/notebooks/transcriptions/loc.00141.html. The reader may also refer to *Notebooks and Unpublished Prose Manuscripts*, 6 vols, ed. Edward F. Grier (New York: New York University Press, 1984), vol. 1, page 74. Hereafter referenced as *NUPM* with volume and page number (1:74).

13 Whitman, Notebook LC #80; see also *NUPM*, 1:76, 77.

14 Whitman, *The Project Gutenberg Ebook of Leaves of Grass.*

15 Whitman, *NUPM*, 6:2046.

16 Whitman, *NUPM*, 1:352.

17 Whitman, *American Bard*, 13.

18 Whitman, "Democratic Vistas," *Complete Poetry and Collected Prose*, 952.

19 Walt Whitman, *Leaves of Grass, 1860*, The Walt Whitman Archive, available at https://whitmanarchive.org/published/LG/1860/index.html, 8.

20 Ibid., 9.

21 For a discussion on the bi-erotic imagination in Whitman's poetry, see Steven Herrmann, *Walt Whitman: Shamanism, Spiritual Democracy, and the World Soul* (Durham, NC: Eloquent Books, 2010).

22 Whitman, *Leaves of Grass, 1860*, 11.

23 Whitman, *American Bard*, 17.

24 Whitman, *Leaves of Grass, 1860*, 13.

25 Ibid., 22.

26 Ibid., 453.

27 Ibid., 371.

28 Ibid., 349.

29 Ibid., 351.

30 Whitman, *American Bard*, 13.

31 Whitman, *The Project Gutenberg Ebook of Leaves of Grass.*
32 Ibid.
33 Whitman, *Complete Poetry & Collected Prose,* 1003. From the 1872 "Preface" to *Leaves of Grass,* which can also be found in Walt Whitman, *Complete Prose Works,* Project Gutenberg, at https://www.gutenberg.org/files/8813/8813-h/8813-h.htm#link2H_PREF3.
34 Steven Herrmann, "Melville's Portrait of Same-Sex Marriage in *Moby-Dick,*" *Jung Journal: Culture & Psyche* 4, no. 3 (2010): 65–89; Steven Herrmann, *Emily Dickinson: A Medicine Woman for our Times* (Cheyenne, WY: Fisher King Press, 2018).
35 Whitman, *American Bard,* 10.
36 Ibid., 9.
37 Whitman, "Democratic Vistas," *Complete Poetry & Collected Prose,* 977.
38 Ibid., 980.
39 Whitman, *The Project Gutenberg Ebook of Leaves of Grass.*
40 Ibid.
41 Whitman, *Complete Poetry & Collected Prose,* 1003. See also the 1872 "Preface" to *Leaves of Grass* in Whitman, *Complete Prose Works,* Project Gutenberg.
42 Whitman, *The Project Gutenberg Ebook of Leaves of Grass.*
43 Ibid.
44 For a full discussion on the four wedding photos see Chapter 14 of my book *Walt Whitman: Shamanism, Spiritual Democracy, and the World Soul.*

Immigration

Chapter 12

An Immigrant's Transit

From a Multicultural Complex to a Multicultural Mind

Lynn Alicia Franco

Late in my adult life, I realized that the cultural complexes of Colombia and Southern California had psychologically entwined with the immigration and proculturation processes that shaped my attitudes and cultural perspectives.[1] This chapter describes a journey of cultural integration, poetically described by Tommy Orange as "we are the memories we don't remember, which live in us ...."[2] The narrative that follows describes a psychological process developed through migration in its historical context, derived not only from personal reflections, but also from analytic work with immigrants and research studies in social psychology and psychoanalysis.

In *Civilization in Transition*, Jung described European cultures as "still having our ancestral spirit ... steeped in history, keeping us in contact with our unconscious" so that great "catastrophes are needed in order to wrench us loose to change our political behavior from what it was five hundred years ago."[3] In contrasting European cultures with American cultures, he speculated that "foreign land assimilates its' conquerors. But unlike the Latin conquerors of Central and South America, the North Americas preserved their European standards with the most rigid puritanism" for which he attributed the American's distinct "discrepancy between conscious and unconscious that is not found in the European ...."[4] There is much to consider in Jung's statement, not only with regard to European cultural complexes, but also for those in the Americas. In this vein, I shall explore the historical antecedents and cultural complexes that contributed to my immigrant multicultural complex.

Five significant psychocultural threads were woven into the fabric of my psyche. The first thread originated in the geography and history of Bogotá, Colombia, which intermingled with the differing cultural values, attitudes, and traumas transmitted to me by my parents. The second thread commenced with the death of my father when I was eight years old, which in addition to being an enormous personal loss, was part of a much larger sociopolitical event that contributed to the third thread, that of my transit when I immigrated two years later to Southern California and began a proculturation process. The fourth cultural thread emerged symbolically when, as an adult, I crossed what felt to me to be a cultural border into the C. G. Jung Institute of San Francisco to become a psychoanalytic candidate-in-training. The liminal experience of this"second transit" activated the fifth thread that I call an "immigrant's multicultural complex" and the task of integrating all the cultural layers of my psyche into my sense of self.

Unraveling the Historical/Cultural Threads in Colombia's and Southern California's Cultural Complexes

First Psychocultural Thread: Historical Legacy in Colombian Culture

Colombia's mineral riches were the siren's call of the heroically entitled conquistadores' quest for wealth and Spain's Catholic dominion over indigenous lands and cultures. According to Enrique Dussel, a 20th-century Argentinian philosopher and historian, "In the Spanish world, and later in the European world in general, it fell to the warrior to establish domination over others. The conquistador was the first modern, active, practical human to impose his violent individuality on the Other."[5] The genesis of this Colombian cultural complex of domination and subjugation originated on May 4, 1493, when Pope Alexander VI issued the "Doctrine of Discovery," a papal edict used by Spain to support full title to lands "discovered" with rights of dominion over its non-Christians communities.[6]

The first accounts of the encounter with the Muisca civilization were written in 1536 by conquistadors and clergy, "both of whom were their mortal enemies, who entered by the sword, neither hearing nor understanding the language spoken."[7] Conquistador Gonzalo Jimenez de Quesada wrote, "One after the other they all fell under your majesty's rule," describing "the native people as having great fear of the Spanish, believing that their gods were punishing them ...."[8]

The Muisca were centrally located in what today is the savannah of Bogotá. Chronicles described them as peaceful agricultural traders, who worshiped the sun and moon ritually in an annual ceremony in which the chief submerged himself in Lake Guatavita, sacrificing the precious gold and emeralds he wore as an offering to the transformational potential of their deities. The conquistadores mythologized the ritual in the legend of "El Dorado," using it to guide their quest. Historians estimate that the wealth looted from the highlands made Quesada's expedition the second-most profitable of the 16th century, after Pizarro's exploits in Peru. Additionally, Catholic Spain rewarded the conquistadores with legal and religious superiority over the indigenous population and their lands, as documented in the *Requerimientos*, which demanded immediate submission to Spain's representatives. The price of survival was religious conversion and peonage. Non-compliance led to brutal reprisal.[9] According to research anthropologist

Linda Tuhiwai Smith, in addition to the actual corporal and material devastation, the cultural consequences of colonialism "positioned indigenous people within new political formations, which ruptured previous relations, strategic alliances, trade routes and ways of communicating with other indigenous nations."[10] Indigenous peoples, according to Smith, "have a close and often intimate relationship with sovereign heads as protectors and great fathers and mothers."[11]

Although the living culture of the Muisca was obliterated, its absence is visibly present, not only in museums, but also psychoculturally in a felt expectation of brutality and a lingering resignation embedded in an abiding religious devotion with submissive respect and fear of authority, as well as a distinct hierarchy of socioeconomic and gender inequities. This legacy left generations of Colombians with a phantom sense that their country holds terrible dangers—that it is a place where internal battles for power between government, guerillas, and paramilitaries are normative and where brutal poverty and displacement of a large proportion of the population continue in silent agony.[12]

One can condense and view almost 500 years of Columbia's history as the creation of a cultural complex characterized by violence and power: from conquest (1536) to independence (1810) to national consolidation (1830) to the Peace Accord (2016). The Conquistadores' legacy continued in the leadership of Simon Bolivar, "El Liberator." As poet José Martí has written,

> You can't speak of calm about a person who never knew calm; of Bolivar you can only speak from mountaintops, or amid thunder and lighting, or with a fistful of freedom in one hand and the corpse of tyranny at your feet.[13]

His grand vision of "Nueva Granada" as a democratically organized territory, held together by religious, military, and legal authority, although successful in obtaining independence from Spain, failed to stabilize warring parties. Bolivar's vision broke apart in 1830 with the formation of the nation states of Colombia, Venezuela, Ecuador, and Peru. Violent disputation over resources and territory continued.

Now let's move forward in time to 1948, when as a child, a riot, known as *El Bogotazo*, contaminated the social, political, and family atmosphere into which I was born. The upheaval continued for 10 years, killing more than 4,000 people and becoming a civil war known as *La Violencia*. Although the violence was eventually halted by an agreement to share political power, a military coup d'état in 1955 was deemed necessary to hold the governing reins steady. Socioeconomic brutality persisted nonetheless. From 1990–2011 overt violence again broke out between multiple warring factions: drug cartels, guerilla groups, and traditional elites, all involving private paramilitary units who vied for dominance. The news media, universities, and church pulpits were subverted to sanction and to promote the quest for dominance among competing power groups. In 2016 a Peace Treaty interrupted the cycle of violence, but this peace is fragile. Threatening the accord are the government's continued assassinations of guerilla holdouts and of those opposing Iván Duque Márquez, the conservative president elected in July 2018.[14] Although judicial forums for truth and justice exist, they too have a political history of legal manipulation and evasion.

The trauma that began with the annihilation of indigenous cultures is one where aggressors and victims inhabit the populations' psychic underbelly. Colombia's cultural complex emanates from a colonial legacy where authority taken and submitted to by both followers and victims has shaped a culture in which domination and submission are normative and underlie repeated cycles of war, defeat, displacement, and incorporation of populations. The death of peoples and cultures, though eerily absent, stamps an ambience of "social death" on the fabric of its society, where belonging requires a submission to the denial of human suffering and brutality.[15] Colombian Jungian analyst Maria Claudia Munevar, who identifies with the victims, has written of this cultural complex as being based on the imposition of brute force solely for the colonizers' own benefit.

> Our ancestors learned through their repeated exposure to violence that the personal power needed to accomplish anything for themselves or their community was not based on the ability to influence others through respect and authority. Rather, influencing others and achieving personal goals can best be accomplished through manipulation, force and violence. ... the failure to guarantee fundamental rights is one of the main causes of a cycle of violence that for many years has prevented Colombians from being able to live together peacefully. ... it is now simply part of our cultural life ....[16]

There are those who identify with the power of a heroic quest in legal, military, and clerical claims of authority, and declare that their actions are taken for the sake of the country. Elements that oppose such authority are criminalized. An ironic aspect of such expressions of power are found in protective, even gracious, patriarchal hands that console the poor, the sick, and the meek, while denying them the dignity of legal and social rights. This "benevolence" protects male honor and gives license for sexual and physical abuse of women.

The myth of *Patasola* (the one-footed one) tells the story of a peasant woman who is raped by her husband's employer and is subsequently treacherously violated by her humiliated husband who chops off her foot and kills himself. In shame, grief, and terror she runs into the jungle becoming demonic—a wild creature who nightly seduces and terrorizes in revenge. Patasola is referenced as the force that overtakes a man's psyche in passion. For a woman she takes on the husband's shame as if her own and downplays her own injury while protecting her husbands' reputation, all of which leads to powerful emotions of vengeance.[17]

In a society in which social and economic inequality are so prevalent, both evil and creative powers are projected, which results in states of envy, vengeance, and victimhood that continue the cycle of violence. Identifying with the victim in need of protection and defense ironically supports every person's righteous aggression. The aftermath and persistent impact of such cultural disrespect and indifference is found in a painful residue that infiltrates everyday life with an unspoken expectation that the poor shall beg and rob, whereas the rich will be arrogant and corrupt.

According to socio-historian Paul Gilroy, "The exploitation of nature and native alike supply a shameful, volatile history, especially where the accusing faces of indigenous peoples appear intact ..."[18] Native peoples without tribal identities, presently known as *campesinos*, are the faces that make up a large portion of Colombia's victimized.

In 1970 Gabriel García Márquez wrote in *One Hundred Years of Solitude*, "A person does not belong to a place until there is someone dead under the ground."[19] In Colombia with so many dead, it is denial itself that has not been buried. Reconciliation requires truth and reckoning with the injury for forgiveness to be truly possible. While contemporary Colombian writers, poets, and artists continue to document their country's tragedies and give expression to Colombia's grief with the hope of penetrating the social denial, the evil within the tragedy also continues to be heroically glamorized in series such as Netflix's *Narcos*.[20] The question remains: how are cultural attitudes reckoned with in a manner that addresses the historical wounds of its cultural complexes?

Second Psychocultural Thread: Personal to National Tragedy

What have I absorbed of Colombia's cultural complexes? What complicates my having a coherent cultural narrative is a mother who herself was an immigrant to Bogotá. She was born of Polish and Russian Jewish immigrant parents who left their homes because of persecution. Psychoculturally she was predisposed to fear and a search for safety, security, and belonging. My father, on the other hand, was born in Colombia of Spanish and Scottish immigrant parents whose families had become part of an elite social structure associated with the anticlerical "Liberal" party. Religiously, he differentiated himself from Colombian's Catholic parochialism, feeling Catholic dogma and ritual to be hypocritical and infantile. My parents' atypical cultural perspectives supported my own capacity to live the cultural paradox of denial combined with living "well" in the midst of economic and social inequality. The death of my father in 1953 not only was a personal loss but also became a national tragedy as the airplane accident in which he died also killed the son of Colombia's president, Laureano Gomez. This accident contributed to a destabilization of the government, which culminated in a military coup d'état that resulted in my being sent from Bogotá to Long Beach, California, unaware that I carried the cultural legacy of Colombia's denial of violence and losses.

The Third Psychocultural Thread: Encounter with the Cultural Complexes of Southern California

George Orwell described California as a

> culture of illusion ... open for schemes and self-inventions, where political language consists largely of euphemism, question-begging and sheer cloudy vagueness ... where millions of peasants are robbed of their farms and sent trudging along the roads with no more than what they can carry; this is called *transfer of population* or *rectification of frontiers.*[21]

Although written ten years before my arrival in 1955, Orwell described the Long Beach I encountered—as a place seemingly without history, devoid of connection and meaning. The absence I felt in Southern California was more than a personal anguish; I was also encountering the region's cultural complex.

Southern Californians seemed to avoid the psychological trauma that abrupt change inflicts by mythologizing the "California Dream" as the path to the future. As early as 1800 promoters began marketing a fantasy designed to ensure prosperity and avoid the bankruptcy speculators feared. Populations considered unsavory, such as Native Americans and Mexicans, were seen as impediments to progress and were simply ignored in promotional rhetoric. The lure apparently succeeded: ambitious investors prospered as the new population in Los Angeles County grew from 30,000 in 1890 to more than 2 million in 1930 to 10 million in 2000.[22] Southern California was a culture of newcomers who had left behind their sociocultural histories, building a society that Italo Calvino described as "incapable of holding a memory."[23]

Although Spain's conquest of this region began in the 1500s, by the mid-1700s, when its empire was collapsing, Franciscan priests continued that conquest, as they converted the indigenous population to Catholicism and used their labor to build missions on the land they had "discovered." In effect, they sanctioned eliminating the footprint of cultures that had inhabited the region for more than 3,500 years. The tribal cultures and identities of those who did not flee or die of illness and starvation were changed from being *Tongva*, *Tataviam*, and *Quechan* (or *Yuma*) to using the mission names where they were indentured as *Gabrielenos*, *Ferandeños*, and *Luiseños*, respectively.[24]

The cultural stamp of patriarchal hierarchy remained after Mexico gained independence from Spain in 1810. Revolutionary ideals, however, had separated church from state, so missions were now on secularized lands that fell to those who became known as *Californios*. They retained title, authority, and social status based on education. Social divisions were not racialized until the United States signed the Treaty de Guadalupe Hildago, in which Mexico ceded its territory. Ownership of land was made easy for incoming Protestant Anglo-Americans; they were supported by claims of Manifest Destiny for territory and social entitlement, displacing indigenous and Mexican peoples with few qualms. The fears and racial antipathies of new arrivals were seized upon by promotional rhetoric designed to offer security and attract their investments; the new emigrants were reassured that "threatening natives" and "morally lax, mix-blooded Mexicans" had already been "domesticated" by the Spanish.[25]

Although Southern California was originally Spanish-speaking, after Mexico's territorial cessation to the United States, legal and economic activities were conducted in English. Informal resistance to marginalization by Mexican-Americans persisted through the use of Spanish in their families and communities, and their cultural identity grew stronger with their participation in WWII. By the 1960s, *Chicanos de la Raza* called for the unionization of farm workers and the establishment of ethnic study departments in public colleges and universities. These solidarity movements were aimed at rectifying the impairment to self-esteem that resulted from the isolation of segregation, which had erased their historical and social legitimacy. Ironically, pride in ethnic identity may have unwittingly aided real estate promoters, who seized upon racial fears and prejudices in the process of selling homes, thereby contributing to ethnically segregated neighborhoods, which further isolated the groups from one another and did little to decrease the social stigma that Chicano identity carried for the "white" population.[26]

As early as 1899 the Los Angeles Chamber of Commerce successfully developed "boosterism" to bring prosperity from tourism, real estate, and transportation. Advertising itself became a powerful industry, selling new dreams as circumstances changed. What did not change was the continued erasure of peoples and cultures as a marketing strategy to promote prosperity. Marketing and public relations became both a profession and an industry in itself. Cultural historian Norman Klein describes Los Angeles as a city where "virtually no ethnic community downtown has been allowed to keep its original location ... the world around them is systematically erased. As identity and community are destroyed, much pain is created ...."[27]

The strong link between racializing identity and economic manipulation through the marketing of the "California Dream" is revealed in the migration history of Oklahoma "white" refugees to the area. Farmers, displaced in the 1930s by economic depression, were hired as cheap labor by Anglo ("white") growers when the unionization of Mexicans farmworkers threatened economic growth. According to Peter la Chapelle, Dust Bowl migrants, who were initially disparaged in this racialized society, assumed a "liminal white" status until economics allowed for "social mobility to disappear them into the white middle class."[28]

By the time I arrived in Long Beach in the mid-1950s, Oklahoma-migrants had shifted to being middle-class suburbanites with cultural aspirations inspired by televised visions of progress. "The California Dream," it seemed, had traded on their prayers for recreation and leisure, privacy and whiteness. Real estate developers created new neighborhoods for a "white only" population, a practice supported by 70 percent of California voters in a "restrictive covenant" deemed legal until 1966 when the Supreme Court upheld the state's right to intervene on behalf of potential tenants and home-buyers who were refused rental or sale due to race. Social commentator Lawrence Culver described the shift as moving "from collective endeavors to increasing isolation and atomization, where gated communities and private security was demanded ... based on a long and troubled history of whites' efforts to restrict and control public space ...."[29]

Because light-skinned ethnic identity is malleable, another group of new-comers, namely immigrant Jews of the early 20th century, were free to re-imagine themselves in the LA image. According to author Neal Gaber,

> Above all things, they wanted to be regarded as Americans, not as Jews: they wanted to re-invent themselves as new men. ... Hollywood Jews embarked on a ruthless and complete assimilation—their lives cut-outs of the American pattern of respectability as they interpreted it.[30]

Although they owned the studios and wielded considerable power, they moved away not only from their Eastern European cultural traumas, but also from the ethnic origins of their ancestors. Gaber adds, "they 'lost themselves'" to the region's cultural complex of manipulatively erasing what was imagined to impede progress.

Southern California's cultural complex was fostered by a small group of opportunists and dream seekers whose social position privileged their own economic gain and vision of the "good life." Clever marketing supported the innovations of modernity, forming cultural ideals that also supported racialized attitudes enacted in regulations, policies, and codes. These new laws discriminated against, devalued, and exploited people of color. Southern California's cultural discontinuity seems to have been intentionally underwritten by manipulative schemes of hope, begat from avarice and the desire for power. For dark-skinned newcomers and for those who were disinherited from their land and culture, memories of physical and psychic pain were not erased with hopeful dreams. As Native American poet John Tetpon decries, the experience of *"being a victim of cultural genocide is a most painful form of suffering because it is unforgettable."*[31]

Prominent in the cultural complexes of both Colombia and Southern California is the obliteration of indigenous culture with the erasure of historical truths. Will greater consciousness of these cultural complexes open these societies to the social mourning needed? And will such grieving support the empathy and mental space for social self-reflections that value emergent creative and relational endeavors? Current concerns and reparative activities are apparent: in Colombia, for example, there are 102 indigenous tribes who are now protected under Colombian law and are reclaiming their cultural sovereignty while they incorporate new traditions with older ones where communal respect and responsibility for land and for each other are valued.[32] Another recent development can be found in groups who were previously engaged with one another in violent conflict, but are now attempting instead to forge a peace accord. The California Dream also may be changing. Recent legal and technological developments support sustainable agricultural practices, integrating values discovered in older practices. Alternative energy sources are being developed, not so much for individual benefit, but for maintaining greater well-being in a modern society.[33] Indigenous populations are reclaiming land rights through legislation, traditional ceremonies, and resistance protests.[34]

An Immigrant's Multicultural Complex

Fourth Psychocultural Thread: Immigration and Proculturation

Although cultural conflicts and disruptions are frequently the basis for cultural complexes, the process of immigration and proculturation itself destabilizes cultural identifications and confronts the immigrant with multiple, often conflicting paradigms and complexes. What I have defined as an immigrant's multicultural complex includes the transit experience itself, which may intensify the disruption of relational, cultural, socioeconomic, and geographical attachments. As such, immigrants in search of community and identity find that they must weave together a narrative of change and continuity that includes the depressive and anxious symptoms of dissociated cultural complexes and more personal anguish and "phantom narratives" of immigrant parents and grandparents.[35]

Immigrants bring with them the fermenting cultural juices of their countries of origin, and often it is those erupting cultural complexes that fuel their emigration. How an immigrant negotiates complexes from the old world and those encountered on new soil, is the lengthy process of *proculturation*, which requires integrating multiple cultural perspectives as identity stabilizes. How a migrant discovers meaning depends on age, internal world, and personal attachments, as well as the social context, cultural identifications, and cultural complexes that the migrant carries psychologically. The impact of the journey on the psyche of a child or adolescent, who may not be sufficiently differentiated from their parents' worldview, initiates a developmental process that includes the impact of migration on the accompanying adults. Inevitably immigration involves many kinds of stresses and losses, and of particular psychological significance is the loss of primary attachments. Death and the circumstances of its occurrence require mourning, a process frequently curtailed by the need to adapt to the demands of a new environment. Grieving my father's death, for example, was interrupted by the political upheaval that followed the accident and by my subsequent migration, where making new connections felt more essential for survival than suffering the pain of his loss.

Anguish for immigrants also occurs when separations from family or when a family member's disappearance remain unresolved. This form of absence may haunt the migrant's psyche with ambivalent longings and depressive anxieties. The circumstances and subjective experiences of the transit itself, such as whether the journey was voluntary or not, the mode of transportation and at what costs, the length of transit, and whether familial ties were maintained or not, have considerable significance to the immigrant. Having to acquire a new language while suffering the insecurity of a broken sense of continuity, along with the interruptions of shared cultural frames of references and shared social mirroring, encumbers the kind of dialogues essential for relational bonds to mature. Many aspects of culture are transmitted intergenerationally, and because much of this communication occurs unconsciously, coping mechanisms used to ease sufferings that are too great to mentalize are transmitted as well.

Adjustments take time and the social mirroring in the host-country's attitudes, cultural norms, and biases impact an immigrant's sense of self. If language, race, or ethnicity are not overtly recognized as defining otherness, which was the case for me, one's felt-sense of foreignness is unknown. Inaccurate social mirroring invites confusion and estrangement and may be experienced as personal inadequacy. When identity remains diffused, it becomes emotionally entangled with shame. Where racial and ethnic biases abound, immigrants are faced with covert negative social mirroring, and experiencing one's self-worth becomes quite challenging. Studies have found that even positive parental mirroring does not adequately compensate for the intensity and frequency of negative social feedback from the broader community.[36] Self-esteem and competency are also impacted negatively by an immigrant's lack of familiarity with norms and social expectations. Learning a new language affects confidence in that effective communication is often difficult. This difficulty inevitably interferes with social connections. Multiple changes in relationships, roles, and environment can lead to acute ego disequilibrium. Using the language of Donald Kalsched, when disorganization, despair, and detachment ensue, an immigrant's soul may depart and take on a life of its own, as if "in a permanent state of alienated captivity."[37] These states invite shame and insecurity, especially if the immigrant is not compassionately received by those in the host culture. Protective mechanisms, such as those described by Kalsched as a "self-care system," may initially compensate for the acuity of pain, but when not understood as transitional coping mechanisms, disavowal may rigidify and burden future generations with emotional and physical symptoms that seem meaningless to the sufferer.[38]

Symptoms of dissociation and detachment may both prompt and help evade deeper terrors felt in being adrift. For one of my immigrant patients finding an internal shore to land on began as she unpacked the underlying circumstances of her father's sullen personality. Like herself, he too had lost the social context and cultural norms when his family immigrated from Turkey to Argentina. In reviewing his history with her, she told me that Argentina at the time was in the hands of a military regime, and he had witnessed his brother's abduction and subsequent disappearance. As we considered how her own psychological states of terror, activated since her immigration to the United States, were similar to her father's, my patient began to experience empathy for her father's "self-care" sullenness and less shame regarding her own panic/paranoid states. With the compassion she felt in our relationship, her isolation diminished and her symptoms subsided.

In the Western world, successful mastery of the turmoil and confusion in adolescence often involves the resolution of emotional conflicts by rejecting certain cultural norms and standards before one's own sense of self consolidates.[39] This trajectory is more difficult for immigrant adolescents who have lost much of their framework for understanding normative expectations. When old pursuits and dreams do not translate into their present realities, the difference stimulates a sense of inadequacy and shame. They isolate themselves from peers or join groups that alienate them from their parents. Many also have parents who are struggling with their own immigrant experiences and are unavailable to mirror their children's precarious search for a new identity.[40]

I immigrated as a child without the empathetic resonance of parents or community to help me process emotions or provide language or meaning for the abrupt cultural and relational ruptures I sustained. The psychic injuries incurred for most immigrants are those of invisibility, discontinuity, and alienation, which may be somewhat ameliorated when psychosocial recognition and relational empathy is available. Learning to hold multiple contexts and cultural paradigms requires the ability to negotiate states of continuity and discontinuity simultaneously.[41] When an immigrant's psychological processes are acknowledged, the "remaking" of identity (a natural process of proculturation) will integrate temporal-spatial discontinuities and unformulated experiences.

Fourth Psychocultural Thread: Culture and Transit Symbolically Revisited

Archetypal psychic forces of belonging and identity formation, shadowed as they are by alienating forces of difference and otherness, are one basis for the origin of cultural complexes. For me, the pressures to adapt erased visible traces of the cultural complexes below my feet. When I crossed the symbolic threshold into the analytic training program, sociocultural disruptions activated in the program offered me the opportunity to grapple anew with unconscious and unformulated cultural complexes from an earlier age. I had entered the program unaware that the "intersectionality" of my own multiple identities—"white" Latina, Jewish/Catholic, Colombian upper class, and poor North American immigrant—would be challenged significantly by the encounter with the relative cultural homogeneity of the Jung Institute, which was established with a Eurocentric cultural bias in the 1940s. [42] Fortunately, the state of "candidacy" is a culturally sanctioned transitional and liminal state where developing consciousness is essential, both to individuation and to certification.

A dream in my second year of training captured the archetypal power I felt in this unfamiliar cultural setting:

> An immense fist breaks through the institute's outer wall as I meet with an evaluating committee of analysts. Alerted to danger, I motioned to the analysts to turn and see what is crashing through the structure, but they ignored my warning and carried on with their business as usual. Awed, terrified, and alone with my vision, I left the room only to find that the institute itself had become an insane asylum. I was lost and while other immigrants suggested options, they were of no use to me as they all involved unwanted deception. I found the empty consulting room of one of the analysts and waited for his return.

Years after I was certified as an analyst, I began to understand the dream from the perspective of my own cultural complexes. The "breaking through" of the immense fist powerfully foretold of my need for greater consciousness regarding the cultural, systemic, and structural violence I experienced as a child. Leaving the dream-room of the evaluating committee where denial was active, alerted me to my unconscious collusion with the cultural complexes of dissociated losses. This dream was also about the sociocultural aspect of group culture, as it contained aspects of the institute's cultural complex. As a candidate, I witnessed a forceful trauma to the community's cultural structure, which especially impacted those in authority. It was also a rupture to the groups' cultural norm, that of avoiding conflict. My dream pointed toward a resulting collective madness that occurs when a group avoids evidence of such trauma. [43] The work of Singer and Kimbles helped me consider how cultural themes, especially at an unconscious level, permeate the boundary between the personal and the group.[44]

Jung wrote about collective problems appearing as personal problems:

> A collective problem, if not recognized as such, always appears as a personal problem, and in individual cases may give the impression that something is out of order in the realm of the personal psyche. The personal sphere is indeed disturbed, but such disturbances need not be primary; they may be secondary, the consequences of an insupportable change in the social atmosphere.[45]

My dream revealed the aloneness I felt when cultural structures breakdown. Metaphorically speaking, my childhood reality of witnessing sanctioned forms of violence along with the denial of intense suffering, threaded through my transit experiences and was reactivated in my experience of the institute's culture. The dream appearance however pointed to the healing that might come if I could find a more inclusive experience of belonging. With this insight, a powerful urge emerged for me to integrate my multiple experiences, languages, and divergent perspectives as being the tapestry of the cultural layer of my psyche.

In analyzing my own cultural integration, I needed to recognize not only the cultural complexes of both Bogotá and Long Beach, but how the transit had impacted me psychologically. I realize that the cultural alienation I first felt when coming to Southern California reemerged in my projections on the C. G. Jung Institute as a "white homogenous" culture. I was largely unconscious that my "whiteness" concealed a cultural estrangement I carried as an immigrant, which I would have felt more overtly had I been a person of color. The myth that the United States is a "melting pot of immigrants" was undermined by the implicit social expectation that newcomers "assimilate" the dominant "white" cultural ideals of America.[46] Language compounds the immigrant's problem of assimilation since words carry emotionally dense cultural meanings and often are not easily translatable. Even when there are commonalities between people, communicating one's inner truth is an accomplishment, and trusting new relationships to endure ambiguity and confusion is rare. During my training, for example, the cultural complex of assimilation reappeared in my struggle to appropriate Jungian concepts whose connotations derived from European and Christian cultures. For me they came with an unspoken conveyance that I "assimilate" a "Jungian" cultural perspective, which felt like a "false-self" adaptation rather than my authentic voice.[47]

Although acute and prolonged suffering of transit may result in significant psychic vulnerabilities, these circumstances also invite resiliency, flexibility, and ingenuity. The process is one of constant tension and the play of multiple cultural complexes and identifications, dynamically circumambulating in "nonlinear, discontinuous states of consciousness in an ongoing dialectic," which in fortunate circumstances can lead to a flexible centering in a successful individuation process.[48] My experiences attest to Wendell Berry's notion that the journey is a spiritual one, not measured in miles, but in an arduous, humbling, and joyful journey by which we arrive on the ground at our feet and learn to be at home.[49]

Soil That Nourishes Multicultural Minds

Idealized and fixed visions of who we are as a people and as a nation may turn out to be false. We are, in fact, in a state of profound flux. What had appeared to be a known and firm cultural ground may actually reveal itself to be in a state of rhizomatic unfolding of interweaving cultures that are in a continuous process of resettlement. This unsettled landscape shifts our attention to emerging subjective and objective realities that are assembling from multiple, divergent, and connected temporalities. For example, more than a third of the inhabitants of the San Francisco Bay Area in California are foreign born, and many more are first-generation Americans, born of immigrant parents.[50] Although American immigration policies historically have been restrictive, the calamity of the 9/11 attack stimulated increased national apprehension and xenophobia. Nonetheless, the complex polycultural communities of residents and immigrants in the Bay Area are engaging interculturally and addressing social problems creatively.[51] Sociocultural complexity, in fact, supports a healthy proculturation process that not only resonates with many immigrants' multicultural minds, but also invites creative mixtures of individuals self-identifying as being of mixed heritage, race, and ethnicity.[52] Social commentator Maureen Dowd described "American identity and American values as fungible at the moment. The guardrails are off."[53] American culture is being reshaped, and the process is activating polarizing cultural complexes. Lest we fall prey to splitting proclivities and merciless repetitious cycles of conflict, we must sustain engagement with cultural differences, long enough for a naturally constructive process to take root.[54] While virtual cyberspace communities are forming more rapidly than most human minds can recognize their shape or meaning, immigrants and their American-born children are forming new communities of multiple internal/external diversities. Social commentator David Brooks describes millennials in terms similar to what I would use for young immigrants: they are "developing a centering synthesis that teaches us that backgrounds are more complicated than simple class or race conflict-stories." Immigrants'

> lives demonstrate that society is a jungle with unexpected connections and migrations and what matters is what you do with your background, the viewpoints you construct by combining viewpoints. Their lives are examples of the power of love to slice through tribal identity.[55]

We must reconceptualize our traditional schemata of culture, depicted as tree-like structures, chronologically, causally, dualistically, and hierarchically organized, to a rhizomatic view where crossroads of complex connectivity, multidimensionality, and imagination exist.[56] This is the soil in which flowers grow—where psychological wounds embedded in immigrants' multicultural complexes nourish rather than deplete subsequent generations' contributions to new cultural forms. Proculturation is a natural, creative, and constructive process of holistic integrity, where human subjectivity dynamically interweaves with cultural systems.[57] A natural polyculturalism is found where there is access to one another's differing perspectives. This is a relational ecology that shares common human ground.[58]

Fifth Psychocultural Thread: Toward Psychocultural Integration

Writing this personal narrative has brought me insight and repair. Cultural ideals and their shadows were clarified as I became aware of how history and heritage had settled into the cultural level of my psyche and shaped my cultural complexes. The psychological dynamics of erasure and denial, both pervasive aspects of cultural complexes in Colombia and Southern California, had entwined themselves in the vulnerability I experienced in my "transit," becoming my immigrant's multicultural complex. As cultural complexes came into being relationally, I observed being both moved toward connection and also away from the pain of marginality, stimulated as it was by differing cultural perspectives. Both denial and erasure, when activated, robbed me (and I believe, rob the surrounding society) of the empathy needed for our multicultural complexities. The integrative process of suffering consciously personal and cultural anguishes and humiliations has increased my compassion for both myself and others; and paradoxically, accepting the vulnerability of my multicultural psyche has created new insights regarding the temporality and fluidity of cultural identifications. This discernment has supported my clinical work with individuals and my work in communities that strive toward the integration of diverse sociocultural perspectives.

Notes

1 Thomas Singer and Samuel L. Kimbles, *The Cultural Complex: Contemporary Jungian Perspectives on Psyche and Society* (New York: Routledge, 2004); Vladimir Gamsakhurdia, "Adaptation in a Dialogic Perspective—From Acculturation to Proculturation," *Cultural and Psychology* 24 (2018): 545–559, https://doi.org/10.1177/1354067X18791977; and Vladimir Gamsakhurdia, "Proculturation: Self-reconstruction by Making 'Fusion Cocktails" of Alien and Familiar Meanings," *Culture and Psychology* 25, no. 2 (2019): 161–177, https://doi.org/10.1177%2F1354067X19829020. *Proculturation* emphasizes the constructive adaptive processes unfolding that integrate a dialogical self and social representations (similar

to Jung's individuation process, which unfolds and integrates personal complexes and cultural complexes). I use this term in agreement with the author's distinction that the traditional term, *acculturation*, is static and mechanistic, whereas *proculturation* takes into account the fluid and integrative aspects his studies revealed.

2 Tommy Orange, *There There* (New York: Alfred A. Knopf, 2018), introductory essay, 10.

3 C. G. Jung, "Mind and Earth" (1927/1931), in *The Collected Works of C. G. Jung, vol. 10, Civilization in Transition* (Princeton: Princeton University Press, 1968), 103.

4 Ibid.

5 Enrique Dussel, *Philosophy of Liberation* (New York: Wipf & Stock Publishers, 1985); quoted in Achim Borchardt-Hume, ed., *Doris Salcedo: Shibboleth*, exhibition catalogue (London: Tate Modern, 2007), 25.

6 Mark Dowe, *The Haida Gwaii Lesson* (San Francisco: Inkshares, Inc. 2017), 27–31. Other European colonizers used the Doctrine of Discovery as the canon of international law as late as 2005; see, for example, the US Supreme Court's finding in *City of Sherril, NY v. Oneida Nation*, which read, in part, "Under the Doctrine of Discovery fee title (ownership) to the land Occupied by Indians when the colonist arrived became vested in the sovereign—first the discovering European nation and later the original states and the United States" (30–31).

7 Jimenez de Quesada and Anonymous, "Lands Loyal to the Bogota Become New Granada," in *The Colombia Reader*, ed. Ann Farnsworth-Alvear, Marco Palacios, and Ana María Gómez López (Durham, NC: Duke University Press, 2017), 26.

8 Antonio Caballero, *Historia de Colombia y Sus Oligarquías* (Ministerio de Cultural, Crítica, 2018), 27–28, 68–69.

9 Eitan Ginzberg, *The Destruction of the Indigenous Peoples of Hispano America* (Eastbourne, UK: Sussex Academic Press, 2018); Linda Tuhiwai Smith, *Decolonizing Methodologies, Research and Indigenous Peoples* (London: Zed Books, 2012), 112.

10 Smith, *Decolonizing Methodologies*, 112.

11 Ibid., 117.

12 "Colombian Conflict Has Killed 220,000 in 55 Years, Commission Finds," *The Guardian*, July 25, 2013; and "More than 260,000 Dead in 70 Years," *The New York Times*, August 2, 2018, report from the National Center of Historic Memory; see also related reports by Silvana Paternostro, "Hell Can be Beautiful," *New York Review of Books*, July 19, 2018; and Omaira Bolanos, "President Ivan Duque, Protect Social Activists," *The New York Times*, August 8, 2018.

13 Jose Marti, "You Can't Speak with Calm," in *Amistad funesta* (Middlesex: Echo, 2006), 39–40, accessed Project Gutenberg, http://www.gutenberg.org/files/18166/18166-h/18166-h.htm; quoted in Maire Arana, *Bolivar, American Liberator* (New York: Simon & Schuster, 2013), xi.

14 *New York Times*, September 13, 2018, from reports on the Ejército de Liberación Nacional (ELN) in the AP and *El Espectador*, August 22, 2018.

15 Orlando Patterson, *Slavery and Social Death* (Cambridge, MA: Harvard University Press, 1982/2018), ix.

16 Maria Claudia Munévar, "In the Shadow of the Virgin Mary," in *Listening to Latin America*, eds. Pilar Amezaga, Gustavo Barcellos, Áxel Capriles, Jacqueline Gerson, and Denise Ramos, 154–165 (New Orleans: Spring Journal Books, 2012).

17 Inés de la Ossa, "La Patasola: Raíces Arquipaleo de la Identidad Femenina de un mito Colombiano," unpublished lecture delivered at the VII Latin American Congress, July 2018.

18 Paul Gilroy, "Brokenness, Division and the Moral Topography of Post-Colonial Worlds," in *Doris Salcedo: Shibboleth*, ed. Achim Borchardt-Hume (London: Tate Modern, 2007), 27.

19 Gabriel Garcia Marquez, *One Hundred Years of Solitude* (New York: Harper Perennial, 1970), 13.

20 Colombian artists such as Doris Salcedo and Fernando Botero, photographer Juan Manuel Echavarría, and writers Gabriel García Márquez, Emma Reyes, Patricia Engel, Héctor Abad, Santiago Gamboa, María Mcfarland Sánchez-Moreno, and Ingrid Rojas Contreras. Nicolas Casey, "City Struggles to Bury Ghost of Drug Lord," *The New York Times*, September 22, 2018, section A1.

21 George Orwell, *Politics and the English Language* (New York: Penguin Classics, 1946); quoted in Leo Braudy, "La, La Land," review of *The Mirage Factory, Illusion, Imagination and the Invention of Los Angeles*, by Gary Krist, *New York Times, Book Review*, June 2, 2018, Sunday Book Review, 59.

22 Lawrence Culver, *The Frontiers of Leisure: Southern California and the Shaping of Modern America* (Oxford, UK: Oxford University Press, 2010), 17–18.

23 Norman M. Klein, *The History of Forgetting: Los Angeles and the Erasure of Memory* (London, Verso, 2008), 27–29; Italo Calvino, *Invisible Cities* (New York: Harcourt, 1974); quoted in Klein, *The History of Forgetting*, 85.

24 John Walton Caughey, ed., *B. D. Wilson Report, The Indian of Southern California in 1852* (Lincoln: NE: University of Nebraska Press, 1995). Also gathered from Wikipedia's use of A. L. Kroeber's documentation from 1907, 1908, and others.

25 Klein, *The History of Forgetting*, 1–29.

26 F. Arturo Rosales, *Chicano! The History of the Mexican American Civil Rights Movement* (Houston: Arte Público Press, 1997), 18, 119.

27 Klein, *The History of Forgetting*, 1–29.

28 Peter la Chapelle, *Proud to be an Okie* (Berkeley, CA: University of California Press, 2007), 23–26.

29 Culver, *The Frontiers of Leisure*, 3.

30 Neal Gabler, *An Empire of their Own: How the Jews Invented Hollywood* (New York, Anchor Books, 1988), 4.

31 John Tetpon, "Of Shamans, My Ancestors, and Genocide," *Native Nation*, July 30, 2018.

32 See BBC internet reports, 2018, under "Muiscas in Bogota."

33 Bill McKibben, "Free California of Fossil Fuels," *The New York Times*, August 9, 2018, A21. The state of California in August 2018 voted to commit to 100 percent green energy by 2045.

34 Los Angeles Native American Indian Commission (LANIC) on "Decolonialization of Public Spaces," http://www.lanaic.org.

35 Sam Kimbles, *Phantom Narratives: The Unseen Contributions of Culture to Psyche* (London: Rowman & Littlefield, 2014), 17.

36 For a comprehensive analysis of studies related to the impact of ethnicity and racism for immigrant children, see Carolina and Marcelo Suarez-Orozco, *Children of Immigration* (Cambridge, MA: Harvard University Press, 2001), 33–37 and 99; Alejandro Portes, ed. *The New Second Generation* (New York: Russel Sage Foundation, 1996); Salaman Akhtar, *Immigration and Identity* (New Jersey: Jason Aronson, Inc., 1999); Karina O. Alvarado, Alicia Ivonne Estrada, and Ester E. Hernández, *U.S Central Americans: Reconstructing Memories, Struggles, and Communities of Resistance* (Tuscan: University of Arizona Press, 2017), 3–4. From 2011 to 2014, there was a surge of unaccompanied migrant children from Central American coming into the United States, which was publicized as a social threat, much like the "anchor babies" of the 1980s. For a personal account, see Francisco

Cantu's *The Line Becomes a River* (New York: Riverhead Books, 2018). As an agent for the US Border Patrol, Cantu describes the terror of 10- and 11-year-old girls crossing alone to meet their mother and teenage boys coming with older brothers who died in the desert in transit (51–54).

37 Donald Kalsched, *The Inner World of Trauma* (London: Routledge, 1996), 106. Also see *Trauma and Soul* (London: Routledge, 2013).

38 Andrew Harlem, "Exile as a Dissociative State: When a Self is "lost in Transit," *Psychoanalytic Psychology* 27 (2010): 460–474; Haydee Faimberg, *The Telescoping of Generations* (London: The New Library of Psychoanalysis, Routledge, 2003).

39 Erik Erickson, *Identity and the Life Cycle* (New York: W. W. Norton & Co., 1980).

40 Suarez-Orozco and Suarez-Orozco, *Children of Immigration*, 33–35.

41 Timur F. Oguz, "Concrete Expressions of an 'Unformulated' Discontinuity," *Contemporary Psychoanalysis* 48, no. 1 (2012): 54–71. For concepts regarding social mirroring, see Sam Kimbles, "Social Suffering Through Cultural Mourning, Cultural Melancholia and Cultural Complexes," *Spring Journal* 78: 213–217; Suarez-Orozco and Suarez-Orozco, *Children of Immigration*, chapter 4, 87–123.

42 Dee Watt-Jones, "Location of Self," *Family Process* 49, no. 3 (2010). Feminists in the 1970s introduced the idea of *intersectionality*, a confluence of multiple identities in each individual, which includes one's social location along with the elevation and subjugation associated with these identities.

43 During this period (1988–1990) several major professional and ethical boundaries were broken between analysts and candidates. At the time of my dream, I was not consciously aware of these violations, but had unconsciously absorbed the trauma and psychological impact in the community. To the memberships' credit, a community discussion, which became known as "the firehouse meeting" was held among analysts and candidates about a year after my dream.

44 Singer and Kimbles, *The Cultural Complex*.

45 C. G. Jung, *Memories, Dream, Reflections*, ed. and recorded by Aniela Jaffé (New York: Random House, 1961), 233–234.

46 Israel Zangwill's *The Melting Pot* was a play staged in 1908. The metaphor of the *melting pot* implies a heterogeneous society becoming *homogenous*. By the 1980s the idea stood for a fusion of nationalities. Ronald Takaki, *A Different Mirror, A History of Multicultural America* (New York: Little, Brown and Company, 1993), 378–428.

47 Donald W. Winnicott, *Through Paediatrics to Psycho-Analysis* (New York: Basic Books, Inc. 1975), 225.

48 Philip Bromberg, *Standing in the Spaces* (New York: Routledge, 1998), 270.

49 Wendell Berry, *The Unforeseen Wilderness: Kentucky's Red River Gorge* (San Francisco, North Point Press, 1991).

50 US Census Bureau, American Community Survey, 2013, https://www.census.gov/programs-surveys/acs/guidance/comparing-acs-data/2013.html.

51 Manuel Pastor, Jennifer Ito, and Vanessa Carter, "California Is America on Fast Forward," The Next California, Haas Institute, April 18, 2018, https://haasinstitute.berkeley.edu/next-california. "By 2040, California will be 73 percent people of color … By 2000, only 47 percent of population was white. During that same period, Latinos grew from 19 percent to 32 percent of the population. Eighty-four percent of Latinos are of Mexican origin. Another growing segment of the population are Asian American/Pacific Islander (AAPI) Californians."

52 Jaee Cho, Carmitt T. Tadmor, and Michael W. Morris, "Are All Diversity Ideologies Creatively Equal? The Diverging Consequence of Colorblindness,

Multiculturalism and Polyculturalism," *Journal of Cross-Cultural Psychology* 49, no. 9 (2018): 1–26, https://doi.org/10.1177%2F0022022118793528.

53 Maureen Dowd, "From Ice Cube to Black Cube," *The New York Times*, May 12, 2018, Sunday Review, 11.

54 Katie Gentile, psychoanalyst and professor at John Jay College, CLUNY, and co-editor of the *Journal of Gender Studies*, from an International Association of Relational Psychoanalysis and Psychotherapy (IARPP) online Colloquium, November 11, 2018.

55 David Brooks, "The Rise of the Amphibians," *The New York Times*, February 16, 2018, A29.

56 William L. Fox, *Unsettled: Art and Environment Conference 2017* (Munich: Hirmer Verlag GmbH, 2017), 178–179. The concept described is based on Neil Campbell's *The Rhizomatic West* (Lincoln, NE: University of Nebraska Press, 2008).

57 Gamsakhurdia, "Adaptation in a Dialogic Perspective," 12.

58 Fabrice Olivier Dubosc, "Co-individuation as an Open Mandala," in *Narratives of Individuation*, eds. Raya A. Jones and Leslie Gardner (London: Routledge, 2019).

National Character

Chapter 13

Our Divisible Nation

In the Grip of an Alpha Narcissistic Complex

Jacqueline J. West

> *I pledge allegiance to the Flag of the United States of America, and to the Republic for which it stands, one Nation under God, indivisible, with liberty and justice for all.*

Most Americans have participated in pledging allegiance to the nation, to its being "indivisible," with liberty and justice for all. "Indivisible?" Not only its indivisibility—but also its capacity to support liberty and justice for all—are currently facing intense and insistent questioning from many voices. What's up?

The United States, as a nation—and as an international citizen—is in a startling state. Within the country, the dis-ease, unrest, and disturbance are palpable; the pervasive violence is relentless. It is a time of chaos, of volcanic polarities, of increasingly exposed racism, along with surprising and dubiously creative restructuring. Meanwhile, the entire world, of which the US is undeniably a part, is in an uproar: plagued by eruptions and strain, dismemberment and fragmentation, along with a startling emergence of mongrel forms of warfare. Both the united and the un-united nations are being asked to redefine themselves, geographically and politically. Some people think this may be ruinous; others think it may be creative, perhaps creative through its destructiveness. Others simply tremble with terror. As informed world citizens, as psychologically minded professionals, and as a nation facing a disordered world, we are being called on, in one way or another, to offer some semblance of understanding about this current reality. This chapter is one way I have chosen to answer this call.

For many of the years I've been practicing as a Jungian analyst, my primary focus has been on the dynamics of individuals. Along the way, however, I began to find myself intrigued by thoughts about the profile of my country, the United States. These thoughts were initially nourished by my parents' deeply liberal political views, which were plentifully expressed in our household. I was born and raised in Colorado but moved to Florida and then Oklahoma as a school kid. These varied states exposed me to worlds that were quintessentially American but curiously different. My first chance to watch a TV program regularly was when our neighbor down the road was watching the McCarthy Hearings each afternoon and she welcomed my siblings and me to the show! Once my parents brought a TV into our own house, I could then watch not only *American Bandstand* but also the endless Western movies that persistently canonized our images of the brave and bold, heroic and victorious gunslingers of the Wild West. I was irrefutably steeped in the romance of the charismatic Lone Ranger, the "Marlboro Man," and in the generalized irresistible confidence of the "American spirit" with its abundant wealth and opportunity. Of course this was alchemically supplemented with my own adolescent highs and lows. Altogether these experiences initiated me into America's persistent complexes. At that point, I obviously did not recognize that I was being coached into a sense of American entitlement, expressed most centrally in the conviction that settling the lands that defined our country led to the birth of an enlightened nation, from its origins through the taming of the West. It was our "Manifest Destiny" that, without doubt, we were to live and prosper in unbounded "riches," including abundant, forever-enough land, minerals, and gold that were ours for the taking.

This induction into the cultural complexes of my country was quite suddenly unsettled when, at the age of 15, along with my parents, my brother, and my sister, I embarked to Pakistan for a two-year adventure. Clearly, though unknowingly, I was primed for an experience that would inspire me to face a vastly wider view of the American story.

As we sailed overseas, I read a book that was popular in 1959: *The Ugly American*.[1] The central "take home forever" points in this book brought out the entitled, dominating, insensitive, and violent sides of the stories I had internalized. It illuminated our shadows that were not so deeply hidden in our cultural complex. This book, along with the remarkable two years in Pakistan, which at the that time had been a country for only 13 years before we arrived, and the amazing experience of traveling in numerous other countries, impacted me deeply. At that time, I had no inkling that I'd ultimately be interested in the cultural complexes of the United States. However, in the innumerable years between then and now, as I found my way into a perspective that invites journeys and reflections into psyche, I became progressively drawn toward extending psychological insights regarding the dynamics of individuals into reflections about the dynamics of this nation where I live. At this point in time, given the extraordinarily chaotic reality in the United States, it seems not only interesting but also essential to reflect on this country.

The United States has become an entity riddled by numerous personal and collective complexes that have been forged out of the dismembered parts of ourselves that have been dissociated, disowned, and split off. As Americans we are capable of functioning with a brave and celebrated persona, but we fail to face the eruption of the dismembered parts of the collective psyche banished into the darkness of our cultural complexes. What is virtually unbearable at this point in time is that these eruptions are appearing, day by day, at an astonishingly steady pace. In effect, Americans are being divided by collective complexes that are crashing into the country's surprisingly frail potential for unity, into its vulnerable "indivisibility."

In this chapter, I will clarify how the United States is tenaciously in the destructive grip of cultural complexes ruled by the dynamics of domination. *Domination* appears in individual and cultural development as an aspect of a particular path rooted in an archetypal force that may be described as *primal* or *potential* action. This is one of several archetypal forces, including *archetypal affect* and *archetypal mentation*, each of which contributes to a different path of development. The consequence of the defensive rigidity of the dynamics of domination is that both individually and culturally we are consistently thrown into chaos and imbalance, dismay and distress, fear and trembling.

The dynamics of psyche that are at play in this pattern of domination can be understood psychologically through an analysis of the archetypal forces that are at work in the formation of different forms of narcissism. By bringing these different forms of narcissism into view, I will describe how the currently intense expressions of narcissistic domination are woven into a pattern of alpha narcissism that disturbs both national and international interactions. Nationally, the grip of alpha dynamics subjects Americans to consistent attacks upon the central values of American democracy: namely truth, justice, and informed delegation. Internationally, it fuels an inflated competitive posture aimed to control others. Alpha dynamics, rooted in predator-prey dynamics, ensure that the individual and collective psyche are tautly strung by relentless polarizations and consistently plagued by either-or tugs of psychic and literal warfare. Pervasively, they threaten the continued quality of life on this planet.

Given the potential consequences of these dynamics, it seems imperative that as Americans we seriously reflect on the impact that our interactions have on the other countries on this planet. Yes, the United States, like every other nation, has a personality. It is an organ within the psyche of the world, to some degree a conscious organ, emerging from the presence of each and every American. And given that each American is a cell in this organ, we each have a unique responsibility to reflect on both our individual *and* our national contributions to the country's cultural dynamics.

So how do we *live with*, how do we *face and work with*, the challenges of these dynamics? First we must deepen our understanding of how clinical perspectives of individual character structures and complexes *can be woven into* an understanding of cultural character structures and complexes. Doing so may strengthen our conscious assessments of these dynamics and strengthen our capacity to face these disturbing times creatively.

The Formation of Complexes

Jung's early work included the development of his ideas about complexes. Key to these ideas are his hypotheses that entering the human world involves an inherent separation, personally from the mother's body, archetypally from a unified state. From this point of view, the moment we are born, we face a profound separation. When an infant is born, the umbilical cord between the infant's body and the mother's is cut. Literally and symbolically what had been one-of-us is now two-of-us. In this moment of birth, the existence of two-of-us delivers the child into the profound quandaries of relationship: the undifferentiated wholeness of one is now dismembered. The child passes through a doorway and enters a perplexing world, a world of "opposites," a world subject to the interminable tensions between conscious and unconscious, creation and destruction, life and death, love and hate, and so on.

Jung returns to the primal dance of the opposites throughout his work, spanning from his earliest emphasis on the structure and dynamics of the psyche all the way through his remarkable voyages into the realms of alchemy. He emphasizes that the emergence of the "opposites" in the psyche leave us in the midst of endless quandaries of relatedness. Relatedness is not easy. In the midst of this ongoing process, experiences emerge that consciousness cannot digest. For the infant, the child, or the adult these experiences may become too painful, too frightening, too overwhelming, possibly even traumatic. And these pieces of psyche are then disowned. They then become dissociated and contained by defensive maneuvers that keep them at bay, out of mind. In effect, paradoxically, we develop ways to keep ourselves fragmented in order to feel safe. The cost is that *we are* then fragmented, indeed dismembered, and we strangle our capacity to develop a sense of wholeness—within and between ourselves and others.

Incarnation is clearly an initiation into a dance with duality—and dismemberment is thus embodied at the core of each of our lives. Intrapsychically, birth and the progressive development of consciousness differentiated from unconsciousness naturally creates a psychic fragmentation, a presence of differentiated elements within psychic reality. The problem is that these differentiated elements are susceptible to being split apart, torn out of relationship to each other, polarized. Briefly, Jung suggested that a complex is formed when these dissociated, fragmented, and split-off pieces of our psyche settle in the unconscious and remain there, not faced consciously. In effect they remain broken off, unreachable, and indigestible—*and* their related unresolved feelings, thoughts, and preverbal memories remain inaccessible to consciousness. When these fragmented pieces settle into the unknown, they gravitate toward and collect around a particular archetype that serves as the core of the complex. The complex then takes on its own autonomous function in the psyche. Clearly, the emergent reality of consciousness as *other than* unconsciousness and the relationship between the two becomes the intrapsychic art of personal development.

The combination of the disowned fragments of psyche with the primal energy of the archetype forges a powerful "creature" within, and to the extent that we continue to reject, ignore, or hide from it, the fragmented nature of psyche is maintained. As the repository of these overwhelming and/or rejected psychic fragments, the complex is not passive. Metaphorically, these raw, denied parts of ourselves fester and eventually claim their space, sometimes erupting as rage, violence, murderous aggression, and so on. These eruptions are typically aimed at others—or at one's own self. When we live in the grip of these dissociated complexes, we cut ourselves off from our own potential wholeness as well as from others who awaken any hint of what we have disowned.

A Portrayal of the Formation of a Personal and a Cultural Complex

It is one thing to understand the development of a complex and to appreciate that complexes tend to ensure our dismembered state—but it's another to *feel* the anguish that stimulates the complex's creation. To summon a felt sense of the creation of a complex, I briefly mention a film I saw recently. This film portrays the creation of a complex sensitively and profoundly and a brief introduction to it evocatively distills this process. The film *Never Look Away* is a somewhat loosely enacted docudrama of a current German artist, Gerhard Richter.[2] This film evocatively portrays a young boy's development of a complex in reaction to a shattering trauma that pervaded the rest of his life. Haunted by the torturous pain he had endured, he eventually relied on his passion for painting to help him turn toward his agonies and he proceeded to create masterpieces that have impacted millions.

This film powerfully elicits an experience of the anguish *and* the emergence of a defensive complex. As the film begins, we meet Gerhard as a young boy who is attending a tour in a museum of modern art in pre–World War II Berlin with his aunt. She is a lovely, sensitive, and eccentric young woman, very attuned to Gerhard who is, in turn, very attached to her. We learn shortly thereafter that the program of eliminating citizens of impurity is already active in Germany under the autocratic and oppressive rule of the National Socialists; the eccentricities of Gerhard's somewhat "different" aunt condemn her to their judgment that she is impure. Soon the troops arrive at Gerhard's home and, in front of the powerless and speechless family gathered in the driveway, forcefully drag the aunt, kicking and crying, out of the house and into their armored vehicle. She is taken away to be sterilized—and subsequently sent to her death in a gas chamber. As she is hauled past the family members and into the vehicle, Gerhard raises his hand to block out what he is seeing. He covers his view of this unbearable scene—but then, for a moment, he moves his hand aside, quickly, and sees them force his beloved aunt into the vehicle. He quickly blocks his view once more. However, just a few seconds later he again removes his hand and all he can see is a blurred, confusing, excoriatingly painful image of her final entrapment.

In the face of his intolerable agony and powerlessness, Gerhard blocked his view and *blurred* his memory of this unfathomable moment. He, in effect, looked away. In the language of complexes, he negated the image, subjecting it, via dissociation, to the unconscious. In that moment, he dismembered himself. Yet, as I mentioned, he did eventually find his way toward making contact with this dismembered part of himself through his art. He painted, over and over again, *blurred* paintings—many of them done over photographs, particularly photographs of his family. Devoting himself to painting after painting of thick paint, blocking the view of what lay underneath, his "practice" became "Never look away."

Continuing this practice for years, Richter steadily addressed the paradox that *we dismember ourselves*: we cast parts of ourselves into our complexes and we then develop various defenses to keep them there. We deny them; we rationalize them away; we develop practices that silence them; we fight them back any way we can. We all *too often support the entrenchment* of the dismembered parts of ourselves and these split-off, disowned parts fester. As they become ever more loaded, they press for expression; they aim to take over. That's when we feel overwhelmed—perhaps terrified that we're "losing it." We may subtly sense at a more primal level that a power greater than us is driving us to do X or say Y, and we may fear we are somehow possessed. But, with a pause and a deep breath, we may realize that in truth it is the disowned, dismembered parts of ourselves speaking up. It is an autonomous complex.

The Formation of a Cultural Complex

Richter's persistent focus on blurring his memories expresses how painful it is to see clearly. This *directly* addresses his personal reality. Simultaneously, his trauma was embedded in the reality of a war, the horror of which stunned every awake soul on this planet. His work thus speaks *indirectly* to the entire world about how not only individuals but also, simultaneously, an identified collective, a nation, can become possessed and unfathomably cruel, forming a cultural complex. It seems clear that Richter turned to painting in order to forge a sufficiently strong self to integrate what was clearly a deep and personal complex—as well as a national cultural one. His daring and persistence make it clear that no matter what nation we live in, it would serve us well to face that *our* collective, our nation, just like each of us, has developed its collection of complexes. The implicit question, then, is what lies in *our* American cultural complexes?

Part I, Our American Cultural Complex: A Review of The Matrix and Meaning of Character

The United States, like every other nation, has a personality with a particular developmental pattern emerging from the presence of each and every American. In 2007, I co-authored a book with a colleague, Nancy Dougherty, titled *The Matrix and Meaning of Character: An Archetypal and Developmental Approach.*[3] A review of this work introduces a clinical and archetypal perspective about the development of personal complexes that leads into reflections about the development of cultural complexes.

We began our work with a clear intention to interweave the depth and richness of archetypal explorations with robust clinical reflections well informed with diagnostic knowledge. Focusing on the archetypal themes that appeared in the various stories and the patterns of a variety of diagnostic categories, we realized that three discrete wellsprings of archetypal energy underlie character structures. The fairytales, myths, and personal stories that we studied taught us that the archetypal forces of affect, action, and mentation were woven throughout these portraits. Each of these forces is truly archetypal, meaning we do not experience them directly, but through their manifestations. These primary wellsprings inspire, inform, and infuse our development, our becoming who we are. Although every person has an identifying archetypal ground, all three archetypal forces, to some degree, are at play in each of our psyches; they are necessary to our wholeness.

As we studied these patterns, we saw that, under the inevitable stress of entering and developing a human life, infants adopt methods to protect and defend themselves. Some, inspired by archetypal mentation, tend *to withdraw from* interactions. Others, informed by archetypal affect, tend *to seek* relationships with whatever and whoever is available. And yet others, informed by archetypal action, tend *to meet the world antagonistically.* These different relationships to others can frequently be seen in the movements of newborns as they adjust to their mother's body during their first contact, hours, days, weeks, and on into life. We found these relational patterns repeated over and over again in stories as well as clinical profiles.

We also recognized that stories and classic diagnostic profiles that shared similar images easily fell into three phases of pre-Oedipal *development.* During the earliest phase, the *primal phase*, roughly from birth to 18 months, infants are occupied with separation. In the midst of sorting out the essential relationship between their nascent consciousness and the archetypal realms, they find themselves exploring the relationship between their infant body and their mother's, their hunger and their satisfaction, their power to affect the world and their powerlessness, the good mother from the bad mother, love and hate, happiness and sadness. The infant's first line of defense is to split experience into good and bad and to get rid of, project, the bad—and a dance of polar opposites begins. As infants continue to encounter reality in terms of ever-changing oppositions, they grapple with the relationships between separated parts. This dance of the opposites has the potential to lead to differentiation, yet it also may lead toward entrenched polarization.

From 18 months onward to roughly 3 years old, the child, primarily through interactions with the mother, is exploring and managing what can be seen developmentally as narcissistic dynamics. Discovering the dimensions of individual presence, in the *narcissistic phase*, children establish their selfhood in the world. They learn, at best, how to integrate the basic narcissistic dynamics of exhibitionism, grandiosity, and omnipotence in a healthy way; at worst these dynamics become employed defensively.

From 3 years to roughly 4.5 years old, in the *pre-Oedipal phase*, the child's psychic attention revolves around the various dynamics that further support the strengthening of a conscious perspective grounded in a more well-defined sense of self. These developments ultimately enable children to explore beyond their primary relationship with the mother, turning toward embracing the father and, subsequently, the larger world.

As children navigate these developmental challenges, they may be faced with experiences that range from personally generative and creative to personally traumatic and destructive. And, as they manage each stage, the particular archetypal wellspring of affect, action, or mentation shapes the emergence of defensive processes that are activated when the child is faced with threatening experiences. Facing grief and rage rather than joy, trauma rather than safety, and abandonment rather than connection, the child develops defenses. In the earliest stage, these defenses are primal archetypal processes that appear psychodynamically as splitting, projection, and dissociation. In the second stage, they are narcissistic defenses, appearing as nonintegrated grandiosity, exhibitionism, and omnipotence. And in the third stage, precognitive entrenched maneuvers, such as denial, rationalization, avoidance, and seduction, emerge.

These differentiations and descriptions of psychological defenses that appear at progressive developmental ages are adeptly described in a book by Nancy McWilliams, *Psychoanalytic Diagnosis*.[4] This work directly influenced our development of the matrix, allowing us to integrate detailed and substantiated differentiations of defenses that previously had not been woven into Jungian theory.

As Nancy Dougherty and I progressively analyzed numerous archetypal and developmental images, stories, and profiles, we gradually realized that when the defense patterns that emerge within each developmental age are infused with an identifiable archetypal wellspring, they create an identifiable defensive complex. What emerged from these analyses was a *matrix* of nine archetypally informed and diagnostically describable personality patterns, each rooted in the force of a particular archetypal wellspring activated at a particular stage of development.

As the pattern of the matrix emerged, we were surprised to see that narcissism has three quite different faces. We had originally imagined that a single narcissistic profile would be rooted in a particular archetypal wellspring, given that this was becoming the case for the other diagnostic profiles. However, as we reviewed our material innumerable times, we consistently found that narcissistic profiles find expression in all three of the relational patterns. Thus, empirically, we concluded that there are three narcissistic character structures: the *counter-dependent narcissist* (archetypal mentation, withdrawing relational pattern); the *dependent narcissist* (archetypal affect, seeking relational pattern); and the *alpha narcissist* (archetypal action, antagonistic relational pattern).

For instance, the boy down the street who won't grow up presents a beguiling image of a counter-dependent narcissist. He experiences an insatiable desire for admiration and adventurous drama, yet he is simultaneously drawn to flying away from direct connection with another. Meanwhile, a narcissistic pattern of defensive seeking—which leads to a dependent narcissistic pattern—might be lived out in patterns of repetitive courting that fail to lead to a dependable relationship. And in the third case, we might be facing an alpha narcissist as we attempt to negotiate with a well-veiled, charismatic, and successful business tycoon. The inherently antagonistic and dominating patterns of an alpha narcissist may emerge most apparently when he is challenged to share or collaborate.

The three faces of narcissism remain generally undifferentiated, not only in an occasional clinical discussion but also, far more prevalently, in public discourse and political debates. This leaves us faced with recurrent riddles, and it robs us of more creative and generative insights that could serve both our individual and national realities. Focusing on the differentiations of narcissism, we find ourselves in a position to free ourselves from the confusion created when they remain undefined. We can then turn toward the task of attending to the psyche of our nation.

The consideration of how patterns of defenses at work in our individual psyches are related to patterns in the psyche of nations has been inspired by the tremendously influential work of Thomas Singer. These ideas appeared first in his book, co-authored with Samuel Kimbles, *The Cultural Complex* and have continued to appear in subsequent volumes.[5] His consistent emphasis on how cultural complexes are the building blocks of our collective psyche, how they are autonomous, rooted in an archetypal core, and deeply laden with unconscious affects, have influenced my remarks throughout this chapter.

Part 2: Our American Cultural Complex: America as an Alpha Narcissistic Nation

With the ideas of the three faces of narcissism at hand, I found myself drawn to the conclusion that the United States is undeniably an alpha narcissistic nation. Alpha narcissism, as I mentioned, is formed when the archetypal forces that underlie *dynamic action* arise in the psyche of an individual or a nation who is not prepared to meet these forces creatively. In the earliest primal phase of development, when this child, or nation, faces a threatening moment, she turns toward "striking out" or "tucking in," and this defensive move tends to develop into an identification with the predator *or* the prey. Generally the predator defends wildly against being prey, whereas the tucked-in victim subjects her life to the eternal and tragic search for someone with the power that she is split off from. This personal inaction reveals her defense against the archetypal force of action that she has protectively disowned.

If development is severely impacted in these very early months of life, infants are likely to find themselves developing either a psychopathic character structure or a fearful, even paranoid, compulsive victim character structure. In the narcissistic phase, these basic dynamics tend to emerge in a person's powerful, even compellingly charismatic drive to dominate or a person's unreflective identification with the "follower" who is readily entranced with someone in power. In each case, the person has disowned an essential source of psychic well-being, casting it into the dark stirrings of the unconscious and into an ensnaring complex. In each case, this entrapped psychic piece is defended against by the split-off opposite that rules the person's life. Predators protect themselves from being prey, and victims hide from forceful action that they have protectively disowned. These people, and our country, are psychically ruled by the same predator-prey alpha narcissistic dynamic complex.

As Americans, when we step back, take a breath, and view our nation diagnostically, it is easy to see the archetypal wellspring of raw action that lies at the roots of alpha narcissism, which has fueled the United States since its birth. These dynamics served both the adventurous settlers and the subsequent inhabitants of these lands—creatively and destructively. Historically, they supplied the forceful energy required to explore and develop, to establish new communities in the face of innumerable raw hardships. Plenty of robust power, a daring stride, and the courage to undertake demanding explorations, as gifts of alpha dynamics, have clearly served the country well. However, these dynamics also inspired the settlers to ruthlessly take these lands from their current Native American inhabitants—at the cost of so many deaths that this process is now quite openly seen as genocide. This raw archetypal energy also fueled a merciless industry of slavery that established a racist rift in the fabric of our nation that we are still struggling to repair. In the midst of all this, our Western "heroes" slaughtered—truly slaughtered—innumerable herds of buffalo that roamed the prairies. To this day, these undeniably destructive early expressions of alpha dynamics lie deep within American narcissism, driving the nation widely and wildly into ruthless domination over and over.

This ruthless determination to dominate continues to appear pervasively in the United States. Not only is there now a well-acknowledged and unprecedented gap between the "haves and have-nots" in terms of money, power, and the ability to obtain justice, huge amounts of our national wealth, both economic and environmental, are in the unregulated hands of people for whom amassing and spending more and more of it is a thrill, a challenge, and yet another star on their shield. Insatiable greed partners with the drive to win each and every time. Alpha dynamics also hold a tight grip on our various forms of national security. When we perceive that our national security is in any way questioned or threatened, not only a determination to protect, but also a fierce determination to dominate, quickly reigns supreme. Within our boundaries, we see a penchant for excessively punitive action applied to the disadvantaged, to those whose vulnerability calls out the predator. Any number of other examples also demonstrate that, in the United States, vulnerability, in any form, is soundly devalued and persistently denied; it is consistently defended against. Returning to my opening remarks about this country's "indivisibility," I see that, indeed, we are deeply divided.

Americans must acknowledge that the country remains consistently intent upon waging numerous international wars that were persuasively presented initially as a determination to rid the world of "evil" and bring democracy to all. Just a few years ago, the fear and despair generated by the boldness of these dynamics was expressed in numerous images of the apocalypse—appearing in the news, films, internet conversations, and so on. And now these wars continue at an alarming rate—even though they are minimally recast as efforts to support the fights for freedom abroad. These aims are expressed with intrepid gallantry accompanied by indisputable assertions that the United States has the strongest military in the world—that the United States is, in all accounts, #1, without question. Sensing the expanding inflation and self-righteousness at the core of each of these national behaviors, many people have recently expressed fear that the United States is becoming an authoritarian, if not fascist, state, and on top of that the United States is recklessly courting an unfathomably destructive war that may destroy our planet.

But how have alpha dynamics become so predominant in the character of the United States? Recall that whereas a number of us are born with a primary root in archetypal action, others are rooted in archetypal affect and others in archetypal mentation. The interrelatedness of these various character structures leads us to enquire, particularly, about the lines of shadow-play, not only between those individuals embodying predator and prey dynamics but also between the three forms of narcissism.

In general, each character structure tends to project its shadow onto those structures that are rooted in the *other* archetypal wellsprings of psyche. Given that an alpha narcissist is attempting to get rid of his vulnerability, he will look for another whom he sees as vulnerable. He will dismiss and diminish the other so as to guarantee that he remains free of this disowned part of himself. Meanwhile, those who are well rooted in the wellsprings of mentation or affect will tend to sense that raw action is so utterly other from themselves that they disidentify with it altogether, leaving the force of archetypal action projected onto the apparently powerful and effective "other," the alpha.

All this rejected and projected archetypal raw action is easily seized and put to predatory use by both alpha individuals as well as by the collective psyche of this nation. This is one of the trickiest dynamics at work today in the United States. Bottom line, those who disidentify with aggression of any sort and then proceed to project it onto alpha individuals as well as onto alpha-spirited collective movements are, in effect, handing over their share of this wellspring of energy—their power—to alpha narcissists. This amounts, in essence, to a collusion with alpha values.

Once we have thrown out parts of ourselves, not only are we psychically much poorer, but also we have lost the possibility—and the responsibility—to maintain a relationship with these disowned parts and thus contribute to their integration. We are left with virtually little capacity to truly own our aggression and therefore assume responsibility for it. Once the citizens of the United States have resorted either to dis-identification from raw action altogether or to identification with the predator, the collective psyche of the nation is rendered ill-equipped to enter into a creative dialogue that might release the country from such destructive oppositional splitting.

Our Participation in Our Cultural Complex

Americans are more at odds with each other than ever—to put it quite mildly. When crippled by our defenses and enveloped in a cultural complex, a significant number of us all too often split off from our own dynamic action, and we then, in effect, gift it to the alpha narcissists who are ready and able to use it for their own potentially cruel agendas. Even though we may well excuse or explain or justify our quietude, or suggest that our lack of participation is "resistance," at a psychic level we're handing a rich, powerful force over to those who thrill in the thrall of the alpha's generally quite violent and cruel dominance.

It seems apparent that to deal with the current predominance of unbridled alpha dynamics in the United States, we must challenge ourselves and each other to assume responsibility for and to address the individual integration of our split, dissociated, and complex-ridden inner selves as well as our complex-ridden culture. Naturally this entails not only developing the capacity to recognize those we've chosen to carry our projections and why, but also endeavoring to withdraw our own projections. Bottom line: when we hold up the mirror, do we each see ourselves wrestling with the predatory beast within? Can we truly see it in ourselves?

Many people fear the United States is becoming an authoritarian country. Fears of global disorder have "come home," and now, for some people, this includes a deep dread that we might well lose our essential democratic values and be faced with totalitarian control. Forecasts of doom aside, it does seem apparent that alpha dynamics not only fuel our country, but that *they also have us in their grip*. In this light, observations and analysis as well as forecasts of increasing instability and even corrosion of our democracy deserve our attention.

Shortly after our 2016 Presidential elections, I was introduced to a well-known play that evocatively portrays, in an imaginary rather than a literal script, how such a take-over may unfold. Late one night, I sidestepped into the distracting wonderland of *The New York Times* in order to explore its endlessly informative and frequently frustrating articles and columns about the State of Our Country. And I met the Rhino. Teju Cole, the author of *The New York Times* piece that caught my attention that evening and has held it ever since, titled his article, "A Time for Refusal."[6] He explored *Rhinoceros*, a play written by the French-Romanian playwright Eugene Ionesco in 1958, in "response to totalitarian movements in Europe."[7] The play is a compelling way for us to explore the captivating power of our alpha narcissistic cultural complex—along with how that power is being enacted in our midst today. Following is a short summary of the play.

The play opens, a street café in France, ... *see if you can let yourself imagine this setting, maybe even imagine yourself being there* ... the protagonist, Berenger, is animatedly talking with a friend when a mammoth rhinoceros comes "thundering down the street, stamping and snorting"! The people gathered there are startled but quite shortly return to their conversations. Soon, however, they are startled once again to see another charging rhino pass by. This time, they stop to say that they are disturbed: "It's outrageous. Something must be done." And then, what they begin to do is argue heatedly about whether there might be just one rhino, not two, and whether the rhino comes from Africa or Asia. They also begin to ponder: some insist that they never believed the sightings in the first place, some acknowledge that they admire the rhino's brute force, others speculate that the rhinos are messengers of liberation.

As time passes, and this event reoccurs, Berenger observes that as the rhino sightings continue to be the subject of pointless dispute, one by one, various people in the town begin to turn into rhinos. Their skin hardens, bumps appear over their noses and grow into horns. Even Berenger's friend begins to rhinoorphisize and Berenger argues: "You must admit that we have a philosophy that animals don't share, and an irreplaceable set of values, which it's taken centuries of human civilization to build up."[8] His friend, who is caught in the delusion that the rhino is somehow related to liberty and "who is well on his way to being a rhino himself, retorts, 'When we've demolished all that, we'll be better off!'"[9] Relentlessly, the number of stampeding beasts increases ... and increases.

The play ends when almost everyone has succumbed to the call of the herd. Berenger, all alone, determined to retain his humanity but racked by doubts, looks into a mirror. Witnessing his own being out of step with the consensus, he slips toward a strange sense of being a monster himself. But he then summons his resolve—and *refuses* to accept the call of the herd.

This play presents a resonating, symbolic picture of the dynamics we seem to be far too close to being in the midst of here and now, at home, in America. In Ionesco's vocabulary, Berenger's capacity to see, face, and refuse to join what was happening around him was his *Refusal*; it was clearly his form of saying "no." The capacity to say NO is essential. It is a basic assertion of self in the face of violation—however subtle, however extreme. This includes a loud NO to our own inner dynamics that inhibit our using our own power responsibly. This capacity arrives when we have sorted out the predator-prey dynamics within ourselves and are not subject to one or the other being split off and lodged in an intrapsychic complex. Then we are able to face the predatory aggression that is in the grip of alpha dynamics and running wild in our country. We may find this NO in words or in action, out loud or written. The key here is that one's NO is rooted in the psyche, deep in the wellsprings of archetypal dynamics interlaced with developmental challenges. Forging the strength to form a NO, we may also find access within ourselves to a truly deep-seated YES—the YES that lights life with active joy, deep security, and a profound sense of love—for ourselves, for each other, and for our country.

Use the Key/Open the Door—and Final Reflections

The value of facing these dynamics within ourselves and within the United States is so central to the points I'm making in this chapter that I want to add reflections about one more story that sheds further light upon our individual and collective complexes. This story is the fairytale titled *Bluebeard*.[10]

Once upon a time—which is to say, right here, right now—an apparently very rich and powerfully seductive man, never mind his peculiar blue beard, arrived in the community seeking a bride. He visited a well-established woman with two daughters, whom he invited to visit him on his estate for a week of "games and gambols," fishing, hunting, and feasting; and, after a knock-out weekend, he proposed to the youngest daughter. She agreed, and she and her sister moved into Bluebeard's castle. Soon he announced that he was going on a journey. Handing his young wife the keys to his house, he invited her to explore each and every room *except* the utterly forbidden one at the end of the corridor. He added, "My orders are to be strictly obeyed, and if you should dare to open the door, my anger will exceed anything you have ever experienced."

After Bluebeard's departure, the young bride found herself increasingly curious about what was in the firmly forbidden room—so curious that she went to the door, paused for a moment, but then unlocked the door. She found herself facing pools of dried blood amidst the hanging, dead bodies of Bluebeard's previous wives, each with their throats cut. Once she could recover her senses, she quickly left the room, and only noticed later that the key to that particular room was stained with blood that could not be removed. When her husband returned and demanded she return the keys, he immediately saw the bloody key and knew she had disobeyed his orders and he proclaimed that she therefore would "take her place" in that same room. She pleaded for some time so she could "say her prayers" and, within the granted minutes, with the support of her sister and of her two brothers who had arrived barely in time, they killed Bluebeard.

Although *Bluebeard* is a French fairytale, written by Charles Perrault, it clearly portrays cross-cultural themes that have appeared globally for centuries. In the interest of the present moment, it takes us straight into the question of both recognizing and facing predatory dynamics. First, I will clarify the dynamics "at work" in the Bluebeard character. Then I will consider the young bride's choice to use *the key* as well as the final outcome of the story. As explained, a person with a predatory character structure frequently appears as an alpha narcissist. This sort of person commands our attention and abundant applause for his victories—which he gets plenty of—and he is ever ready to knock out, if not kill, anyone in his way. Determined to dominate everyone and everything in his path, he feeds off constant one-up maneuvers that highlight the other's defeat. His persistent attacks rely not only on physical threats, but also on soul murdering ruthlessness woven with threads of humiliation, lies, and relentless provocations.

When Bluebeard handed his new bride the keys to his house, he invited her to explore each and every room *except* the utterly forbidden one at the end of the corridor. He added, "My orders are to be strictly obeyed, and if you should dare to open the door, my anger will exceed anything you have ever experienced." As the tale proceeds, the young wife, guided by her curiosity, steps *toward* knowing her mysterious husband, toward facing who she has married. She does not turn away from this challenge; she turns toward it. And, once she has opened the door, she is faced, from one angle, with startling and vivid evidence of her husband's lethal, repetitive, entrenched pattern of killing off his wives. She has faced who he is. From another angle, she is simultaneously asked to see who she herself is. The fact that she did choose to use the key to open the door exposed the truth that up to this point she had been seduced by his *apparent* power and generosity; she'd taken no action to find or form her own reality. Right from the beginning, she had allowed him to write the script, and consequently, she had been prey to his dominance and was now facing being prey to his primal predatory hunger. Reflecting on this moment in this tale, analytically we can see that she had projected her own archetypal action onto him, dynamically handing energy to his predation while she left herself blindly entrapped in her own unquestioned lack of action. But by choosing to open the door, she chose not only to face his predation but also to break out of her previous collusion with it.

Yes, this part of the tale, opening the door, is a memorable gem, story-wise. But then? Let's stay with it for a moment. What *does* happen next? The young wife tries to hide her newfound liberation, but she is caught. Nevertheless, she then comes through well enough: by incorporating some of the trickster's magic, she scores a bit of time and she and her support system manage to kill Bluebeard.

Let's take a deep breath and consider this: In terms of our individual inner worlds, our personal relationships, and the state of our nation's psyche, is this *really* what we need? Is this *really* what we want? Do we choose, yet again, to see killing the *other* as the answer? The game is so prevalent: call it kill or be killed—or call it win or lose—it rules our lives, it rules our country. It is another way of clarifying that as a nation we are in the grip of an alpha narcissistic complex deeply and defensively rooted in predatory archetypal action.

Ultimately, this game ruled the young maiden in this tale also. She clearly joined the game of kill or be killed—and became the killer. Fight to kill or flight to avoid does not transform this dynamic; neither fight nor flight releases us from this game; neither takes the next step toward hold-ing both sides of the split archetype. And I'd like to emphasize, again, how trenchant this game is in our nation.

What's at stake—in the tale and in life—may be truly about being killed off, but in our lives it is more subtly about being beaten in the competitive game that runs so much of our world. Many of us attempt to be minimally involved in this setup; when we smell this sort of "winner takes all" men-tality, we back up—and out. We live with our impotence, symbolically as prey. Or we identify with the winner and join the herd. In each case, we all too often deny ourselves access to the forceful energy that lies under this profile. Indeed, when we join the game, we hand over our own creative action to either a loser, victim complex or a winner, predator complex.

It is essential that we now ask ourselves: Have we wrenched ourselves free of the possession of this underlying zero-sum game? Are we actively addressing the polarized grip of the alpha narcissistic complex that lurks inside our political lives today? Are we free of the insistent warfare that we engage in internationally—criminally—day after day, year after year? Our crass and crude determination to be #1 consistently wins and dominates economically, militaristically, *and* environmentally.

Yet there *is* an entire wellspring of sheer action at the core of these dynamics that the predator employs destructively and defensively against the terror of being vulnerable in any way, against the terror of being prey. However, this wellspring is available for us all to use creatively. This energy is the source of creative action. But to keep this archetypal wellspring within reach, we need to step toward it—not away from it; we need to own it and use it, not give it away.

The young bride's story teaches us that we may take a first step toward revealing the predator and claiming our own action, but what is the next step? There is something else calling from a much deeper level, calling us to find another way, truly another way; and I think it is related, at least in part, to freeing ourselves from the win-lose story. Finding this "other way" may include recognizing that opening the door to, that is, becoming informed about, relentlessly destructive actions is only the first step.

It is then up to us, individually and collectively, to turn inward, exploring our own relationship with the polar opposites of predator and prey—as well as the similar polar opposites that spring into tension in our affects and imagination. We each must face our own complexes. We each must forge access to our capacity to dig for the awesome archetypal forces that we have buried, that we have defended ourselves against, to meet them, even when they appear shameful or threatening, and to then contain them. Only we can do this and in this way create the possibility of a synthesis of the polarized opposites. And this synthesis and containment of the opposites can generate a release from both individual and collective complexes.

Truly understanding the potential power accessible to us through such psychological work is a first and essential step in loosening the grip of America's alpha narcissistic complex. Developing an individual relationship and collective relationship to our aggression that renders it creative rather than destructive may well be one of the most effective and responsible steps we can take. Asserting our knowledge about transformation through the development of integration and balance within psyche would be, in itself, a form of creative aggression, one we can enact with conscience. I think this has been, historically, an essential challenge for the human race, and it is, *right now*, an increasingly demanding—and potentially evolutionary—challenge in this country.

Notes

1 Eugene Burdick and William Lederer, *The Ugly American* (New York: W. W. Norton & Co., 1958).
2 *Never Look Away* [*Werk ohne Autor*], directed by Florian Henckel von Donnersmarck (Walt Disney Studios Motion Pictures, 2018).
3 Nancy J. Dougherty and Jacqueline J. West, *The Matrix and Meaning of Character: An Archetypal and Developmental Approach* (London: Routledge, 2007).
4 Nancy McWilliams, *Psychoanalytic Diagnosis, Second Edition: Understanding Personality Structure in the Clinical Process* (New York: The Guildford Press, 2011). The first edition of the book was published in 1994.
5 Tom Singer and Samuel Kimbles, eds., *The Cultural Complex: Contemporary Ideas on Psyche and Society* (Hove: Brunner Routledge, 2004). Other titles in the series include *Europe's Many Souls: Exploring Cultural Complexes and*

Identities, Placing Psyche: Exploring Cultural Complexes in Australia, and *Listening to Latin America.*

6 Teju Cole, "A Time for Refusal," *The New York Times*, November 11, 2016, Notebook, https://www.nytimes.com/2016/11/11/magazine/a-time-for-refusal.html.

7 *Rhinoceros*, written by Eugene Ionesco. Premiered in 1959 in Düsseldorf, Germany.

8 Ibid.

9 Ibid.

10 Charles Perrault, "Bluebeard" in *The Great Fairy Tale Tradition: From Strapola and Bazile to the Brothers Grimm*, ed. Jack Zipes, 732–735 (New York: W. W. Norton & Company, 2001).

Chapter 14

The Child in 21st-Century American Film

John Beebe

Archetypes' formal qualities may be timeless, but film reveals that archetypes are not like ancient figures in a museum, eternally the same. They have their own interest in development. Culture changes them and they change culture; there is interaction between form and fashion. Jung called this "the play of the archetypes."[1] It's that play that movies have almost magically managed to convey since they were invented, that is, starting with the short 1895 black-and-white documentary the Lumière brothers thought to produce to introduce their invention, showing *Employees Leaving the Lumière Factory*.[2] In fact, these workers in Lyon are shown ending their workday in their Sunday best clothes. They had dressed for the occasion of being in the first moving picture! Perhaps it had dawned on these *fin-de-siècle* first-movie subjects that the new medium held the power to move them forward into the new century; they were already projecting themselves into that future in a 20th-century way.

That same playfulness has begun to attend the way American film in the 21st century is addressing subjects that 20th-century moviegoing taught us to take for granted, as if they were too archetypal to change much in essential meaning. One of these subjects, a trope that would seem to be eternally fixed in our memories of films that have foregrounded it, is what it means to be a child. Recent films from directors working in the United States have begun to convince me that the child of the 20th century, who in films from *The Wizard of Oz* to *E.T.* was ready to set sail toward an eternally renewing future, is rapidly being left behind in favor of a new archetypal image of what the childhood prerogatives permit. American *auteurs* who are presently choosing to direct their attention to the 21st-century child are revealing this emerging person to be someone who is choosing, with equal archetypal decisiveness, to anchor him- or herself firmly in the present.

Comparing the image of the child in the 21st century to the image of the child in the 20th century is a bit like establishing postmodernism's relation to modernism, which requires a recognition that the one derives from, and depends on, the other. Because we're probably now in post-postmodernism, we've already begun to forget the 20th-century child archetype's debt to the modern movement, which set the stage, as if for all time, for every futurity to come. Not just 1979, the International Year of the Child, but the entire 20th century was the Century of the Child, of the magic of emergence from the past. Consider, for instance, the power of Freud's idea of infantile sexuality, which made the infant in all of us sexy, that not so obscure subject of desire. And how many of us would have become Jungians if we hadn't read *Memories, Dreams, Reflections* and gotten that wonderful sense of how Jung's child self was father to the man who discovered individuation?[3] Similarly, the modernist wars, World Wars I and II, led to Anna Freud's work on the surprisingly robust developmental lines of displaced children and John Bowlby's indispensable work in attachment.[4] The 20th century, replete with international psychoanalytic work on the child that reached our shores, made Americans smarter and smarter about the child in all of us. I can name as influences that significantly affected my own work as a Jungian analyst practicing in San Francisco, D. W. Winnicott, Melanie Klein, Erich Neumann, Erik Erikson, Margaret Mahler, Michael Fordham, and Heinz Kohut, and I know that not one of these major contributors to my own analytic understanding could have opened his or her particular window on depth psychology without privileging some aspect of the development of the child as the way into new psychological theory.[5] By the time my generation got to the neuroscience of the child and the relational science of infant observation made immediate by Daniel Stern and Beatrice Beebe in the last part of the 20th century, the Century of the Child had exhausted its understanding of what "the Child" could mean.[6]

At times of theoretical standstill I often turn to film to move my own stuck images forward. So, I invite you to start our fresh look at the child archetype with a recent American movie, *20th Century Women* (2016). The film is told from the point of view of Jamie, an alter-ego for the director, Mike Mills. Jamie, an earnest boy bent on trying to grow up, is 15 years old when the action around that interesting process starts for him, in 1979, with the spontaneous combustion of the family car.[7] As his mother's assumptions about what she could keep running go up in smoke, *20th Century Women* develops an interesting irony about the 20th-century child in adult fantasy. The focus of the film is the inscrutably stuck and stubborn personality of Jamie's mother, Dorothea. Played by Annette Bening with a lingering 1930s Amelia Earhart androgyny, Dorothea is a divorced, heterosexual woman who thinks that romance with a man ought to be as it was in *Casablanca*, when a man had to respect a woman's agency.[8] Although she is not happy alone, she is confident that she knows how to live. She has a problem, however, figuring out what a 15-year-old boy needs to become a romantic success in the late 20th-century world that she recognizes has been reorganized by a feminism beyond her own.

Dorothea has turned the capacious, ramshackle turn-of-the-century Santa Barbara, California, home that she is slowly renovating on her salary as a commercial artist into a rooming house for what she might think of as rugged modernist individuals like herself. Ever forward-looking, she has decided that she wants two young women—one a paid boarder and the other, her son's slightly older best friend—to coach Jamie in all the ways of the emerging post-feminist America that she finds herself resistant to adapting to. The two women accept the challenge to educate Jamie in the skills he is going to need to enter a dating world in which male privilege has been reduced to an anachronism.

A culminating image of what mother and son are both inviting themselves to get into occurs in the summer of 1979. A mix-raced group of young Santa Barbarans have come over for one of Dorothea's dinners, and they are crowded in front of her little television to watch and listen to Jimmy Carter deliver his "Crisis of Confidence" speech.[9] This was Carter's last-ditch defense of his costly and unpopular environmentalist policy on energy and of his visionary national goals for conservation that were deemed at the time naïve and old-fashioned. Mills's screenplay describes Carter's tone of voice that night as "strangely vulnerable," but by today's standards it is unusually direct for an American president to address the shadow of capitalism, the insidious materialism that Carter could see taking over America and that he had the courage to condemn. Carter was shaming Americans for their selfishness and failure to uphold higher ideals, but even in doing so he seemed subliminally to realize, as the filmmaker invites us to see by focusing on the president's face and voice, that this was a losing strategy that would actually help to elect Reagan the following fall.

What Carter was trying to address, at a time when Jungian thought had begun to speak to many Americans as never before, was the meaning-hunger of the developed world, a minority concern that was becoming urgent at just that time. This was the period when many people in America read Jung, or listened to Joseph Campbell, to reconnect with renewing images of meaning. For the first time some were reading Jung's 1940 essay, "The Psychology of the Child Archetype," in which he put forth his view that "One of the essential features of the child motif is its futurity. The child is potential future."[10]

Although Jamie doesn't realize this, this is his mother's image of what his life should be about. Director Mike Mills, who wrote his own screenplay, has made it clear in interviews that he had a mother very much like Dorothea, and I suspect he chose the name he gave Annette Bening's rendering in this film after the Dorothy of *The Wizard of Oz*, who epitomized America's image of itself in 1939, a child in the long history of the world, poised insecurely but hopefully, for a flight into a future in which it could manage to remain itself even as it came of age in the eyes of other nations.[11] Forty years later, Dorothea, the lone supporter of Jimmy Carter at her gathering, is beginning to realize she is on the losing side of history.

In this scene in Dorothea's home, Carter, reading his script for television, says,

> As you know, there is a growing disrespect for government. The schools, the news media, and other institutions. This is not a message of happiness or reassurance. But it is the truth. And it a warning ... It is a crisis of confidence. We can see this crisis in the growing doubt about the meaning of our own lives and in the loss of a unity of purpose of our nation. Too many of us now tend to worship self-indulgence and consumption. But we've discovered that owning things and consuming things does not satisfy our longing for meaning.[12]

"All our main characters," director Mills's script tells us, "are watching [Carter's] strangely vulnerable speech." One of Dorothea's carpenters, invited for the occasion, says "Oh, he's screwed. It's over for him." Only Dorothea finds what Carter has said "beautiful."[13]

Afterward, when everyone sits down to dinner, Abbie, the boarder, who has agreed to teach Jamie, and a photographic artist who affects a Sex Pistols style, probably uses too many drugs, and has been experiencing problems with her reproductive organs, falls asleep at the table. Dorothea asks that someone wake her up. Abbie counters, "I'm menstruating." Dorothea protests this disclosure, but Abbie, entering her role as a life teacher for Jamie, says, "You want to have an adult relationship with a woman you need to be comfortable with a woman having her period. Say menstruation like there's nothing wrong with it—menstruation."

Under repeated prompting, Jamie and the other men at the table all, in turn, say "Menstruation." This leads to even more self-revelation by another young woman at the table, Julie. Julie is Jamie's best friend, the other slightly older contemporary of Jamie's that Dorothea has also nominated to be his mentor in coming of age. Julie sometimes sleeps over in Jamie's room but will not have sex with him. At the dinner table, she reveals that she is not a virgin and empowered by Abbie's frankness describes being deflowered at age 14 in graphic detail: it was "fairly painful sex in his van parked in the street, just spit in his hand for lubrication ...."

After Dorothea calls this Judy Chicagoish dinner party to a halt, with a dry "Show's over girls," she goes into the kitchen to try to have her own heart-to-heart talk with her son.

"Jamie," she says, "we need to, there's a lot of stuff happening, I'd like to know what's going on with you. This has all been a lot for us to deal with."

Making "an exasperated gesture," Jamie delivers the *coup de grâce* on all this to his mother, the "modern" woman who is no longer even relevant: "I'm dealing with everything," he says. "You are dealing with nothing."

This is what so many of us said to our parents after 1964, the year that Jamie was born. We thought we were carrying the responsibility that our parents had ducked. The confrontation with our parents, which in California particularly led to a huge "generation gap," presumed that we were the better heroes. It did not challenge the heroic ideal that had made theirs "the greatest generation." Sexually, emotionally, and politically, that "greatest generation" was perceived as avoiding everything, and we were the ones dealing with all of it. The only difference between my own adolescent self and Jamie's at 15 was that he was mannerly enough to deliver this rebuke to his mother just once. I think I had the conversation fully 1,000 times with my own divorced mother.

In *20th Century Women*, the closest person Jamie has to a father figure is Billy Crudup's character, William, the perfect 1970s soft male. It's fun in the light of Rebecca Solnit's recent work on the lingering sexism of men who have chosen to be "fair" to women to watch him mansplain.[14] At the dinner table after the importance of menstruation is broached by Abbie, William mentions, in the most seductively gentle way, that sex can be especially exciting to a woman while she is menstruating; it can ease the pain. In such a man, when he tries to be fatherly, the father archetype is not present, nor is the anima. He is more like a green snake in the garden of feminism. The best that can be hoped is that he is not lethally poisonous.

The attempt in this movie to use feminism as a kind of father is interesting, and we hope the compliant Jamie is not actually trying to undermine that. But, aside from him, the message of the film is that the presence of a father is essentially out of the question for Jamie and his generation, so often raised by single mothers, and the mother is not good enough either. It will be up to sister-figures to educate him and up to him to demand his rights to a sexuality of his own. This developmental configuration made the late 20th-century child feel like he was still some kind of hero.

Onscreen, of course, there was a man trying to be a father and that was Jimmy Carter. It's shocking to see him, in the year before Reagan was elected, articulate so much of what's still wrong today in our time of the loudmouthed Trump. A gargoyle, President Trump is a reminder of what a long run the false father has had. He is an avatar of the decomposing structures that René Girard called attention to in the last quarter of the 20th century, during the time of what the Marxist postmodern critic Fredric Jameson calls "late capitalism."[15] Carter expressed the problem directly for Americans and was discarded by the American collective. The end of the 20th century was replete with discredited attempts to be the father, not least those of Bill Clinton, who threw the moral high ground of his presidency away while undermining the electability of his likely successor, Al Gore, through his inappropriate relationship with Monica Lewinsky, a White House intern.

The 21st century began in America with the expectation that any American father figure would turn out to be a false father. The child in the 21st century begins with that premise, not with the idea of reconciling with, or redeeming, the lost good father that would make the son's and daughter's efforts to stand up to the unrealized 20th-century mother worth it. Jamie's confrontation with his mother seems like a period piece now, a Carter-era gesture that is finally futile.

Let us turn now to the 21st-century version of a similar situation, a son living alone with a twice-divorced mother. In Richard Linklater's *Boyhood*, which was filmed with the same cast over a series of 12 summers, the central character is an American boy, Mason, whom we follow from the age of 6, when he is in the first grade, to 18, when he is about to start college.[16] When the film opens, his father, played by Ethan Hawke with *puer* charm and a traveling salesman's hapless patina of promises that are never delivered upon, has gone to Alaska to find himself, leaving Mason's mother behind in Texas with their two children to support.[17] She is smart and willing to plan, though she must complete her education to the master's level to realize her ambition of becoming a college professor. The loss of a masculine role model, fortunately, is not a disaster for Mason. He approaches it with an effort to be philosophical, even at six years of age.

There is something immediate, embodied, and deeply feminine about Olivia, his 21st-century mother (played by Patricia Arquette), that is quite different from the buttoned-up physical presentation of Annette Bening as Dorothea in *20th Century Women*. As *Boyhood* begins, Olivia is outside her son's school, comfortably, yet purposefully, striding toward him. Six-year-old Mason is lying on the grass, gazing up at the sky.[18]

"Hey, love bug. You ready?" she greets him.

Scrambling to his feet he says, "Yeah. Hey, guess what, Mom?" as they walk together toward their car (one that will be capable of taking them home, unlike Dorothea's which combusts in the first scene of *20th Century Women*). "I figured out where wasps come from."

"Oh, yeah?" Olivia asks, with an open mind that is accustomed to Mason's ingenuity.

"Well, I think it must be if you flick a rock into the air just right, it'll turn into a wasp."

Unlike Dorothea, confronted with something that doesn't make sense, Olivia says, "That's cool." And to Mason, that makes her a cool mom.

It's clear that we're in a very different time, when a mother and son do not, primarily, have a corrective relationship on either side, but an existential one, which privileges and enjoys immediacy. It's on this basis that Mason's mother can go on to give the feedback she got from her meeting with Mason's teacher and challenge his overconfidence in his own ideas. As she drives, she remarks, "Hey, I had a good meeting with Miss Butler this time. I kinda liked her."

MASON: "What did she say?"

What follows is a series of critical observations about Mason that Olivia, with admirable detachment, reports the teacher having made. He fails to hand in his homework (though he always does the work). He stares out the window all day.

MASON: Not *all* day.

Finally, it emerges that Mason broke the teacher's pencil sharpener by forcing rocks into it.

MASON: I thought if it could sharpen pencils, maybe we could sharpen rocks.
MOM: ... [W]hat were you gonna do with a bunch of sharpened rocks?
MASON: I was trying to make arrowheads for my rock collection.

Part of the charm of this beautifully played scene is that it is so relatively empathic a conversation between rather opposite kinds of thinkers. In the typological terms Jung introduced for analyzing consciousness, Mason's mother occupies a typically American extraverted-thinking position.[19] Throughout the 12 years of the film, she consistently aims at establishing an adaptive logic within Mason, to give him a chance at a reasonable life, whereas Mason, the introverted thinker, is mostly eager to try out his ideas, however inexplicable they are to others. His goal is not self-correction but interesting conversation, and if he can't have that with his mother, he'll look for it elsewhere. His is a commitment to dialogue, and despite his frequent misunderstandings of other people's feelings, his approach to sharing ideas is relational rather than prescriptive. For the most part, this charms his mother.

Later in the film, however, the agreeable spirit of their jousting relationship will have to break down. Mason is ready to leave home to start college, and the differences in the way he and his mother conceive of life makes it hard for them to separate graciously.

In one of the movie's key scenes, Mason, who has gotten a scholarship to a state university on the strength of his photography, is in the final stages of packing to leave home for his first months of college. In one of the boxes he has packed, he discovers a framed photo that he knows he didn't put there. It's a picture he took when he was 15. Realizing that his mother has slipped it into the box, he confronts her about it, insisting that he doesn't plan to bring it along. She protests, reminding him that it was his very first effort as a photographer. Mason replies, "Well, I mean, all the more reason to leave it behind, right?"

The ruthlessness of this drives his mother to dissolve into tears, and the speech that emerges is a valediction to her planful 20th-century thinking:

This is the worst day of my life ...
    You know what I'm realizing? My life is just gonna go, like that! This series of milestones. Getting married, having kids, getting divorced, the time we thought you were dyslexic, when I taught you how to ride

a bike, getting divorced AGAIN, getting my master's degree, finally getting the job I wanted, sending Samantha off to college, sending you off to college ... You know what's next? Huh. It's my fuckin' funeral!

The poignance of this scene for the mother is obvious (and, indeed, playing her role in it with frank sincerity won Patricia Arquette the Academy Award for Best Supporting Actress). There is, however, also a poignance for the child who has grown up in the 21st century, with neither a father nor a father's anima to guide him toward expressing himself in a truly related way.[20] As played with great naturalness by Ellar Coltrane, Mason is still the thinking-type little boy who's been raised to say to his mother what he thinks, but is still not capable of evaluating her ideas. The result is the one-sided thinking of the self-taught. This is not as sad a thing as first meets the eye, for it is typical of the 21st-century child. One bit of psychoanalytic dogma that even post-Freudian developmental psychologists of the 20th century insisted on was that the father's availability is critical to the child's learning how to think. This could be, as Andrew Samuels says, the "father of whatever sex," but a third person is needed to stand in the father role outside the charming dialogue between mother and child so that the solipsism of thinking only within that relationship can be critiqued.[21] As Mason reveals in his insensitivity to his mother, even a thinking-type son needs to find some way of evaluating his ideas before he speaks and acts on them. But as we will also see, as Boyhood proceeds to individuate Mason's different path to thinking in a related way, this is not going to come from a father.

The abject but not hopeless aspect of 21st-century American fatherlessness is the subject of the opening third of another recent film that spans two decades of its central character's development. Moonlight, which won the Academy Award for Best Picture, is like Boyhood in carrying a leading character, Chiron Harris, through several stages of his struggle from child to adolescent to young man within the black underclass in Miami, Florida.[22] When we first encounter Chiron (pronounced in African American patois as shy roan), he is 10 years old and being chased by bullies. The boys he runs from are bigger, two or three years older, and armed with sticks. They know him as "Little," and they're all yelling "Get that nigga!" though they are African American too.[23]

The actor playing Chiron, Alex Hibbert, was 11 when filming began; and because he is small, frightened-looking, and silent, he comes across on screen as no older than 7 or 8 years old, the very image of the abject, scapegoated child. Like Mason in Boyhood, he has a single mother who is struggling to make it, one who is not at all up to the challenge of raising a son who might not be able to defend himself. She is herself not at all stress-tolerant: she is addicted to crack cocaine. Appropriately, the first father figure who comes on the scene for Chiron is a cocaine dealer. He finds the boy hiding in a crack house. Chiron will not speak directly to him for the longest time, but the dealer takes him under his wing, feeds him, and lets him stay a night in his pretty lady friend's place. Direct and natural, she is successful in getting the boy to open enough to tell her that "They call me Little," revealing a self that not only keeps its own counsel but also is fiercely protective of its own identity. This is one of the essential characteristics of the 21st-century child's early adaptation, and even the temporarily intimidated Chiron is already looking forward to the powerfully self-directed man he will grow up to become.

The drug dealer, however, must return the stubbornly shy little boy to his mother, who though grateful to have him back and safe, implies with a look that any further interest the man might show in him would have to be sexual. Disgusted by her attitude, the dealer returns long enough to teach little Chiron to swim, an essential ingredient of his future ability to cope on his own in a world in which he will never be popular. This initiation into a successful, if lunar, masculinity, which *Moonlight* reveals as a surprisingly robust introverted ability to cope with living in the shadow, also stands as a symbol for the move away from solar enlightenment versions of masculine development that would insist that mastery is outward facing and socially recognized.[24] But the sympathetic dealer who protects the boy from internalizing homophobia, also becomes Chiron's mother's crack dealer, and so Chiron himself grows up to be a drug dealer, big and tough, who calls himself "Black." Because Chiron remains secure in his introverted feeling, however, at the end of the film, he can declare his heart from within as someone who has always been true to his core identity. *Moonlight* at first seems like little more than an unusually touching rendering of ghetto initiation into an outsider identity reminiscent of depictions in the 20th century of children who are not fortunate in their parents or their social circumstances. I might mention, beyond American films, such alienated midcentury children as Antoine Doinel in Francois Truffaut's *The Four Hundred Blows* and Billy Casper in Ken Loach's *Kes*, whose free will and agency emerged out of existential despair.[25] There is a different, more hopeful tenacity to Chiron, however, a rootedness in feeling that suggests he will not remain just a child given little to build upon. Instead, as *Moonlight* progresses, no less than Mason in *Boyhood*, Chiron proceeds to makes an identity out of what he has and becomes a successful loner—"Black." The key to his adaptation is his stubborn fidelity to his inner depths, which extends to his only friend, a chum who is also gay and, in adolescence, gives Chiron his sole early sexual encounter and his only experience of what it feels like to love another person. At the film's end, these young boys have grown into men who have both served prison terms, but the old connection remains alive between them. They have survived emotionally, and they are not victims. The mature extraverted feeling of the friend can accept the planful extraverted thinking that introverted-feeling Chiron finally expresses by sharing his truth that they have always been together in his heart. *Moonlight* leaves us with the sense that the social attitude that is "most truly compatible with American individuation" has one again declared itself before our eyes in an American movie.[26] This time it is a 21st-century construction by black American men of a masculine standpoint that has emerged from very down low in the 20th-century shadow, where sexual relationships between men, especially among African Americans, had been expected to remain, but can now, as *Moonlight* illuminates, give image to what it would look like to heal the social fabric for all of us.

The 21st-century's American child is capable of building on what's at hand and not throwing what's presented away, which is quite different from having to carry the image of futurity for one's parents, the way 20th-century children so often felt they had to do. We find the ability to work with what's at hand already present at the age of six in the 2012 film *What Maisie Knew*, directed by Scott McGehee and David Siegel.[27] The heroine, Maisie, a privileged first-grader growing up in Manhattan, is an American reinvention of the heroine of Henry James's astonishing 1897 book, which some have called the first modern novel, in that it turns entirely upon the consciousness of the character rather than the conditions against which she has to strive.[28] James's fiction depicted Maisie as a morally precocious 11-year-old whose parents have divorced and all but abandoned her to the care of their new spouses. These adults (predictably for a James novel) fall in love with each other, using their caretaking responsibilities for Maisie as excuses to meet, and Maisie eventually figures this out. What Maisie finally knew was not only how much she was being used, but in American tran-scendentalist fashion, how also to rise above the resentment this knowledge might have stirred up in her long term. In the novel, she escapes this danger by simply renouncing her desire for more priority in parental fig-ures' lives than she has. What she most of all has figured out is how to be generous when significant others are selfish. James's irony in creating a psychological compass that is better than the betrayals of life usually let us shape is at its peak in this novel, and the pattern that produces Maisie's moral perfection is brilliantly drawn, but the story leaves Maisie little chance to assert more than consciousness. In the American film setting of 21st-century Manhattan, Maisie's mother and father are more conscious of the need to appear to be caring for Maisie, but they are, in fact, just as abandoning as in James's novel. And their new partners are also, as in the novel, much nicer to the girl and genuinely interested in her. The story turns not on her consciousness that all of the adults in her life come and go, but in her willingness to engage with them from the standpoint of a self that knows what's good for itself and thus is willing to give them a chance to see what they can be for her. Maisie's resilience is beautifully conveyed by the star, Onata Aprile, who was six years old when the shoot-ing started, and coolly delivers a pitch-perfect performance as a child who always knows what she wants.

In the film, Maisie's mother is a rock star who is often on the road; her father is a rock promoter who is often out of town. When Maisie's father marries the governess, who has been taking care of Maisie and delivering her to her father on her father's pick-up days, Maisie is consoled by the fact that she can be the flower girl at their wedding. But she is ill prepared, when she returns to school, to find that her mother will not come to pick her up, but rather has sent a man Maisie hardly knows, a tall, good-looking bartender named Lincoln, who seems sweet but hapless. He tells her that he has just married Maisie's mother. As we watch the film, the hasty remarriage of Maisie's mother is obviously a retaliation engineered to spite Maisie's father and his new wife. But to Maisie, her mother says of Lincoln, "I will tell you a secret. I married him for you." As aging rock star Susanna Nun, Julianne Moore is even more offensive than Ida Farange, the mother in James's novel, who is too busy going off to play billiards with men in other cities, to be available as a mother, though she nevertheless demands absolute loyalty from her daughter. Moore's Susanna is worse because she is so present in her absence, and witchy to everyone else but Maisie, in a way that creates anxiety. It is a relief to watch Maisie begin to bond with Lincoln in the moments when Susanna is not trying to smother her with narcissistic relatedness to upstage Lincoln, and it is painful to watch Susanna punish them both for surviving her.

In fact, though it is Susanna who is trying to perfect the too predictable tracks on her new album by recording them again in her home studio, it is Maisie and Lincoln who create an aesthetic mood together. At first, Maisie is drawing by herself. Lincoln shows interest, and she tells him she is making a castle, adding that she doesn't know how to show the bridge that goes down over the moat. Lincoln encourages her to try, but it becomes clear that what she wants is for him to co-create the drawing with her.

MAISIE: I can't do it. You do it. ...
LINCOLN: Okay. Well maybe you can ... draw some animals in the moat ... some dangerous animals so people can't swim across. Crocodiles and polar bears and stuff that will eat you.[29]

In this way, the two begin to create a trusting space together. Later, Lincoln, after asking Maisie if she is hungry and if she likes eggs, makes something lovely for Maisie to eat, using his skills at fashioning bar food to fluff up a pair of boiled eggs into a pleasing presentation, complete with what looks like a fresh basil leaf with each of them. Then he says, "Here we go. *Bon appetit.*" Maisie is somehow affected by the gesture and keeps looking at the now beautiful eggs without eating them.

LINCOLN: I thought you said you liked eggs.
MAISIE: I don't want to ruin it.

At such moments, Maisie's extraverted intuition and Lincoln's extraverted sensation come together to create an aesthetic attitude, which, like the draw-bridge, releases Maisie from being a princess imprisoned in her witchy mother's castle, allowing the little girl to make a confident entry into relations with the world.

The *aesthetic attitude*, along with the *social attitude*, the *religious attitude*, and the *philosophical attitude*, are the four traditional cultural attitudes introduced by Joseph Henderson that can give us a coherent and effective way of navigating the difficult and alienating culture around us.[30] In films of the 21st century, American children are capable of joining with each other to create a cultural attitude that can sustain them, one that is not just good enough for now, but rescues the very point of *now*, in that it lets one be with others who can also be present to the moment of their individual adaptation. This is a solution to living in the world in which each self not only knows what's good for itself but also is not afraid to let a kindred self know that it knows. Thus is created a new kind of family of individuals who trust each other's orientation to survival. Not infrequently this is accompanied by the construction of a cultural attitude that as few as two can share to make possible a viable worldview of their own.

The culminating moments of *Boyhood* express this capacity with unusual clarity. Mason has arrived at Texas State University and his extraverted roommate Dalton has already planned a trip to catch the late afternoon at Big Bend, where the sunset is spectacular. He has also provided Mason with a girl to accompany him on the outing, a friend of Dalton's girlfriend Barb, who has brought psychedelic brownies for them all. This girl, Nicole, teaches dance. That makes sense because she is graceful and lovely, though quite as introverted as Mason. He asks her what forms of dance she teaches and learns that her favorite is tap because of the freedom it gives the dancer to create steps and sounds.

The children Nicole teaches are six to eight—fully 21st-century American children. They have not known any other century. For a few moments Nicole and Mason say other things, as Dalton and Barb, some distance away, are whooping it up in their extraverted way over the arriving sunset. The extraverted couple's noisy exclamations welcoming the environmental beauty that has now surrounded them are funny, but they spur Nicole to voice a quieter credo that ends the film in a 21st-century way.

NICOLE: You know how everyone's always saying, "Seize the moment?"
　　　Mason nods yes.
NICOLE (CONT'D): I don't know, I'm kinda thinkin' it's the other way around.
　　　You know, like, the moment seizes us.
MASON: Yeah. Yeah, I know. It's constant, the moments, it's just … it's like
　　　always right now, you know?
NICOLE: Yeah.

The script says that they "trade smiles," but they have actually traded psychological places, because we are used to Mason doing the introverted thinking, and we can believe that Nicole normally steers by introverted feeling, establishing the value of what's happening. But as she offers introverted thinking, and he listens to her idea, so different from his mother's 20th-century extraverted-thinking expectation that "there would be more," Mason grants what he withheld from his mother, introverted-feeling approval of the young woman's thought. They have created a philosophical attitude for a new century, in which the abundance of opportunities to live in the moment offsets the scarcity of resources ahead and behind the young people of America today.

These American children, growing up to begin to teach the first children born in the 21st century, are not holding the image of futurity that Jung had seen in the 20th century as the archetypal role of the child.[31] Rather they are holding the present, not least because the future is so fraught.

Not long ago, a mother I know was trying to have a conversation with her son. She was in her early 40s, and he was in his mid-20s. It wasn't going well. Finally, to cut through the barrier that had seemed to come up between them, he said to his mother, "You know, we have problems." He did not mean that he and she had problems communicating that might require counseling. He was explaining to his mother, who had been holding a 20th-century perspective that was not working for him, even though he had originally been born in that century, that the "we" of his entire post-millennial Generation Z was in crisis. After what happened to our confidence in pensions in America when one of our signature cities, Detroit, the home of the American automobile industry, declared bankruptcy and suspended payment of pensions in 2013, no one in America could be positive that they'd really have a pension when they retire, even if they are enrolled in a plan. People are not sure there is going to be water by midcentury. And how much longer are countries feeling challenged going to merely *threaten* nuclear war?

Luigi Zoja, a Jungian analyst trained originally as an economist, put it this way five years ago, speaking from a European perspective: "The present generation of parents is the first since the Renaissance that cannot look forward to a better future for their children."[32] I think this applies equally to Americans. That comment made me see my own 61 years of individuation in the 20th century in the light of what my 20 years of growing on in the 21st century have taught me. My issue, and that of most of my contemporaries in the 20th century, was to stop being what Jungian analysis had taught me to call in Ovid's Latin a *puer aeternus*, an eternal boy, unquestionably divine in potential—I was to grow up, finish school, complete things I'd started, and make myself real. Most of my contemporaries and I thought all we had to do was stop being adolescent and everything would be all right. I'm glad it has finally dawned on me, as my years in the 21ˢᵗ-century approach their majority, if the number 21 still means anything, that nobody believes anymore that the future is where it's at. Rather, the ability to make the most of the present, which welcomes the child in all of us, is the gift of the wise, no longer heroic, child.

Notes

1 C. G. Jung, *The Collected Works of C. G. Jung*, vol. 14, *Mysterium Coniunctionis* (New York: Pantheon Books, 1963), 401.

2 *Employees Leaving the Lumière Factory*, directed by Auguste Lumière and Louis Lumière (Lumière, 1895), Short film.

3 C. G. Jung, *Memories, Dreams, Reflections*, ed. Aniela Jaffé (New York: Pantheon Books, 1963).

4 Anna Freud, *Indications for Child Analysis and Other Papers, 1945–1956* (Madison, CT: International Universities Press, 1968); John Bowlby, *A Secure Base: Parent-Child Attachment and Healthy Human Development* (London: Routledge, 1988).

5 Donald W. Winnicott, *The Child, the Family and the Outside World* (New York: Perseus Books, 1992); Melanie Klein, *Envy and Gratitude & Other Works 1946–1963* (New York: Delta Books, 1975); Erich Neumann, *The Child* (Boston: Shambhala Books, 1990); Erik Erikson, *Childhood and Society* (New York: W. W. Norton & Co., 1950); Margaret S. Mahler, *The Psychological Birth of the Human Infant: Symbiosis and Individuation* (New York: Basic Books, 1975); Michael Fordham, *Children as Individuals*, 3rd ed. (London: Free Association Books, 1969); Heinz Kohut, *The Restoration of the Self* (Madison, CT: International Universities Press, 1977).

6 Daniel N. Stern, *The Interpersonal World of the Infant: A View from Psychoanalysis and Developmental Psychology* (New York: Basic Books, 1985); Beatrice Beebe and Frank M. Lachmann, *The Origins of Attachment: Infant Research and Adult Treatment* (London: Routledge, 2013).

7 *20th Century Women*, directed by Mike Mills (A24, 2016), Motion picture.

8 *Casablanca*, directed by Michael Curtiz (Warner Brothers, 1942), Motion picture.

9 Jimmy Carter, "Energy and the National Goals" (popularly known as the "Crisis of Confidence" speech), televised address to the American people on July 15, 1979, three years after accepting the nomination of his party to run for President of the United States. Transcription by Michael E. Eidenmuller, 2008, accessed June 4, 2019, www.American Rhetoric.com.

10 C. G. Jung, "The Psychology of the Child Archetype" (1940), in *The Collected Works of C. G. Jung*, vol. 9i, *The Archetypes and the Collective Unconscious* (New York: Pantheon Books, 1959), 278.

11 *The Wizard of Oz*, directed by Victor Fleming (Metro-Goldwyn-Mayer, 1939), Motion picture.

12 Carter's speech, "Energy and the National Goals," is heavily edited in the film. For the original, see the transcription by Eidenmuller, https://www.americanrhetoric.com/speeches/jimmycartercrisisofconfidence.htm.

13 *20ᵗʰ Century Women*, screenplay by Mike Mills, http://scriptfest.com/home/wp-content/uploads/2017/01/20TH-CENTURY-WOMEN.pdf.

14 Rebecca Solnit, *Men Explain Things to Me* (Chicago: Haymarket Books, 2014).

15 René Girard, "René Girard: Interview," *Diacritics* 8, no. 1 (1978): 31–54, doi:10.2307/464818; Fredric Jameson, *Postmodernism, or the Cultural Logic of Late Capitalism* (Durham: Duke University Press, 1991).

16 *Boyhood*, directed by Richard Linklater (IFC Films, 2014). Motion picture.
17 Marie-Louise von Franz, *The Problem of the Puer Aeternus* (New York: Spring Publications, 1970).
18 *Boyhood*, screenplay by Richard Linklater, https://images.amcnetworks.com/ifc filmsawards.com/wp-content/uploads/2014/11/Boyhood-screenplay-11-14-FINAL.pdf.
19 John Beebe, *Energies and Patterns in Psychological Type: The Reservoir of Consciousness* (London & New York: Routledge, 2017).
20 John Beebe, "The Father's Anima," in *The Father: Contemporary Jungian Perspectives*, ed. Andrew Samuels, 95–109 (Washington Square, NY: New York University Press, 1986).
21 Andrew Samuels, *The Political Psyche* (London and New York: Routledge, 1993), 133–135.
22 *Moonlight*, directed by Barry Jenkins (A24, 2016), Motion picture.
23 *Moonlight*, screenplay by Barry Jenkins, http://www.dailyscript.com/scripts/MOONLIGHT.pdf.
24 John Beebe, *Integrity in Depth* (College Station, TX: Texas A&M University Press, 1992), 91–95.
25 *The Four Hundred Blows (Les quatre cents coups)*, directed by François Truffaut (Cocinor, 1959), Motion picture; *Kes*, directed by Ken Loach (United Artists, 1969), Motion picture.
26 Beebe, *Energies and Patterns in Psychological Type,* 108.
27 *What Maisie Knew*, directed by Scott McGehee and David Siegel (Millennium Entertainment, 2012), Motion picture.
28 Henry James, *What Maisie Knew* (London: Penguin Classics, 1897/2010).
29 *What Maisie Knew*, screenplay by Carroll Cartwright and Nancy Doyne, https://www.springfieldspringfield.co.uk/movie_script.php?movie=what-maisie-knew.
30 Joseph L. Henderson, *Cultural Attitudes in Psychological Perspective* (Toronto: Inner City Books, 1984). I have analyzed these cultural attitudes in terms of Jung's theory of psychological types in Chapter 6 of my book *Energies and Patterns of Psychological Type.*
31 Jung, "The Psychology of the Child Archetype."
32 Luigi Zoja, "Uncivilization without Transition?" (lecture given at "Analysis and Activism: Social and Political Contributions of Jungian Psychology," London, England, December 6, 2014).

Environment

Chapter 15

A Tale of Two Cultures

Climate Change and American Complexes

Jeffrey T. Kiehl

Climate Disruption and Psyche

There is growing recognition that Earth's climate system is radically changing before our eyes. No longer do we look to the future anticipating climate disruption; floods, droughts, fires, and mass migrations of humans and nonhumans are here, now. We struggle physically and psychologically to deal with all that is unfolding and what is predicted to come. As science has shown, we are the origin of the current climate disruption and oncoming future climatic chaos. What is required of us is no less than a transformation of consciousness concerning our relationship to the world. In particular, we are tasked with understanding our collective resistances to actions to address this issue. In particular, the constellation of cultural complexes presents a fundamental barrier to action within the United States. As discussed in this chapter, the roots of this problem are archetypal, for as Jung states, "The driving forces of a psychological mass movement are essentially archetypal. Every archetype contains the lowest and the highest, evil and good, and is therefore capable of producing diametrically opposite results."[1] It is no wonder, then, that America is split around climate change, an issue that evokes such strong emotions. Given this situation, consideration of cultural complexes of climate change is essential. As Andrew Hoffman, professor of sustainability, points out, "We must acknowledge that the debate over climate change, like almost all environmental issues, is a debate over culture, worldviews, and ideology."[2] Here, I explore the climate change debate through the lens of analytical psychology, with special emphasis on how cultural complexes contribute to the polarization around this issue. I present findings from social sciences research to support my analysis of two cultures within the US. I then provide mythopoetic and archetypal descriptions of these two cultures, and conclude with the role analytical psychology can play in helping to work with the cultural complexes connected to climate disruption.

Where We Are Now

Earth is warming at a dramatic rate, and the dominant cause of this warming is human activity. Through the burning of fossil fuels with accompanied increases of atmospheric carbon dioxide, humans are strengthening Earth's greenhouse effect, which is a key process regulating the temperature of the planet. Over 85 percent of our energy needs are generated through the burning of fossil fuels. The continuing rise in global population accompanied by a rise in per-capita energy use has led to a 45 percent increase in the levels of atmospheric carbon dioxide since the Industrial Revolution. If population and energy use continue to grow at rates similar to past decades, then within 80 years carbon dioxide levels will triple above preindustrial levels. It has been over 40 million years since Earth's atmosphere contained this much carbon dioxide. Earth's climate at that time was one of extreme warmth, severe storms, ocean acidification, and massive sea-level rise. Not only the human species but also many others have never lived in such a climate. It is important to recognize that unlike the geologic past in which greenhouse warming occurred over hundreds of thousands to millions of years, our current warming is taking place over a century.

Forty years ago, scientists began to warn the public of the consequences of continued increases in greenhouse gases. In spite of these warnings, little action has taken place to address climate change. The longer humanity waits to address the issue the more difficult it will be to avoid the worst consequences of climate change, including increased severe heat waves, rising costs of storm damages, increased sea level with the displacement of millions of people, severe drought, loss of agriculture, increases in vector-borne diseases and increased mortality, and a projected loss of more than 50 percent of world species. The planet has already warmed by 1.8°F since the mid-1800s. Unless rapid action is taken, the warming will likely exceed 5°F or higher within 80 years, which would be devastating to life on Earth. The science of climate change is sound, and the technologies exist to move us off of fossil fuels, yet we do not act. Many countries have worked hard to create an international agreement to limit global warming to no more than 2.7°F. Presently, there is only one country that rejects this international accord, and that is the United States, which historically has contributed more to the global increase in carbon dioxide than any other country. Currently, the United States is the second largest emitter of greenhouse gases behind China. China has signed the international accord and is actively working to move to renewable sources of energy; meanwhile US government officials claim there is no scientific consensus on the issue, and the US president claims that climate change is a "hoax" perpetrated on the American public to either bring more money to science and/or to impose government control on the lives of American citizens.

Where does the American public stand on the issue of climate change? The Yale Program on Climate Communication and the Center for Climate Change Communication at George Mason University have tracked the public's perception of climate change for over a decade. The PEW Research Center has also carried out polling on the issue of climate change for over a decade. According to a 2016 PEW poll, 48 percent of US adults agree with the statement that "Earth is getting warmer mostly due to human activity."[3] A March 2018 study by the Yale and George Mason groups found that 59 percent of registered voters agreed that "global warming is caused mostly by human activities."[4] There is a strong political divide within these findings, in which 84 percent of liberal Democrats agreed with the statement, whereas only 26 percent of conservative Republicans agreed that the warming was due to human activity. What is most disturbing is the public's perception of the scientific consensus on climate change. Research has shown through independent studies that 97 percent of the scientific community agrees that Earth is warming and it is due to human activity.[5] However, when the public is asked if scientists agree on the cause of warming, 49 percent state that there is no consensus within the scientific community on the issue. This near 50/50 split within the United States has held steady for over a decade. Clearly there is a tremendous disconnect between the reality of scientific consensus and the perception of this consensus.

The United States has historically been reluctant to take legislative action to reduce carbon emissions. While many other nations have long since accepted the science and have moved on to discussing solutions, the United States remains stuck on arguing whether humans are causing the planet to warm. The US debate on what we should do about climate change evokes volatile emotionality. Climate scientists have been compared to terrorists and threatened with physical harm, and their families have been verbally assaulted. Politicians who run on campaigns seeking action on climate change are deluged with heavy negative ad campaigns and are often defeated.

Not all Americans reject the facts of climate change due to political position; many struggle with the affective reactions surrounding the issue. For the past few decades, I have given numerous public presentations on the science of climate change to groups ranging in size from 25 to 500 people. My experience over the years has made it clear that climate change is a highly emotional issue for Americans. I now make it a practice to stop after 20 minutes of presenting the facts on the issue to ask people how they are feeling. The answers to my question cluster around the following emotions: hopelessness, helplessness, anger, guilt, denial, defiance, and dissociation. People ask: Given the immensity of the problem, how can I make a difference? How can this be happening? I can't believe this is happening? I feel guilty for how I have contributed to this problem. These strong feeling-toned reactions around climate change are not only felt by individuals, but also by society as a whole and, as such, define cultural complexes as proposed by Thomas Singer.[6]

The Yale group has carried out detailed studies of how Americans' responses cluster around six groups that they call "The Six Americas," denoted as: Alarmed, Concerned, Cautious, Disengaged, Doubtful, and Dismissive.[7] In their March 2018 poll, the Yale group found that 51 percent of the American public identified as either Alarmed or Concerned about global warming, whereas 21 percent were Doubtful or Dismissive about the issue. Another 21 percent of the public identified as Cautious about global warming, whereas only 7 percent were Disengaged by the issue. These findings, on one hand, are encouraging, in that slightly more than half of the public understand that global warming poses a serious threat, but on the other hand it is also clear that more Americans need to be engaged to act on the issue.

Importantly, action on climate change requires that it be viewed as a higher priority than many other threats or concerns. A 2016 poll by the Yale group asked each of the "Six Americas" to rank order the issues they wanted to be addressed by the next elected president. Not surprisingly, there are stark differences among the rankings across the "Six Americas." For those who are Alarmed, protecting the environment, addressing global warming, and developing clean energy are the top three priorities. For those who fall into the Concerned category, the economy, healthcare, and terrorism are the top three concerns. For those identified as Doubtful, the top three concerns are the economy, terrorism, and the federal budget deficit. For the Dismissive group, the priorities are terrorism, the economy, and gun rights. Only 17 percent of the American public fall within the Alarmed category, and they are the only group who place addressing global warming as a top priority, whereas the other five Americas place addressing climate change as a lower priority compared to issues like the economy, healthcare, and terrorism. It is important to note that these various issues are not independent of one another and are all affected by climate change. In the next section I will explore why such polarization exists around the issue of climate change, especially in terms of America's cultural complexes.

The United States could be a leader in addressing the problem. Yet, the United States is the one country avoiding action. Avoidance behavior is rooted in psychological processes best addressed through a comprehensive approach to psyche, that is, one that considers both conscious and unconscious processes. I feel that it is only through such a depth psychological approach that we will be able to address the root cause of climate change. Our inner psychic dissociation is manifesting in the outer world as symptoms such as climate change. Given climate change is a collective issue, understanding the role of American cultural complexes is paramount with regard to this issue. Climate change is the greatest challenge humanity has ever faced, and if we fail to address it, then we bequeath terrifying trauma on generations to come. We have a moral and ethical responsibility to not let this happen.

The "Two Cultures" and Climate Change

Before exploring American cultural complexes, I summarize findings from the social sciences regarding the US reaction to climate change, for there are close parallels between social science findings and an analytical psychology view of climate change, in particular regarding American cultural complexes and polarization around this issue.

To begin, Cultural Theory, based on the work of British anthropologist Mary Douglas, proposes that social groups can be described by the degree to which 1) individuals identify as a member of a group, or bond within the group; and 2) members of the group accept imposed structure or accept rules for the group.[8] These two "axes" of group structure lead to four types of group behavior denoted as 1) fatalists, 2) individualists, 3) hierarchalists, and 4) egalitarians. Fatalists tend to isolate and not participate in groups, whereas the remaining three types lead to coherent social cultures. The three cultures react to perceived risk differently, which affects how they relate to nature and the issue of climate change. Studies find Americans cluster around two of these social structures: *hierarchical individualists* and *egalitarian communitarians*. The first group values individualism and order within society; the second group is more attuned to others within the group and outside of the group. In terms of how these two groups view nature, individualists believe nature is resilient to change, whereas communitarians view nature as fragile to external forces. I believe we can look at these ideas in terms of the degree of connectivity, which reflects the intensity with which individuals and groups connect to others and the natural world. On one end of the spectrum are those identified as highly independent; at the other end are those who identify as highly interconnected. Cultures foster belief systems that lie somewhere along this spectrum of connectivity. The challenge for individuals and groups is to value and respect people whatever their degree of connectivity. Clearly, such valuing will be quite challenging for those who identify as highly independent.

From a Jungian perspective, we can view a group's affective, feeling-toned reactions to risk as indicators of cultural complexes. Individualists are invested in strong defenses against the outer world. They believe the natural world will take care of itself and are invested in protecting themselves and their families. They fear for themselves and those close to them. Communitarians are more empathically attuned to others and this attunement extends out to the natural environment, which they view as needing protection. They fear harm to the natural world and others and look for support from the collective. What are the cultural complexes that reflect these two group dynamics? The image of the rugged individual immediately comes to mind in terms of the first group. Those who identify with this group value freedom, personal rights, and an expectation of one's ability to be self-reliant. The image of the helper comes to mind with regard to the second group. Those who identify with this group value community, collective support, and believe that we are "in this together." I argue that these two images reflect the two dominant cultural complexes in America.

Dan Kahan used Cultural Theory to show how these two groups react to information about climate change.[9] He finds that hierarchical individualists reject the science of climate change, whereas egalitarian communitarians more readily accept the science. In fact, the higher educated the individualists, the more likely they are to reject the scientific facts concerning climate change, indicative of a constelled cultural complex:

> The cultural cognition theory ... posits that persons who subscribe to a "hierarchical, individualistic" worldview—one that simultaneously ties authority to conspicuous social rankings and eschews collective interference with the decisions made by individuals possessed of such authority—can be expected to be skeptical of claims of environmental and technological risks. Such people, according to the theory, intuitively perceive that widespread acceptance of such claims would license restrictions on commerce and industry, forms of behavior that Hierarchical Individualists value. In contrast, persons who hold an "egalitarian, communitarian" worldview—one that favors less regimented forms of social organization and greater collective attention to securing individual needs—tend to be morally suspicious of commerce and industry, which they see as the source of unjust disparities in wealth and power. They therefore find it congenial, the theory posits, to see those forms of behavior as dangerous and thus worthy of restriction. On this view, then, we should expect Egalitarian Communitarians to be more concerned than Hierarchical Individualists with climate change risks.[10]

Essentially these two cultures are highly invested in their respective ideologies, and those who are more educated are even more invested in their ideology and will resist any information that threatens their belief system—a behavior that is indicative of a cultural complex. Important to note is this behavior exists at both ends of the connectivity spectrum. Note also that these two groups' affective response to climate change is quite different. Individualists exhibit anger and aggression when confronted with climate change information; communitarians express subdued sadness and grief. The flow of psychic energy for the individualists is directed out toward the climate change messenger, whereas the flow of energy for the communitarians is more often directed inward.

Another approach to understanding cultural structures is that of Michele Gelfand who considers what is defined as "tight" and "loose" worldviews in American society.[11] Harrington and Gelfand

> contend that differences among states reflect a core cultural contrast that has been studied in anthropology, sociology, and psychology: the degree to which social entities are "tight" (have many strongly enforced rules and little tolerance for deviance) versus "loose" (have few strongly enforced rules and greater tolerance for deviance).[12]

Furthermore,

> Tight societies have more authoritarian governments, more media restrictions, less civil liberties, and greater use of the death penalty; have much more constraint in everyday situations; and have citizens who exhibit greater prevention-focus, cautiousness, impulse control, need for structure, and self-monitoring ability relative to loose societies. Tight societies have also experienced a greater number of ecological and historical threats, including fewer natural resources, more natural disasters, a greater incidence of territorial threat, higher population density, and greater pathogen prevalence compared with loose societies. Such threats increase the need for strong norms and the sanctioning of deviant behavior, which help humans coordinate social action for survival. In contrast, loose societies have fewer ecological and historical threats and can "afford" more deviant behavior.[13]

The dyad of "tight" and "loose" is analogous, in many, but not all, ways, to the dyad of "individualists" and "communitarians," respectively. Similar to the latter dyad, tight cultures focus on defending against perceived threats using hierarchy and rules, whereas loose cultures are less ruled based and are more accepting of variations in social behavior. Harrington and Gelfand carried out a survey of the United States to identify regions of the country that were either more tight or loose and found that "tightness–looseness is predicted by a number of ecological and historical factors across the 50 states, including natural disaster vulnerabilities, rates of disease, resource availability, and degree of external threat ...."[14] This is an interesting finding given Jung's observations about how psyche is connected to geographical location. Is it possible that cultural complexes are rooted in the physical conditions of a specific region? Gelfand and colleagues argue that it is the presence of threat in the environment that shapes the degree of tightness or looseness for people living in these regions. It is also of interest that a new area of social science termed *geographical psychology* has been established to explore how collective psychology is rooted in specific locations.[15]

From these findings we would expect "tight" cultures to be more defended against the reality of climate change, whereas "loose" cultures to be more open to the facts of climate change. Indeed, when one compares the geographic maps from the Yale studies to those of Harrington and Gelfand, the regions of tightness are predominately regions where the cultural complex of rugged individualism prevents one from viewing "humanmade" climate change as difficult to accept. Whereas regions where looseness predominates correlate with those where people accept the reality of climate change.

Finally, let us consider research on the construction of social identity as it relates to consumption and material possessions.[16] American culture is deeply rooted in the consumption of material goods. For example, the average American consumes three to four times more than the average European. The rise of consumerism in America, especially over the past 60 years is well documented, which includes how advertising connected self-worth to the things one can buy and own. The *Age of Mad Men* shifted Americans' relationship to material things in significant ways. Americans now use material possessions as a substitute for meaningful attachments and our culture of materialism feeds upon itself, in that the desire to own more prompts one to buy more.[17] How is this cultural belief system connected to climate change? It takes energy to make material goods and transport them around the world, and planned obsolescence of these material goods ensures never-ending need. High consumption of material goods requires tremendous amounts of energy, which currently is fossil-fuel centric. Thus, the rising increase in global per-capita consumption linked to self-identity is an important driver in increased greenhouse gas levels.

The production and consumption of material goods is a central component of capitalism that links a free-market economy to climate change, and the belief in a free-market society is central to the cultural complex of hierarchical individualism. Charles Waugh points out that

The value of rugged economic self-reliance and distrust of outside authority combine to express the fear that government agencies, scientists, and representatives are using climate change as a way to tell him what to do and to take his money. The nexus of corporations, politicians, and conservative media make the situation worse by presenting irrational opinions about individual rights and misleading pseudoscientific information as rational counterarguments to the scientific certainty of global warming, but to an extent, they are successful because they play on a distrust of authority that has been enshrined in a culture and history that many Americans believe began with the Declaration of Independence. At the same time, Americans are inundated with corporate messages to indulge their sense of individual importance, to enjoy what they think they have earned, and ignore requests made for the common, global good.[18]

This rugged self-reliance comes from the

> United States' frontier history, whose mythology has been perpetuated by popular culture since the late eighteenth century. In brief, these stories feature individuals who go out into the wilderness with just the right tools and supplies and turn that wilderness into civilization. These are the stories of early explorers like Daniel Boone and Davy Crockett, but also of western cowboys like Wyatt Earp and Wild Bill Hickok who are portrayed as individuals who struggled heroically to tame the frontier.[19]

The perceived threat to the mythic rugged individual by environmentalists has led to a reaction on the part of the corporate sector, in particular the fossil-fuel industry that feels most challenged by the facts of climate change. For example, Aaron McCright and Riley Dunlap have identified anti-reflexivity as a major determinant in the US's rejection of climate change science.[20] *Reflexive modernity* is a movement to help address the problems (social and environmental) that arose from modernity. Thus, *anti-reflexivity* is any action that opposes attempts to address the environmental wrongs of modern technology, like climate change. The anti-reflexive strategies employed to counter action on climate change include sowing seeds of doubt about the science of climate change and arguing that any action on climate change would lead to economic devastation. Psychologically, anti-reflexivity is a defense mechanism used to maintain the dominance of the rugged individualism cultural complex.

This section has reviewed some of the leading social theories proposed to explain why America has resisted (and rejected) the reality of climate change and has opposed any action on the issue. Each of these social theories presents a tale of "two cultures," in which, on the one hand, there is a group that feels threatened by the facts of climate change and resists action; whereas, on the other hand, there is a group that accepts the threat of climate change and wants action. Thus social science research supports the existence of two constellated cultural complexes within the American psyche. What analytical psychology brings to the social sciences is a mythopoetic approach to view these structures in terms of image and metaphor, which allows us to relate more intimately with these complexes.[21] Most importantly, analytical psychology offers approaches to working with these cultural complexes to minimize their dissociating influence on the American psyche. Succinctly, within the heart of America beats two cultures that have polarized the nation around many important issues, including the most existentially threatening of all, climate change.

Cultural Complexes, Archetypes, and Climate Change

The strong emotional reactions to the news of climate change, including irrational defensiveness and avoidance concerning the issue are indicators of constellated cultural complexes. The archetypal depths of these emotional reactions are profound. For as Jung states, "The archetype corresponding to the situation is activated, and as a result those explosive and dangerous forces hidden in the archetype come into action, frequently with unpredictable consequences."[22] Personally, when I reflect on what is happening in terms of the science of climate change, current environmental disruptions, what is projected to happen in the future, and finally the rejection of these realities by a substantial number of Americans, I feel tremendous sadness coupled with a sense of looming loss. Our experience of current loss (the increased destructiveness of fires in the West and storms in the East) and anticipated loss (rising sea levels and storm-surge damages, displacement of life, extinction of species) evokes feelings of sadness, despair, fear, and anxiety. We would expect from the previous section that the two cultures experience loss in quite different ways.

The individualistic reaction to perceived loss is a desire to protect out of fear. The individualist "circles the wagons," which is an interesting image rooted in iconic figures from American Western films often centering around the rugged individual, an archetypal hero figure easily constellated in the American psyche (see also Jensen).[23] It is an image connected to the wide-open spaces of the Wild West—the expansive frontier calling to be explored—and exploited—by such individuals. This is an archetype directly connected to America's geography. The Western hero, as maverick, rides out into the frontier, protecting himself and his family. These are heroes who are relatively detached from the surrounding world. They believe everyone is on their own and should "pull themselves up by their own bootstraps." They often appear distant, caustic, and can be aggressive. They are loners. Interestingly, the figure of the rugged individual continues to be a dominant image in American films—consider Harry Callahan in *Dirty Harry*, Gordon Gecko in *Wall Street*, Laura Croft in *Tomb Raider*, Ripley in *Alien*, and Hans Solo in *Star Wars*, to name a few. Over time the wide-open spaces of the Wild West have been replaced with the wild financial markets on Wall Street and the vast expanse of outer space. The rugged individual seeks frontiers and refuses to be fenced in.

The other image appearing in American Westerns is someone who helps to protect and bind communities together. Here one finds the archetypal image of the helper who cares for and provides support for others. The helper in the Western story may be a woman who not only cares for her family, but also rallies the wider community. This role also appears in the form of the saloon "gal" who has a heart of gold, for example, Kitty in the 1950s television show *Gunsmoke* or Trixie in *Deadwood*. The character can also be the quiet country doctor or sheriff who defends the community against mob rule. The image of the helper also exists in current films such as John Keating from the *Dead Poets Society*, Erin Brockovich, and Wonder Woman. Note that for the hero, the image tends to be singular;

whereas for the helper, the image is more inclusive, indicating a dyad of independence and interdependence. I posit that these metaphoric images represent the two dominant cultural complexes of the American psyche, a dyad that has played out throughout American history.

It is important to recognize both positive and negative dimensions of any complex. The positive manifestation of the individualistic (independent) complex is the establishment of order, protection, and potential meaning. The negative manifestations of this complex are separation, control, rigidity, misuse of power, and aggression. This negative polarity is perhaps most evident in the horrific decimation of native peoples and nature in America. The positive qualities of the communitarian (interdependent) complex are inclusiveness, caring, empathy, and sensitivity to nature. Americans have also carried a deep sense of community within their religions, which continues today in the form of spiritual practices that value the natural world. The negative manifestation of this complex is overprotectiveness, indecisiveness, too much fluidity, and lack of boundaries often leading to disorder. The optimal situation is one in which both positive poles of the dyad are active. From the perspective of analytical psychology this ensures a dynamic engagement in life and access to the archetypal energies residing in the collective unconsciousness. It is when one pole dominates over the other that dysregulation occurs. When those who identify as wholly independent dismiss, denigrate, or deny the importance of communalism, then destruction lies nearby. Equally, when those who identify with communalism attack independence and wish to eliminate it because it is viewed as no longer useful, then disruption arises. As Jung noted, one-sidedness is the source of, at best, neurosis and, at the worst, collective annihilation.[24]

I would like to point out the connections between the cultural complexes of individualism and communalism and the dominion and reciprocity psyches described by Jerome Bernstein.[25] There is clear overlap between the dyad of these cultural complexes and the psychic paradigms described in Bernstein's writings, in which dominion is associated with the patriarchy, duality, power, and anthropocentrism, whereas reciprocity is associated with balance and harmony. Clearly, there is more to explore with regard to the connections between these two approaches to understanding the Western psyche.

Jung felt that at the core of any complex resides an archetype, which is true for cultural complexes as well. Jung also argued that archetypes and instincts are integrally coupled with one another. What are the archetypal cores of the cultural complexes of individualism and communalism? I believe that at an instinctually deeper level this dyadic cultural complex carries the characteristics of independence and interdependence rooted in the biological forms of competition and cooperation. In developing his theory of opposites, Jung states, "I ... occupied myself with tracing [oppositions] down to something fundamental. I started with the primitive idea of the flow-ing out and flowing in of energy ...."[26] Here Jung is referring to psychic energy, the energy that sustains our psyche and our relationship to the outer world. However, this term *energy* could also represent the internal use and competition for sources of energy by an organism, or the exchange of energy between an organism and its environment, for the flow of energy is essential for all life forms.

Biologists have recognized that the most optimal setting for evolution is one that not only involves "survival of the fittest," or *competitive independ-ence*, but also involves the process of *cooperative interdependence*. These two processes work to ensure a self-regulatory evolution strategy, which optimizes adaptability to changing environments. This dynamic regulatory dyad appar-ently arose quite early in biological development for it is observed at the level of microbes.[27] For billions of years, life has involved a dance between I and WE and is perhaps the oldest archetypal polarity. According to Jung arche-types express themselves first and foremost in image; indeed, archetypes are the "unconscious images of the instincts themselves."[28] So it is not surprising that the instinctual pattern of competition-cooperation has given birth to an archetypal pattern that exists in life forms today, including humans. Ernest Lawrence Rossi has noted the importance of these processes and calls them the "archetypes of life."[29] With the development of language and use of sym-bols, humans were able to develop culture, which accelerated our evolutionary process. Yet psyche continues to carry the archaic, instinctual competition-cooperation dyad in the image of the cultural dyad of individualism-communalism, and in its varied nuances this dynamic dyad has remained active throughout human history.

For example, from an anthropological perspective, hunter-gatherer societies were more rooted in cooperation than competition, for at those times the social unit was sufficiently small and the environment sufficiently threatening that creating and maintaining close social bonds was critical for survival. With the establishment of agrarian societies more hierarchical structures developed to manage the increased complexity of a larger social body, includ-ing the diversification of tasks. Communities still needed to be interconnected, but connectivity became more dependent on structure and authority, which means that at any given time both poles of the cultural dyad existed. There was never a time when one of these poles disappeared. There were times when the tendency for individualism dominated over communalism, while at other times the reverse was the case. One generation may move more toward the individualistic end of the spectrum of connectivity, whereas the next gen-eration may move to the communalistic end of the spectrum. Cultures have exhibited fluidity through time. However, what does appear to be historically true is that Western civilization has trended toward increased individualism over time, especially since the Enlightenment when the rights of the individual became paramount. Nowhere was this truer than in the foundation of the

United States. Given this increasing drift toward one-sidedness, it is not surprising our collective dissociation has grown over the past two centuries.

If the psychic images of competition-cooperation are the archetypal cores of the cultural complexes of individualism-communalism, why are these complexes more active in America as compared to other countries in the world? If this dyad is truly archetypal in nature, then why aren't they more present in other places? First, it is important to recognize that these two archetypal cores are active around the world. In fact, the worldwide accelerated emergence of nationalism over the past decade indicates that the cultural complex of isolationism and individualism exists in other places. Second, the prevalence of this dyad in the American psyche has been facilitated by both the physical and philosophical landscape of America. The American Frontier Thesis of Frederick Jackson Turner continues to be a persuasive argument for America's development.[30]

Ours is a time of increased investment in the story of independence and separation. We have turned away from a belief and experience of our interdependence with others. We have turned to a myth of absolute materialism and separation. This is the fundamental root of our problem. It is pervasive in cultures around the world, but nowhere more so than in the United States, owing to a combination of factors: 1) the country was founded on personal freedom; 2) it had a culture that fostered growth and expansion; 3) it had the physical space, the great Western frontier, to accommodate expansionism; 4) it was rooted in a religion that promoted dominion over wilderness; and 5) this religion also encouraged hard work and accumulation of wealth by individuals.[31] If you combine all of these factors (and there certainly are more), then you have the United States, which grew in size, wealth, and political might. This growth has been aided by technological innovation, spurred on by a new generation of rugged individuals (Steve Jobs, Bill Gates, Elon Musk). The price paid for following this path of ultra-individualism is loss of community and spiritual impoverishment.

Working with Cultural Complexes

Activated complexes lead to a collective state of dissociation. The dominant activated cultural complexes are those of individualism and communalism, also framed as competition and cooperation, respectively. These complexes also couple with other complexes such as money and over-consumption to support a dissociated state. The purpose of this chapter is to discuss the evidence for the two dominant cultural complexes and how they prevent acceptance of the reality of climate change. A secondary purpose is to suggest how, using analytical psychology, we could work with these activated complexes—the goal being to place the collective in a more balanced, sane state with the unconscious and the outer world. Given that dissociation is a nonrational state of psyche, any purely rational linear approach to addressing climate change will be limited in success (as evidenced by our present state of stasis around action). Analytical psychology recognizes the importance of the nonrational and thus opens ways of working toward integration and action. Nonrational approaches include collectively working with dream images, fantasies, and synchronicities. Furthermore, Jung argued that, "... the symptomatology of an illness is at the same time a natural attempt at healing."[32] Thus, by working with our complexes, which manifest as symptoms, the process of healing takes place—a healing that addresses both inner and outer symptoms related to climate change.

We stand at the edge of a deep, dark abyss in a state of collective dissociation. It is no exaggeration to state that we are on the brink of a major collective collapse. Using the best estimate of Earth's climate sensitivity to increased carbon dioxide indicates we need to transition off of fossil fuels within less than 20 years to avoid catastrophic destruction. This task seems impossible given the current collective inertia to change, especially in the United States.

What to do? How do we begin to work with the American cultural complexes connected to climate change? One thing is certain, if we do nothing, then we are committing future generations to terrible suffering. We have a moral and ethical responsibility to do everything possible to reduce suffering. Depth psychology comes with an ethical responsibility, for it opens our eyes to the reality of the unconscious with all of its blessings and curses. We have eaten of the tree of knowledge and cannot turn our backs on our knowing. Jolande Jacobi states that

> The inability to distinguish between contents of the conscious mind and those stemming from the unconscious complex ... constitutes a great danger; it prevents the individual from properly adapting himself to his inward and outward reality; it impairs his ability to form clear judgements, and above all thwarts any satisfactory human contact.[33]

Thus, we are tasked with identifying our cultural complexes and working with them to avoid the "great danger." What follows are suggested paths forward to work with cultural complexes. I am not naïve in believing that these will be adopted by many people, nor do I feel these suggestions are comprehensive. However, based on my work on this issue for close to 40 years now, I feel they are worth exploring and discussing.

Little can be accomplished within the federal government given the psychological and political impediments existing at that level. The best chance for behavioral change is at the local community level, evidenced by current state and city commitments on climate action. However, even these smaller communities find themselves ensnared within a web spun by our conflicting dominant dyadic cultural complexes. Imagine members of the analytic community working within small communities to help identify activated cultural patterns in these groups. Imagine conversations not solely centered on political differences, but on working with the deep-seated psychological barriers to progress on climate change, most importantly on the constellated cultural complexes. I argue that as analytical psychologists we have well-honed approaches that can be employed to effectively work with and hopefully even through these psychological barriers.

One approach would be to form small groups to create new stories around what is happening now and imagining the world that we would like to bestow to future generations. The power of story is universal. Through imagination, rich in image and metaphor, we could collectively connect on a deeper communal level. This group activity could explore the stories that weave the two cultural complexes together. Another approach would be to form small climate dream groups to listen to what the unconscious is telling us about the world and how it is changing. I have been a part of such a group for the past two years, and it has been a powerful way to sit and work with the feelings around climate change.[34] Another approach is to connect mindfulness practices with working with complexes. Mindfulness practices focus on becoming more aware of the mind's activities, including images, affect, and thoughts that emerge from the unconscious. Although the practice is not focused on dwelling on an image during meditation, discussion of images, especially those connected to collective issues, could be explored after the meditation practice. One particular practice, giving-taking, includes a component that connects individuals to the greater community, which could also be integrated into working with cultural complexes. These are only a few approaches involving community that could help us recognize and engage with the cultural complexes hindering action on climate change.

Final Thoughts

I have explored only a few ideas that relate American cultural complexes to the issue of climate change. My research was guided by my personal desire to understand why it has been so difficult to connect Americans to this issue. I have used social science research from a number of sources to show how pervasive and polarized this issue really is in the United States. These results indicate that two cultures exist within the US that correlate with the two political parties. The two cultures—individualism-communalism or independent-interdependent—are in a state of extreme affective polarization. This heightened level of affect and emotionality is indicative of psychic complexes. These cultural complexes are also linked with Americans' obsession with consumerism, which reinforces the demand for energy and associated changes to Earth's greenhouse effect. Furthermore, these complexes are rooted in the archetypal images of hero-helper that pervade American history. I believe that these archetypal motifs represent more archaic biological instincts of competition-cooperation. These fundamental processes are alive and active in the psyche of Americans and are maintained and reinforced via cultural belief systems. Their power and prevalence in the United States are due to a combination of factors, including roots in European Enlightenment thought, *laissez-faire* capitalism, and a frontier myth fostered by America's unique geography.

A critical question is: where do we go from here? Knowing that cultural complexes are active around the issue of climate change, what do we do? As analytical psychologists we have worked with our own personal complexes and those of our analysands. Jung provided descriptions of how complexes appear in psyche and how, through the personification of these complexes and engaging with them, we can redefine our relationship with the complex. Can we work with cultural complexes in a similar manner? I believe this is possible, but it needs to be done at a group level. By bringing communities together to identify and work with cultural complexes we may be able to build bridges across the two cultures. If nothing else, we will bring these complexes out of the shadows.

The analytic community can play an important role in this process, given our experience in working with complexes. For this to happen, more individuals within the analytical psychology community need to actively engage with social issues like climate change, which thrusts them into a place of discomfort, for often they are more comfortable with an analytic container built for two. However, we are in a new world, where if we do not act soon, that analytic container will be under assault from a destabilized environment. Flood waters will be lapping at the consulting room; the office thermostat will be unable to keep the room at a reasonable temperature; severe storms will prevent analyst and the analysand from reaching the protectiveness of that container. The analytic community has an ethical responsibility to face the cultural complexes within themselves, their communities, and the nation.

Acknowledgments

I thank the following people for very stimulating conversations that have contributed to my formulation of this chapter: Robert Romanyshyn, Jerome Bernstein, Andrew Szasz, and Robert Stayer.

Notes

1 C. G. Jung, "Epilogue to 'Essays on Contemporary Events'" (1947), in *The Collected Works of C. G. Jung*, vol. 10, *Civilization in Transition* (Princeton: Princeton University Press, 1978), 474.
2 Andrew J. Hoffman, "Climate Science as Cultural War," *Stanford Social Innovation Review* (Fall 2012): 32.

3 Cary Funk and Brian Kennedy, "The Politics of Climate," Pew Research Center, October 2016, www.pewresearch.org.
4 A. Leiserowtiz, E. Maibach, C. Roser-Renouf, S. Rosenthhal, M. Cutler, and J. Kotcher, "Climate Change in the American Mind: March 2018," Yale University and George Mason University (New Haven, CT: Yale Program on Climate Change Communication).
5 Peter T. Dorn and Maggie Kendall Zimmerman, "Examining the Scientific Consensus on Climate Change," *EOS* 90, no. 3 (2009): 22.
6 Thomas Singer, "The Cultural Complex Theory: Scientific and Mythopoetic Ways of Knowing," in Joseph Cambray and Leslie Sawin, eds., *Research in Analytical Psychology: Applications from Scientific, Historical and Cross-Cultural Research* (London: Routledge, 2018), 69–82.
7 Edward Maibach, Connie Roser-Renouf, and Anthony Leiserowitz, "Global Warming's Six Americas 2009: An Audience Segmentation Analysis," Yale University and George Mason University (New Haven, CT: Yale Program on Climate Change Communication).
8 Mary Douglas and Aaron Wildavsky, *Risk and Culture* (Berkeley: University of California Press, 1983); Virginie Mamadouh, "Grid-Group Cultural Theory: An Introduction," *GeoJournal* 47 (1999): 395–409.
9 Dan Kahan, "Cultural Cognition as a Conception of the Cultural Theory of Risk," in Sabine Roeser, Rafaela Hillerbrand, Per Sandin, and Martin Peterson, eds., *Handbook of Risk Theory: Epistemology, Decision Theory, Ethics and Social Implications of Risk* (New York: Springer, 2012), 725–759.
10 Dan Kahan, Maggie Wittlin, Ellen Peters, Paul Slovic, Lisa Larrimore Ouellette, Donald Braman, and Gregory N. Mandel, "The Tragedy of the Risk-Perception Commons: Culture Conflict, Rationality Conflict, and Climate Change" (2011), Temple University Legal Studies Research Paper No. 2011–26; Cultural Cognition Project Working Paper No. 89; Yale Law & Economics Research Paper No. 435; Yale Law School, Public Law Working Paper No. 230. http://dx.doi.org/10.2139/ssrn.1871503.
11 Michele Gelfand, *Rule Makers, Rule Breakers: How Tight and Loose Cultures Wire Our World* (New York: Scribner, 2018).
12 Jesse R. Harrington and Michele J. Gelfand, "Tightness-Looseness Across the 50 United States," *Proceedings of the National Academy of Sciences* 111, no. 22 (2014): 7990–7995. DOI: 10.1073/pnas.1317937111.
13 Ibid.
14 Ibid.
15 Peter J. Rentfrow, ed., *Geographical Psychology: Exploring the Interaction of Environment and Behavior* (Washington, D.C.: American Psychological Association, 2014).
16 Russell W. Belk, "Possessions and the Extended Self," *Journal of Consumer Research* 15 (1988): 139–168.
17 Francine Russo, "Our Stuff, Ourselves," *Scientific American*, May 2018, 67–71.
18 Charles Waugh, "The Politics and Culture of Climate Change: US Actors and Global Implications," in M. A. Stewart and P. A. Coclanis, eds., *Environmental Change and Agricultural Sustainability in the Mekong Delta* (New York: Springer, 2011), 90.
19 Ibid.
20 Aaron M. McCright and Riley E. Dunlap, "Anti-reflexivity: The American Conservative Movement's Success in Undermining Climate Science and Policy," *Theory, Culture & Society* 27 (2010), 100–133.
21 Singer, "The Cultural Complex Theory."

22 C. G. Jung, "The Concept of the Collective Unconscious" (1936), in *The Collected Works of C. G. Jung*, vol. 9i, *The Archetypes and the Collective Unconscious* (Princeton: Princeton University Press, 1980), 98.

23 Phyllis Marie Jensen, "American and Canadian Cultural Complexes Compared," *Jung Journal: Culture & Psyche* 12, no. 2 (Spring 2018), 91–108.

24 C. G. Jung, "Commentary on the Secret of the Golden Flower" (1968), in *The Collected Works of C. G. Jung*, vol. 13, *Alchemical Studies* (Princeton: Princeton University Press, 1968), 15.

25 Jerome S. Bernstein, "Different Realities: What Is Reality and What Difference Does It Make?" *Psychological Perspectives* 61 (2018), 18–26.

26 C. G. Jung, *Introduction to Jungian Psychology: Notes of the Seminar on Analytical Psychology Given in 1925*, ed. Sonu Shamdasani (Princeton: Princeton University Press, 2012), 86.

27 Shiri Freilich, Raphy Zarecki, Omer Eilam, Ella Shtifman Segal, Christopher S. Henry, Martin Kupiec, Uri Gophna, Roded Sharan, and Eytan Ruppin, "Competitive and cooperative metabolic communities," *Nature Communications* 2, no. 589 (2011): DOI: 10.1038/ncomms1597.

28 Jung, "The Concept of the Collective Unconscious," 91.

29 Ernest Lawrence Rossi, "The Life Archetype," *Psychological Perspectives* 27 (1992): 5–13.

30 Frederick Jackson Turner, *The Frontier in American History* (New York: Holt, 1893/1920).

31 Bernstein, "Different Realities."

32 C. G. Jung, "The Structure of the Psyche" (1931), in *The Collected Works of C. G. Jung*, vol. 8, *The Structure and Dynamics of the Psyche* (Princeton: Princeton University Press, 1980), 312.

33 Jolande Jacobi, *Complex, Archetype, Symbol in the Psychology of C.G. Jung* (Princeton: Princeton University Press, 1971), 16–17.

34 Bonnie Bright and Jonathan Paul Marshall, eds., *Earth, Climate Dreams: Dialogues with Depth Psychologists in the Age of the Anthropocene* (Depth Insights, 2019).

Healthcare

Chapter 16

Biomedicine

Its Cultural Complex and
Its Dispiriting

Richard M. Timms, MD
SENIOR FELLOW HARVARD'S INITIATIVE ON HEALTH, RELIGION, AND SPIRITUALITY

The social forces over and within biomedicine have been increasingly dominated by impersonal and bureaucratic factors as demands for greater coverage, cures, and efficiencies have taken precedence. As organizations have flourished, controls and capitalization have achieved remarkable results and made significant progress throughout all medical specialties, perhaps excepting mental health, addiction, and other psychosocial-related medical fields. Correspondingly, social capital, spirituality, religion, and soulfulness are now stepchildren within biomedical culture. One secondary result is the dispiritedness and burnout among medical professionals, "a public health crisis" according to the *Boston Globe*.[1]

This cultural trend, or cultural complex, has been termed biomedicine's *technical imperative*, implying its emotional content and its focus on curing diseases and healthcare delivery through technological and organizational advances. This complex has fostered impersonal forces, depression, and burnout among medical professionals. Most physicians believe that medical care should be better integrated with competent spiritual and religious (R/S) support. However, the separation between biomedicine and R/S has reached its greatest dissociation.

The more subjective, relating, and caretaking the orientation of a healthcare deliverer, the more he or she may be adversely affected by this technical imperative. Likewise, those nurses and physicians involved with the greatest degree of R/S and subjective issues may feel the greatest conflict with the increasingly technical and bureaucratic focus in healthcare.

Biomedicine's cultural complex is driven by powerful archetypal energy, an altruistic ethos that energizes efforts toward technical cures, efficiencies, and reasonable care for everyone. Humanness is proving that this ideal is an allusive goal, although biomedicine's relative consumption of the gross national product has tripled over the past half century.

Who would know this evolution of biomedicine better than the nurses and physicians who have worked in the field for four decades? I interviewed 47 of them to gain their insights.

The Professionals

Important to this analysis and understanding was the selection process, the personal interviews, and the questions. All MDs and RNs were referred by their colleagues after posing the following question to a variety of working MDs and RNs in different locations in Northern and Southern California, a location chosen in order to limit travel time and costs: would they recommend a respected clinical nurse or clinical physician who has been practicing for more than 30 years? Forty-seven professionals were subsequently referred. All 47 were interviewed. No one declined nor was excluded. I introduced myself to the referrals as a recently retired professor of research medicine and board-certified internist. Each was informed that the interview would be anonymous as to person and workplace, last 30 to 40 minutes, and take place at a time and place of their choosing. My goal was to gain their insights regarding the trends in clinical medicine during their work years.

Twenty-nine MDs and 18 RNs were interviewed; 41 of them were still working. The average length of clinical practice was 38 years. They lived and worked in 27 different practices and work locations. Twelve RNs worked hospital or emergency settings, whereas six worked in outpatient medicine. The MDs worked in 23 different specialties, the most (3) from family practice/internal medicine. The RNs worked in 12 different primary areas, the most (3) from outpatient medicine. In order to broadly cover clinical medicine, once I had interviewed two referrals from a certain work specialty, I asked the referring professionals to refer someone from other specialty areas.

I defined two terms for all subjects. A *trend in medicine* was defined as a significant and noteworthy pattern of change that consistently affected work behavior, situation, or attitude. *Spirituality* was defined as that aspect of humanity that refers to the way individuals seek and express meaning and purpose, and the way that they experience connection to the moment, to the significant, and to the sacred.

There were a total of 46 questions; of those questions, 45 were asked of all subjects; one question was posed to RNs only. The questions spanned six categories: workload, control or empowerment, integration of work and personal life, work-related economics, work-related meaning, and insights into "supra-medical practice trends," which were defined as overarching cultural trends that affected participants' work yet originated and occurred primarily at a cultural level above or beyond the field of medicine.

Results

Most RNs and MDs perceived that their work hours had not significantly increased over their careers. Only 9 out of 47 replied that their workload had increased. This finding is consistent with the California Board of

Nursing survey. It appears that trends in total worktime is not the culprit causing greater dispiritedness among medical professionals.

Their work has changed, however, and their work environment is more stressful. A variety of questions supported this conclusion. Participants were asked to consider their worktime divided into three segments:

1. **Personal worktime:** worktime spent interacting with patients or their families in the office, during procedures, or outside one's office such as in hospitals, clinics, or office.
2. **Technical worktime:** worktime spent on patient records, dictating, ordering and analyzing tests, reading reports, and all other nonpersonal-worktime related to specific patients.
3. **Other worktime:** neither personal worktime nor technical worktime. This is medical worktime that is unrelated to specific patients. Examples are educational work and committee work.

Of the participants:

- 41 out of 47 (87 percent) of the interviewees indicated that their *personal worktime* had decreased.
- 43 out of 47 (91 percent) indicated that their *technical worktime* had increased.
- Of the third worktime allocation, *other worktime*, responses were mixed among same, increase, and decrease with no majority answer.

Consistent with these findings, 34 out of 47 (72 percent) fully agreed that "during the latter time of their careers they were spending more time on objective, scientific issues of healing versus time on subjective aspects of healing." Of the respondents, 9 out of 47 replied maybe and only 3 out of 47 disagreed; 1 out of 47 did not know.

Interestingly, 17 of the 18 RNs reported that their personal worktime had decreased. None of the respondents reported a decrease in technical time. The majority of these medical professionals, 32 out of 47 (68 percent), fully agreed that there is more emotional stress in the work environment than three to four decades ago; 9 of 47 (19 percent) responded maybe; 4 of 47 (9 percent) disagreed; and 2 of 47 (4 percent) did not know. Eighty-five percent (40 of 47) fully agreed with the following statement: "My colleagues are more disenchanted or disconnected from their practice of medicine as compared to 30 or more years ago." In summary, their technical worktime has increased without an increase in total worktime. This insight was nearly universal from RNs. Both MDs and RNs observed that their work environment has become more stressful. They noted this trend among their colleagues as well.

Control and Empowerment

Sixteen questions dealt with work-related control. More than two-thirds of these professionals "fully agreed" with the following statements:

- My workload seems less under my control than three to four decades ago.
- There are more administrative burdens that are beyond my control.
- Medicine is more often practiced in large groups managed by nonmedical experts.
- There is more sophisticated credentialing and regulation.
- There has been an increasing separation of physicians and nurses from operational control.
- My work is more complex, in part, related to outside controls such as JCAHO (Joint Commission on Accreditation of Healthcare Organizations), Medicare, and other third-parties that define my work.
- The major trends in medicine over the past three to four decades have not been intentionally brought forth by physicians, nurses, or their managers. These trends were caused by larger cultural or economic issues.
- During the latter decade of my career, in contrast to earlier in my career, I have been more likely to miss a meal or a break than to miss inputting requirements of data or patient-care information.

When workers experience growing demands and controls from their supervisors or from those at higher levels of power, and if they struggle to meet these demands, they become dispirited. There is an established link between empowerment at work and job satisfaction, enthusiasm and burnout. Medical professionals and their patients encounter more specialized strangers within more complex bureaucracies and controls. The increase in technical time and in having to interface with strangers and bureaucracy fosters less social capital and causes increased dispiritedness. Social capital relies on a worker's personal network and how these networks interact and support one another. Social capital increases when work conditions and connections foster goodwill, trusted transfers of information, a reasoned sense of control, collegial friendships, and work-related enthusiasm. These professionals have experienced a decline in social capital, however.

Integration of Work and Personal Life

Only 15 of 47 (32 percent) of health professionals agreed with this statement: "It is more difficult now to integrate their personal and medical life than three to four decades ago." Of the respondents, 17 of 47 (36 percent) disagreed with this statement and 15 or 47 (32 percent) replied maybe. These responses, along with the fact that work hours have not increased, suggests that changes in the integration of work with personal life are not the primary cause of greater work-related stress, burnout, and reduction in social capital or further dispiritedness.

Work-Related Economics

These interviewees had a mixed response regarding trends in economic rewards. The majority (25 of 47, or 53 percent) of MDs and RNs replied that there was no significant change in their economic rewards. A minority (12 of 47, or 26 percent) stated that they must work harder for the same level of income, and (10 of 47, or 21 percent) replied that it has become easier to make economic rewards with a relative improvement in their economic rewards. A higher proportion of RNs (39 percent) than MDs (10 percent) reported an improvement. These responses suggest that changes in economic rewards are not a significant cause of the trends of dispiritedness.

At a broader cultural and economic level, these professionals (83 percent) fully agreed that "medicine's overall economic importance had multiplied during their practice life." They (81 percent) agreed that "the major trends in medicine have not been intentionally brought forth by nurses, physicians, or their managers. These changes are primarily secondary to bigger cultural or economic issues." Only 1 of the 47 respondents disagreed.

The Liabilities-Related Atmosphere

Nearly two-thirds of the interviewees, 30 of 47 (64 percent), fully agreed that there has been a trend toward a greater liability atmosphere in their medical work. Of these, 9 of 47 (19 percent) replied maybe and 7 of 47 (15 percent) disagreed. Interestingly, only a bare majority, 24 of 47 (51 percent), fully agreed that the liability atmosphere affected their thoughts and actions.

Meaning and Spirituality

Twenty of the 47 work-related questions reflected on the meaning of respondents' work. The responses indicate that the trends in medicine have resulted in a less meaningful work culture.

Ninety-four percent fully agreed that there is less time for nurses and physicians to listen to their patients stories, experiences, and concerns. Eighty-seven percent fully agreed that their colleagues are more disenchanted with or disconnected from their practice of medicine as compared to 30 or more years ago. Eighty-one percent noted "more emotional stress in their work environment."

A majority noted a growing separation from the continuum of healthcare. Nearly all agreed that specialization is more apparent, that they are less involved with the continuum of healthcare, and that listening to the experiences of patients and their stories is more often lateraled to specialists such as social workers, psychologists, or psychiatrists. Eighty-three percent fully agreed with the statement, "Studies suggest that health professionals now have a higher rate of work dissatisfaction and burnout in contrast to decades ago. This observation coincides with my work-related insights." Seventy percent of interviewees fully agreed that "medical institutions do not prohibit spiritual practices but they do not actively support them either." Fifty-three percent noted a trend toward a more secular atmosphere, and 64 percent felt that there is a trend toward dying becoming a more technical than soulful event. Seventy-three percent disagreed with this statement: "a distancing between medicine and spirituality is a good thing." One open-ended question asked for their most memorable work-related experience. The importance of spirituality is suggested by the observation that a majority of these MDs and RNs chose a non-cure event as the most meaningful one.

All of these interviewees were in the second half of their adult lives, a time when there is greater consciousness about what is meaningful. Older RNs show a higher percentage of dissatisfaction with their work. Other investigators found that medical work has become less meaningful and more stressful. Dr. Sandeep Jauhar writes in the August 29, 2014, *Wall Street Journal*, "In surveys, a majority of doctors express diminished enthusiasm for medicine and say they would discourage a friend or family member from entering the profession. In a 2008 survey of 12,000 physicians, only 6% described their morale as positive."[2]

The pattern of responses from these 47 senior medical professionals suggests definable reasons why MDs and RNs feel that their work is less meaningful, exclusive of economic rewards, total work hours, or their ability to integrate their work with their personal lives. The dispiriting trends are associated with a decrement in personal worktime and social capital coupled with an increase in technical worktime. Their work seems more difficult and less under their control. Their time is more specialty focused and less connected to continuities of care. They are less connected to the personal experiences of their patients and colleagues.

The meaning or spirit associated with their work has diminished.

These professionals recognize that many important trends in medicine have originated from a cultural level beyond their field or practice. Consider the responses to these statements:

- "I have noticed that medicine's overall economic and cultural importance has multiplied": 38 of 47 fully agreed, 8 of 47 maybe, and 1 of 47 did not know.
- "In my medical work over the past three to four decades I have noted a more secular atmosphere": 21 of 47 fully agreed, 13 of 47 maybe, and 9 of 47 disagreed, 4 of 47 did not know.

- "The major changes in medicine over the past three to four decades have not been intentionally brought forth by nurses, physicians, or their managers. These changes are primarily secondary to bigger cultural or economic issues": 37 of 47 fully agreed, 9 of 47 maybe, 1 of 47 disagreed, 0 of 47 did not know.

The following summarizes the responses from these senior medical professionals:

- The major trends in the culture of biomedicine since the 1960s stem from changes that are beyond the control of these professionals.
- They feel less empowered.
- Bureaucracy has increased.
- The trends in total economic rewards for medical work are not downward. They may have improved for RNs.
- Work hours have not increased.
- Worktime is more technological, with less time spent on patient experiences, coping, and spiritual issues.
- Specialization is more apparent.
- Experiences with continuity of care have diminished.
- Credentialing, regulations, and organizations are more complex.
- There is an atmosphere of greater liability risk.
- Connections with colleagues and social capital have diminished.
- They feel more stressed.
- Their colleagues seem more stressed.
- The work environment is less meaningful.
- Further distancing between medicine and the spiritual is not a good thing.

These conclusions are summarized from group responses. Group conclusions do not apply at the individual level where exceptions existed to nearly all conclusions. These conclusions should not be a surprise. Today's work experiences and related effects within the culture of modern biomedicine have been recognized in an array of medical and lay articles, which are noted in the endnotes.[3]

What are the origins of this dispiritedness within our biomedical culture? One family practitioner interrupted my questioning to explain, "I used to feel like the captain of my rowboat. Now I feel like a galley slave rowing someone's battleship." This is a telling image regarding the evolution of biomedicine's work culture.

The underlying powerful or archetypal forces influencing biomedicine began many decades ago, forces interpreted as a "technical imperative." Medicine has its own community with external appearances, shared assumptions, and a collective nature. Since the mid-20th century, the culture of biomedicine has rapidly changed under the influence of new technologies, greater efficiencies, top-down controls, and healthcare-related coverage demands. Universal caretaking obligations carry a heroic ethos and a cultural complex that have been allowed to unbalance biomedicine. This imbalance is associated with reductions in meaning, social capital, and the subjective aspects of healing within medicine's work culture.

To better understand the force of medicine's cultural complex we look back to the introduction of the universal right to quality healthcare. This goal or privilege had little cultural traction until the second half of the 20th century. In the late 1940s the World Health Organization first supported the right to universal healthcare within its Declaration of Universal Human Rights. In the 1960s President Kennedy supported universal healthcare as a moral imperative. Medicare legislation in 1965 was an organizational and controls milestone. President Nixon politicized the ethos of a scientific victory with his 1971 "War on Cancer" announcement. Our nation's often altruistic spirit, which has driven the desire for universal healthcare, the search for cures for diseases, and a technical imperative have supported remarkable advances in cure rates, organizational developments, medical efficiencies, and preventive measures. Our nation became the world's leader in medical science. Other nations benefited from its discoveries and advances. One of many noteworthy examples was the translation of bio-scientific research on the toxicity of tobacco into public health education, taxation, and associated regulations. Healthcare issues less amenable to technology have floundered. Our shoddy caretaking of the mentally ill is an example. A second example is the technology-driven costs and resources that are wasted on terminal cancer patients.

A Psychological Understanding

Understanding the trends in medicine energized by its cultural complex and its technical imperative starts with medicine's timeless balancing symbol, the *caduceus*. The upright, often winged staff entwined with snakes has been a ubiquitous symbol of medicine for centuries. The staff symbolizes scientific rigor, vertical thinking, and rationality that brings light to the darkness of illness. This bright, upright, sky-level power has been mythologized by the healer god Apollo. The Hippocratic oath, until its modernization, began with "I swear by Apollo the physician."

In contrast, the snake or snakes of the caduceus symbolize grounded intuition, regeneration, mystery, and the power of intuitive insight. A winged staff entwined with snakes was Hermes's symbol. Hermes was the healing messenger, the god of journeys, messages, stories, and creative ambiguities. Hermes lords over that which cannot be fully defined or understood in pure scientific terms. He featured the nuances of speech and story. We need Apollo for the impeccable science and Hermes for the caretaking of the spirit, for the stories and messages that attend every illness and medical encounter. Earthiness, connection, and care of the soul are alien to Apollo.

There are many enduring stories of cultures and individuals who aggressively pursue cures or address injustice yet find themselves contending with imbalance. Is bioscience and related efficiencies the one path to quality healthcare for all citizens? This is a bright Apollonian path. Under influences of medicine's cultural complex, its archetypal forces have separated and become unbalanced. This separation is exemplified by the growing split between medicine and R/S, a unique feature of the last 100 years.[4] Medical professionals are the victims of this imbalance and the loss of control and have, therefore, become dispirited. The balance that escapes them is symbolized by the caduceus.

Are there answers to the loss of meaning within medicine's cultural complex? The first answer is greater consciousness of the cultural complex. The separation between the admirable advances in curing diseases and the subjective aspects of healthcare raises the issue of values as nurses and physicians are pushed to greater technological orientations.

A second answer centers around the premise that meaning, social capital, and R/S are vital elements of healthcare, exclusive of technical cures, efficiencies, information management, and material rewards. Unfortunately, the quality and quantity of professional time spent on the subjective aspects of caretaking are difficult to measure and weakly reimbursed. Nonetheless, our cure and procedure-oriented healthcare system needs proof that clarifies where, when, and how increases in subjective caretaking improve outcomes in employment, social capital, costs, and patient care. Who within our healthcare culture will push for the support of meaning, social capital, and professional experiences aside from cures and efficiencies? Will our nurses and physicians continue their march into technical roles or will they also be trained, employed, evaluated, and rewarded regarding their roles in the broad aspects of caretaking?

The third answer to the perceived reductions in meaning and social capital lies in addressing professional empowerment. Whether RNs and MDs are employees, providers, or professionals, greater involvement as a group and as individuals with regulations, organizational developments, and other aspects of their work environment remain important to social capital and the prevention of burnout. The waves of top-down regulations and requirements accompanying medicine's technical imperative have been oriented to cures and efficiencies. The results in efficiencies or outcomes have not been impressive to the 47 professionals I interviewed. Only 40 percent of these professionals agreed that "their patient-related work had become more effective or efficient than three to four decades ago." This is a troubling sign from experienced frontline staff.

Is one answer found through greater material rewards, perhaps corresponding to measurable improvements in cures and efficiencies? Of course, these professionals care about efficiencies, curing diseases, and related material rewards. However, improving material rewards and cure rates may be weak antidotes to reductions in meaning and empowerment. Given the evolving work culture, it is likely that these professionals will seek greater increases in material rewards per work hour in reaction to the diminution in meaning and related subjective rewards.

What about adaptation through medical training? Might the dispiriting associated with modern medicine be neutralized by training more technological MDs and RNs, specialists with less interest and expectations regarding the meaning, empowerment, and social capital of their profession? Are younger MDs and RNs better adapted to the trends of modern medicine? These interviewed professionals observed that newly trained RNs and MDs express less interest in subjective aspects of their work and more interest in boundaries and materials aspects. Whether this is a trend for younger RNs and MDs was not investigated. It would be interesting to ask young MDs and RNs their related impressions.

One path toward addressing the dispiritedness of medical professionals lies in organizing and supporting caretaking groups. The success of diversified caretaking groups within hospice and palliative-care programs suggests this solution. The work experience goal of caretaking teams might allow associated RNs and MDs more access to the breadth of caretaking possibilities and the continuum of care. Such groups can be structured to better balance or share technical time, specialty demands, and subjective issues of caretaking.

These professionals are receptive to improvements in subjective aspects of caretaking. This opinion is reflected in the high percentage of those who feel negatively toward the separation of medicine and spirituality. I emphasize that "spirituality" was defined in its broadest sense as that aspect of humanity that refers to the way individuals seek and express meaning and purpose, and the way that they experience connection to the moment, to the significant, and to the sacred. These professionals are aware that the subjective and relationship aspects of caretaking are being sacrificed in favor of enhanced technical worktime focused on prevention, cures, and knowledge management.

A variety of medical work experiments are underway that address the issue of meaning, social capital, and empowerment for MDs and RNs. Efforts toward improving balance within the medical profession face a major challenge because of the momentum and energies underlying its cultural complex. This research suggests that material rewards, however important, are neither the problem nor the best solution to dispiritedness. Increasing material rewards without other changes may lead to more MDs and RNs choosing part-time work in response to a dispiriting work environment. Because the technological, bureaucratic, knowledge management, and efficiency aspects for these professionals are likely to increase, solutions need to come from creating and empowering caretaking structures and rewards that support social capital, meaning, and R/S in balance with preventive and curing responsibilities.

Notes

1 Priyanka Dayal McCluskey, "Physician Burnout Now Essentially a Public Health Crisis," *Boston Globe*, January 27, 2019, https://www.bostonglobe.com/metro/2019/01/17/report-raises-alarm-about-physician-burnout/9CGdUc0eEO nobtSUiX5EIK/story.html.

2 Sandeep Jauhar, "Why Doctors Are Sick of Their Profession," *The Wall Street Journal*, August 29, 2014, https://www.wsj.com/articles/the-u-s-s-ailing-medical-system-a-doctors-perspective-1409325361.

3 J. B. McKinlay and L. D. Marceau, "The End of the Golden Age of Doctoring," *International Journal of Health Services* 32, no. 2 (2002): 379–416; Heather K. Spence Laschinger, Joan Finegan, and Judith Shamian, "Promoting Nurses' Health: Effect of Empowerment on Job Strain Work Satisfaction," *Nursing Economics* 19, no. 2 (2001); John C. Goodman, "Why Are Doctors So Unhappy?" *Forbes*, September 11, 2014, https://www.forbes.com/sites/johngoodman/2014/09/11/why-are-doctors-so-unhappy/#7fc2f9ea1771; T. D. Shanafelt, S. Boone, L. Tan, L. N. Dyrbye, W. Sotile, D. Satele, C. P. West, J. Sloan, and M. R. Oreskovich, "Burnout and Satisfaction with Work-Life Balance Among US Physicians Relative to the General US Population," *Archives of Internal Medicine 172*, no. 18 (2012): 1377–1385; Lisa Esposito, "How Heathcare Providers Combat Compassion Fatigue," *US News & World Report*, April 27, 2016; as well as the previously referenced Jauhar, "Why Doctors Are Sick of Their Profession," and McCluskey, "Physician Burnout Now Essentially a Public Health Crisis."

4 See Gary B. Ferngren, *Medicine & Religion: A Historical Introduction* (Baltimore, MD: Johns Hopkins University Press, 2014); and Michael Balboni and Tracy Balboni, *Hostility to Hospitality: Spirituality and Professional Socialization within Medicine* (Baltimore, MD: Johns Hopkins University Press, 2018).

Index

Page numbers in italics refer to figures. Page numbers followed by "n" refer to notes.